The Conspiracy of the Young

The Conspiracy of the Young

Paul Lauter and Florence Howe

MERIDIAN BOOKS

The World Publishing Company

New York and Cleveland

A MERIDIAN BOOK

Published by The World Publishing Company

Published simultaneously in Canada
by Nelson, Foster & Scott Ltd.

First Meridian Printing—1971

An original World Publishing Company hardcover

Library of Congress Catalog Card Number: 78-115809

Printed in the United States of America

WORLD PUBLISHING
TIMES MIRROR

Acknowledgments

We should like to thank two editors—James Wade and Peter Ritner—who two years ago persuaded us to interrupt a book on education to write this one, and who urged us to finish it during the past six months. We were able to do so because many friends in the movement and among our colleagues and students helped us. We name most specific acknowledgments in the text or notes. Here, we want to thank others who supplied us with materials, information, or unpublished manuscripts: Richard Flacks, Todd Gitlin, and Steve Weissman on the West Coast; James Brann, William Neumann, and Alice Rossi of Baltimore; Steve and Joan Baratz and Steve Bookshester of Washington, D.C.

We want to acknowledge particularly the research done for chapters 6, 9, and 10 by Goucher College students Deborah Stone, Andrea Friedman, and Dorothy Watson. We are grateful to two other Goucher College students who typed the manuscript—Laura Schneider and Dana Schelling.

To our friends, comrades, and families who suffered our absences and our abrasive presences, we also say thank you. Most of all, we appreciate our students—in Mississippi, Chicago, Washington, Massachusetts, and Maryland—for all they have taught us.

Paul Lauter and Florence Howe

Baltimore
March, 1970

Contents

Contents

The Conspiracy of the Young

1

Service and Rebellion

On New Year's Day, 1970, a small plane passed close over the Badger gunpowder plant near Baraboo, Wisconsin. The plant, which makes munitions for Vietnam, had been in the past an occasional target for antiwar demonstrations; a 1968 summer march from Madison, some thirty-five miles to the south, had ended with a few arrests for civil disobedience as demonstrators tried to climb over the outer fences. But when the stolen Cessna-150 swept above one of the main powder-making units, it dropped a number of homemade firebombs. The bombs failed to ignite, though others set in the following week seriously damaged military facilities on the University of Wisconsin campus.[1]

These were by no means the first bombings aimed at military or corporate targets in the United States: ROTC buildings have been destroyed at Stanford and the University of Washington, draft boards in New York and Ohio, high-tension towers in Colorado and California, an ammunition plant in Hanover, Massachusetts—to name just a few events. For carrying out bombings of corporation offices at Rockefeller Center and Wall Street, four people in New York City are under indictment, and half or more of the F.B.I.'s "most wanted" list now consists of revolutionaries. Seven more young activists have died in bomb incidents during early March, 1970. But the aerial bombing of a powder plant just a few hours after the seventies had begun seems to have been meant as a symbol. It may prove to be one.

When we began this book almost two years ago, it was with the

3

idea of explaining a generation at war with its elders. Adults we knew —colleagues, friends, parents, parents of our students—were angered and baffled by young people, by their marches and slogans, their clothes and hair, even their music. We thought to explain the history of that war, to illustrate the unequal terms of the conflict, to persuade adults that it was *not* a contest between generations, but of values. Thus we planned first to describe three movements for social change that young people had organized—in Mississippi, on the campus, and against the war—as well as their experience in the Peace Corps; second, to analyze those (adult) institutions—schools, the law, and the draft, in particular—most involved in controlling young people; and finally, to reject as "solution" such proposals for handling youth as national service and to offer alternatives based on the principle of self-determination rather than on control. Perhaps, we thought in optimistic moments, we might even convince adults that the values of their children are ones they share or might want to share.

Events have cooled our initial optimism: the end is nowhere in sight; probably we are only at the beginning of a far longer war, much of which will be fought between the old and the young. In the Chicago streets in 1968, young people were perhaps impatient, but even as spectators in the 1970 courtroom of the "Conspiracy Eight," they refused to contain their anger. What began in the early sixties as protest or pleas for social change has, as we enter the seventies, become a test of power. All over America, the lines are being drawn.

When in 1960 John Kennedy offered youth an imperative for action—"Ask not what your country can do for you, ask what you can do for your country"—he could not, nor could they, have imagined the decade's end in rebellion. For Kennedy's was no revolutionary call; rather, it revived an ideal of service that had most fully been developed in middle-class Victorian England. Earlier in the 1800's, Englishmen began to note the power of individual accumulation, of private greed, set loose among them; the transformation of England's "green and pleasant land" into drab, slum-pocked sprawl continued through the century. And the citizenry seemed mean-spirited, selfish: "Getting and spending, we lay waste our powers," Wordsworth had written. In opposition to the self-interested doctrines of private profit, and to alleviate some of the misery their application had produced, Victorians developed an ethic of service. Service could take many forms—from the Salvation Army to the Royal Navy. Especially for women, service became charity—home visits, workers' education, temperance campaigns—all designed to alleviate the lot of the poor. For men, the ethic meant devotion not to private gain but to public good in government service: colonial administration in India, the Home Office, the military. A career in "service" thus became not merely an avocation for ladies or gentlemen, but a legitimate and even admirable calling. It was, indeed, Kennedy's own.

The ethic of service functioned well within the established social order, either to carry out the policies of existing institutions or to relieve somewhat the suffering these caused. With respect to helping the less fortunate, service located the source of misery in the character of the miserable, in their drunkenness, improvidence, or ignorance. The obligation of social-service work, therefore, was to relieve suffering not by questioning, let alone attacking, its social and economic causes—as, for example, Marxist social critics might do—but, in the name of improving character and education, by training the poor in the virtues of middle-class society: promptness, dependability, sobriety, obedience, literacy. Not incidentally, these were also the virtues an industrial system required of its workers. In the same way, those in public service were not called upon to question the premises of colonial policy, for example, though they might work to moderate its harsher effects. Such service, while carried out with the most liberal spirit, has served, as Raymond Williams shows, "at every level, to maintain and confirm the *status quo.*"[2]

This is *not* the concept of service about which we will write in this book, and though it is a somewhat awkward phrase, we will use "service for change" to describe our alternate view. Two chief differences must be stated at the outset. First, instead of preserving institutions, young people in service for change have worked to transform them; second, because they located the sources of misery or powerlessness in institutional oppression rather than in the nature of the poor or the oppressed, their chief goal has been self-determination or the "liberation" of those groups. When hundreds of volunteers went to Mississippi in 1964, for example, their function was neither to relieve the poverty of a few black people nor to improve Mississippi's governmental services. Southern whites recognized the volunteers as "outside agitators" interested in disrupting Mississippi's central institution, white supremacy—and they were quite correct. The main idea of that summer's project was to start a "move-ment" in a state that had not changed for a hundred years or more. Volunteers brought some books, clothing, skills, and money into Mississippi. Some may also have brought their guilt. But their first function was to break the color line, and their second, to help black people establish the principle of self-determination, denied to them for centuries.

We are, of course, abstracting or generalizing a decade's ex-perience, and we will spend the next four chapters reviewing aspects of its history. But we wish here to make clear the framework within which young people have worked for change in this country. Neither the older form of service nor yet rebellion outright, service for change implies the kind of tension that exists when one works both to improve the quality of others' lives (and one's own) and to trans-form the institutions that control them. Let us put alongside each other two quotations that illustrate this contrast between the older idea of service and service for change. First, a group calling itself the National Service Secretariat defines national service:

> National service as a concept embraces the belief that an opportunity should be given every young person to serve his country in a manner consistent with the needs of the nation—recognizing national defense as the first priority—and consistent with the education and interests of those participating, without infringing on the personal or economic welfare of others but contributing to the liberty and well-being of all.[3]

Then, from a counterinstitution founded by young people called Vocations for Social Change:

> Vocations for Social Change is based on two great hopes. We feel that there is a great need for institutional change in this country so that ordinary citizens can have greater control over the forces that limit their lives. We believe that it is possible for far-reaching change to occur in this country if enough human energy is devoted to the task. At the same time, we are greatly concerned about the quality of our lives and the lives of our fel-low citizens. *We want our work to produce change in the society and we also want it to provide meaning for us.* Similarly we hope that others can work towards and achieve this kind of confluence.

> This means that we view a job as a focus for individual involvement, not a way to earn some money to do things with.[4] [Italics ours.]

Beyond the obvious similarity—both passages appeal to young people by offering them some activity—the differences illustrate not only opposing values, but ones bound to conflict. The most obvious clue is the language itself: "as a concept embraces the belief" opposed to "We believe"; the official rhetoric that pronounces, in passive voice, that "an opportunity should be given," the giver invisible, contrasted to the personal style of people directly stating their beliefs, hopes, and desires and asking others to join them. The official passage indirectly proposes that nothing is really to be changed; the personal passage that changing institutions is the goal. And while the writers of *Vocations for Social Change* do not specify the institutions, they are clear about the vehicles of change: human energy and a drive to control one's own life. The idea of controlling one's own life, what we call the principle of self-determination, leads to a critical concern with community and the "quality" of life in the United States. As Adrian Abel, a student leader in the strike at New York State University at Buffalo, put it: "The reason I support self-determination is because it's a first step toward serving the community instead of big business." The focus on quality and community gets to the main point: the work we do ought to be meaningful, not alienating or time-wasting, but productive personally and in an effort to improve the lives of others. Idealistic? Perhaps. Nevertheless, chief values of a generation of activists have been self-determination and meaningful work. The values of the two passages conflict precisely here: in defining what constitutes "meaningful" service— service for whom?—and on who makes that decision. Vocations for Social Change makes it clear that the priorities are to be decided by people themselves, in the work they do together. The National Service quotation assumes national priorities, specifying defense as the first of them. Young people will be fitted into such priorities ("consistent with their education," to be sure), but there is no sign of who will do the fitting, let alone who has decided national priorities. Or that defense is at the top of the list.

Such were Secretary of Defense Robert McNamara's assumptions when he told the American Society of Newspaper Editors, meeting in Montreal in May, 1966, that the United States had to find new ways of using the time and talents of its youth. Internal peace and security, as well as the development of the third world, demanded teachers, health and social workers, policemen. Though the military must continue to tap many young men, McNamara said, shouldn't others be given an opportunity for serving the nation? Shouldn't the resources of their energy and imagination, so well demonstrated in the Peace Corps, be put to solving America's—and the world's—problems in what could be called a "draft without guns"?

Taking his cue from the Defense Secretary's view of young people as a "national resource," a University of Chicago sociologist, Morris Janowitz, estimated roughly how 1,800,000 military and national-service conscripts could annually be put to work dealing with national needs.[5] Each year, Janowitz proposed, 150,000 conscripts might be assigned to a National Teacher Corps, 100,000 to a police cadet corps, 150,000 to health and domestic "peace corps" projects —all of this aside from at least 615,000 to the military and another 400,000 who, in Janowitz' words, "have been failed by our society" to a national Job Training Corps. Or here, in more modest estimates offered by the National Service Secretariat, is a similar distribution of the resources of youth among existing institutions:

Federal Programs

Job Corps	50,000
Peace Corps	15,000
VISTA	7,000
Teacher Corps	3,000

Non-Federal Programs

Education	50,000
Health	50,000
Community Service	50,000
Conservation	90,000
Libraries	5,000
Other	5,000
Total	325,000[6]

On scales so large it is difficult to talk about particular jobs. How might 325,000 (or more) young people be used as a national resource without disturbing the institutions of power or even the job market? A note attached to a similar set of estimates made for eight selected cities by the National League of Cities suggests one pattern:

> Job Descriptions: It is proposed that the volunteers will fill positions not now being filled by the "law of the open market" or which may not now be listed on organization tables. Examples of work are: teachers' aides, hospital aides, recreation assistants, library aides, administrative interns, police cadets, urban beautification and social work assistance. The types of jobs should not be of a "make-work variety." The work must adhere to Federal Civil Service Commission standards with respect to involvement in political activities and related endeavors.[7]

In simpler terms, these are to be jobs that no one *wants* to do. If they are not to be of the "make-work variety," and if they are not to conflict with the job market, what can they be but uninteresting or unpleasant? And, lest a young person undertake such dreary work as a basis for organizing change, they are not to involve "political activity." A single job description for a "driver-observer," provided as "exemplary" by the National Service Secretariat, further defines such work:

> The primary purpose is to provide transportation by taxi, bus or private automobile to institution residents or agency clients in cooperation with the planning of the social worker. In addition to driving, the volunteer will observe the general reactions of his rider to the situation and make other observations as suggested by the supervisor.[8]

In short, the work proposed perverts the task of chauffeur into that of spy.

It is true enough that more sophisticated proposals and analyses focus on fitting the young (college-educated, to be sure) into different kinds of slots: teacher, nurse, youth-worker, even, within limits, community organizer—the jobs that many Peace Corpsmen or VISTA volunteers perform. These "service" jobs are neither useless nor uninteresting, though they have often proved more frustrating than fulfilling to young people, for reasons we shall detail in subsequent chapters. But one basic cause of their limitations is how they are conceived by adults who design them. A middle-aged manpower specialist, at a conference on national service, offered a comment on such "service" by recalling his own experiences:

> When I think back to when I was eight years old and was sent by my mother to take a bowl of beans to an elderly blind lady down the street, I went not because I wanted to but because my mother wanted me to and because this was expected of me. I think these are the earliest roots of "voluntary service" for me.[9]

The view that equates service with charity is familiar enough, and a suggestion that young people be set to work bringing contemporary versions of beans to the poor and the handicapped is probably no worse, from the point of view of youth, than the McNamara-Janowitz view of them as a national resource to be exploited for manpower. In some fundamental respects the two views come together, since they both answer the question: If we had these kids for two years, what could we do with them that would absorb their energy without disturbing or altering the nation's basic political, economic, or social arrangements?

That all such proposals for "dealing with" youth rely on documentations of national needs, moreover, leads us to conclude that designs for youth service mask—and only thinly at that—confessions of national failure. What greater acknowledgment of institutional failure than to say we must conscript 400,000 men each year to save them from the public schools and the slums? Or that conditions of health and welfare are so poor for so many that we must conscript 150,000 young men each year into projects of community uplift and another 100,000 to help maintain order where justice does not prevail? One could hear, moreover, in the same Montreal speech in which he praised youthful service, Mr. McNamara's praetorian boast that the United States "has devoted a higher proportion of its gross national product to its military establishment than any other major free world nation"; and his estimates that by the year 2000 the per-capita yearly income in about forty of the poorer nations might reach $170, while in the United States, which continues to swallow some half the world's resources, per-capita income will have grown from the present $2,700 to $4,500.

Young people in 1960 listened to President Kennedy's call for their energy and commitment, for their idealism in service to the goals of their country. As the early rapid growth of the Peace Corps makes plain, they were willing to "serve."[10] If the young have become cynical about "national priorities" they were being called upon to fulfill, that was because they saw the meaning of "national defense as the *first* priority" expressed on the lives and soil of the Vietnamese. At first there was the fact that drafted Americans were dying in Vietnam; later there was compassion for the destruction of that distant land and people and anger about the consequent neglect of the poor and the black here at home. In whose interests were national priorities set, and by whom? Robert Bly angrily connected American affluence at home and murder abroad in a poem developed during a series of national poetry readings in the spring of 1969 "celebrating resistance" to the war:

> It's because a hospital room in the average American city now
>   costs $60 a day that we bombed hospitals in the North
> It's because the aluminum window-shade business is doing so
>   well in the United States that we roll fire over entire
>   villages
> It's because the milk trains coming into New Jersey hit the
>   right switches every day that the best Vietnamese men are
>   cut in two by American bullets that follow each other like
>   freight cars. . . .
> It's because tax-payers move to the suburbs that we transfer
>   populations.
> The Marines use cigarette lighters to light the thatched roofs
>   of huts
> because so many Americans own their own homes.
>
>> (from *"The Teeth-Mother Naked at Last"*
>> San Francisco: City Lights Books, 1970)

James Rouse, Jr., Yale 1967, son of the president of an important and creative Baltimore architectural firm, had thought of joining the Peace Corps. But the training program turned him off:

> The feeling was clear by the end of the program, that if I was going to do community development work, the people who needed me weren't the poor people of Costa Rica but the white middle class. It seemed hypocritical of me to go overseas and help hungry people when I came from the kind of white middle class community which is the cause of most of the world's problems due to its insensitivity to them.[11]

He wanted to live in a manner that would not integrate him "into a system which perpetuates white superiority." For he felt that "a political movement is developing, a recognition of the fact that the underlying assumptions of the institutions are the things we object to. Therefore working through the system becomes a meaningless act."[12] Thus he became a conscientious objector, leafleted for the grape boycott, grew his blond hair long, taught a course in "Suburban Problems" at a freedom school for whites, wore patchy jeans, marched for the Catonsville Nine, moved into the city. "What white youth senses," he argued,

> is the bankruptcy of a society based on the worship of quantitative aspects of man. That's what the hippie and student movement is all about. They seek to build a life that re-emphasizes spiritual values.

For some adult Americans, James Rouse, Jr.'s language, his life style and politics hardly suit his pedigree and diploma. He may seem to be an oddity if not an "extremist." In fact, he is perfectly representative of many young people. The essentials of his views are shared, moreover, by thousands of others more brushed and suited than he, those, for example, who took the more traditional routes of working for Robert Kennedy and Eugene McCarthy in the 1968 presidential campaign. *New York Times* reporter Steven V. Roberts interviewed many of these "smart and sophisticated" young people shortly before the Nixon administration took office. He found that for large numbers "traditional careers and traditional goals will no longer suffice. They want 'to do something' more. to *make social and political change their major, if not their total occupation.*" "It does seem clear," Roberts continued, "that there is a vast cadre of young people who want neither to 'drop out' of political and social activity nor feel the best way to promote change is through physical demonstrations and disruptions. But they are still looking for a peaceful alternative." They recognize that whites cannot organize the black and Puerto Rican communities; thus many envision their roles as providing "technical assistance to poor people." "'The basic idea,'" Roberts quotes a former Kennedy aide as saying, "'is to put our professional abilities on the side of the dispossessed. This is not a new idea, but *what is new is how many of us have no faith that the traditional institutions*—the universities, for example, or the Federal Government—*would do these things.' "*[13] (Italics supplied.)

To feel conviction diminish about the good intentions of U.S. institutions, to query whether universities *or* the federal government would take "the side of the dispossessed" (which side are you on?) is, in other words, to be "radicalized." When people speak of the radicalization of youth or, as we do, of their movement from older forms of ameliorative service to service for change, they are describing the process whereby "involvement" in the lives of poor people, for example, leads to consciousness about, then confrontation with, such institutional causes of poverty as racist housing or educational policies. What young people discovered in the Peace Corps as well as in Mississippi or northern ghettos was that patching over the symptoms of poverty with some temporary comfort was all they could do: to eliminate the sources of misery, they would have to begin to challenge American institutions. Such challenge naturally leads to deepening, more permanent clashes between young people and the institutional structure of U.S. society. It is worth remarking that, ironically, John Kennedy's effective appeal helped set in motion a challenge to the conceptions of national security and social stability which he shared with McNamara, Janowitz, and the National Service Secretariat.

There are, of course, other theories to explain the "alienation" or "rebellion" of youth. Among them, the most crude is Lewis Feuer's assumption that youth in revolt are acting out oedipal conflicts with their fathers and other authority figures. We would not deny that the young people we describe here are in rebellion against many contemporary American values. But the work of sociologists and psychologists, notably Richard Flacks, suggests that the "generation gap" is an insufficient and basically misleading concept. Interviewing University of Chicago students and their parents, Flacks "discovered that there *was a substantial continuity between the basic values and aspirations of the two generations."* He writes:

> I believe this continuity can be summarized by saying that both the activists and their parents were hostile to the self-denying, competitive, status-oriented individualism of bourgeois culture, and sought a way of life which emphasized self-expression, humanism, openness to experience and community. In addition,

both the students and their parents were substantially disaffected from the political system—though the students, of course,
were more thoroughly alienated than their parents. It seemed
clear to us that the students, through their activism, were for the
most part attempting to fulfill and extend an ideological and cultural tradition which was already present in their families, rather
than rebelling against the values with which they had been
raised.[14]

Our own experience bears out Flacks's findings. During the summer
of 1964, for example, parents in the North provided the major
sources of support and bail for most of the Mississippi volunteers—
and not just out of anxiety for their children. Increasingly now in black
communities, we find evidence that parents—traditionally strong supporters of school authoritarianism—are encouraging and aiding their
children's agitation for different schools.

Young activists, those whom *Fortune* calls "forerunners" and
Flacks "the young intelligentsia,"[15] are products of America as well
as rebels against it. That fact may be obscured by the tendency of
American institutions—from political parties to school textbooks—
to trivialize differences and thus to smother struggle by emphasizing
the "norm" of consensus or compromise. American intellectuals who
argue that Western pragmatism has established an agreed-upon
direction for U.S. society, and that it only remains, with the end of
ideological conflict, to work out technical problems and to train tech-
nologist-leaders, must needs ignore the often direct and brutal repression of serious dissent—from the Palmer Raids of 1920, through
the McCarthy period of the 1950's, to the Panther raids in 1969.
There has, of course, always been a dissenting culture in the United
States, fluctuating in its strength, but steadily opposed to the values
of material acquisition, puritanical competition, and arbitrary authority. Some of our greatest works of literature—*Walden,* "Song of Myself," "Howl"—celebrate an alternative culture. In the past, its
political expressions—radical abolitionism, the woman's suffrage
movement, turn-of-the-century Socialists and Wobblies, the WPA
—have attracted masses of Americans. We do not imagine that young
people are, on the whole, aware of this history. But to present the
youth movement in terms of a "generation gap" is to suppose that
their elders and ancestors have uniformly accepted a single set of

values and assumptions. Obviously, material, competitive, authoritarian, white, and male values have dominated our history. But to imagine that everyone has shared them is an absurdity that only the most frightened or subservient intellectuals could devise. As a contemporary expression of the conflict of values and power in United States society, the youth movement is peculiarly American in its eclectic mixture of Marx and utopianism, collective responsibility and individualistic assertion, political engagement and smoky escapism.

Certain contemporary conditions have helped to popularize this cultural conflict and to give it a distinctively youthful character. Flacks suggests, for example, that material security has permitted many youths to be "experimental, risk taking, open to immediate experience, relatively unrepressed" (p. 13). The contrast between the relative ease with which money may be earned today and the traditionally asserted values for success—hard work, abstinence, and obedience—has led young people to legitimate skepticism about such traditions. Rising college enrollments also have contributed to the rapid spread of insurgent values, since students' exposure to them in reading and in life style will obviously be much greater at college than in their home neighborhoods. Finally, the burden of carrying these alternative values has depended heavily on the young, because their immediate forebears were largely demoralized and rendered inactive during the 1940's and 1950's, both by disillusionment with Russian communism, in which many had set great faith, and by the attacks of militant anticommunism, into which many former friends and liberal colleagues had descended.

Describing the current tensions in United States society as a war between the old and the young suggests also that young people will "grow out of it." When Rennie Davis, one of the Chicago "Conspiracy Eight," threatened to organize the children of federal prosecutor Thomas Foran into a domestic Viet Cong, he was obviously not talking about a two-year period of "alternative service" or a Peace Corps, but of a lifelong alternative to the values of Foran or Judge Julius Hoffman's court.

This means, in the first place, that service for change is not an "interlude" or "moratorium" between childhood and adult responsibility, during which young people can test out competency and interest, develop identity and commitment, before "settling down" to family and career. To be sure, the translation of youthful "involvement" into a life of meaningful work is not easy. In Chapter 12 we attempt to document the search of young adults for continuity and thus to dispute the "moratorium" theory. For while it may have been liberally intended to win space for youthful testing and discovery in a nation where adolescence was "vanishing," the theory has also been used to put down activists for "carrying on adolescence beyond 30," and to justify accepting the status quo of adult careers as a norm.[16] Infantilizing youth has been one means of controlling it—a means obviously less successful in a day when high-school dropouts can edit underground newspapers.

It is finally useless to dismiss youthful rebels by charging them with adolescent authority problems or by expecting their rebelliousness to fade away, because in the past five years there has come into being a large "counterculture," with its own developing counter-institutions, mores, values. Its existence has been an encouragement (some would say an incitement) to young people to "do their own thing," organize their own resources. But perhaps more important, it has provided for those who "drop out" of accepted modes—of school, dress, career—something to "drop into": not a crash pad or a place to hide, but a life style and a set of loosely shared assumptions and attitudes that support them in what adult society might call their "deviance." The judgments of that adult society, of psychiatrists, social workers, teachers, parents, can now be "appealed," and the instincts that drive a young person from the shelter of Marin County or Westchester to the streets of Berkeley can be supported by the presence of others, by music, in print. It means that young people do not identify themselves as "dropouts," or only in the same sense that they repossess epithets like "freak" for praise.

The spread of this youthful counterculture has been phenomenal. We are not thinking only of the half-million who turned up at the Woodstock festival to dig the music and each other, to smoke grass, and to make love for a brief saturnalia; or the probably greater numbers who sang "give peace a chance" in Washington on November 15, 1969. *Fortune* magazine's detailed survey of youth early in 1969 concluded that "behind the small and visible activist minority is a much larger and generally 'invisible' minority of forerunners holding similar dissident attitudes." Some 2,300,000 young people, *Fortune* estimated, make up this "forerunner" group.[17] Far greater numbers accept at least some of their values—opposition to the war and the draft, for example—and join in some of their activities. In 1969, before its split, Students for a Democratic Society was an avowedly revolutionary organization; yet chapter meetings at the University of Wisconsin and Harvard might attract as many as a thousand people, and national estimates of young people who paid dues or participated in chapter activities spiraled up from 30,000.

We have already mentioned some of the developing values of the counterculture: self-determination, a willingness to commit one's full human resources to institutional change. We would underline the word "developing," for it is obvious that little is absolute and fixed in the youth movement, and that conflicting interests within it—over dope, for example—generate part of its dynamism. But a number of directions, in addition to those we have mentioned, seem established in the counterculture.

One is its emphasis on community rather than the competition and separation of urban life or the multiversity. Communal living arrangements and collective styles of work vary wildly, from religious "Kibbutzim" preparing for the coming-in of the Aquarian Age to the revolutionary "struggle collectives" like those of the Black Panthers or the SDS Weatherman faction; from cottage-craft industries or organic farms to halfway houses for addicts or runaways; from the People's Farm to the People's Store to the People's Clinic; from underground newspapers to "free" schools. For some, the meaning of communal life, as Stephen Gaskin wrote in a recent issue of *Motive,* "is to stay loose, groovy, high, happy, and compassionate, to manifest the kingdom here and now, with or without the assistance of drugs." This vision emphasizes sharing of experience—of drugs, swimming in the moonlight, of one's own freaks, impulses to walk or make sundaes, or simply of silence—with an intimate group which "vibrates" together. For others, collective organization involves eight-hour debates about politics and intense criticism of individual work and ideas. Underneath these differences, however, are common practices: sharing income and goods, rejecting privacy both of property and for self, arriving at personal decisions through collective discussion. What is fundamental is the collective mode of arranging and assessing one's life.[18]

The steady trouble to which living communes have been subjected has also taught young people that just for the right to exist in the United States groups which do not accept the norms must struggle. Many communes have moved to the country or the suburbs, partly because there communards can afford patches of land or big, rambling houses, partly to avoid building inspectors, cops, narcotics agents, landlords. But harassment follows. "We could cut off our hair and do it the easy way," a resident of a Madison, New Jersey, commune said, "but now I know what it's like to just walk down the street and have people hate you."[19]

The sense of being together under siege provides the counterculture with something of its insurgent character. We experienced it in Mississippi in 1964 and in Montgomery later, as did students occupying Sproul Hall in Berkeley or Hamilton Hall at Columbia. John Holt describes the sense of what we might call "solidarity" among youth on a larger scale. Older people ask why the young, even those uninterested in politics or the movement, can't just mind their business and stay away from where the trouble is. "The students gather where the police are," Holt responds,

> first, because their friends are there, because they feel a solidarity with them, because they want to see what happens to them and share in it. They have a sense that history is being written at such places, and every whole man wants to be a part of the history of his own times. Also, they go as witnesses. They know that the police can be counted on to lie—and, in general, authority supports their lies—about what happens at these occasions.[20]

Holt's observation helps explain why, for example, young people almost never turn each other in for drugs, and why drug busts therefore extend youth's solidarity and foster their general mistrust of authority.

Such values, as we have said, were always present in United States society: "underground" papers, insurgent journals, and bohemian and revolutionary colonies have existed in many parts of the country. But it is probably true that at no time in the past has an insurgent counterculture generated institutions so widespread among young people, nor the sense that an underground, with its own services, communications, and style, functions everywhere in the nation. A young person from Baltimore arriving in Atlanta can quickly tune in to the local scene, find a pad, strangers who are not strangers, movement action if he wants it. The counterculture is thus not an "object" over there, a record one listens to. It is rather a movement in which young people participate and work.

The counterculture is widespread in another sense: in time. It includes those who were nineteen or older in 1960 and are growing into or past their thirties, who can recollect the deadness of the fifties and how Kennedy's call, for all its ambiguities, seemed at least a step toward freedom worth taking. It also includes those young activists now in their early twenties for whom the single initiating experience might have been the demonstration at the Pentagon in October, 1967. One warm day and one cold night were their Mississippi Summer, their siege under fire, their training in nonviolence. "Don't throw things," the experienced told the young. "Don't fight back. Keep cool. Cover your head this way, and talk to the soldiers. Try to get them to respond to you as a person." On and off all that night the chant was "Join us, join us." People watched, angry but peaceable, as friends were dragged through the lines, beaten by federal marshals and noncoms. Many, even as they learned the discipline of nonviolence, sitting in the cold up against the line of troops, vowed that they would no longer accept passivity in the face of attack.

Others of the same age, like the Kennedy aide we quoted before, came to the counterculture during the 1968 Presidential campaign. Not just in Grant Park and in the streets outside the Conrad Hilton, but intellectually, for example, from a full-page ad in *The New York Times* placed by the pro-McCarthy Coalition for a Democratic Alternative. "IS THE WHOLE THING A FRAUD?" huge letters across a voting booth asked:

> On November 5th, the great moment will finally arrive. . . .
> After four years of grinding your teeth in frustration and helplessness,
> You will go into that voting booth, draw the curtains, and you will be able to choose freely between . . . Hubert Humphrey and Richard Nixon.
> WHAT A CHOICE.
> What a free election.
> What an example of how the people in a democracy pick their president.

What a way to unify the country for the four years ahead.

What an object lesson for those who've been saying all along that "You can't beat The System."

. . . Many Democratic delegates are now concerned that a Tweedledum-Tweedledee choice between Humphrey and Nixon will alienate a large portion of the electorate, who might turn away from the democratic process in disgust. . . .

This is not some docile banana republic in Central America or some "People's Democracy" in Eastern Europe.

This is the United States of America. And they're not going to take away our right to a free election and get away with it. [July 21, 1968.]

What further was there to be said?

For those in nursery or grammar school in 1960, the path to the counterculture was different yet. Eight or ten years ago the founders of SDS—some of whom are today among the "Conspiracy Eight"—addressed themselves to a few hundred students at most. When Tom Hayden and Rennie Davis spoke in their Chicago courtroom in February of 1970, their audience included not only their contemporaries, but a new generation on the campus, another in the high schools, and still another, even younger. In 1970, these young people arrive in an already polarized world. Those who were nine in 1960 cannot remember the fervor of the nonviolent movement, the bus rides and lunch counters, the singing of "We Shall Overcome." They have grown up watching slaughter on TV, violence in the streets of Chicago, and hate, as the New Jersey communard said, in the faces of ordinary neighbors. They "join" the counterculture rather by nature than by decision or trauma, and they learn about its dynamics in a way different, and certainly more rapid, than their older friends. Confrontations with sheriffs and police in Mississippi were, if not new to us in 1964, certainly not the norm of our daily life. Of course, we are white, but even white youths these days, wherever they may be, seem virtually born mistrusting schools, authorities, "pigs"; and they can tell you why.

In February of 1970, for example, more than one hundred Baltimore high-school students were arrested, many tear-gassed and maced, in a series of demonstrations. A group of primarily middle-class black students in all-girls Eastern High School had petitioned over several months for the removal of an allegedly racist teacher. Finally, the students confronted the teacher with their charges, a crowd gathered, police were quickly called in, and eight girls roughly arrested. Outside, male students from nearby City College High School, who tried to cross the street to join with their sisters, were blocked off by police lines: pushing began, a few rocks flew, immediately the gas came down on the students. A few days later at the Polytechnical High School, the pride of the city system, 150 students barricaded themselves in the cafeteria; 95 who refused to leave were finally hauled off to jail. Angry parents and teachers met, the school board began investigating, students formed a city-wide Central Committee and issued demands: amnesty, ridding the schools of racist teachers and policies, indicting brutal police, black studies. Knowing where such confrontations have led in other places, worried school and city authorities have moved to meet at least some of the demands, though everyone understands that the school unrest and the quick police resort to gas symptomize much more fundamental problems.

It took us ten years, the experiences of Mississippi, jail, the Pentagon, to learn what many of these young people can tell you about America. For many more, the learning took place in the course of their service for change, the work we shall describe in the four following chapters. And in chapters six through ten, we spell out some of the lessons that have emerged, primarily about the oppressive character of the institutions that shape and control the lives of young people. Those lessons the latest generation moving into the counterculture learn almost by instinct, from their day-to-day confrontation with institutions in the United States. And they understand that the American way of youth is to combine lavish provision, mostly private, with increasingly harsh control, mostly public.

The more immediate and younger "radicalization" of students helps to explain why at least 38,911 college students were involved in 221 protest demonstrations between January 1 and June 15, 1968.[21] And why, by the following year, protests had spread downward so that, according to Professor Alan Westin of Columbia University, three of five high schools in the United States had had some form of student action, and even 56 percent of the *junior* high schools had been affected by such protests. Or why, as 1970 began, few urban high schools did not have permanent guards, many of them armed, stationed inside.

Nor does the spiral of service, confrontation, and violence seem likely to be reversed in the near future. In 1965, little came of the efforts of a tiny group called the "Deacons for Defense" to arm black communities in Louisiana and Mississippi. But in 1970, the program of the Black Panther party calling for armed self-defense begins, even to whites, to seem reasonable, even as, or perhaps just because, the ranks of the Panthers have been decimated by police attacks. At the same time, the student movement has had its first martyr to police violence, James Rector, shot and killed during a police attack on People's Park demonstrators in Berkeley, California. The Weatherman faction of SDS, marching under the slogan "Bring the War Home," did precisely that during a series of attacks on property and "pigs" on Chicago's Gold Coast during October, 1969. And even the forms of nonviolent direct action in the white movement have shifted from individualistic draft-card turn-ins or burnings to a widening succession of attacks on draft-board files carried out by groups calling themselves the New York 8, the Boston 8, the Beaver 55, and the East Coast Conspiracy. Within such groups one finds no "generation gaps"; though three of the Beavers are nineteen, another, a women member of the Medical Committee for Human Rights, is forty-four years old. There are, of course, many in the movement, many young people, for whom the calls for a "revolutionary army," the "Wild in the Streets" tactics, the whole accession of violence in a movement dedicated to peace and justice seem irrational romanticism or signs of despair which can generate only reaction and a return to the quietism of the 1950's—if not to more active forms of repression. But we have found, nonetheless, a certain underlying solidarity, a kind of excitement, a thrill of support, even among those fearful or rejecting of terrorism against property or even "pigs." We recall the earlier awkwardly sympathetic rejection of the "provocations" of card-burners and of freedom riders. Do the few bombers, Panthers, Weathermen, express one logical, if fearful, extension of the institutional challenges of service for change?

But of course for most people, most young people included, the present questions do not center on whether violent disruption of the American economy and society is justified by the American past or practical in the American present. In his essay on guerrilla warfare

Che Guevara points out that people become revolutionaries only when they have no other choices. True, some leaders—like Che himself—who might personally have led comfortable lives take on, like the public servants of another context, revolutionary roles because of deep commitments to end oppression, primarily of others. Such men and women are often persuaded to rebellion by the effects of present policy—like the United States war on Vietnam—or by the perception of historical trends, such as the role of white, American power in enslaving, destroying, or keeping down people of color. But most people become revolutionaries, let alone take up arms, only when they see that course as less disastrous for them than a continuation of present misery. It is not just dread of death, as Hamlet suggests, but inertia mixed with realistic doubts about the advantages of change that

> . . . puzzles the will,
> And makes us rather bear those ills we have
> Than fly to others that we know not of.

Governments are not changed for "light and transient causes"; and mankind is indeed "more disposed to suffer while evils are sufferable, than to right themselves by abolishing the forms to which they are accustomed."

Whether or not revolutionary ideology or revolutionary organization broaden in this country will depend, we think, on whether the society can be transformed in response to the kinds of demands raised by blacks, Puerto Ricans, Chicanos, Indians, and others who have been excluded from the mainstream, by women coming to consciousness about their subservient roles, and by young people engaged in service for change. When service was regarded as a brief semieducational stint, a year or two at doing good, small change, small progress could be satisfying. But when service for change becomes a permanent commitment, a way of life supported by a flowering counterculture, the commensurate change demanded of institutions is much greater. That requires not just opening a storefront clinic, but shifting the *power* over it, and over local hospitals, to community control. That requires not just admitting some few more qualified black students to college, but reorganizing admissions, curriculum, and educational objectives to make universities serve the great mix of people in our country, and not primarily the social managers. It seems to us a sign of our times that there are more young Americans in Cuba as we write, serving the Cuban people by cutting sugarcane, than went to Mississippi in the summer of 1964. It remains to be seen whether they are already beginning to write the sequel to this book.

Notes

[1] See *The New York Times,* January 11, 1970.

[2] *Culture and Society* (New York, 1966), p. 329.

[3] "Introduction," *National Service, A Report of a Conference,* ed., Donald J. Eberly (New York: Russell Sage Foundation, 1968), p. 6.

[4] "Introduction," *Vocations for Social Change Newsletter,* #2 (July, 1968), p. 3.

[5] Morris Janowitz, "The Logic of National Service," *The Draft,* ed., Sol Tax (Chicago, 1967), pp. 79–87.

[6] "A Plan for National Service," *National Service, op. cit.,* pp. 525–26.

[7] *Ibid.,* p. 547.

[8] "A Plan for National Service," mimeographed document of the National Service Secretariat, November, 1966, pp. D1–D2.

[9] *National Service,* p. 158.

[10] By 1967, a million applications had been made to Kennedy's Peace Corps, VISTA, and the Job Corps. A Gallup poll, conducted in April of that same year, found that the service imperative had broadened in young America: nearly 3,500,000 of the nation's 6,500,000 college students were interested, Gallup reported, in working in programs like VISTA. See *The New York Times,* June 12, 1967.

[11] Barbara Gold, "James Rouse, Jr.: In Quest of Justice," in Baltimore *Sun Magazine,* January 19, 1969, p. 6.

[12] *Ibid.,* p. 7.

[13] "'Smart and Sophisticated' Young People Who Aided Kennedy and McCarthy Seek New Energy Outlet," in *The New York Times,* January 5, 1969.

[14] Richard Flacks, "The Revolt of the Young Intelligentsia: Revolutionary Class-Consciousness in Post-Scarcity America," draft of an essay to appear in Norman Miller and Rod Aya, eds., *Revolution Reconsidered.* Earlier work by Flacks and by Kenneth Keniston confirms this observation. See Richard Flacks, "The Liberated Generation," *Journal of Social Issues,* XXIII (1967), pp. 52–75; and Kenneth Keniston, *Young Radicals* (New York, 1968).

[15] "By 'intelligentsia' I mean those engaged vocationally in the production, distribution, interpretation, criticism and inculcation of cultural values." This group includes not only teachers, writers, and artists, but students preparing for careers in public service as well as the "helping professions"—that is, professionals in what we have broadly called "service."

[16] One of the best statements of this idea appears in an otherwise useful if subjective essay by Erik H. Erikson, "Youth: Fidelity and Diversity," in Erikson, ed., *The Challenge of Youth* (Garden City, N.Y.: Anchor Books, 1965), pp. 3–4, 10: ". . . in all youth's seeming shiftiness, a seeking after *some durability* in change can be detected. . . . This search is easily misunderstood, and often it is only dimly perceived by the individual himself, because youth,

always set to grasp both diversity in principle and principle in diversity, must often *test extremes* before *settling* on a *considered course.* These *extremes,* particularly in times of *ideological confusion* and widespread *marginality of identity,* may include not only rebellious but also *deviant,* delinquent, and self-destructive tendencies. However, all this can be in the nature of a moratorium, a period of *delay,* in which to test the rock-bottom of some truth before committing the powers of body and mind to a segment of the existing (or a coming) order. . . . But what I have called a psychological moratorium, of some form and duration between the advent of genital maturity and the onset of *responsible adulthood,* seems to be built into the schedule of human development." We have italicized a few of the words and phrases that lend themselves to a trivializing of young activism.

[17] *Fortune* magazine, Special Issue on "American Youth: Its Outlook Is Changing the World," 79 (January, 1969), p. 68.

[18] In *Culture and Society* (New York, 1966), pp. 325–26, Raymond Williams contrasts the central ideas of "bourgeois" and "working-class" culture. The former, he says, "marks that version of social relationship which we usually call individualism: that is to say, an idea of society as a neutral area within which each individual is free to pursue his own development and his own advantage as a natural right." The latter, he continues, "whether it is called communism, socialism or cooperation, regards society neither as neutral nor as protective, but as the positive means for all kinds of development, including individual development. Development and advantage are not individually but commonly interpreted. The provision of the means of life will, alike in production and distribution, be collective and mutual. Improvement is sought, not in the opportunity to escape from one's class, or to make a career, but in the general and controlled advance of all. The human fund is regarded as in all respects common, and freedom of access to it as a right constituted by one's humanity; yet such access, in whatever kind, is common or it is nothing. Not the individual, but the whole society, will move."

We would not suggest, of course, that most young people who have adopted collective or communal styles of life and work have significant relationships with the working class. But Williams' analysis is equally pertinent to a non-working-class culture that is, nevertheless, antithetical to the values of bourgeois society in the United States. In this respect, the clash between communal and individualistic values takes on far more significance than the usual press accounts of communes might allow us to believe.

[19] *The New York Times,* August 26, 1968.

[20] "The Radicalizing of a Guest Teacher," in *The New York Times Magazine,* February 22, 1970, p. 65.

[21] Report of a survey conducted in the fall of 1968 by the National Student Association. Their report did not include the massive disruption of Columbia University, nor a host of other actions involving less than thirty-five students. In fifty-nine of the demonstrations, NSA reported, school buildings were taken over; ten involved "considerable violence."

2

Freedom Summer—Mississippi

On February 1, 1960, four young men walked into the F. W. Wool-worth store in downtown Greensboro, North Carolina, to have a cup of coffee. They were not served; they left when the lunch counter was closed. When they returned the next day, they had with them students from colleges in Greensboro other than their own, North Carolina A & T. They sat at the lunch counter waiting in vain for the white waitress to attend to them. Within two months, this scene—elaborated with arrests, tear gas, white toughs, cigarettes ground into necks, ketchup poured over clothing, jeering, beatings—was played out in over eighty communities and on the television screens of millions of American homes.

It seemed an improbable place for a revolution to have birth, a shabby five and dime, with its bitter, watery coffee, and its greasy hamburgers. But in the year that followed, over 50,000 people, mostly black, had participated in such demonstrations; over 3,600 had been jailed; the Student Nonviolent Coordinating Committee (SNCC) had been organized; the color line had been thoroughly punctured and a Presidential election deeply influenced. A new picture of the young southern Negro, assertive, determined, willing to suffer for change, impressed itself on the United States, and especially on his peers, white and black, north and south. And the fundamental pattern of the youth movement, which persists even in these more complicated days, was established just as the youthful Kennedy era began.[1]

There was nothing precisely new in the Greensboro sit-in. Segregation had been brought under pervasive attack by the Supreme Court's 1954 school decision. Nonviolent direct action had become a not unusual tool of protest, especially since the 1955 Montgomery bus boycott. A "Freedom Ride" had been tried by the Congress of Racial Equality (CORE) as early as 1942. Students had even sat in at public facilities in Oklahoma, Kansas, and elsewhere. But the Greensboro action caught up and gave shape to a gathering impulse for change. Repeated, the Greensboro incident became a sit-in movement.

The nation, and especially its youth, was emerging from the quiescence and privatism of the 1950's. There were other signs of stir: early ideas about a Peace Corps, campus protests against ROTC, demonstrations for a nuclear-test ban. Dr. Spock was beginning to be worried. John F. Kennedy spoke to, and in some measure for, many of these newly awakened young people. His message of concern to Mrs. Martin Luther King, Jr., after Dr. King had been arrested in an Atlanta sit-in, was one of the decisive events of his campaign. The sight of well-dressed—it was very important then that they *were* well-dressed—young men and women laying their lives on the line, suffering scorn and injury because they took constitutional guarantees of equal treatment seriously—that sight helped galvanize these stirrings into a potent movement.

Right from the beginning, as this movement began to enlist northern white students in support actions and, a bit later, clergymen in the freedom rides, it was a movement for social and political change. It entailed, to be sure, personal sacrifice for the sake of others, a kind of "service" therefore, at least in the case of whites, and even, in some respects, of the young northern blacks who left teaching and graduate school to work in the South. Whatever the sacrifice or service, however, young people aimed not simply to improve the conditions under which black people lived, but to eliminate the fundamental institution of segregation. Thus even by the time John Kennedy said "ask what you can do for your country," the answer of many young people, shaped by the sit-ins, was "Change it."

The political thrust of the sit-ins was confirmed by 1961, when much of the civil-rights movement turned toward voter registration, even as the freedom rides continued to batter segregation in public facilities. For while the desegregation of lunch counters or bus facilities spoke to the pride of southern Negroes, it affected very little the basic conditions of their lives. Deprived of the vote since the turn of the century, they had few resources to combat the economic and political forces that kept them in subservience. Restoration of the vote was viewed as a vital weapon in combatting injustice and gaining equal protection of the law. According to strategists in the movement, moreover, voting was so fundamental a right that a campaign to ensure suffrage was expected to win endorsement by large numbers of Americans, even in the South, and eventually by the Congress. But restoring the franchise to southern blacks, let alone a life of economic and psychological dignity and wholeness, required more than a voting-rights bill, more even than the heroism of young SNCC organizers tramping through the dust and terror to persuade people to go down to the courthouse and "regis."

Just how massive the task was became clear in Mississippi. There in 1960 the average annual income of Negroes was $606, only 29% of the meager $2,023 of Caucasians. The chances of black babies dying within the first year of life were twice that of white babies; in some counties the infant-mortality rate approached that of "underdeveloped" countries in which Peace Corps volunteers were soon to be working. Two-thirds of all houses in which Negroes could live were found by the census to be "deteriorating" or "dilapidated"; over 90% had no flush toilets, no bathtub, and no shower. As of July, 1963, not a single black person was registered to vote in nine Mississippi counties; in twenty-six other counties, less than 1% were registered. In Amite County, more blacks had been murdered for their associations with civil-rights activity than had been allowed to register.[2] But no litany of statistics, nor even works as expressive as James W. Silver's *Mississippi: The Closed Society,* could fully communicate the weight of so many years of oppression and terror. One volunteer seeking "freedom registrations" described a conversation with a "woman in a terrible house who said, 'I can't sign no paper.' Lester then asked her, 'How will the pay for jobs and the homes ever get better unless we get together. Negroes have to do something to get something.' She said, 'I ain't no Negro, I'm a nigger. The Boss Man, he don't say nothing but nigger girl to me. I'm just a nigger, I can't sign no paper.'"[3]

Dealing with such realities clearly involved more than bringing people to the courthouse to register, even if that could have been done massively by the hundred or fewer civil-rights workers in Mississippi during 1962–63. In the first place, of the 60,000 black people who attempted to register between 1961 and 1964, only about 6,000 were actually inscribed on the voting rolls, and most of those in relatively enlightened areas. Resistance had, if anything, stiffened in the deep South, and, as Professor Silver pointed out, there was little reason to believe that "the closed society will ever possess the moral resources to reform itself."[4] Beyond that, voting was but one problem: poverty, illiteracy, poor health, exclusion from federally sponsored programs, etc., had to be encountered if real changes were to come about, and if gains made on one front were not to be lost on another. The movement needed resources outside itself. It turned in two directions, toward the federal government and the services of volunteers—lawyers, doctors, teachers, and students.

A working "Prospectus for the Mississippi Freedom Summer," prepared sometime in the spring of 1964 by an anonymous SNCC "field secretary," put it this way:

> Either the civil-rights struggle has to continue, as it has for the past few years, with small projects in selected communities with no real progress on any fronts, or task forces of such a size as to force either the state and the municipal governments to change their social and legal structures, or the federal government to intervene on behalf of the constitutional rights of its citizens.

In fact, few people, including the writer of that prospectus, had any illusions about large-scale federal intervention in Mississippi. On the other hand, it was clear that a "massive Peace Corps-type operation," as one recruiting brochure described it, might change the quality of national response to events in Mississippi, and thus provide more energy and scope to the civil-rights work. As the prospectus said,

Previous projects have gotten no national publicity on the crucial issue of voting rights, and hence, have little national support either from public opinion or from the federal government. A large number of students from the North making the necessary sacrifices to go South would make abundantly clear to the government and the public that this is not a situation which can be ignored any longer. . . .

And it was certainly true that the FBI hopped beyond deliberate speed when a bomb threatened an office in Shaw, Mississippi, where Len Edwards, son of a California congressman, was visiting as a summer volunteer.

At least because of the variety and inclusiveness of its programs, the Mississippi Summer Project of 1964 was the most unified and ambitious effort the civil-rights movement in the South had attempted. It brought together, however temporarily and disputatiously, all major civil-rights organizations—NAACP, CORE, SNCC, the Southern Christian Leadership Conference, as well as other private, church, and legal groups—under the umbrella of the Council of Federated Organizations (COFO). It involved about 1,000 field workers, including over 700 student volunteers, blacks and whites, some veterans of the movement, many novices, not in a day's march, but in a complex two-month program. It engaged participants at a variety of levels, from performing basic services—health and legal care, teaching literacy—to the most dangerous and direct political organizing, especially voter registration. It challenged white supremacy at its citadel, in Mississippi. And it provided a model of the varied, imaginative, and courageous work to which young people since have been willing to give themselves.

Though it came into being under the aegis of COFO, the summer project was the brainchild of young SNCC and CORE activists, who supplied most of the day-to-day leadership as local and state project directors. Young, mainly black, and veterans of the civil-rights movement in the South and elsewhere, they were a remarkably diverse group. There were black northern intellectuals—Bob Moses, James Forman, Stokely Carmichael, Ivanhoe Donaldson, for example—who had abandoned the usual ladders of graduate school or teaching and had turned instead "for the duration" to the southern movement.

Other black movement people, however, were almost as transient as the summer volunteers, since they were lending their time and talents for particular projects, before returning north. Similarly, there was a smaller group of whites drawn to the southern civil-rights movement either temporarily or permanently, many of them women —Mary King and Casey Hayden, for example—responsible for key office positions. There were also southern intellectuals and young southern ministers like John Lewis and James Bevel, whose special commitments to a philosophy of nonviolence were deeply respected but not always shared by other young Mississippians. Finally there were black southern youths, whose whole lives were the movement: subject to extreme pressure from local courts and juvenile authori- ties, from draft boards and from terrorists who knew them and their families, their firsthand knowledge of Mississippi was of crucial im- portance.

The diversity was not easy to hold together, but the understated style of SNCC leadership and the equally quiet contribution made by adults like Staughton Lynd helped to set a tone that provoked as little internal conflict as possible. If the coalition of black and white, northern intellectual and southern day laborer was fragile, it was also essential to the summer project, since all skills and strengths were essential. Summers have a way of ending: this summer could not do that. The leadership knew that they could not hold their coalition beyond the summer; nor could they reproduce themselves locally in one summer. Their function was, therefore, to serve and strengthen local leadership where it existed and to find it and set it into motion where it did not. They were catalysts.

The summer's strategy emphasized political organizing rather than direct action to test compliance with public-accommodations laws. Initial plans included voter registration, freedom schools, the Free Southern Theatre, as well as an elaborate network of long-dis- tance WATS (Wide Area Telephone Service) line telephones and citizens'-band radios that provided the basis for security arrange- ments. Plans also included the use of hundreds of northern volun- teers, chiefly college and graduate students, as well as some adults to help organize the training programs—for example, on the campus of Western College for Women in Oxford, Ohio. All adults, it ought to be emphasized, who worked with the Freedom Summer did so within the framework established by its young leadership. That the summer project was primarily initiated and implemented by young people for young people (and not by adults for youth) helps account for its character—its mystique, its impact on the volunteers, as well as some of its ambiguities.

The Mississippi Summer Project organized four interrelated programs—community centers, freedom schools, voter registration, and freedom registration—and several special services, such as legal and medical aid and research on federal programs. It was expected that where community centers were located or built, they would provide space for freedom schools and classes on prenatal care or literacy; that part of the freedom-school curriculum would involve students in canvassing for voter registration; that young researchers would discover how federal funds might be acquired for the support of community centers, for economic experiments like cooperatives, and eventually for such community-controlled projects as the Child Development Group of Mississippi (CDGM). The COFO leadership hoped that, together, these programs would provide trained local leadership and open avenues—physical, psychological, economic, and legal—for organizing black political power in the state.

Two community centers had been opened before the summer project, in Meridian and Greenwood, during the winter of 1963–64. Conceived as permanent institutions, they roughly combined elements of the old-fashioned urban political clubhouse and of new suburban community centers. Like the latter, they provided a place for kids to congregate, dance, talk, read, and study—generally relax and have a good time. In most Mississippi communities, where there were no such places for young Negroes, this function grew in importance as the summer went on, and the original two centers became thirteen. They were also to have regular recreation programs, movies, and classes in sewing and typing. But they were to function additionally as political centers for meetings, voter-education classes, and as places, moreover, where the resources of the civil-rights movement could be offered to the constituency it was trying to organize and activate. Here people could come, not only for help in registering or applying for welfare, but for legal advice, even for food and clothing.

It was perhaps some kind of instinctive understanding of the inherent danger to white supremacy of any possible locus for political action in the black community that led a group of Ku Klux Klansmen and Neshoba County "law enforcement" officials to mark the director of the Meridian community center as one of their prime targets. Surely the ping-pong table, the typewriters, the sewing machine, the newly installed 10,000-book library in that five-room center run by Mickey and Rita Schwerner were by themselves innocent enough. Even the small political meetings and voter-education classes were hardly then directly threatening to white Mississippi. But the community centers provided, for people who normally met only in church, bars, or social clubs, a nucleus for the political organization of the Negro community. Thus at the very beginning of the summer, when Mickey Schwerner, James Chaney, a local black youth, and Andrew Goodman, a white volunteer from New York in Mississippi only one day, drove up to neighboring Neshoba County to investigate a church burning, they were waylaid, beaten, shot, and buried. Though their bodies were not discovered for some weeks, it was clear to the summer volunteers, just arrived from or on the point of leaving their training program in Oxford, Ohio, and their thousands of sympathizers around the nation, that the three were, in fact, dead.

The murders were, in many respects, no surprise, certainly not to SNCC veterans who had so often been beaten and jailed, and had seen co-workers shot down in towns with names like "Liberty," no less ironic than the "Philadelphia" into which the three had disappeared. But, of course, for the nation the murder of two northern white youths was a different matter altogether from the killing of an obscure Negro like Herbert Lee or even the ambush slaying of NAACP leader Medgar Evers. The outrage expressed in newspapers and in Congress, the efforts displayed by the FBI and by U.S. Navy personnel in seeking the three, and the President's own expression of concern no doubt helped restrict violence during the remainder of the summer; nevertheless, COFO's running summary of incidents, ranging from threats and arrests to church burnings, beatings, and attempts at murder, just from June 16 to August 13, filled thirty-two legal-sized pages.

The volunteers themselves and those who anxiously watched the Mississippi Summer Project from afar could not help noting one irony. "There wouldn't be this fuss," they said to one another, "if it had been Chaney alone." That said something bitter about the United States, but the murders and the subsequent experience of violence and terror, which hardly a person connected with the Summer Project was spared, said more. For most of the whites, Freedom Summer marked the first time they had lived in hostile territory. Soldiers understand this experience, from Vietnam particularly, where there is little safety and less relaxation, for the "enemy" is here and everywhere. But for these young people the hostile territory was in their *own* country, the "enemy" were people who looked like them, had at least white skin in common; the enemy appeared in a pick-up truck with a shortwave antenna and no license plates, or in a sheriff's dusty car. The danger mounted the closer to downtown streets and courthouse steps one ventured. And in many places the nonviolence of the project survived only behind the quiet screen of guns manned each night by local black men. It is not easy, we think, to exaggerate the impact on hundreds of middle-class American students of this discovery, not in books or reports or on TV, but in life: you were physically in danger in your own country, and often at the hands of white police charged with upholding the law and the peace. For some, and through them many more, Mississippi 1964 was the beginning of the road to Chicago 1968.

Another lesson which the murders enforced was the radical connection between the innocent-seeming service of running a community center and the more fundamental challenges to racist power. The volunteers discovered that to set up a library or a day-care center, to conduct literacy, first-aid, or nursing classes—their primary jobs in community centers—was to risk their lives. Who could object, one wondered, to the Ruleville Center? A young white girl changed the diaper on a black baby in a small room lined with books. Two other infants crawled on an old blanket nearby. In a front room other small children scrawled crayon indifferently on scraps of paper or on the floor. Outside, half in shade, a circle of eight Negro women and two old men sat with two denim-clad volunteers, bent forward, explaining a section of the Mississippi Constitution that might be part of their voter-registration test. On the porch between these groups, a black SNCC field secretary repeated with unconcealed irritation a report of arrests in nearby Drew to two clean-dressed young whites—the FBI. And in Ruleville, a volunteer wrote:

> Violence hangs overhead like dead air—it hangs there, and maybe it'll fall and maybe it won't. Sometimes it's directed at people in the movement, sometimes it's indiscriminate. Cars

have been roaming around; seven or eight vigilante trucks with their gun racks and no license plates have been seen meeting at the city dump. What will they do? When? Something is in the air, something is going to happen, somewhere, sometime, to someone. . . . A few nights ago cars roamed the streets, empty bottles flew from their hands, striking cars and homes. They were empty that night—the next night the bottles were loaded— exploding as they hit the church and setting it afire.[5]

The fear of violence taught other political lessons. You walked along a black street in Jackson, even late at night, and all the people on porches, or out for a breath of air, said hello. You felt safe in the black community, almost as safe as a black person. It was in a perverse sense the end of the color bar: white volunteers were secure in the black community, provided whites didn't decide to organize bombings. You were a transient and you weren't black—you were what southern whites still called a "nigger-lover"—but life under siege, even the security precautions you had to memorize and follow, most of which blacks knew by instinct, allowed you to share the life of blacks in a racist society. However temporarily and illusorily, you also felt a part of the black community because it welcomed and sheltered you. If you didn't look into a mirror for some days or weeks you began to forget you were white. Freedom-school students included you in their "we." Some of their mothers saw to it that you had a hot meal each day. And in a few special instances, you caught a glimpse of community that urban, middle-class Americans don't usually see.

Harmony, an aptly named black rural community in Leake County, was one notable example. For nearly a century, black people in Harmony had owned and farmed their own land, using some equipment cooperatively. But certain aspects of their lives—their children's schools, for example—were not under their control. After their freedom school had been denied the use of an old school building which had once belonged to them, the farmers decided to build their own center. In a matter of weeks, a 30- by 60-foot frame building had been erected on a piece of land given by one member of the community for "the sum of one dollar" to an elected board of trustees. Every day at noon, work ceased and the local men and teen-agers, the volunteers, visitors passing through, and children gathered alongside the rising wood two-by-fours. Seven or eight women set out fried chicken, catfish, peppery potato salad, tea, and the inevitable kool-aid. Plates were pressed into strange hands; the ladies checked to see that everyone was comfortably stuffed in the 100-degree sun. One of the volunteers, a redhead from Detroit, squatted around the building plans with a small circle of black men, all of them dusted by the wood they had been sawing and hammering. A freedom-school teacher repeated French phrases for two children. And our hostess, who had introduced herself to us with a strong handshake and the name Dodson, carefully explained the relationship of various people to her folk, where they had come from in Alabama after the Civil War, and the new plans to boycott schools. The Leake County Negro schools had been suddenly scheduled to open three weeks early, partly to destroy the freedom school and partly to prevent desegregation, which had been ordered by the courts for that fall. Their community, Mrs. Dodson told us, had been the first in Mississippi to push for integration.

Volunteers were absorbed in curious ways into the community's life. An orthodox Jew managed to maintain his eating habits in the kitchen of a black family. A young couple from Milwaukee learned to ride mule bareback. And one young male volunteer slid out the back window of his bedroom if he wanted an evening out with local males—rather than worry the black family he lived with. Harmony was a special place, although not unique. Elsewhere in Mississippi, northern volunteers were also captivated by the sense of community:

> Now that I have worked with people to change the society in which they live, I know what I want to learn about societies and how other people have changed theirs. . . .
> I guess the thing that pulls me back [to Mississippi after the summer] most are the people who made us a part of their community. People I knew in Mississippi could honestly and unselfconsciously express affection in a way that few people I know in the North are able to do. They did not have to be "cool" or "one up" or "careful. . . . " In Mississippi I have felt more love, more sympathy, and warmth, more community than I have known in my life. And especially the children pull me back.[6]

Indeed, it was the children who made the freedom schools probably the most satisfying and emotional component of the summer project. Originally planned for about 700 high-school students in no more than twenty-five schools, there were by midsummer forty-one schools enrolling 2,135 students ranging in age from three to twenty-three, but including others as old as eighty-two. The Hattiesburg schools alone were flooded with over 600 students. In August an additional nine freedom schools opened in Jackson, with about 500 students enrolled. Over 200 volunteers taught full-time in freedom schools for one or both of the three-to-four-week sessions, and in many of the schools older students, visitors, or local adults also became teachers. Though most of the schools did not continue beyond the summer, the establishment of a large and varied "school system," under conditions of harassment and deprivation, was a major accomplishment.

In spite of their unexpected proliferation, the freedom schools remained in style and content very close to the initial vision of them projected by Charles Cobb. Cobb, a quiet Howard University student who had come south to work as an SNCC field secretary, believed that black Mississippians had to break out of the slavery imposed by their "schooling." "This is the situation," he wrote:

> Learning here means only learning to stay in your place. Your place is to be satisfied—a "good nigger."
> They have learned the learning necessary for immediate survival: that silence is safest, so volunteer nothing; that the teacher is the state, and tell them only what they want to hear; that the law and learning are white man's law and learning.
> There is hope and there is dissatisfaction—feebly articulated —both born out of the desperation of needed alternatives not given. . . . Here is the waiting, not to be taught, but to be, to reach out and meet and join together, and to change.

Education in Mississippi schools is "geared," as Charlie Cobb put it, "to squashing intellectual curiosity and different thinking," to creating passive, compliant "good niggers." "All education is political," we wrote after that summer; "it is inescapable that the educational system furthers the political, that the kind of learning the individual gets depends completely upon the role he is supposed to live."[7] The political task of the *freedom* school (the words themselves in 1964 seemed paradoxical) was to release students from the passivity that Mississippi schools had fostered and to provide them with skills and experiences which might encourage them to maintain their activity. Freedom-school education was "geared" to build leadership for a movement designed to change Mississippi.

How to devise a structure that would open up the idea of education for young blacks? That would turn "school" from a means of fettering them into a means of making the "students . . . a force for social change in their own state"? There was no point to having white, authoritarian teachers (or novices) replace the black authoritarian Mississippians that students knew in their regular schools. Even using the word "school" was risky. That cycle had to be broken. The students themselves had to be set in motion so that they might see learning and knowledge as potentially useful to changing the conditions of their lives—if only because knowledge was also the power of consciousness and the confidence to act. Or, as an "Overview" of the summer's plans projected it, "the purpose of the freedom schools is to create an educational experience for students which will make it possible for them to challenge the myths of our society, to perceive more clearly its realities, and to find alternatives—ultimately new directions for action." Those were no mean lessons to teach. And for a complex of historical and social reasons, the freedom schools taught those lessons not only to thousands of black Mississippians, but to hundreds of (mostly white) volunteers, who returned to their colleges in the fall with a new understanding of their own education.

Cobb and the others who planned the freedom schools used a number of novel devices and one traditional one unconventionally. First, there was the context of the schools. The physical setting of church basements, or, where these were not available, stores, houses, or even lawns, helped to generate a nonschool atmosphere. But more important was the "political setting," so to speak. The schools were an integral part of the summer's challenge to the white power structure: harassment and repression, facilities threatened or hit with bombs, students and teachers arrested—such incidents provided a special urgency to school discussion. More immediately even, many students and teachers were involved outside of freedom school in voter registration or in canvassing for school integration. The unity of education and politics was thus guaranteed.

Second, the planners of the freedom schools trusted in novices as teachers, reasoning quite correctly that though they had been taught in authoritarian modes, they were young and hence likely to be less rigid about teaching. There was also voluntarism and its concomitant informality: no school that called itself "freedom" could compel attendance. No one had to come, and once there, no "attendance" was taken. You came if you wanted to, you stayed if you were interested, and you left if you felt like leaving. Your teacher, moreover, was "Tom" or "Judy," who shook your hand, called you by your first name, and said how glad he was to meet you. In your "class," your teacher sat with you in a circle, and soon you got the idea that you could say what you thought and that no one, least of all the teacher, would laugh at you or strike you. Soon, too, you got the idea that you might disagree with your teacher, black or white, and get a respectful hearing.

Clearly, the freedom-school teacher was not to be an omnipotent, aristocratic dictator, a substitute for the domineering parent or the paternalistic state. He was not to stand before rows of students, simply pouring predigested, precensored information into their brains. Indeed, one of the teachers' main problems was to learn to keep quiet, to learn how *to learn* with the students. In the democratic and creative sense that Wordsworth understood when he described the poet as "a man among men," the freedom-school teacher was to be a student among students. The teacher did not have all the answers; his creativity depended on his ability to listen to his students as much as or more than they listened to him, to discard the formal classroom procedures in which he had been drilled for years, and to respond with feeling and imagination as well as with intelligence and good humor to the moods and needs of the group. He had to understand that a thirteen-year-old who had survived her years in Mississippi understood, however fearfully or inarticulately, a great deal about her world. The freedom-school teacher was not to be a professional manipulator, but a concerned questioner—who really wanted to hear what students had to say, and who would himself be led by their responses to think and act. For these reasons, a traditional device was used unconventionally: a thick mimeographed packet called "Curriculum"[8] included not only materials (on black history, for example, or the Mississippi power structure) and suggestions about how to devise other materials, but also instructions about *how* to teach.

The citizenship curriculum, a discussion of which filled many mornings at freedom schools, was frankly a response to the repressive society Charlie Cobb has described. It was aimed at meeting two basic needs of students: first, a need for identity and hence activity; second, a need for information. The "facts" of history, in terms of dates, people's names, places, events, as well as the interpretations of history—all this had been denied to them, and denied particularly in relation to their own lives as American blacks. Not only was black history unknown to them but even the history of the civil-rights movement was known only in bits and pieces, largely through television, since their newspapers were notoriously uninformative. Their need for identity and activity was organically one with the need for facts. It had to do with what happens when an individual begins to know himself as part of history, with a past and a potential future as well as a present. What happens when an individual begins to assess himself as a human being? The aim of the citizenship curriculum was to assist the growth of self-respect, through self-awareness, both of which lead to self-help. In this way, the curriculum at the center of the freedom schools was avowedly a program for leadership development.

There were seven units, arranged in a "developmental"[9] order, that is, one that "begins on the level of the students' everyday lives and those things in their environment that they have either already experienced or can readily perceive, and builds up to a more realistic perception of American society, themselves, the conditions of their oppression, and alternatives offered by the freedom movement."

1. Comparison of students' reality with others' (the way the students live and the way others live)
2. North to freedom? (the Negro in the North)
3. Examining the apparent reality (the "better lives" that whites live)
4. Introducing the power structure
5. The poor Negro and the poor white
6. Material things versus soul things
7. The movement.

These units were supplemented with others on Negro history; the persecution of the Jews by the Nazis; carefully researched information about the Mississippi white power structure.

Teachers were urged not to lecture, to arrange their classes in circles, and to ask particular kinds of questions.[10] The curriculum supplied two sets of questions to be kept constantly in the minds of teachers and to be introduced frequently to the students:

> The Basic Set of Questions:
>> 1. Why are we (teachers and students) in freedom schools?
>> 2. What is the freedom movement?
>> 3. What alternatives does the freedom movement offer us?
> The Secondary Set of Questions:
>> 1. What does the majority culture have that we want?
>> 2. What does the majority culture have that we don't want?
>> 3. What do we have that we want to keep?

Such questions were quite distinct from the usual school recitation. In the first place, they were "open"—that is, there were no single, prepackaged answers that teachers were to listen for or to require students to memorize. The idea was, indeed, that no one could have a single, ultimate answer to any or all of the questions, for the questions' purpose was to evoke not only response but also students' search for definition and identity. In the second place, the questions were based on what students already knew from their own lives— that is, they could begin to respond, they were already equipped. And third, essential to such questions and such response is the process of discussion itself. The hidden assumptions behind a reliance on discussion are, first, that talk—*saying the words*—is a necessary step for discovery of self and social identity. Further, the *public* discovery—saying the words in a group—might lead to action, if not at once, then later.

While the discussion circle was not successful everywhere, we saw it work in church basements and on lawns. The circle opened with nonthreatening questions: "How do you feel about . . . ?" or "How would you feel if . . . ?" Seated and relaxed, the teacher waited several minutes for a response, listened seriously to those that came, and asked others whether they agreed—without attempting to settle disputes, should they arise, but rather to provoke students to think about them deeply: "Why do you feel this way?" or "Why would any- one feel this way?" The teacher deliberately silenced his own point of view and worked only to move the discussion along, encouraging the shy ones to speak up, clarifying the opposing views of the talkative ones. There was no pressure to "cover content," for the content was the process of trying to make sense of the social and political world you were living in—you students and you teachers. It was trying to make connections between your feelings and the objective conditions of your life.

At first, of course, students were distrustful of the situation generally. Some were also shy before their peers as well as frightened of their teachers. But of course they all had feelings, and they all had some words with which to describe them. And eventually the moment came, unnoticed and passed over, when a student could say easily to his (white) teacher or to a fellow student, "I disagree," and explain why. As for us, college teachers of English, we had never known a comparable experience. It was as freeing for us as for our students, because the key questions applied as much to the lives of volunteers as to students, and the classrooms were as liberating from our schooling as from theirs.

Some of our own experience was with a relatively young group—eleven-to fourteen-year-olds. After describing their own houses, they went on to describe the houses of whites in Jackson that many of them had seen either because they had themselves worked as domestics or because their mothers did. When asked what changes they would like made in their own houses, their answers varied from additional rooms to more yard space; no one thought in terms as grandiose as the "white" houses they had described, and most of them thought of their houses as "comfortable." On the other hand, they were certain that their (segregated) schools were inferior, even when they admitted that the buildings were new. They resented their hand-me-down textbooks, they suspected their teachers of inadequacy, and they complained particularly about the repressive atmosphere. In their schools, they reported, no questioning or discussion was allowed, except in rare instances when they and a particular teacher knew they were "taking a chance." Of course, they knew little or nothing of conditions in white schools, either in Mississippi or elsewhere, beyond their impressions that these, somehow, were "better."

In another school, a discussion started with "What do you think of the editorial in this Jackson *Clarion-Ledger?*" Or, "If you were writing a letter to the editor, what would you say? Let's go ahead and write them." The students also talked about the "law" the Jackson paper said it upheld, whether they supported that law, and when or whether they were justified in breaking it. The teacher explored with them the differences among statutory, constitutional, and "natural" laws which they were likely to encounter in their lives.[11] Or in other schools, an opening question was, "Which is your favorite freedom song? Why? What does freedom mean to you?" Students wrote in essays on freedom, "Freedom is to be able to go in." Or "Freedom is like when you make $40 a week and a white man with the same job makes $100, you should make $100." Alice Jackson, a sixteen-year-old from the Gulf Coast, in a Jackson freedom school wrote:

> I want to walk the streets of a town
> Turn into any restaurant and sit down,
> And be served the food of my choice,
> And not be met by a hostile voice.
> I want to live in the best hotel for a week,
> Or go for a swim at a public beach.
> I want to go to the best university
> And not be met with violence or uncertainty.
> I want the things my ancestors
> Thought we'd never have.
> They are mine as a Negro, an American;
> I shall have them or be dead.[12]

There were other methods suggested to evoke activity and expression. The power structure might be approached through the question "What would you have to do to get the street in front of your house paved?" Students and teachers role-played town councils and school boards at work, the Mississippi legislature and the U.S. Congress, picket lines and voter-registration canvassing, a discussion between a white employer and her black maid whose husband had just tried to register. Debates were among the most popular activities in the schools. One visitor described a debate between the two freedom schools at Palmer's Crossing, a rural community outside Hattiesburg, on the subject: "Resolved: that violence is necessary to obtain civil rights." The points of the debate, which indicate some of what the freedom students were studying, were outlined in a letter:

Affirmative:

1. It's too late for nonviolence. NV can only work if it can reach the conscience (e.g., Gandhi and the British). The white

conscience is dead. The Jews practiced NV against the Nazis and were exterminated.

2. Violence has been successful in Africa—we must show the white man we aren't afraid. Haiti got freedom by violence— Joseph Saint led slaves to freedom after a revolt.

3. Violence shows people you aren't happy even if you don't win.

Negative:

1. Negroes should not stoop as low as whites.

2. We're outnumbered—life is a very precious thing—we can save lives by NV.

3. Love creates community between brother and sister.

4. Negroes have come a long way through NV (e.g., the Civil Rights Bill).

Rebuttal Negative:

White man's conscience isn't dead—I don't believe it, and neither do you. Frederick Douglass may have fought, but he fought harder with words. U.S. isn't 100% against us, or how would Civil Rights Bill have passed?

Rebuttal Affirmative:

People are afraid of use Civil Rights Bill—if you really believe it, you'd all enroll at Hattiesburg High (white). [This caused shouts of laughter.] People pick on you if you're NV—what good did it do Medgar Evers?[13]

As this debate suggests, the freedom-school curriculum's most substantial statement of values, "Material Things and Soul Things," took as its central idea the society that is "humane" because it is "nonviolent." Blacks, of course, are no more naturally violent or nonviolent than any other people. But these students, brought up on the edge of a volcano, named as their heroes the leaders of the nonviolent movement, Martin Luther King, Jr., Medgar Evers, and, when they knew him, Gandhi as well.

But more important perhaps than heroes was the question of how or whether the freedom schools could produce young black leadership. That problem was fundamental for a number of reasons. In the first place, much of the very mixed cadre of black leadership that had organized Mississippi Summer was preparing to move on—

to Bogalusa, Louisiana; to Lowndes County, Alabama; to Syracuse, New York. Nor could movement be sustained on the spirit of voluntarism alone, on temporary altruistic commitment, whether by northern blacks or by whites. The volunteers injected energy, academic knowledge, enthusiasm, caring. Simply by living with black families, whites shattered patterns of behavior baked by hundreds of years of daylight segregation. They were catalytic; they were loved. Those that returned to northern campuses carried with them ideas about education and politics and an imperative to work for the liberation of black people and of themselves as well.

But those that stayed or returned, still loved, also became troublesome—white and bossy in personal relationships, overwhelming with their ability to get *things* done, still strangers who would leave. By the winter, local people were commenting that whites smoked in church sanctuaries, dressed shabbily, came and went. By the summer of 1965, the day of the white volunteer was done in Mississippi: drifters populated the once terrifying freedom house in McComb, and the citizens'-band towers stood silent and useless.

These developments would not have been surprising to the young black staff that projected the citizenship curriculum. The section "North to Freedom?" was rooted in their understanding that the main objective for many, if not most, young blacks in Mississippi was to get out—to Los Angeles, to Chicago, to the Army, to a northern college—anywhere, but out of Mississippi. Did they anticipate as well, we wonder, that the energetic young "shock troops" would encourage their freedom-school students, implicitly or explicitly, to follow them north?

Mississippi whites were only too happy to have them go; one-way bus tickets north were offered by many White Citizens' Councils. More important, job opportunities, even the most laborious and menial, were being cut back in heavily black areas like the Delta. Many of our students expressed a wish to go north to college, in part because they suspected that Negro colleges in Mississippi were as inadequate as their public schools, and also because they wanted the experience of learning in an integrated group. They were articulate about the need for communication between black and white: the freedom songs they sang every day—"Black and white together/We shall not be moved," for example—were not simply words to be mouthed. But there was also the rationalization and wanting to leave.

On the other hand, some of them had been reading with us from the works of Richard Wright and James Baldwin of the Negro in Chicago or Harlem; and they knew they were living through a summer which had brought riots to northern cities, though not to Jackson, Mississippi. They questioned the condition of blacks everywhere, and many of them concluded that it was probably better to stay in Mississippi and work to improve things than to imagine that things were better in another place. How many will maintain these commitments in the face of Mississippi's realities remains unclear.

If the spirit of the Summer Project was best expressed in the freedom schools, its pulse was established by the political program. In the early stages, voter registration was the focus. Organizers tramped tediously from house to house—often under the hostile eyes of local sheriffs and cruising cars of whites—asking, persuading, cajoling people to go down to the county courthouses, the only places in Mississippi where applications for voter registration were accepted. Voter education and literacy classes were established, rallies were held. And then registration workers accompanied individuals or, on "Freedom Days," whole groups to face the sheriff and often angry crowds gathered outside the courthouse. In a sense, these trips to the courthouse were symbolic exercises designed to show that people were unafraid and determined to vote. When they were in at all, registrars predictably failed most black people by using the complex voter-registration requirements, which included the interpretation of any of the 285 sections of the state Constitution. During late June and most of July in Greenwood, 144 Negroes went to the courthouse, 123 managed to get in to take the test, and two were passed; in Canton, twenty-two went and took the test, none passed; in Hattiesburg, seventy went, five passed. By contrast, in Panola County, where a federal voting registrar had been installed by the courts, two SNCC workers alone helped 237 black people register in one *week,* and by August over 600 had been registered. In most places, applicants found their names published in the local paper, ostensibly to permit others to challenge their moral character as potential voters, but realistically to let the white community know which blacks were challenging their political monopoly. Consequently, people going down to the courthouse were not only subject to harassment and arrest during their pilgrimage, but to economic reprisal, threats, and physical intimidation afterward. The attempt to register, however symbolic, had real and dangerous effects. Indeed, voter registration was considered the most risky assignment for volunteers. The positive effects were equally real, however: in building the courage, enthusiasm, and solidarity of the adult black community; in bringing into clear national view the fact that Mississippi systematically disenfranchised black people; and in providing the kinds of public confrontations without which, it seemed, national attention could not be kept on the civil-rights struggle.

Partly in response to the slow frustration of voter-registration work, but primarily to support the challenge of the mostly black Mississippi Freedom Democratic Party (MFDP) to the (white) Mississippi delegation to the August Democratic National Convention, emphasis shifted about midway in the summer to "freedom registration." Canvassers then went from house to house asking people who wanted to vote to enroll on "freedom-registration" forms similar to those to be used by federal registrars. The results were, at first, encouraging: in the places cited above, Greenwood, Canton, and Hattiesburg, 3,384, 2,000, and 3,373 Negroes respectively registered on such forms by August 1. But the point of freedom registration—to impress distant courts or even more distant national Democratic-party officials—was never as immediate or vivid as voter registration. The numbers enrolled were never, finally, as high as expectations. Somehow, perhaps by the very challenge it had so long presented, the regular institution of voter registration, however racist, however corrupt, retained its authority. Though it provided a legal basis for a challenge to the white Democratic convention delegation and to the election of segregationist Mississippi congressmen early the following year, freedom registration never did take root.

Mississippi Summer's political program moved to a visible climax at the Atlantic City convention of the national Democratic Party. There the integrated Mississippi Freedom Democratic Party demanded acceptance as the only legitimate representative of the Mississippi people; they won recognition from many state delegations and were acclaimed by much of the convention. And all across Mississippi itself, black people watched in delight as their friends and neighbors and representatives spoke their piece for the Credentials Committee, for state delegation caucuses, and for national television. Liberals, led by Joseph Rauh, then attorney for the Freedom Party, attempted, as they saw it, to consolidate these largely unexpected gains by working out a compromise to seat the regular delegation and two representatives of the MFDP. The compromise was angrily opposed by SNCC staff and finally rejected by the Freedom-Party delegates as "tokenism." For the young staff and volunteers, the whole Atlantic City effort became a bitter charade. Their case, they felt, was self-evident: blacks were excluded from Mississippi's political processes; the documentary evidence was overwhelming. Even on prudential political grounds, seating the regular Mississippi delegation made no sense, since it was clear that Goldwater would take the state and the few others like it, and that the theoretically Democratic delegates would, in fact, support him.

Moreover, it was impossible to forget that three of their number had died that summer and that others had been beaten and still others had been murdered in prior summers. Compromise seemed a betrayal of those deaths, of so many other sacrifices, beatings, risks. Their cry was then still "Freedom," but it was "Freedom *now!*" How could others who had not walked the hot streets of Greenwood, experienced the terror, seen Neshoba County sheriff Cecil Price laugh and spit as the three bodies were being searched out presume now to preach compromise? The political processes epitomized by the convention seemed to many Mississippi veterans at best a sham.

One may find these attitudes naïve, or, as Tom Wicker did in *The New York Times* four years later, puritanical. Seen another way, however, they are perfectly natural reactions of young people who have risked their lives and futures to the political conditions adults take for granted: where alignments are shifting, tentative, partial; where Ribicoff and Eastland claim the same party; where yesterday's castigated target becomes today's esteemed colleague and party leader. There is irony in the discrepancy between the total commitment necessary to reach the convention floor and the impossibility of turning such commitment to compromise. If there were moralists among the back-slappers at Atlantic City, it was Mississippi which had moralized them.

Atlantic City also clarified another ambiguity of the summer's political program. Unlike the freedom schools and the community centers, voter registration was aimed at generations of Negroes older and more settled than the COFO staff or volunteers. It was not, as some people charged, that radical staff at Atlantic City had persuaded naïve local people to reject the compromise; once its token character was clear, most of the Freedom-Party delegation had genuinely opposed it. What comes into relief, oddly, perhaps only now, in retrospect of 1968, is the distance there always was between the young, roaming the Boardwalk, cadging tickets to the gallery to shout support for Fannie Lou Hamer: support, finally. "For whom do they really work?" some delegates were tempted to ask about the denim-clad young people who haunted their comings and goings, who slept on the beaches, and who mocked the Democrats' dignity, even while they asked their vote. The futures of these young people were tenuously connected, if at all, to the resurrection of Democratic political life in Gothic Mississippi. Where were they to be in 1968, an Atlantic City soothsayer might have asked, when Mrs. Hamer and Mr. Henry were seated as Humphrey delegates in the Stockyards auditorium? Yet they had taken their present in their hands and delivered it into the Mississippi fire. Why? Weren't there things to do closer to home?

The question rankled in 1964. Volunteers, particularly, were forever put to explaining why they had come to Mississippi. The question seemed impertinent, the answers obvious. Yet the question had hit upon a truth, though perhaps not of the sort originally meant. Reflecting on their devotion to other peoples' lives and politics, some of the volunteers and the staff began to find, indeed, that their own struggle had not yet begun, in their own lives, with the institutions that affected them. Whether or not they had "changed" Mississippi, they had learned something of the struggle and the ambiguities of change.

And of course Mississippi gave even more to the volunteers. Our experience in the freedom schools—in learning to teach by asking, in discovering radical connections between school and life—led us to raise some fundamental questions about the quality and nature of our own northern schools. It was no accident either that many of the leaders of the student rebellion at Berkeley that next winter were Mississippi veterans, nor that among the most prominent demands of the Berkeley students was that education at the University of California become more relevant and humane.

Some of the whites and most of the blacks who experienced the maneuvers of Atlantic City drew additional conclusions. White friends in high places were not to be relied on, whether they called themselves liberal lawyers or liberal senators, or even whether they said in the halls of Congress, "We *shall* overcome." For when it came to the count, the Freedom Democratic Party got tokens, and white, racist Mississippi got the delegates. The white volunteers got the publicity; the black staff would be left to pick up the pieces. The only power on which blacks could rely finally was the power they themselves could organize. The white volunteers filtered north from Mississippi; a few white SNCC staff members stayed on even into the following year. But by the time the Johnson-Humphrey team stood to receive the accolades of the assembled Democrats, the steps from a civil-rights to a black-power movement were already hastening.

Notes

[1] For a detailed history, see Martin Oppenheimer, *The Genesis of the Southern Negro Student Movement,* Ph. D. dissertation, University of Pennsylvania, 1963, and "The Southern Student Movement: Year I," *Journal of Negro History* (Fall, 1964), pp. 396–403; and Howard Zinn, *SNCC—The New Abolitionists* (Boston: Beacon Press, 1964).

[2] See 1963 Report of the U.S. Commission on Civil Rights; *Congressional Weekly,* July 5, 1963; U.S. Bureau of the Census Report for 1960; among other sources.

[3] *Letters from Mississippi,* ed. Elizabeth Sutherland (New York: New American Library, 1965), p. 62.

[4] James W. Silver, *Mississippi: The Closed Society* (New York, 1964), p. 155.

[5] *Letters from Mississippi,* pp. 139–40.

[6] *Ibid.,* p. 205.

[7] Florence Howe, "Mississippi's Freedom Schools: the Politics of Education," *Harvard Educational Review,* XXXV (Spring, 1965), p. 144.

[8] The packet of mimeographed curriculum materials, circulated to freedom-school teachers before they came south, was mainly prepared on the basis of a conference held by the National Council of Churches March 21–22, 1964. The curriculum contained three divisions: ideas for teaching academic materials, mathematics, English, etc.; ideas for organizing recreational and cultural events; and the "citizenship curriculum," which we will discuss in some detail.

[9] We are not going to describe the "academic" curriculum, but it, too, was developmental: "The value of the freedom schools will derive mainly from what the teachers are able to elicit from the students in terms of comprehension and expression of their experiences. The curriculum should derive from the students' background, and all aspects of classroom activity should be an outgrowth of their experiences." "A Note to the Teacher" further urged as useful instructional materials "the actual problems of communication and analysis which the student encounters in his daily life, e.g., how to write a leaflet, how to calculate the number of eligible voters in a community."

[10] So central was this process of questioning that one of the few vaguely accurate news stories about freedom schools in Mississippi's hostile press reported that "the underlying aim of the 'citizenship curriculum,' a COFO worker says, is to teach the Mississippi Negro to question—to question the written word, to question the radio, not to believe everything heard." Biloxi-Gulfport *Herald,* July 10, 1964.

[11] See Howard Zinn, "Schools in Context—The Mississippi Idea," *The Nation,* November 23, 1964, and reprinted by SNCC; and Liz Fusco, "To Blur the Focus," unpublished mimeographed pamphlet.

[12] First printed in *Harvard Educational Review,* XXXV (Spring, 1965), p. 157, then as part of *Freedom School Poetry* (Atlanta: SNCC, 1965), p. 43. Al-

most every community had a freedom-school newspaper—in which such essays and poems were published—mainly written, edited, and mimeographed by the students, and distributed by them to the community, sometimes at the risk of arrest. In Jackson, a group of students from the Blair Street Freedom School collected poems from their own and other papers and sat through many hot afternoons typing them and deciding which to include in the *Freedom School Poetry* anthology (much later published by SNCC).

[13] *Letters from Mississippi,* pp. 103–04.

3

The Peace Corps

For the nine years of its existence, the Peace Corps has stood as a symbol of the nation's commitment to the idealism of youth. It has had, of course, other specific functions. The enabling legislation, passed by Congress on September 22, 1961, established three such objectives: to provide necessary manpower for developing countries, to improve the image of the United States abroad, and to promote among Americans a better understanding of other peoples and other cultures. But the power of the Peace Corps has rested less in its ability to do these three jobs or other, similar tasks than in what was expressed by its mere existence. For it seemed to say that U.S. society not only approved of, but was willing to encourage and support, the commitment of its youth to improving the lives of people overseas. U.S. rhetoric, from the first Roosevelt through Wilson and the second Roosevelt, had always claimed that we were devoted to the aid of peoples less fortunate than we. But in fact American youth had gone abroad—except in the notable service of a few small voluntary agencies—mainly as soldiers whose relations to other people were occasionally helpful but, in retrospect, mostly self-serving if not downright imperial. Thus the Peace Corps seemed, at last, to put American money and manpower where its mouth had been—on the side of development, progress, and the ideals of international order.

In fact, the Peace Corps's investment of the dedication and talent of young Americans (if not of the money of older Americans) has been considerable. By 1968, over 35,000 Americans, whose average age was twenty-four years, had seen or were involved in Peace Corps service. Over 13,000 volunteers were overseas in some fifty-nine countries. The agency's budget had climbed to $110 million in 1967, and it has been hoping for small but steady increases since. Though over half the volunteers have taught, there are roughly 100 job categories (300 if one includes every subcategory); and the job descriptions are almost as various as the individual volunteers. They include work with Malawian counterparts, to use the language of the Corps's 1967 congressional presentation, to "conduct health surveys, administer tests and treatments, and visit, exhort, and persuade patients, thus providing the necessary and usually missing follow-up which means saved lives instead of wasted resources"; helping organize and manage rural cooperatives in Peru; running summer schools in the Philippines; farming demonstration plots in India; forming mothers clubs in Chilean urban slums and providing lectures and demonstrations for mothers on sewing, finance, health, and nutrition; helping staff a nationwide educational television program in Colombia.

Whatever the value of these enterprises for the host countries, they have been of great importance to the volunteers. Some have learned what freedom-school teachers learned—that before one can talk, one must listen, that in order to teach, one must first learn. An instance often cited is the volunteer who discovered that her lectures on preventive medicine were incomprehensible and irrelevant; the Africans with whom she was working had their own theory of disease and treatment, and it was only after she began to understand their frame of reference by listening to their questions and language that she could begin to see the value of their forms of cure and how what she had to offer might usefully fit into their patterns of care. Or again, a girl who had tried to impose a cooperative on Chilean peasants "listened to what the barefoot *campesino* had to teach us about his world and its problems," and she

> . . . began to understand as the peasant began to articulate— for five hours without a stop—why a co-op was not possible *now* and what he needed in order first to live and then to enter the modern world. He had no horse to reach a central meeting place

regularly, and to walk meant walking miles in mud and cold to return with a bad cold to an unheated straw hut where illness meant nothing—no doctor, no pills, nothing but the communal grave if you had not the constitution to survive. A co-op needs some financing if it is to function, but the small farmer had nothing—nothing but "in-kind" produce to buy salt and sugar and an occasional bus trip to the nearest pueblo. . . . He understood the life-or-death world he lived in, and his attitude was "show me that my life and my family mean anything to you of the world of doctors and food and adequate housing and education-fine words."[1]

Some Peace Corps volunteers have questioned whether the "taxpayer is getting his money's worth"; at the same time, they have usually insisted that their "experience . . . was well worth it" for them. More severe critics, including those who claim to have been "radicalized" by the experience, learned something of the "realities of poverty, with its underlying apathy, violence, and chaos," of "the difficulties—economic, social, political, and emotional—which people face in building a nation in the twentieth century," of the "potential of people breaking out of the apathy imposed by centuries of poverty and serfdom," of "the inadequacies in the actions and goals of our own government."[2]

Perhaps because of its own critics, perhaps for other reasons, the Peace Corps's popularity among the young has badly declined. In December, 1967, recruitment officials announced that applications had dropped 30 percent from their peak number in 1966, despite the addition of twenty-five former volunteers to a regular recruitment staff of ninety-three. *Newsweek* reported the drop as more severe—50%, not 30%.[3] Beyond a decline in numbers, there was a decline in quality. Some Peace Corps officials described the 1967 volunteers as more "bland" than heretofore, though former volunteers suggested that the Corps's own selection policy, which eliminates "radical" or even outspoken candidates, was chiefly to blame. Wherever the responsibility may truly lie, the director of the Peace Corps in Ethiopia was complaining, at about the same time, and in an official journal, that new volunteers were less committed to the Corps and its ideals, but were joining because it was better than other alternatives open to them, including the Army.[4] As if those recruitment problems were not sufficient, on campus, the Peace Corps has met hostility less intense, obviously, than that directed at Dow or Marine recruiters, but not different in kind. During the fall of 1968 at least two Peace Corps recruiters were effectively prevented by demonstrators from doing their campus business. By 1970, they were being physically threatened on some campuses.

For the first time, too, the Peace Corps has come under considerable printed attack. Some critics have questioned its competence, charging that the volunteers are mostly unqualified, unskilled, and untrained generalists, and that the Corps sends overseas those who by chance have been recruited rather than people with skills needed by the host countries. Arnold and Marian Zeitlin, two former volunteers, have pointed out, for example, that though Ghana needed math and science teachers, only thirteen of the fifty-one volunteers sent fit that description, however remotely. Volunteers in Ghana taught history, which was precisely what Premier Kwame Nkrumah did not want.[5] There are too many Ph.D.'s in the Peace Corps, the Zeitlins have complained, and no plumbers. A recent book by David Hapgood and Meridan Bennett, *Agents of Change,* takes the first really "close look at the Peace Corps" (as their subtitle puts it). And though they have hopes for the future, and praise for many individual corpsmen, they conclude that "as a contributor to development in the third world, the Peace Corps can make no great claims to accomplishment." Their stories of bumbling volunteers and bungling bureaucracies make sometimes hilarious, but finally sobering reading.

More fundamental criticism has been made by those young people who have come to see the Peace Corps as "simply another arm of U.S. foreign policy," the primary expression of which is Vietnam. They begin with the simple observation that "the entire Peace Corps budget of about $105 million a year is less than the budget for two days in Vietnam."[6] Articles have begun to appear in college newspapers and alumni magazines complaining, for example, that for the United States the Peace Corps is "a pretty salve to its foreign-policy guilt and the Iranians can take advantage of an opportunity to cultivate American friends or can dismiss us as meddling foreigners (the concept of altruism is so foreign to them, they cannot believe we're simply there to help them—and maybe they're right)."[7] Most outspoken is a new organization of some 3,000 former Peace Corpsmen, calling itself a Committee of Returned Volunteers. "The spirit of the group," one of their leaflets passed out during the demonstrations at the Democratic convention in Chicago says, "is informed by a sense of outrage against the increasingly militaristic policies of the United States, concern with the ineffectuality of present foreign-aid programs, and the conviction that there is something fundamentally wrong in our repression of indigenous attempts to revolutionize societies of the third world. It is this outrage, concern, and conviction which now leads us to question the role of the Peace Corps."

It is as easy and as dangerous to underestimate such questioning of and opposition to the Peace Corps as it has been to exaggerate its achievements. Some members of the agency have attributed such problems to malcontents, a radical fringe, or temporary malaise generated by the Vietnam war.[8] But to dismiss or trivialize the new rush of criticism is to mistake the Peace Corps's crucial and fragile symbolic role—or to misunderstand the significance of such symbols. Governments depend upon certain institutions and symbols to maintain their legitimacy and their citizens' devotion. These symbols express commitments of public power and authority to certain shared values and goals. And they help evoke and command loyalty not only to such goals but also to the government and to the society itself. Federal civil-rights legislation, for example, whatever its concrete effects on the lives of black people, has functioned this way. Similarly, whatever its usefulness to underdeveloped countries or to the United States, the Peace Corps's importance rests on its power through much of the 1960's to evoke widespread loyalty and commitment from the young. The Peace Corps remains the largest single employer of new B.A.'s in the country. Even in 1967, the agency received 35,000 applications. But a decline in the Peace Corps's prestige, in its legacy of Kennedy charisma, so to speak, symbolizes, in a fairly obvious way, an erosion of trust in and allegiance to the federal government among young people.

The Peace Corps's problems have grown, in part, from contradictions in its initial purpose and from serious defects in its performance. But these, in turn, are rooted in the fundamental character of American foreign policy, and looked at closely, they can tell us a good deal about why that policy has been so significant in generating rebellion against it.

The initial ideas for a "Point 4 Youth Corps" or an "International Youth Service Agency" developed partly from the tradition of overseas volunteer service fostered by private or religious agencies like the American Friends Service Committee (AFSC) or the International Farm Youth Exchange. Such agencies and the international "work-camp" movement allowed young Americans to express their concern for the aspirations and well-being of the rest of mankind. But these efforts were quite small; in forty years of work, for example, the AFSC and the Mennonite Central Committee, two of the most active agencies, had placed only about 10,000 volunteers overseas, many of them in refugee-relief work.[9] The second root of what became the Peace Corps was the effort of the United States government after World War II to promote the development of nations in the "third world" through a variety of mechanisms, including the International Cooperation Administration, the Export-Import Bank, the Development Loan Fund, and through United Nations programs like the Expanded Technical Assistance Program. It seemed to a number of people during the late 1950's that a national program of service abroad might at once enlist the idealism expressed in voluntary-agency projects and contribute to the national goal of helping other nations help themselves by providing them with vital manpower. Finally, in 1959, Congressman Henry S. Reuss and the late Senator Richard L. Neuberger introduced bills to study the advisability and practicality of such a venture. Such a study was mandated by law in June of 1960; at the same time, Senator Humphrey introduced a bill, which did not receive Senate consideration, actually to establish a Peace Corps.

Those were, it must be said, innocent days. No one seemed to see it as likely that young idealism, the needs of developing nations, and the interests of American foreign policy might *not* be served together. It seemed simple enough:

> We must offer our technical skills, asking neither favor nor profit in return. We must show them how to get ten times or a hundred times as much from their land as they get now. We must show them how to conquer those diseases and insects that kill their crops and animals and children. We must show them how to conquer malaria and hookworm and dysentery and venereal disease and plague. We must help them as they struggle up out of their hell. We must go to their sides and help them. There is no substitute for the real, living, loving person rubbing elbow to elbow with the people who toil. . . . We must have 100,000 technically trained men of unimpeachable integrity over the world, to

help people help themselves. We must give or loan money when these technicians call for it.[10]

The influential Colorado State University study (which grew out of the Reuss-Neuberger bills) quoted this passage almost as its motto. But it also suggested, with more wishfulness than realism, that "American business [is] increasingly engaged in meeting its social responsibilities abroad. . . ." (Sect. 1, p. 2). (The fact was that American business was primarily engaged in more than tripling its earnings on foreign investment between 1950 and 1965). Some of those who prepared the Colorado State report had had long experience in voluntary agencies; their work and thought perhaps best exemplified the spirit out of which the Peace Corps grew. Yet even these men and women did not challenge their own assumption that "Peace Corps volunteers will be transmitting something perhaps even more important than technical skills. They will be carrying with them a typically American quality of knowing how to organize for effective action. . . . Even young Americans normally have had experience in organizing to get a job done. Yet this quality is one which may often be lacking from peoples emerging from other culture patterns and paternalistic outside rule" (Sect. 3, pp. 3, 4). Thus even this fine study assumed the fundamental rightness of American methods, the purity of American motives, and the decency of American institutions—or, at the very least, the ability of American youths to perform valid tasks divorced from the ugly realities of foreign policy.

While the promoters of the Peace Corps idea felt that the Corps should serve the American goal of "developing" poorer nations and should relate closely to the efforts of other agencies working toward that goal, they also saw the danger of the Corps's identification as another arm of America's militarized, anti-Communist foreign policy. Professor Max Milliken of MIT, for example, suggested in an independent memorandum for President-elect Kennedy, that the Corps not conduct overseas operations directly, but contract projects out to voluntary agencies and educational institutions. Relatively independent agencies, Milliken and others argued, could more easily experiment, and could capitalize on the goodwill and experience that might be developed abroad. They urged movement toward an international Peace Corps under United Nations auspices; they proposed that overseas projects be planned and supervised by binational commissions; they also warned that the Peace Corps must not become a propaganda tool, an intelligence arm, or a "mere 'Cold War' weapon, a skillful device to win allies and combat totalitarianism" (Sect. 3, p. 7).

Yet the idea for a Corps that emerged from the 1960 Presidential campaign and the actual agency that came into being on March 1, 1961, were open to all these abuses. In presenting the Corps in a speech just prior to the election (November 2, 1960), Senator Kennedy pictured it primarily as a Cold War weapon. "The Lenin Institute for Political Warfare," he warned, "exports each year hundreds of agents to disrupt free institutions in the uncommitted world. . . . Already Asia has more of the Soviet than American technicians. . . . They know the country, they speak the language—and in Guinea, Ghana, Laos, and all over the globe, they are working fast and effectively. Missiles and arms cannot stop them—neither can American dollars. They can only be countered by Americans equally skilled and equally dedicated. . . ." In part this echoed Senator Humphrey, who had spoken of the Corps as a means "to combat the virus of Communism."[11] In part, this was Kennedy's campaign rhetoric. Kennedy did continue to emphasize the need for skilled technicians who could make meaningful contributions to the development of the host country. And he appointed to the Corps imaginative people who, if they shared assumptions about the superiority of American organization, did not accept such State Department dogmas as, for example, that the United States "is not disposed to favor large loans of public funds to countries not welcoming our private capital."[12]

Nevertheless, the Peace Corps has been, in practice, not the creature envisioned by its progenitors. The notion that the Corps's actual work should be done through voluntary agencies did not survive the first few months' politics. A few projects were contracted out to agencies like CARE, but religiously affiliated organizations were excluded, and the Corps's staff, like many other New Frontiersmen, soon began to feel that it could do the job better by itself. The idea of organizing a truly international service corps under UN auspices also soon disappeared. Kennedy had spoken of the need to obtain "technicians," under which he included "engineers, doctors, teachers, agricultural experts, specialists in public law, labor, taxation, civil service." But even in its heyday, most Peace Corps volunteers were graduates of liberal-arts colleges with degrees in history, literature, sociology. Half of them teach; another quarter work in "community development," which can mean almost anything, but has seldom been dependent upon technical skill. Slightly more than 10% of the volunteers work in agriculture, slightly more than 11% in health, and somewhat under both those percentages come to the Corps with skills in such areas.

It is not that the Corps is unaware of such limitations or that it has not tried to effect changes. But its culture remains that of white, middle-class America, its prime recruiting targets B.A. generalists from good liberal-arts colleges. Only 3% of the volunteers in the first five years were not college graduates. A black auto mechanic from Harlem has probably less chance of getting into the Peace Corps—assuming what is unlikely, that he would want to—than into Columbia University. And he has still less chance, given the Corps's methods of screening and training, the style of life it enforces, the assumptions it insists upon, of staying. Not surprisingly, under these circumstances, the recruiting rhetoric of the Corps has come to emphasize not the struggles of developing nations but the desirability of the experience for young people seeking identity. "You'll find out who you are"— the radio add in Baltimore runs to a slightly alien rendition of the song "Who Am I?"—"what you are, what kind of guts you've got." You will be helping to overcome poverty and disease, the broadcaster adds, but in the context of extending the narrow experience of white, middle-class college graduates.

And so the program comes to resemble those teacher-training enterprises in which novices are forever cutting their pedagogical teeth on ghetto children. Or, more awkwardly still, it becomes a training ground in which tomorrow's elites learn better to impose their assumptions and priorities on the under classes. As the returned volunteer we quoted above, who had "learned" so much listening to the articulate *campesino,* all too accurately put it: "My basic premise is that a Peace Corps-type experience can teach the future teachers, planners, economists, policymakers, and bureaucrats how to make the immense knowledge at our disposal relevant and communicable to underdeveloped peoples" (*Barnard Alumnae Magazine,* p. 5). "Relevant" and "communicable," experience has well taught us, are finally translatable into "accepted by." Thus, a secondary purpose of the Corps, the extended education of certain young Americans, has become what Hapgood and Bennett have called "the clearest result of the Peace Corps experiment."[13] A less friendly way of putting it would be to say that the Corps's main accomplishment has been in providing on-the-job training for tomorrow's administrators of the American Empire.

In addition, the Corps has not, on the whole, been able to maintain the difficult stance of cooperating with other "positive" American overseas efforts while not being identified with or submerged in the general thrust of United States foreign policy. Dean Rusk had said that "the Peace Corps is not an instrument *of* foreign policy because to make it so would rob it of its contribution *to* foreign policy."[14] But that distinction has come to seem increasingly disingenuous. In Bolivia, Peru, Colombia, and elsewhere, the Corps works very closely with USAID. That liaison has not always been a happy one: in some respects the heavy AID resources tend to corrupt both the spirit of the Corps and its ability to do the kind of work it can best do (see Hapgood and Bennett, pp. 91–92). But perhaps more fundamentally, the relationship to AID illustrates one of the ways in which the Peace Corps is incorporated into and used by the powerful agencies that determine America's foreign policy. The Department of State reviews and approves all projected Peace Corps projects. Thus it should be no surprise that the Corps has in the last two years left Guinea, Gabon, and Pakistan, which have become increasingly independent of the United States; its contingent in socialist Tanzania had faded from 400 to 11 by the beginning of 1969, and in Nigeria from 750 to 90. At the same time, the Corps has begun new projects in South Korea and Paraguay, two dictatorships heavily dependent upon the American military.

The amalgamation of the Peace Corps and other foreign operations of the government is being extended under the administration of the new director, Joseph H. Blatchford. He headed ACCION, a privately supported development program in Latin America; well-documented scuttlebutt among former PCV's is that corpsmen were once instructed to avoid ACCION projects because the organization was thought to be funded primarily by the CIA. However that might be, Mr. Blatchford is clearly committed to redirecting the Peace Corps toward fulfilling specific roles *within* developmental projects organized by larger government agencies. In addition, Undersecretary of State Elliot J. Richardson has asked State Department bureau heads to look for ways of interchanging personnel among agencies like the Peace Corps, AID, and the U.S. Information Agency.[15]

Host countries have been especially sensitive to a shift in the avowed role of the Peace Corps. For instance, Julius K. Nyerere, President of Tanzania, has said recently that "the Peace Corps has changed its character. Some of its idealism has gone out, and now? Now it is a problem."[16] Overseas suspicion of the Corps has been fed by incidents like that in Chile, where a Communist-party deputy made public a 1966 memorandum supposedly from Peace Corps official William E. Moffett to all Latin-American Peace Corps representatives. The memo indicated that "payment for items of information supplied to PCV's by the local population" had been increased "so as to interest both the sources and the PCV's themselves." And it expressed interest in information "concerning students, leftist groups and parties, the attitude of the local population to the Peace Corps program, the names of persons most antagonistic to the U.S.," among other things.[17] Whether or not the memorandum is, as has been charged, a forgery (it is remarkably clever and appropriate if it is), the implication that PCV's have gathered data for other U.S. agencies fits the experience of many previously innocent volunteers, "debriefed" after stints in the countryside. No wonder, then, that a poster on the bulletin board of the editor of one of Nigeria's leading newspapers asserts: "Not a single man in Nigeria should have doubts as to the Peace Corps. It is a corps of spies and American imperialists."[18] Or that the conservative newspaper *El Tiempo* of Bogotá, Colombia, speaks of the Corps as "Marines with velvet gloves." Or that bombs were planted in the Corps' office in Guatemala.

Thus the Corps has emerged, despite the admonitions of some of its founders, as a "soft" cold-war weapon. But more important, perhaps, than specific instances of its absorption into imperial strategy is the sense of many young people who, as a former volunteer put it, "ask how they can volunteer for an organization called the Peace Corps run by a country which is also running the most monstrous war in history?"[19] It would be hard to exaggerate the impact of Vietnam on the morale of the Corps and attitudes toward it. We have already cited the contrast between the Peace Corps's $105-million yearly budget and the costs of the war. Those figures have become a popular symbol of feelings about the Corps. Ninety-two volunteers in Chile signed a mild "Negotiations Now" petition in 1967 and precipitated a public row involving the highest levels of the State Department. Similar incidents occurred in the Dominican Republic and Turkey in 1969, and other volunteers throughout the world have expressed their opposition to the war and consequent disenchantment with the Corps. And even Ray Holland, the Corps' recruiting director, acknowledged that there was an "increasing reluctance on the part of young people to become associated with the U.S. government, which they see waging a war they cannot support."[20]

The Peace Corps' activities in Thailand provide a case study of how the war-dominated interests of American foreign policy have come also to dominate the corps. In its 1967 congressional presentation, while acknowledging that volunteers were being pulled back from less friendly nations, the Corps boasted that plans were being completed to "mount a program of social change and economic development in the critical north-east sector" of Thailand. It is, of course, precisely in that long-neglected area that a small Communist-led insurgency has been developing despite the relative affluence of the rest of the country. The real role of the 400 PCV's in a country where at least 40,000 American troops are at war becomes clear in a letter from a volunteer stationed in Thailand. The comments of the former volunteer who printed the letter in an article perhaps better than anything else we have read express the anguish of a young person, wishing to work good in the world, but caught in a machine that inexorably incorporates her into its computerized horrors:

"I hope you include for ALL to read that there are some of us who actually cry when we see what the U.S. military policy is doing to this country. Tell them about all the Thai teachers who leave their schools to become interpreters and clerks at our military bases at three times their original salaries. Tell them about Thai agriculturalists who desert their experimental stations, who desert their work with the farmers to work at our military bases. Their job is to make the base beautiful and pleasant to the eyes. They now get five times their original salary. Tell them about the Thai engineers who leave their road, dam, and bridge construction jobs to build runways and supply houses for our military bases. They now earn seven times their original salaries."

The sad thing of course is that in Thailand, the enormous American military and paramilitary build-up makes the job of a

Peace Corps volunteer virtually meaningless. The very volunteer who wrote that pained letter has, willy-nilly, become part of an enormous American disruption of Thai life and society.[21]

Unfortunately, the Corps's work is not, in fact, likely to be "meaningless." For in the context of northeast Thailand, it cannot help but become the carrot of "development" to balance the military stick in that brutal process, familiar to us from Vietnam, known as "pacification."

Two fundamental problems are underlined by this volunteer's experience in Thailand. First, the testimony the Corps was to embody of America's commitment to the ideals of international justice and progress has been thoroughly subverted by the louder, bloodier testimony of our guns and planes. That at least thirty-eight PCV's have been recalled from assignments to be drafted for the war dramatically illustrates U.S. priorities. And in at least one case, that of Bruce Murray in Providence, Rhode Island, evidence introduced in his suit against the Corps and the Selective Service System strongly indicated that he had been separated from the Corps and illegally processed and drafted by his local board because he chose to express his opposition to the war.

Second, as Hapgood and Bennett have cautiously put it:

Whenever the United States sends people or money into another society, the act is tinged with imperialism, however mild. Questioning the purpose of American efforts abroad can be painful; the Peace Corps experience has forced many to do just that. Volunteers have asked, on occasion, if there is really a difference, except in degree, between dropping napalm on Vietnamese to convert them to our form of politics and dropping Peace Corps teachers on Africans to convert them to our form of education. [P. 30.]

From one point of view, of course, that is simply hard-headed realism, to be accepted along with the "legitimate needs" of American business overseas. But that rationalization does not deal with the idealism on which the Peace Corps has depended, both for volunteers and for its symbolic function. And it raises even more sharply the question of what the Peace Corps has actually been able to accomplish.

In statistical terms, the volunteers' contribution to education has been impressive; indeed, education is "the Peace Corps's biggest business," as an official leaflet puts it. In 1968, for example, 6,200 PCV's helped teach 700,000 children and train 55,000 teachers, who, within two years, will be instructing ten million children in Africa alone. Given the usual assumptions of Americans that "education" in any form and at any time is good, such a return seems excellent business. But the value of the Corps's teaching program, which looks so good on paper, has come under sharp attack recently with respect both to what it does and whether it is of real value to the people it affects.

The Corps assumes "that a college graduate has a good foundation of *what* to teach—his college major or minor—and that he has the ability to learn *how* to teach."[22] In practice, the first of these assumptions has proved extraordinarily naïve—few things could be more irrelevant to the schooling needs of developing countries than most American undergraduate curricula. The experience of one former volunteer we interviewed might serve to illustrate the problems. Like the majority of volunteers, she was a recent graduate from a liberal-arts college; her assignment, teaching English in a Philippine town. Once there, her first discovery was that local people wanted, insofar as they were at all aware that Peace Corps help was available, aid in ceramics and marketing to develop home industry. This was not an unusual discovery: other volunteers have similarly reported overwhelming local needs in health, sanitation, and agriculture. But her program had been planned by Manila, which, if it did not listen to local demand, was at least in touch with what the Peace Corps had to supply. At another level, however, Manila was indeed listening to local demand: the head of a powerful family, who owned the land on which the school stood, who hired most of the teachers, and who was President of the "PTA," wanted a Peace Corps volunteer. For him it was a matter of local status; it didn't matter much what got taught.

Very well, then, she was to teach English. Volunteers all over the Philippines—and Asia and Africa—were doing that. But as she looked around at her students and their lives, she began to ask "Why"? What had English to do with them? It was the language of the elites, mostly in Manila, which few of her students would ever even visit. Like the "new math"—which some hundred volunteers were busily introducing—or her very presence, some smattering of English might provide a little competitive status. It might help the natives to communicate better with the Americans who came in to run the local Del Monte packing plant. But it could not significantly improve or even change the conditions of peoples' lives. It provided them with neither skill nor power. It all began to seem a waste. And though she continued to do her job, many other volunteers she observed did less and less, putting in their two years, some of them avoiding the Army, most feeling guilt and anger at the Peace Corps.

At the root, the problem was not a matter of the volunteers' inadequacy nor the Corps's and Manila's bad planning, but of the assumptions which have informed the Corps's education program, especially the notions about the relationship of education to development and to change. It has become clear, in recent studies, that even during the industrialization of the United States, "education was not the driving force in industrial development." Rather, in the hands of the elites who controlled both schools and industry, education became a means for disciplining the work force, for training into working-class children elementary habits of regularity, obedience, acceptance, and restraint. Schools also were used to promote and maintain the status of those elites, by institutionalizing their values, assumptions, and forms of knowledge: the ability to speak "correct" English, for example, or knowledge of the "classics" or the "facts" of history.[23] Schools in almost every country where Peace Corpsmen teach were set up by former colonial masters. They retain colonial systems of rote learning, which even the most innovative Corpsmen, in two seasons or so of co-teaching, are not able to change. They maintain colonial assumptions about what accumulation of facts it is necessary to know in order to pass the examination, in order to enter the class of clerks, in order to avoid the sweaty labor of the mass of people, in order to gain what small status is available for a colonial. Should the Peace Corps, under such circumstances, be fostering—and in a way imposing—heavy investment in an education that produces more elite-oriented students rather than fulfills immediate needs of people, and the developmental needs of the nation? President Julius K. Nyerere of Tanzania, responding in part to the excessive number of Peace Corps teachers in his country's schools, provided an answer increasingly shared by leaders of developing nations. According to a *New York Times* report (February 3, 1969), President

Nyerere wrote that it was "useless and dangerous to prepare primary-school pupils for secondary education when there was room in the secondary schools for only one of every eight who had gone that far." The President felt that practical skills, for jobs or farming, ought to be emphasized, and that for the Peace Corps to help finance and stimulate a major investment in an American style of education was of no service to his country.

Tanzania's response, which has been followed by other countries and, in some measure, by the Corps itself, raises not only the question of whether PCV's should be teaching, but also what and how they might teach. No less than the older colonial masters, Americans have through schools imposed their own assumptions, as well as their language. The Corps's recruiting brochure speaks of the values young Americans bring into education:

> Reasonably well-educated young Americans with unusual energy and motivation are a liberating force to the young in any pre-technological or transitional society. Their tools are their elementary habits of health, pragmatic thought, optimism, and geographical horizons.

These are values (cleanliness, Fordliness) a young, white American can afford, but they have all too seldom been relevant to his African or Asian student—or even to many ghetto students back in the States—who must pass examinations that usually demand rote-learned information. Nor, on the other hand, are habits of loose-jointed and often wasteful "pragmatism"—"try it out, and if it doesn't work, take another"—very pertinent to nations which must hard-headedly and painfully move out of subservience in a world they have little to be optimistic about. Or again, here is Harris Wofford, formerly one of the Corps' most experimental staff members, explaining why "the teaching of English is the single most important thing that the Peace Corps does in Ethiopia or Africa." Hapgood and Bennett report that:

> He hailed Ethiopia's decision to make English its language of higher learning, and he went on: "When Ethiopia has fully arrived in the twentieth century . . . it will certainly have its disagreements with us, but the disagreements will be in our terms of discourse." (Note that "our." It refers to Americans, not Ethiopians. An Ethiopian might not be so charmed by the prospect

that disagreements with the Americans will be in what to him are foreign terms of discourse.) Wofford raised his sights: "Let me shoot higher—a long shot. English may well be the best language for twentieth-century development. . . . You can't be well read in English without learning something about due process, equal protection of the laws, freedom of speech and self-government." It was indeed a long shot. Today Ethiopia, tomorrow the world! [Pp. 53–54.]

In short, what the Peace Corps teacher brings to Ethiopia, or to Colombia, or to the Philippines, can be regarded as something of a gift horse, showy, youthful, desirable by twentieth-century Western fashions, but finally a positive danger to the growth and culture of nations in the third world. No wonder, then, the Tanzanians, who see themselves as socialists, felt it was wrong "to have their children taught by the children of capitalism" (*The New York Times,* February 3, 1969).

To be sure, the Corps has done more than simply advance the cause of "cultural imperialism." It has in recent years consciously tried to introduce innovative methods of teaching, to "break the rote barrier," to emphasize problem-solving approaches, and, especially in areas like science, to relate the student's new understanding of process to his immediate environment. In its own training programs and increasingly in the field, the Peace Corps has adopted more open, experimental forms of instruction. It has, in a few rare instances, succeeded in introducing genuinely useful changes into school systems. And there have, of course, been excellent teachers among the volunteers, who will be remembered and probably loved by local children. But the Corps has run not only against its own fallacious assumptions about education, but against the fact that schools serve the society as structured; they do not change the structure. The Philippine town mentioned previously was dominated by the presence of the "Philippine Packing Company" plant, in reality owned and run by Americans. The Americans, on rotating overseas duty, had their own local preserve, with its pine trees, its golf course, its shade and cool. Even so, they received "hardship pay," whereas the Filipino, with a larger family and greater needs, could not advance into a top executive position. That was a much more fundamental problem, the Peace Corps volunteer discovered, than learning English, or even than organizing women to make ceramic pots at home. Yet that problem was not part of her job, nor any Peace Corpsman's. For, as Warren W. Wiggins, the deputy Director, had put it: "Stay out of local politics—but produce change."

The question, of course, is whether that can be done. Right at the heart of the Peace Corps's developing ideology is the belief that it can. Indeed, Wiggins has insisted that the changes a volunteer could "encourage" are "so great that we might as well talk about revolution."[24] Andrew Kopkind quotes another high Peace Corps official: "Our mission is essentially revolutionary. The ultimate aim of community development is nothing less than a complete change, reversal—or revolution if you wish—in the social and economic patterns of the countries to which we are accredited."[25] And former director of the Peace Corps Jack Vaughn himself told a State Department audience that everything about the PCV, "his reason for going there, his performance, his personality, what he's after, what he prays for, is revolution, is change, is democracy."[26] In part, according to Wiggins, that has meant encouraging a form of "participatory democracy": helping communities develop political groups and teaching people how to participate in the political life of their country. But more concretely and more realistically that has meant, in the words of the Corps' Sixth Annual Report, that the goal of community development is "to create a sense of identity among the people served by the volunteers by promoting the concept that self-help is both a desirable and possible method for improving their lives."

Knowledgeable critics of the Peace Corps, like Hapgood and Bennett, have contempt for most of the educational projects and serious misgivings about most of the unfocused and paternalistic "community-development" efforts of untrained volunteers. But they hold out reasonable hope for a "wholistic" approach developed by Michigan State's Institute for Community Development that emphasizes careful study and selection of projects, integration of resources, teamwork, and limited but meaningful goals. Such an approach has been tried in Chile and in Colombia, two countries, American officials have hoped, that might display an "alternative to Castro" or another form of socialist revolution in Latin America.

Colombia has been one of the Peace Corps's largest operations. About 2,000 volunteers have served there; as of June, 1968, the contingent was 576, including 187 in education and 283 in community action. In Colombia, the Corps has worked closely with a major USAID effort to establish an educational TV network, rationalized as a force for national unity. Almost 300,000 people have lost their lives in political and family violence over the last twenty years in the country. "Now the nation's leaders," the Peace Corps told the American Congress in May of 1966, "see in educational TV a powerful force to help weld the people into one nation." In Colombia, moreover, the Peace Corps had the additional advantage of being able to work with an indigenous and relatively successful community action program, *Acción Comunal.* The *promotores* of that organization had by 1967 organized some 10,000 local "Juntas" or boards, not all of which were, to be sure, active, but most of which had managed to develop one or another kind of community project, building roads and schools, installing electric systems, or even establishing health posts and religious shrines. Some of the boards had taken on administrative responsibility for agricultural improvement and adult education, and to some extent they had begun to form an organized pressure group on the government.[27] Thus a Peace Corps volunteer could be integrated, in many instances, into an existing structure and could work along with the local *promotores* instead of dropping as a thorough alien into the countryside. In addition to all of this, U.S. aid to Colombia from 1962 through 1968 totaled $732 million, one of the major efforts to build a showcase for the Alliance for Progress.

Yet Senator J. W. Fulbright issued a study at the end of January, 1969, which shows that the social and economic goals projected in 1962 have in no measure been met.[28] The study reports, for example, that Colombia's gross national product has risen only 1.2% annually, from $276 to $295 per person, compared with the Alianza goal of 2.5%. The number of functional illiterates, despite educational TV and the Peace Corps's investment of teachers, has risen from five million to more than six million. Agrarian reform has not even reached 15% of the landless people. "The country's social structure," according to the report, "remains essentially unchanged, with close to two-thirds of the population not participating in the economic and political decision-making process." "The rhetoric of the Alliance for Progress was lost in the arcane world of international finance," the report says, and it concludes that U.S. assistance has only helped Colombian governments to "postpone making more basic reforms."

Obviously, the Peace Corps cannot be blamed for the evident

failure of reform in Colombia, nor even for the fact that its efforts to educate cannot even keep up with the birth rate. But that is not the point. Because the Corps is, for better or worse, an integral part of American efforts overseas (especially in a country like Colombia, where it is so closely tied to USAID), it shares the fate of those efforts. Like the Alliance for Progress, it held out to young people glowing hopes for change. That the goals have not materialized has meant for some idealists that they have had to learn "what to make of a diminished thing." A letter from a couple who had gone to Colombia with the Peace Corps partly out of commitment, partly to avoid the draft, tells much of that story:

> We went to Colombia with the Peace Corps, after climbing mountains and scaling rocks for three months in New Mexico. We began with educational television (after I had my gall bladder removed) in Barranquilla, a large port city on the Caribbean coast. We went around to the various elementary schools which had TV sets donated to them by AID and tried to teach the teachers how to use the sets themselves and how to utilize the programs which came over them. The reception of programs (I speak of technical reception) was poor, and we felt rather like junior AID officials. In fact, a remark you once made echoed repeatedly through my brain—it concerned Jane, who went to Chile to teach in the university—you said she wanted to "learn about life," but she never would learn that way, the universities being the exclusive region of the *ricos,* the poor you said could never go to the universities. You were right, of course, the poor weren't to be found in the universities. In fact, they were seldom found in the primary schools above the third grade. And so, we gave up the convenience and comfort of the city (good transportation, electricity, running water, convenient doctor, telephone, and daily mail service) and moved out into "el campo." In the campo we had no running water, horses were the transportation in the immediate area, to get to the cities, we had to hitchhike or wait (in 110-degree sun) up to three hours for a broken-down bus to pass. It took three hours to get to the mailbox (usually empty) and four hours to get to the nearest telephone, should a doctor be necessary. We bathed in the irrigation ditches with the rest of the people. Seven children starved to death in our village. I should add that it was the former site of the United Fruit Company headquarters in Colombia, when the Fruit Co. was operating on a large scale. They had pulled out, however, before

we arrived. Needless to say, the UF Co. was a benign and kindly father and mother figure to the peasants who (intentionally or unintentionally) stifled all initiative in the people. Our task was a difficult and miserable one—a community-action project, we organized juntas and tried to convince the peasants that they were valuable human beings, and quite capable of doing things for themselves. Our success was limited—to overstate the situation —an aqueduct in one village, a basketball court in another, a bridge for one, a road repair for another and the beginnings of a CARE school restaurant in another. We did manage to make quite a few friends, convince many *campesinos* that all Americans aren't materialistic money-grubbers and that someone does indeed care, we learned Spanish, and I guess the really biggest lesson we learned was about poverty—the culture of poverty and what it does to a person, indeed to a nation. I could wax on forever about it, but I think you understand (I don't think very many Americans have the slightest conception of real poverty, *I* certainly didn't before I went into the Peace Corps). Anyway, to continue, we suffered a lot physically and emotionally, there was a lot of disease, a lot of loneliness and tremendous amount of frustration, and we picked up some scars from this experience which we can never shed (both physical and emotional again). However, I can say, without qualification, that it was worth it, a thousand times over. I'm awfully grateful to have had the experience. Thank you, JFK. I would not, however, recommend it for everyone.

Probably most Americans who have served in the Peace Corps, like the letter-writer, do not regret those years. Young people in service rarely regret hard work, shock, some hardships, if they feel a sense of accomplishment. That sense for Peace Corps volunteers is, typically, one of marvel that "soft" Americans could endure even a modified version of the lives of the poor. That sense is also mixed with futility and undirected anger: what had they done for those poor? For finally, they can "thank JFK" only for the Peace Corps's contribution to their own lives: the strength they gained under stress, the Spanish they learned, the friends they made.

The Committee of Returned Volunteers have come to another view, in part through focusing their attention not on their own education per se, but on their political function as emissaries of the

United States around the world. Participating in the demonstrations at the Democratic National Convention in August, 1968, CRV members handed out leaflets that described themselves and their "Position Paper on Vietnam." We quote from the latter paper because it outlines the route from service in the jungles of Colombia to the rebellion in the streets in front of the Hilton.

> . . . We chose to work in programs like the Peace Corps because we thought that through such channels we could support the forces of constructive change, rather than those which maintain the status quo of wealth and privilege for the few, and poverty, hunger, and disease for the many. . . . Although in most instances we went in order to serve, we found that we had more to learn than to teach, more to receive than to give. We affluent Americans were exposed to the realities of poverty, with its underlying apathy, violence, and chaos. We were caught up in the tension between modernization and tradition. . . . We felt the aspirations and frustrations of people caught up in the process of development. . . . As we learned to understand the societies of those different from us, we began to be able to view our own society from the perspective of others. We came to see the inadequacies in the actions and goals of our own government. As a part of this process we began to realize that there are ambiguities inherent in United States-sponsored programs like the Peace Corps. Although its name indicates a goal of serving the forces of peaceful change, we wonder whether the Peace Corps's effect has not at times been to impede rather than accelerate the movement into a future of greater abundance and full political participation. . . .

The route is typical enough: from the experience abroad to an intellectual understanding of U.S. global policies and a redefined view of U.S. society at home and abroad. And yet, the leaflet's tone is relatively gentle, charging the Peace Corps only with "ambiguities" or occasional error. By the fall of 1969, the CRV had adopted a resolution describing the Peace Corps as "an instrument of U.S. domination" over the third world, one that operates in a dozen different, elaborated-upon ways to support "the status quo in the countries to which it sends volunteers" and to support "the worldwide vested interests of U.S. business and the U.S. government." There is no longer any hedging in the new document, though there is a tinge still of reluctance—as some of the same people who in 1960 had stood outside the Michigan Union in the late hours of a campaign night applauding John Kennedy's call for a Peace Corps, who had done their two or more years of service, now in 1969 "come to the unavoidable conclusion that the Peace Corps should be abolished. . . ."

Notes

[1] Gaile P. Noble, in the *Barnard Alumnae Magazine,* XVII (Spring, 1968), p. 7.

[2] Committee of Returned Volunteers, "Position Paper on Vietnam," 1968. The Committee of Returned Volunteers is composed mainly of veterans of the Peace Corps and of voluntary programs conducted by private agencies like the American Friends Service Committee.

[3] *Newsweek,* 71 (January 15, 1968), 23. On the day after the Nixon administration took office, the Corps' Washington office reported a record of 700 applications for the twenty-four-hour period. But recruitment since has proved no easy matter, and the number of volunteers has been sharply cut back. In February, 1969, the Corps was reporting about 13,800 volunteers serving abroad and the expectation of training some 8,500 in the course of the year. By the end of 1969, however, the Corps reported a total of 10,151 volunteers in service, *including* trainees, a drop of perhaps one-third. The reduction does not, of course, reflect only difficulties in recruitment; the Nixon administration has apparently wished to cut not only the administrative structure of the Corps back, but its volunteer staff as well. *New York Times,* February 2, 1969; January 4, 1970.

[4] David Berlew, "The High Art of Staff Leadership," *Peace Corps Volunteer,* VI (November, 1967), p. 2.

[5] "The Peace Corps Isn't Doing Its Job," *Saturday Evening Post,* CCXXXIX (January 1, 1966), p. 7.

[6] See Marjorie A. Donnelly, in the *Barnard Alumnae Magazine,* XVII (Spring, 1968), p. 8.

[7] Carol M. Japha, in the *Barnard Alumnae Magazine,* XVII (Summer, 1968), p. 18.

[8] See *The New York Times,* February 2, 1969.

[9] Colorado State University Research Foundation, Maurice Albertson, director, *The Peace Corps,* Final Report, prepared for the International Cooperation Administration, Fort Collins, Colorado, May 1961, Sect. 1, p. 5.

[10] Frank Laubach, *Wake Up or Blow Up* (Westwood, N.J., 1951), pp. 109, 133; as quoted in Colorado State University Report, Sect. 1, p. 2.

[11] *U.S. Congressional Record,* 86th Congress, 2nd session, March 15, 1960, p. 5682.

[12] State Department Bulletin #22, 1950, cited in Frederick Clairmonte, *Economic Liberalism and Underdevelopment* (Bombay and London: Asia Publishing House, 1960).

[13] David Hapgood and Meridan Bennett, *Agents of Change: A Close Look at the Peace Corps* (Boston and Toronto: Little, Brown, and Co., 1968), p. 220.

[14] Quoted in Harris Wofford, "The Future of the Peace Corps," *Annals of the American Academy,* #365 (1966), p. 131.

[15] *The New York Times,* May 6, 1969.

[16] *The New York Times,* February 3, 1969.

[17] *Committee of Returned Volunteers Newsletter,* III (November, 1969), #8, p. 15.

[18] *The New York Times,* June 2, 1969.

[19] Marjorie A. Donnelly, the *Barnard Alumnae Magazine,* XVII (Spring, 1968), p. 8.

[20] Interview with the San Francisco *Chronicle,* December 13, 1967, quoted in C. D. Berreman, "The Peace Corps—A Dream Betrayed," *The Nation,* CCVI (2/26/68), p. 264.

[21] Marjorie A. Donnelly, *op.cit.,* p. 8.

[22] "Teachers in the Peace Corps: From Rote to Reason," an official Peace Corps publicity flyer.

[23] Michael B. Katz, *The Irony of Early School Reform* (Cambridge, Mass., 1968), pp. 88–93.

[24] See *Newsweek,* LXVI (November 8, 1965), p. 66.

[25] Andrew Kopkind, "How Fares the Peace Corps," *New Statesman,* LXXI (2/11/65), pp. 184–85.

[26] In a talk at the Department of State, September 22, 1965, quoted by Harris Wofford, "The Future of the Peace Corps," *op. cit.,* p. 132.

[27] See Matthew Edel, "Mobilizing Human Resources: The Colombian Community Development Program," in Frank T. Bachmura, ed., *Human Resources in Latin America: An Interdisciplinary Focus* (Bloomington, Ind., 1968), pp. 19–35.

[28] See *The New York Times,* February 2, 1969, and *I. F. Stone's Bi-Weekly* of February 24, 1969, for useful summaries. The entire 865-page study is available as *Survey of the Alliance for Progress,* Compilation of Studies and Hearings of the Subcommittee on American Republics Affairs of the Committee on Foreign Relations, United States Senate, 91st Congress, 1st session, Senate Document #91-17 (Washington: U.S. Government Printing Office, April 29, 1969).

4

Service on the Campus: The Free University Movement and Educational Reform

—The ideal university is a community of controversy, within itself and in its effects on communities beyond.

(*The Port Huron Statement*, 1962)

—In short, we were more interested in learning from the process than in being processed.

(The New Alabama Experimental College, 1969 catalogue)

Students turned relatively late to their own campuses and to questions of their rights, powers, and responsibilities. The slogan "a free university in a free society" was not coined until late 1964, and the first "free universities" were not founded on campuses until late 1965. But anyone who has lived or worked on a campus knows how difficult it is to accomplish slight alterations of protocol, let alone real change. Academic machinery stresses continuity and repetition: even the annual publication of catalogs, with a printer's deadline six months in advance of their appearance, acts as an impediment to change. Whether initiated by students, faculty, administrators, or the Ford Foundation itself, changing the university has been more difficult than establishing the entire Peace Corps. Indeed, the Peace Corps decided to develop its own training programs precisely because university-organized programs proved so hidebound, self-serving, and in the worst sense, academic.

Apart from the university's resistance to change, there is also its power to make or break students' futures. It is not surprising, therefore, that they were for a considerable period of time unwilling (or unable) to convince each other that the risk was worthwhile. And yet, with this last matter in mind, it is understandable that once convinced—once students saw not only that the university needed to be changed, but also, to put it bluntly, that it could not toss all of them out—the movement has been more rapid than any other we can point to.

Beginning in 1965, whenever students organized a series of study groups they could call "courses," they could and often did announce themselves as a "free university," "free school," or "experimental college." Though its forms have varied, the free university has functioned as an institution parallel or adjacent to a particular university. Its purpose, quite simply stated, has remained critically utopian: as students' leaflets or catalogs usually put it, this is the way a university should be; or, grandly, this is what we'd like to turn the university into. The chief ingredients have been self-determination and community, to be achieved through freedom, individuals' real interests, social and political responsibility, and democratic participation. Catalogs have listed courses pell-mell, their content naturally reflecting and reinforcing the students' vision. No course is too unconventional; no teacher (sometimes called "organizer") unqualified; no student unacceptable. Ideally, the classroom becomes a democratic community of learning and the institution a larger but still democratic community in which hierarchy is abolished and government is attempted through committees and mass meetings. Anyone may organize a course; the only criterion is the interest of its participants.

As an institution and as a movement, the free university has been partly invisible and not easy to trace, since with rare exceptions its student founders have not looked for publicity beyond their local recruitment needs, nor have they, until recently, evaluated their efforts. When free universities succeed, they simply continue; when they fail, they disappear, sometimes to be born again in another generation of students. We have collected materials on nearly one hundred free universities.[1] In the spring of 1969, it should be added, the National Student Association claimed to know of more than three hundred of them. Even the conservative *College Management*[2] used the number 157. However many there are or have been, free universities have embodied some of the best educational ideas produced by young people during the sixties, and have provided an arena for some of their most creative organizing. At the same time, tracing the forces that have produced, as well as prevented and co-opted, them will tell us much about how the student movement has grown, and where that as-yet-uncompleted growth is likely to lead.

THE MOVEMENT'S ROOTS

In 1962, on relatively quiet campuses, two documents appeared to proclaim the failure of higher education and to affirm its significance as a potential lever for social change. The first of these documents, a sixty-three-page pamphlet called *The Port Huron Statement,* was written collaboratively by founders of Students for a Democratic Society (SDS). The second, a one-thousand-page volume called *The American College* and edited by Nevitt Sanford, was the result of nearly a decade of cooperative effort by prestigious scholars. Certain similarities between the documents are remarkable. Sanford deplores the fact that colleges are of more benefit to their students socially and economically than intellectually, let alone morally and politically. The authors of *The Port Huron Statement* view the university as "tragically" indistinguishable from any other institution that passes on "the stock truths of the day," and they indict students for passivity: "Almost no students value activity as citizens. Passive in public, they are hardly more idealistic in arranging their private lives: Gallup concludes they will settle for 'low success, and won't risk high failure.'"[3] At the same time, the authors conclude that "the universities are an overlooked seat of influence": "no matter how dull the teaching, how paternalistic the rules, how irrelevant the research that goes on . . . the university [is] a potential base and agency in a movement for social change." Sanford also assumes that "colleges have the task of influencing the youth of the country, in directions set by the higher ideals of our culture." Though he readily admits that most institutions have been unable to carry out their mission, he is optimistic about the university as an "agency . . . of initiating change" in the society at large. Sanford asks the key questions: "Who, then, is to reform the colleges? And how is such reform to come about?"[4]

It is in the answers to these questions and to one other—"Who is the college to serve?"—that differences between the two documents emerge. These differences begin to explain why, seven years later, a factionalized SDS has largely left the campus to confront "pigs" in the street or to demonstrate outside factories, while some of the same professors who contributed essays to *The American College,* and many others besides, are now joined to a slick and well-funded magazine called *Change* ("the new language of higher education"). The differences also suggest why recently cloistered campuses are today in a state of controversy verging on explosion and why such innovations as the abolition of examinations and grades are now being proposed and accepted by faculty and administrators alike as panaceas for the pacification of a potentially or actually unruly populace. Or why, in 1970, faculty and administrators are talking with students about "community" government on campus, or student-initiated rules, discipline, and censorship boards, or about a curriculum organized around students' "interests."

In 1962 *The American College* narrowly addressed its own constituency and its own interests: the faculty were advised to reform higher education, and the method proposed was research. But the work offers no sign of urgency. Morton Deutsch makes this explicit in the Foreword: the book "charts the way into relatively unexplored territory," using as "central thesis . . . that scientific method, more than any other procedure known to man, provides the basis for intelligent change: for change based on systematic knowledge rather than on improvisation, hunch, or dogma." He is thus helping to found the new education industry. The function of such an industry—whom is it to serve?—Deutsch, like the rest of *The American College,* leaves unspecified. It is evidently assumed that "systematic knowledge" leads automatically to "intelligent change," that the "scientific method" ensures purity of motive: scientists and social scientists, having set ideology aside, work without bias or self-interest, certainly without explicit political purpose. Thus, *The American College* effectively proposes to establish the university as a laboratory, and as in most laboratories, the approach to problems is "objective." Somehow, moreover, the university-laboratory is equipped to produce the product to reform not only campuses but also society at large—if only faculty are energetic about their research and if only the rest of us are patient about waiting for results and are trusting about the character, morality, and politics of U.S. scholars. The book's aspirations for the American college are especially congenial to a traditional and "liberal" view of the university. The view interprets the customary separation of town and gown as an opportunity for enlightened academic reformers to function. The university is not merely to be a retreat from an imperfect world, but a laboratory from which will come curative prescriptions. In such views, the university remains a clean place; the world, polluted. But only vaguely, or by implication, polluted. It is important to note that *The American College,* perhaps because it reflects and reports the scholarship of the fifties, does not mention the civil-rights movement nor the concept of service we have been describing. Students are "subjects" of studies; the worlds of poverty, social inequality, racism, etc., are invisible.

Town and gown are not separate in the view of the *Port Huron* writers: if one word were needed to describe the university, that word would be "complicit." The university not only mirrors a defective society; it serves and fosters the defects: poverty, racism, capitalism, and the cold war, not to mention bureaucracy that denies people power over their own lives. Having labeled some university research as "irrelevant," the writers of *The Port Huron Statement* describe a new burgeoning business on campus:

> . . . the extent to which academic resources presently are used to buttress immoral social practice is revealed, first, by the extent to which defense contracts make the universities engineers of the arms race. Too, the use of modern social science as a manipulative tool reveals itself in the "human relations" consultants to the modern corporations, who introduce trivial sops to give laborers feelings of "participation" or "belonging," while actually deluding them in order to further exploit their labor. And, of course, the use of motivational research is already infamous as a manipulative aspect of American politics. But these social uses of the universities' resources also demonstrate the unchangeable reliance by men of power on the men and storehouses of knowledge: this makes the university *functionally tied to society in new ways,* revealing new potentialities, new levers for change. [Italics ours.] [p. 61]

Service on the campus became—for SDS in its early days— educating generations of students about the "new" complicit function of the university. The method proposed involved traditional academic processes, though distinguishably different ones from those called for by *The American College:* "real intellectual skills ... deliberativeness, honesty, reflection" are prescribed as "working tools" necessary for the formation of a "new left in America." Such a new left would function on campus to "start controversy across the land," emphasizing "nonviolence as a condition of conflict," and presumably recalling the university to its ideal state as a "community of controversy." SDS, it is important to note, saw the university as both open to change and needing change, for it "permits the political life to be an adjunct to the academic one, and action to be informed by reason."

The writers propose the barest sketch of ambitious goals to be accomplished through "national efforts at university reform by an alliance of students and faculty":

> They must wrest control of the educational process from the administrative bureaucracy. They must make fraternal and functional contact with allies in labor, civil rights, and other liberal forces outside the campus. They must import major public issues into the curriculum—research and teaching on problems of war and peace is an outstanding example. They must make debate and controversy, not dull pedantic cant, the common style for educational life. They must consciously build a base for their assault upon the loci of power. [p. 63]

The program unites two distinct objectives: changing the campus, and making it a base for changing society. Change on the campus involves both democratization of the bureaucratic structure and politicizing the "style of educational life." Bringing "major public issues into the curriculum" and bringing students into "fraternal and functional contact" with movement groups outside the campus make explicit those implicit and invisible connections the university already has established with the social order. The ingredients are all present for the "free university," though there was no mention of it in *Port Huron.*

Only five pages of the pamphlet are devoted to the university as such, a fact that further clarifies the difference between it and *The American College.* The pamphlet assumes that politics is not an activity restricted to voting once a year and on matters disconnected from the campus. Rather, politics establishes an intellectual's apprehension of his society. The pamphlet, for example, connects poverty, the structure of corporate power, the cold war, *and* the university; whereas the book, in contrast to the wholeness that students now demand, illustrates the fragmentation characteristic of higher education. The pamphlet says to students: your society functions as an organism to maintain itself unchanged; you need to grasp how the whole organization—including the university—institutionalizes oppression, especially of the poor and the black. Your education denies you that vision; even your professors are blind to it. But you can understand and you can teach others.

But how to manage this process? How to put the theory to work, given the usual rigidity of the curriculum and other realities of campus life? The Mississippi Summer of 1964, Berkeley, and the teach-in movement that began in the spring of 1965 provided educational models and experience. The freedom schools allowed hundreds of college students to build and teach a relevant curriculum that made connections between education and political action. Even if the summer did not change the condition of Mississippians' lives, it did change many students' perceptions of their campus and their own lives. Some of these students returned to Berkeley to participate in the Sproul Hall sit-in in the fall of 1964, where, as Mississippi veterans, they proclaimed "the right to set the conditions in which they themselves lived and worked."[5]

The mocking "Free Speech Carols"—"Hail to IBM," "We Three Deans," "O, Come All Ye Mindless"—composed during the Sproul Hall sit-in make explicit how the university had become, for Berkeley students at least, an oppressive institution.

> Masters of Sproul Hall announced the news today,
> Students have no rights except to idle play . . .
> Why not use the sandbox, try some basketball,
> If you want some clean fun, buy an Oski doll.

> From the tip of San Diego,
> To the top of Berkeley's hills,
> We have built a mighty factory
> To impart our social skills.
> Social engineering's triumph,
> Managers of every kind
> Let us all with drills and homework

Manufacture human minds.
Make the students safe for knowledge,
Keep them loyal, keep them clean,
This is why we have a college,
Hail to IBM machine.[6]

If the student was, in point of fact, not a "nigger"—since he was a member of the privileged middle classes—on campus, he was hardly his own master. His personal and political freedom was controlled by antiquated rules not of his own making, his study dictated by an irrelevant curriculum not of his own choosing and by faculty disdainful of teaching—and with it all, his identity mocked by the IBM card he carried. If he didn't like it, of course, he was always "free" to go elsewhere . . . to any one of a number of similar institutions. But wherever he went, he would find the same impersonal, irrelevant, and constricting education. Of course, he was also "free" to drop out altogether—into the waiting embrace of General Hershey. The "classes" held in Sproul Hall have been self-consciously referred to as the first "free university." Whether they were or not, they provided what Mississippi had—the peculiar intensity and joy of learning under siege that you were capable of taking a hand in your own education.

The free-speech movement, which began partly as an effort to aid and recruit for the southern civil-rights struggle, also provided immediate insight to the connection between the character of university education and its political objectives:

Oski dolls, pom-pom girls
UC all the way,
Oh what fun it is to have
Your mind reduced to clay,
Civil rights, politics, just get in the way,
Questioning authority, when you should obey.

The university was not simply an "irrelevant" institution; it mirrored a corrupt society. In the next few years, the mirrors would reflect the scandal of Michigan State's key role in aiding the Diem regime to establish a police state in Vietnam; the willing cooperation of most universities with the Selective Service System; revelations about secret war research on campuses; and the presence of only a few privileged blacks on prestigious campuses. The Vietnam war hastened the discovery that the university was of critical importance to U.S. society and quickly radicalized generations of students who learned firsthand of the university's complicity in their manipulation as "youth resources"—some being channeled to serve the "national interest" on campus, others, mostly from black, poor, or working-class families, channeled to Vietnam.

For some of those in Sproul Hall, the FSM was a first attempt to challenge both curriculum and decision-making processes, to "restructure the university," as it later came to be called. For others, however, attempting simply to reform campus life was to avoid the more pressing problems of race, war, university expansionism, to misplace one's political talents and social responsibilities. A tension developed in the student movement, which alternately pressed for campus reforms and organized off-campus involvement in broader social issues. From the mid-sixties on, the history of this crowded movement reveals a contradiction between two modes: reform the university so that it may function to change society; fight directly for social change and against the university because all it can ever do is serve a corrupt society—unless that society is itself changed. Those in the movement were agreed on the necessity for change. But some were committed to reforming, perhaps to using, but at any rate to remaining at, the university; while others demanded that students seriously committed to a new America leave the campus for work in the civil-rights movement or for organizing in urban areas with SDS's Economic Research and Action Project (ERAP).

The Vietnam teach-ins during the spring of 1965 reiterated this growing idea that the universities should become more "relevant," not to "national interests" defined by corporations and government, but to the social issues of the day. And they provided still another model of a temporary parallel institution for those thinking about university reform. Their immediate *raison d'être,* like that of the freedom schools, was moral and political. As Louis Menashe and Ronald Radosh, editors of *Teach-Ins U.S.A.,* account for the movement, teach-ins came out of the "anger" of scholars who "felt betrayed" by a president they had worked hard to elect: who had promised peace and initiated the bombing of Hanoi on February 7, 1965.[7] The teach-ins demonstrated the usefulness of the university as public forum even as they pointed out the limitations of the university's curriculum and concept of education. For a period of several hours to several days, on hundreds of campuses that spring, thousands of students and faculty met—outside of the classroom—to hear "dialogue" for and against U.S. foreign policy in Vietnam. On a subject of immediate concern and potential action, professors turned their best scholarship and, what is even more significant, their moral and political judgments, even passion. In fact, it began to seem increasingly impossible to many students and faculty members in 1965 to omit moral and political judgments from rational discussion of foreign policy. How, then, they began to question, was it feasible to omit controversy from the classroom?

The models of the Mississippi freedom schools, of Sproul Hall, and of the teach-ins provided some basis for student activists to test the theory that reforming the university could be a useful means of changing society. And for a year, beginning in late 1965, longer in some places, they began to organize to change the campus and the conditions of students' lives, especially by founding counterinstitutions called free universities. At the SDS national convention held during the summer of 1965, the "free university" appeared as an important topic for debate and planning, despite the fact that no free universities had yet been established on campus. Several unpublished convention documents[8] suggested possible patterns for free universities: teach-ins, "counter-classrooms on campus to meet the deficiencies of specific courses," and "intentional . . . cooperative communities." No one suggested that SDS chapters as such turn themselves into "free universities" on hundreds of campuses. Nor was there agreement about formalizing such yet-to-be-born institutions: "to try such synthesis," the writers of the workshop reports claimed, would be to "stifle many of the breakthroughs presently being made on campus." Characteristically, the SDS formula was "let each chapter decide."

Much of the discussion in the workshops attempted to redefine an ideal university—especially over against the despised "multiversity" described by Clark Kerr, the president of the University of California. A central concern was whether "the atmosphere of the free university [is] more important than the subjects discussed." One report suggested that the words "free university" be dropped in favor of "free educational atmosphere," and that as a corollary, political education be conducted at "institutes" set up for that purpose. Those

who espoused this view were indicating their approval of the pluralistic university, which allowed free expression or exploration of
many, if not all, points of view. Understanding that most U.S. universities, in fact, gave only lip service to this ideal—excluding practicing
Marxists, for example—these students were loath to do the same. In
keeping with the spirit of *The Port Huron Statement,* their vision of
a "free university" would give real meaning to the word "free."

Others challenged that view by pointing out that to separate
"political education" from "free atmosphere" was to fall into the same
error of standard institutions that divided politics from education.
They argued that politics—left politics—had to inform any educational experiment. (In practice, as we shall illustrate, both of these
patterns were attempted.)

If a "free educational atmosphere" is open to all points of view,
why not to all sorts of people? In the 1965 SDS workshop, "free"
also meant that anyone might attend a free university and that there
were to be no prescribed—only internal—measures of success or
failure. The ideal university ought to function at the service of those
who need it, and when they do, rather than organize a series of
hurdles through which its clientele must pass to be certified. Extending the idea of pluralism from curriculum to admissions and standards
is the crucially radical idea of the free university movement.

If the free university is open to all sorts of people, then might
some not learn or be taught in ways different from the standard curriculum and methods of the classroom? One workshop focused on affect rather than cognition, on varieties of communication beyond
or apart from language. Is education "only for the theoretician and
the ideologue?" What about those who "speak with their bodies and
eyes, with intonation and speed?" "Who is tacitly presupposed as
constituency for the free university," a key question asked, "when
the emphasis is placed on subjects and forms which require high degrees of articulateness and intellectualization?" And finally, the most
familiar question of all—"What is relevant to our lives?"—assumed
that the student is a reliable judge of his educational needs.

The thrust of this early discussion was prophetic. The idea of a
"free educational atmosphere" extended the earlier ideal of a "community of controversy." While most of the free universities founded
by SDS in 1966 and 1967 were at least intentionally pluralist with
regard to political courses, they were successfully pluralist in other

curricular respects: catalogs included courses in painting, politics, body movement, and community organizing. As significant as the creation of countercurriculum was the redefinition of the ideal university as an egalitarian rather than an elite institution where modes of learning other than the verbal and intellectual might be accommodated and whose standards of admission might be flexible and open.

Following the 1965 SDS convention, discussions in *New Left Notes* and a short-lived free-university newsletter preceded the formation, late in 1965 and early in 1966, of a handful of free universities. Political activists on the West Coast and SDS members elsewhere took a leading role in these and perhaps a dozen others founded later in 1966 and early in 1967, in that brief period of unity between political activists and educational reformers. After 1967, the radical left and the blacks moved into confronting university complicity in the war and in racism, while, at about the same time, the free university movement, transformed into a program for educational reform, began to take hold not only of the imagination of large numbers of students untouched by politics, but also of the interests of faculty and administrators.

THE LONG LIVES OF TWO FREE UNIVERSITIES

In the fall of 1965 and the spring of 1966, a small number of campus-based free universities were founded, two of which proved especially significant to the movement. Unlike most of the early free universities, San Francisco State's Experimental College (EC) and the University of Pennsylvania's Free University (FUP) were still in existence four years later. Their early success, even notoriety, established them as particular models for emulation by other campuses.

Like most early free universities, these were begun by student activists who were consciously part of a larger movement for social change. The Free University of Pennsylvania was founded by a group of SDS members, though the SDS chapter continued its independent existence. West Coast groups organizing free universities were all, in the manner of SDS students elsewhere, involved in off-campus political action as well as in on-campus educational reform. "VOICE," the group that founded UCLA's first experimental college in 1966, for example, was a multi-issue organization, having as part of its interest "conditions or activities outside the university," including rent strikes to counter discriminatory housing and antidraft organizing.[9] Jim Nixon, one of the student-activists who founded the Experimental College, describes his own history: "I spent a long time in the Peace Movement and in various radical groups, and I found a sense of profound impotence in trying to tackle that [peace] issue."[10]

Both the Experimental College and the Free University of Pennsylvania placed their sights on changing the lives of students on campus and the conditions of the classroom. Both institutions also organized themselves consciously so as not to resemble the models most visible to them: San Francisco's New School and the Free University of New York (FUNY).[11] The basic idea of the Experimental College was cooperation with the establishment, not separation from it. The organizers of the Free University of Pennsylvania were explicit in their dislike for FUNY. Both FUP and the EC adopted the position that anyone can organize a course: that is, despite the radical politics of the founders, all political views were to be tolerable. The Experimental College announced early that there would be a course in Goldwater politics, but then had to cancel when their "organizer" disappeared. The Free University of Pennsylvania offered Herman Kahn a chance to teach a course when FUNY turned him down. But in practice, the political curriculum of these two free universities (and others) was overwhelmingly left, for at least two reasons: the glaring omission from any standard curriculum of courses critical of and committed to changing the norms of U.S. society; and second, the politics of the students willing to organize courses.

San Francisco State's Experimental College

The founders of the Experimental College aimed consciously to reform San Francisco State through collective political activity named educational reform. They were putting their experience in the peace and civil-rights movement to work on "a new style of revolution." Jim Nixon, one of the founders, described himself and some of the others as "young intellectuals" who had "rebelled against the anti-intellectualism" of academe. Like the writers of *The Port Huron Statement*, their analysis of U.S. institutions was "rather bleak." In one of three experimental seminars begun by Cynthia Carlson (later Nixon) in the fall of 1965, a series of conversations reminiscent of those in Mississippi freedom schools began what was later to be called at San Francisco State the "quiet revolution." Jim Nixon describes these:

> We tried to ask what it was we wanted. What kind of education did we want? . . . We reacted against the system; we wanted to be free. . . . If you take students and have them sit in classrooms and receive information, if all of the rules are laid down for those students and they don't have an opportunity to participate in making the rules, you are teaching the students to be passive and receptive. The teacher stands up and lectures about freedom to a group of students who are sitting and taking notes and listening to him in a situation which he structured. They don't learn much about freedom; they learn a lot about sitting and listening to somebody talk. [Pp. 50–51.]

The conversations established as goal the changing of education at San Francisco State:

> We wanted students to take responsibility for their own education instead of having the institution believe it was supposed to meet the needs of students. We wanted it set up so students would come to meet their own needs and come to learn about their whole being, to learn how to think, to learn how to lead, to learn how to be agents of change in the society. What we need to do is educate people who are able to take control of social change and wrest it around to human needs. [P. 51.]

The model for education is one the founders had learned from Mississippi and from political organizing: put people into motion; change the process from passive to active. As serious organizers with ambitious goals, the founders extended their conversations to include a careful analysis of "formal and informal power structures" at San Francisco State and two other seminars: one on "community organizing in which we learned some of the techniques"; and another which "tried to question whether most ordinary students—ones who weren't outside of society—could come to question and evaluate the institution they had just joined. . . ." (P. 51.)

Their chief tool (aside from tact and shrewd politicking around the campus) was what can be called "process," a reliance on dialogue and group interaction, the same tool that, in fact, helped them to decide to begin the EC in the first place. Thus, they saw as primary the continual need to prepare more leaders. Course "organizers" were trained in advance or through being part of a staff that met regularly to make policy decisions and to continue personal development in sensitivity as well as staff rapport. The original group was able to grow from twenty to fifty in the space of a year. The teacher education program built into the EC included weekend retreats and technical assistance from faculty with credentials from the National Training Laboratory, as well as an early summer (1966) of planning and conference-organizing.

The emphasis on process permeated and, in fact, united all aspects of the EC's curriculum. All teachers (mostly "students"), called "organizers," learned that their job was to guide or help students to "state their needs and concerns." Once students knew what they wanted to learn, the organizer helped them "define a method of procedure appropriate" to their needs. "In order for this procedure to work," some of the initiators comment, "everyone in the learning community must become aware of his own behavioral processes and sensitive to the needs of others."[12] The model is obviously related both to that proposed in the Mississippi freedom schools and (later) to the one proposed by Harrison and Hopkins for Peace Corps trainees.[13] The model is also identical with that proposed by Carl Rogers, founder of the Rogerian school of psychotherapy, in a paper, now republished widely by the student press and the National Student Association, called "Graduate Education in Psychology: A Passionate Statement." Rogers' name appears from time to time in early press accounts of the Experimental College. His model emphasizes the necessity for the learner (or the patient) to take responsibility for his learning, even to grow conscious of how and when it occurs. The teacher's job, as Rogers defines it, is to provide "resources which stimulate the desire to learn rather than in planning a guided curriculum." (Rogers uses the word "facilitate" to describe the process that helps learning to take place.) Logically adhered to, the model turns students into teachers or at least effects an ambiguity about their traditionally defined roles. As Jim Nixon puts it, teaching is one way to "learn a tremendous amount": "If you have to teach something, you have to really know it." (P. 51.)

If teacher education formed the backbone of the Experimental College, good bureaucratic arrangements with San Francisco State finished the skeleton, and an extremely varied curriculum fleshed out the body. Even in its first real semester, the spring of 1966, about sixty of its 350–450 (depending on sources) students registered in twenty-two courses received official credit from the college. One ready-made mechanism, in the form of "independent study," served the aggressive student who wanted course credit for his work at the Experimental College. Before the first spring was over, the college administration had created new course numbers in each department that allowed a faculty member to invent and teach experimental courses. These might be given inside the Experimental College, or they might even be initiated by students.[14]

The fall 1966 program was a phenomenal success. In its second term of existence, the Experimental College registered 1,200 students. An additional $15,000 had to be found for the budget above the $6,000 that had been allocated to the Experimental College by the student government.[15] Money was important to the Experimental College because their idea of an organized and committed staff called for salaries. The staff was paid from $50 to $150 per month for teaching or office work—an extraordinary feature that few free universities imitated until recently. The arrangement promoted stability and thus allowed considerable strength to the experiment. It meant that students—undergraduates or graduate students, recent graduates or nonstudents—could do a "movement" job of some importance and live on a subsistence wage. It meant that the EC was not an extracurricular activity that one did on top of a full program of courses and a part-time job—with all three areas of one's life fragmented. Rather, EC staff could spend full time creating an institution: taking courses, teaching courses, promoting the EC among faculty, working up evaluation procedures and follow-ups. The significance of this arrangement is hard to overestimate, especially when one looks at the free universities that died of anarchy between 1966 and 1969.

By late 1967 and early 1968, enrollment in the Experimental College was over 2,000, nearly 15 percent of San Francisco State's student body. The popularity of the Experimental College depended on its curriculum, by then more than seventy courses. That curriculum was, almost from the start, not a potpourri but a series of courses organized around the educational philosophies of the staff. The idea was that "individuals wishing to test some specific educational notions were encouraged to develop integrated areas of learning and investigation around their personal educational philosophies." (Bass, etc., p. 7.) Not unexpectedly, the "areas" (a euphemism for "departments") developed were interdisciplinary and sometimes overlapping. Thus, for example, there were, in the fall 1966 catalog, three dance or body-motion courses listed in three different areas, and literature courses in most of them. Various devices served as unifiers for each area, from relatively obvious themes as in "communication" or black studies to more complex "Styles of Thought."

It is difficult to describe what was, in fact, under constant revision. "Anyone can try to organize a course on anything," the catalog announced. "The only requirement is that he accurately describe what he is trying to do. The students make the final decision about whether a proposal becomes a course, by signing up to attend, or not." One might submit a proposal to a particular "area" or simply as an independent course. Areas, moreover, also shifted from term to term, even after they became "programs" in the fall of 1967. But a pattern is evident and useful: most of the courses and areas and programs reflect three semiautonomous interests of the staff that the Experimental College attracted and held together as well as the general interests of students at San Francisco State and in the broader movement for educational reform. These may be described as youth or "hippie" culture; politics and community organizing; and the educational process itself. To a greater or lesser degree, all the courses and areas are activity-oriented: participants talk, act, create, organize as much, or more than, they read or prepare papers.

Youth or Hippie Culture

More than anything else, perhaps, the free-university movement is known for its extension of the curriculum into hippiedom. Or, one might wish to argue, for its creation of hippiedom, though the argument is beside the point here. Thus, the ubiquitous jokes in university circles about "Zen Basketball," a course that appeared in the Experimental College catalog of spring 1967—and was still a joke to the editors of *College Management* in January, 1969. From all reports, the course-listing was itself a joke—a private response: "If that's what they want, let's give it to them!" All jokes aside, however, the free-university movement (along with other underground media—film, newspapers, music) has helped to identify, codify, and spread what by 1970 can be called either a "counterculture" or an independent culture of the young. Most of its categories and nomenclature are present in the early catalogs of the Experimental College.

At least two of these categories are not difficult for adults to understand, for they are extensions or variations of contemporary culture. First, the psychological introspection that emerges as an interest in one's self and one's relations to others. When an Experimental College leaflet announces as one aim, "to strive for . . . interpersonal relationships and awareness, absolutely necessary acquisitions for individual fulfillment and a healthy society," it is rephrasing rhetoric that most colleges also use. But the courses that the Experimental College catalog lists bear little resemblance to curricula in psychology or sociology—"Gestalt Therapy," for example, or "Seminar in Modes of Awareness and Intra-Group Communication," or body-motion courses, or one, called "Competition and Violence," that attempts to connect psychology and politics:

> This course will consider the psychology of competition of both groups and individuals. Some personal and group competition situations will be created to provide material for meaningful discussion. We will also consider the roots of violence in societies. Inter-cultural comparisons will be made. Lectures will be used solely to provide information and to stimulate discussion. Dialogue will not be forsaken for monologue. The course content and grading procedure will be determined by the class. The course will meet once a week for three hours. Organizers: Joe Borankin and Mervin Freedman.

As "courses," these are unique, since their subject is not a "body of knowledge," but rather a group of bodies. That is, what might be conceived of as "group therapy" or "counseling"—roles that colleges have assumed openly or covertly, though uneasily—is here unblushingly a "course." What students are saying is that they are interested in themselves as subjects of study and investigation. They don't want to adjust or to be adjusted; they want to work out a way of recognizing themselves and others in connected ways. Such courses may include the traditionally forbidden subjects of drugs and sex.

Like adults, the young are also interested in their roots, their relation to others on the planet, past or present. Not surprisingly, they have turned away from history—which in high school at least is blatant dogma they can recognize as lies—toward what has seemed esoterica to adults, Oriental religion and mysticism. The Experimental College catalog is never without a dozen or more courses in "Zen Koans and Stories," for example, or "Tai Chi Chuan Yin Form," as well as other forms of the esoteric. Students' interests may seem perverse to those who have filled college catalogs with their own, but there is ample reason for students, sated by the hypocrisy of a Christian and democratic society systematically murdering its own people and foreigners, to turn to the East. If one has to point to precedents, Thoreau, Emerson, and Whitman are available. Closer at hand, however, are the Beats of the 1950's, those cultural oddities who ruffled a passive decade. It is no accident that Allen Ginsberg can fill halls with thousands of students in every large city and small college town in the country. Ginsberg chants and reads, chants and reads, chants again: the performance is ritual and intellectual. The young audience moves readily through allusions to politics, pot, sex, karma, and the cosmos. From the fall 1966 catalog, a course called "Dance of Joy: Seminar in the Ecstatic Style of Cosmic Consciousness" describes the feelings of wholeness and health that students are (were) seeking as well as several historic antecedents:

> For many of us this is a time of dancing and seeking joyous unity. We have attempted to become one with the universal rhythms, to commune with the whole, and with each other. Our glimpses of revelations have moved us to place the radiant dance of being as the goal of our consciousness. In this course we will study such groups as the Chassids and the Sufis, the Orphics, Shakers, and the American Indians—people who have attempted to establish their life with one another on the foundations of divine truth; communities which have danced and loved as paths to the ultimate.
>
> Additional work will be done with the writing and teaching of such various recognized masters as Sri Aurebinde, Sri Ramakrisna, Gurdjieff, Guatama Buddha, Jesus the Christ. The struc-

ture of the class will develop organically from the participants. Time will be spent listening to the music and attempting the dance. In addition, guest lecturers will be invited to participate. The class will meet twice a week for two hours. Organizer: Ian Grand.

While participation is a feature of both categories of courses we have described, for a third category it is essential. We might call the category "play," because play is serious business to the young. In the beginning, "play" courses involve the performing arts; later the idea is extended to "Cottage-Craft Industries" and even to games like "Cosmopoly" and "Introduction to Frisbee." Two ingredients are essential: humor and a desire to be part of the present, or as one course description puts it, "Art: The Super Present":

> . . . Various presentations will include: Happenings, light-sound, theatre, artists' visits, motorcycles, music, noise, "excursions," dance, etc. Participation will be either by papers or products (painting, sculpture, or sympathetic media). Credit by individual arrangement for those who want it. The course will meet once weekly for two hours. Organizer: Michael Cookinham.

Other courses in "Disc Jockey Analysis," "Concrete Poetry," "Op Art," or "Street Poetry" sound somewhat more familiar, obviously related to drama and writing workshops, painting and music courses, now beginning to burgeon on liberal-arts campuses where the "applied" arts were, with rare exceptions like Bennington notwithstanding, usually relegated to "extracurricular activities."

Politics and Community Organizing

More than a third of the courses offered by the Experimental College in 1966 were political, and though that proportion seemingly diminished in the next several years, the decline was more apparent than real, since courses and "areas" became independent projects and organizations that maintained a relationship to the EC. We must add also that the separation of cultural from political is not always a useful distinction: we include as "political," for example, what was probably the first black-studies department, the area called "Black Culture and Arts," a series of five courses in the fall 1966 catalog, four of which were "cultural." Other political courses, on nonviolence, for example, or "The College and War," like the courses described in the category of culture, attempt to make connections between the values of students and the society they live in. The area title for these and other courses ("C.O. Counseling," "Evaluating Organizations Working for Change," "Contemporary Soviet Civilization") is "The Institute for Social Change." Most of these are discussion courses, though a few call for "situations outside the classroom for laboratories to test theory."

An important group of four courses (in the fall of 1966) functioned wholly outside the classroom. One of these was called "The Miseducation of the Negro":

> Working through the tutorial program and a few selected schools in the black communities, we will make firsthand critical evaluation of classroom situations and textbooks in the context of a miseducational process that treats the American Negro student as a nonentity. . . . The course will consist principally of field work, with individual students observing classes in schools in the black community. Reports will be prepared periodically and discussed by the class. A final report will be required of each student. Organizer: Gerald LaBrie.

Three others were organized under the area title "Urban Communities and Change." One, called simply "Oakland Project," asked for "people of Mexican-American background and Negro students" to help set up "classes in minority-group history for East Oakland high school students and dropouts." Another, called "Field Techniques of Establishing Rapport," was a course in practicing how to break into "an unfamiliar environment." The third, called "Neighborhood Renewal," was described as a "range of possibilities for working with a San Francisco neighborhood that is trying to build community-based alternatives to Redevelopment. . . ." The course organizers, Donna Mickleson and Sharon Gold, described their goals in terms of four assumptions about community organizing. Their language is worth quoting, since it unites the jargon of the new left with that of the new educational reformers, the "process" people we will discuss shortly:

> —that students can learn most about communities by making them the environment of learning.

—that knowledge can and ought to be gathered in response to the needs of people actually living in communities and desiring to actively influence and control the decisions that direct their lives.

—that teaching and learning are mutual processes; the public housing resident is just as much an expert on public housing as the student of pressure legislative politics may be an expert. The bugbear of submissiveness to authority has all too long been frighteningly real in the way people have bowed before science and "expertise" regardless of the sort or amount of relevance they had to a given situation.

—that the single most profound change that could take place— in urban renewal or welfare policy or developing recreation programs or whatever you choose—would be to transform the process of decision making to dispel impotence and decentralize power so that people can become active participants rather than passive recipients of policy.

It is not surprising that the organizers of these courses were Mississippi veterans, nor that the courses led, in a year, to the formation of political organizations.[16] Thus, creating an "environment of learning" is no different from, and what is more, leads to a "response to needs of people." The desire to bring "power to the people" in the form of "participatory democracy"—in Mississippi or in San Francisco—is an ancestral form of the desire of students to bring power to themselves on their campus. Conversely, the model for the Experimental College—a student-centered curriculum and teaching strategy—is identical with the model proposed by early SNCC and SDS organizers for political work and freedom schools. There is, finally, very little *formal* difference between asking a group of welfare mothers about their needs and resources and then helping them to plan their organizing tactics and strategies, on the one hand, and, on the other, asking a group of students what they want to learn and helping them to decide how to procede.

The Educational Process

Which brings us back to the Experimental College's original interest in process. The area called "Styles of Thought" that in the fall of 1966 included fifteen of the sixty-eight courses is, in one sense, the least homogeneous of all. Held together under the rubric of experiment are such diverse courses as "Martin Buber"—which calls simply for "a dialogue at the I and Thou Coffee House"—and "College Union Workshop," in which students are to work out the "theory and practice" of "designing a 'Union' for the college"; as well as seminars in the methodology of related traditional disciplines (zoology, psychology, and anthropology, for example, in "The Study of Animal Behavior"). What connects all of the courses is the goal of activating students without sacrificing "content." As Cynthia Carlson Nixon, the area organizer, put it, the courses were to create an environment that would allow students "to develop the ability to direct their own learning"; thus, they would acquire not only "bodies of information" but, more importantly, "thinking skills."

Ideally, students trained in "thinking skills" might organize their own courses. It may be useful to mention again that the term "thinking skills" takes for granted a process that allows students to make connections between the way they feel and the way they think. The ambitious goal of the Experimental College is, after all, to create independent, *connected* individuals who understand not only how they think and feel, but how their society works. Process, the Experimental College's key idea that decentralized responsibility by placing it in the hands of student/learner/teacher/participant, thus functions both with regard to the personal needs and cultural interests of students as well as their political commitments to social change.

In terms of growth, vitality, student interest, and educational and political ferment, the Experimental College was a "success." From another point of view, its effects have been more ambiguous. The founders believed that educational process was more important than course content per se, that process might, in fact, be used to control content and thus to effect their conscious goal—university reform. They were clear about pushing the parallel institution as imaginatively and exhaustively as far as it would go. To change San Francisco State, they needed to attract large numbers of students who might in turn then serve to accomplish two different ends: to force the rest of the college to reexamine itself and then change; and to gain from the college official recognition as a credit-granting body. The growth of the Experimental College was phenomenal, but the second goal was more easily accomplished than the first. "Anybody can organize a course" was one of the two initial slogans that the Experimental

College began with, and this one obviously appealed to students. The other slogan, "blackmail the institution with quality" (Nixon, p. 52), somehow did not work on the official college departments in the same manner. The success of the Experimental College as an innovative educational institution was not translatable into political power. In fact, the history of the experiment illustrates the ultimate powerlessness of the parallel institution with regard to a host. It can be argued that the Experimental College allowed San Francisco State to stay just as it was until other forces took hold in 1968.

In short-range terms, it may be that the Experimental College acted as a catalyst for those forces by welcoming and at least temporarily absorbing into its programs the work of political activists. Jimmy Garrett, a veteran of Mississippi's Freedom Summer and a former SNCC organizer in Los Angeles, entered San Francisco State as an undergraduate early in 1966, and according to James Brann, approached Jim Nixon about "money for black student courses and ghetto programs."

> "My words came back to haunt me later," said Nixon. "I told him we could give him some money but he had to produce some real programs and really work at it.
> "He really worked."

"The effects of the black-run courses," Brann continues, "combined with experiences in the ghetto tutorial program, produced a mounting dissatisfaction among San Francisco State blacks with the existing American educational system."[17] The experience inside the Experimental College clarified for blacks that they had to be in charge of their own educational programs as well as those for high-school students.[18] A central issue of the San Francisco State College strike thus flowed naturally from that experience: "immediate establishment of a Black Studies Department with 20 full-time faculty members . . . free from interference by college administrators or the state-wide board of trustees which oversees all 18 California State Colleges."[19]

In general, the San Francisco State strikers' demands for autonomous third-world studies programs and for open admissions followed logically from the educational philosophy of the Experimental College. The central principle is self-determination—in the classroom and in the community, whether student or organizer. Anyone can organize a course; anyone can take a course; there are to be no grades. Learning is an internal process of discovery in which only the learner can validate his experience—or demonstrate it perhaps in an action. In fact, therefore, learners or students decide what is to be learned and then set their own standards for achievement. If some students can initiate and organize courses and set their own standards, why not *any* students? Why not a group of black and third-world students? Why not?

The question is apparently scandalous, but it follows readily and logically from fundamental free-university premises. The logic of free universities leads directly to the breakdown of the university as a trainer and channeler of elites. The logic leads directly to open admissions and to self-determination by students of the content and quality of their education.

In reality, the logic led to the demise of the Experimental College. For its support of the strike, the college's funds were withdrawn from its control. In the fall of 1969, the students held a press conference and announced that they could not operate "in a repressive atmosphere." James Brann wrote recently of San Francisco State's current atmosphere:

As long as I have known it—since 1966—the place has had an unusual atmosphere—almost tangible vibrations. This year the vibrations are cold, heavy, damp, and very tangible as one steps off the trolley at the gate. The spirit of the lines of police formations persists. It's almost as if the lines were still there, but invisible—and in a way that's true. There are many undercover plainclothes types—some with "cop" written on their forehead as they sit together and drink coffee in the cafeteria.[20]

How, then, to summarize the Experimental College's service to the campus and to educational reform? Away from its own campus, its national press after the fall of 1966 fired the imagination of students in other colleges, some of whom even traveled specially to visit its courses. These and the language of its catalog were widely copied elsewhere. But the Experimental College remained somewhat unique, especially because its emphasis on process, on building cadre or staff to teach in a particular manner, was something not picked up easily. For the most part, until relatively recently, that was ignored. Similarly, the Experimental College's ambitious approach to the institutional problems of educational reform was also not easily exported. Rather, most free universities founded in 1966 and even in 1967 used the EC's rhetoric and some of the curricula but the form—or lack of structure—of the Free University of Pennsylvania.

The Free University of Pennsylvania

One of the founders of FUP was also among those responsible for exposing the University of Pennsylvania's involvement in chemical-bacteriological-warfare research. Bob Brand's attitude toward a free university, nevertheless, was non- or anti-sectarian. "A university is a place," he told us, "where all kinds of courses ought to be taught. If you're going to discuss ideas, you have to discuss *all* ideas. We've never refused a course. Rockwell could teach here."[21] When questioned about his politics, Brand insisted that he could and did separate them from the few administrative chores he performed for the free university. He and several other founders saw their roles as deliberately nonpolitical, and in the free university's second term voluntarily gave up SDS sponsorship in favor of an enlarged "coordinating committee" open to all who would work on it. All announcements and brochures state that the Free University of Pennsylvania "espouses no ideology or point of view beyond its own tenets of operation."

The coordinators' job was to issue a call for course organizers, print the list for circulation, name a time and place for registration, and assign meeting places for courses. After that, the free university was on its own. There were, after all, no fees, exams, grades. There was, in fact, no follow-up except of the most informal, accidental variety. The chief complaint, when we visited in the spring of 1967, was that the drop-out rate seemed to be high—a guess was 50 percent—because classroom procedures were typically no different from usual, except that students were lecturing instead of professors.

Unlike the Experimental College, and typical of most free universities, there was no system of internal education built into the scheme. The main idea, Leo Kormis said, was no rules, no structure, no organization at all. But who sets policy? "There is no policy" was the steady answer we received, "no policy—that's our policy!" If people wanted the free university to continue, it would; if not, it wouldn't.

The relationship to the University of Pennsylvania was also a loose one. The university supplied rooms and facilities, and no one was paid for teaching. "Money," the members of the coordinating committee told us, "has not been a problem." In a procedure quite the reverse of the Experimental College's, the organizers themselves contributed money as well as time. In the beginning, for example, Steve Kuromiya's profits from the sale of a *Collegiate Guide* helped cover the relatively modest annual budget of $300, spent mostly on publicity and printing.

The aim of the SDS-initiated project in the fall of 1965 was "to destroy the image of grades and authority" and "to give people a different idea about education by example." "Just sitting in a different kind of classroom" would, the initiators thought, "clue people in that Penn was not doing the job" it should. And to some extent, they were quite correct. Though their anarchy contrasts remarkably with the organization of the Experimental College, it is possible to note some effect on their university host. In fact, it may be that the effect of a free university on a host institution depends not so much on the organization of the free university as it does on the vulnerability of the regular college curriculum to any kind of criticism.

The initiators expected that about 125 people would register for the twenty-four courses that had been set up in the spring of 1966. Instead, more than 750 people turned up and, in a manner "quite exciting" to see, "courses began springing up" to double the original number. The initiators described their curriculum as "too contemporary, controversial, broad or narrow to be part of the university curriculum." The courses included "Black Power," "The New Left," "Contemporary Education," and "American Youth in Revolt."

In preparation for the fall of 1966, the committee "started making bridges to the rest of the world," by soliciting course offerings from the community around the campus and by making "a real effort to get non-students on to campus." Thus, their curriculum included "Psychedelics and Getting High" by two members of Timothy Leary's Neo-American Church, four courses offered by the Institute of Jewish Studies, a course on the Warren Report by a staff member of the

American Civil Liberties Union, and a course on contraception offered by Planned Parenthood. There were five different courses concerned with aspects of socialism or Marxism. Registration soared to a
thousand and included a high enough proportion of off-campus
people to worry the university authorities. "We challenged the university's concept of property," the organizers claimed, "suddenly
non-students were using facilities." Though the organizers talked in
1967 about finding nonuniversity facilities, they solved their problems in quite another way—by turning the free university, in its third
year, over to the student government. Thus, as the *Daily Pennsyl-
vanian* put it on February 13, 1968, "the Free University has solved
most of its administrative chaos and can concentrate on providing
free courses for faculty and students alike." The "community," even
as a word, has disappeared.

The effect of the free university on the University of Pennsylvania is not easily measurable. Its organizers point out that the free
university served the campus atmosphere by "keeping good students
on campus" and showing others that there was more to intellectual
life than "five easy Penn courses and drinking." Probably Leo Kormis'
skepticism is more to the point: "We provided a safety valve, and the
university realized it, by offering what they could not." At the beginning of the free university's second year, Penn announced that it was
offering ten free noncredit seminars to a limited number of undergraduates. The courses were to be "voluntarily" staffed by professors and to meet evenings in their homes. Registration was overwhelming, the free university organizers reported, and the titles and
descriptions of the courses were lifted from the free university.

Other effects are less visible and nonmeasurable except in terms
of the larger movement for educational reform. That is, the rhetoric
used in free-university leaflets and campus press accounts helped to
popularize the ideas of "taking an active role" in one's education and
eliminating the "hierarchical relationship which weakens the student-
teacher one." But the organizers themselves were critical about their
own effectiveness in spreading new educational ideas beyond the
coordinating committee. As Leo Kormis put it, "We've broken down
the stereotype of teacher as authority, but we haven't gone on to a
new view of education. People come to an interesting series of lectures and not to participate in their own education."

In fact, the curriculum has come to depend more and more on

visiting lecturers, gimmicks, or the esoteric, though Bob Brand and several others tried, in December, 1966, to reorganize the free university so as to begin creating courses that might help to develop "a freshman science curriculum" or "a different approach to the study of economics." Nothing remotely like that occurred, for reasons that are not obscure when one considers the organization necessary for the Experimental College to have moved in this direction. Instead, the number of political courses declined steadily from two-thirds of the curriculum in the fall of 1966 to one-half in the spring of 1967 to one-seventh in the spring of 1968. And no courses in educational theory took their place. The spring 1968 courses included a number that might appear in any general-education catalog—speedreading, for example, conversational Italian, or a course on James Joyce. But more than half the courses listed were jazzy or esoteric, new movements into hippiedome: languages like Swahili, Gaelic, Brazilian Portuguese, and Cakchiquel (classical Mayan); titles like "Engineering Theology," "Reality Contact," and "Bullshit"; and favorite performers like Ira Einhorn offering, instead of "The World of Marshall McLuhan" or "Analogues to the LSD Experience," both very popular in previous semesters, a new course entitled "How Does One Occupy a Space?"

The development is different from the Experimental College's. Politics and ideology, missing from the Free University of Pennsylvania as an institution, also gradually disappear from the curriculum. Not surprisingly, they are replaced by the diverse extrapolitical interests of the students: personal development and creativity, esoteric drug and religious experiences, exotic languages and cultures. Under the direction of the student government, the free university, once envisioned as a means of changing the university, now functions in its service.

EARLY AND LATE MODELS: THE MOVEMENT'S GROWTH AND DECLINE

A vision of the university's relationship to the larger community outside was the most significant feature of some thirty "early" free universities founded either by SDS members or other radical activists. San Francisco State's Experimental College provided one model, since a significant portion of its curriculum was at first dedicated to the poor, black, and third-world communities surrounding State, and since the activity of community organizing was conceived as a legitimate "course." Most early free universities included at least one such course in their curriculum—at Bowling Green State University, for example, it was called "Perrysburg Heights Community Involvement Project."[22] The Free University of Pennsylvania's cool rhetoric and nonideological line provided another early model in its deliberate effort to bring the community as teachers or students onto the campus. Seattle's founders took a similar stance: students, they said, "demand a relationship between learning and their own moral concerns," presumably in the community outside the university. The founders of Stanford's "The Experiment" offered education "in a larger context and perspective" than the regular curriculum, in an effort to help students understand themselves, their society, and the relationship between the two.

On the whole, the rhetoric used to describe the relationship of these early free universities to their host institution was more militant than the Experimental College's. They announced themselves as "protest counter-institutions to the *un*free universities" (Seattle, fall 1966); or as attempts to "reach students dissatisfied with standard "Multiversity education" (Minnesota, January 1967) or simply as geared to "destroy the irrelevant university" (Ann Arbor, January 1966). And whether they asked the university for facilities (Minnesota, under SDS sponsorship) or decided to be independent in that regard (Ann Arbor, Seattle), they saw themselves as hostile challengers of university standards and procedures.

They solved the problems of finances and bureaucracy in various eclectic ways, or they disappeared within a year as did the Free University of Ann Arbor and Princeton's Experimental College. Some charged a token membership fee—from two dollars at the University of Minnesota to ten dollars at Stanford's Experiment. Others relied on the energies of a single student founder to run the bureaucracy. More ambitious was the attempt at democracy in the form of mass meetings of participants once or twice a month, as at Seattle and Minnesota. At Seattle also, funds collected by charging a nominal fee for courses paid two or three full-time coordinators a monthly stipend of fifty dollars and rented a house off campus where all courses met. Obviously, there was no single organizational model. Obviously, too, most free universities finally depended on the range of courses they could offer and on the interests of the students in them.

Initially, the proportion of political courses was high. At the University of Minnesota's free university, two-thirds of the seventeen courses were political, including the ubiquitous "Vietnam" and "C.O. and the Law." Seattle's curriculum, the first to include a political course on "Women in Society" (fall 1966), also included "Conservative Libertarian Theories" and "National Unity Through Class Struggle," taught by a "Marxist lecturer, organizer of the Freedom Socialist Party." Other interests were also represented. At Bowling Green, for example, five of the eight courses—an "Alienation Seminar" and four workshops in folk dancing, film production, journalism, and theater— contributed to counterculture on the campus. Seattle's first free-university meeting was organized by student activists who were surprised and delighted to find in attendance some "pretty non-political types" who "gave the Free U. of Seattle a broad base," and "kept it from becoming a sectarian tool of radical local politics."[23] Seattle's curriculum, which began with nearly equal numbers of political and hippie courses (13:12), doubled the hippie ones almost at once. These tended to move in a direction similar to San Francisco State's, into crafts, film-making, and toward the mystical and introspective.

Very few course descriptions included the educational focus of San Francisco State's Experimental College, even in so limited a form as Ann Arbor's "nondirective seminar." Though the rhetoric of free universities decried the authoritarianism of most classrooms or the "hierarchical" relationship between students and teachers, these problems were not attacked by engaging students in the process of teaching. Rather, the organizers found different adults to serve as teachers. Most of the (unpaid) teaching staff at the Free U. of Seattle were local poets, artists, photographers, film-makers, and technicians, or local radical Negroes, pacifists, leaders of the American Civil Liberties Union, or "outstanding local experimental educators." The effect was to offer an alternative idea of "expertise"—the man or woman in action—rather than the stereotyped university scholar. Though this is especially striking at Seattle, it is also apparent at the Free University of Pennsylvania and elsewhere in the effort to open the university's tower to the town.

Only relatively few of the early free universities survived, and those which did (with the striking exception of San Francisco State) grew large at the expense of service to the wider society. To some student critics it also began to seem doubtful that the free university could or would serve to change the campus. By 1967 it was clear to early enthusiasts like Michael Rossman that, given the intransigence of faculties, "Radical change within the system is impossible. . . ." He concluded that "The free-university approach seems a dead end to me: parallel institutions are tremendously wasteful of energy, and compete at a disadvantage."[24] In early 1967 also, Carl Davidson, the national vice-president of SDS, came to the same conclusion. Though the free universities may be successful especially "in an immediate internal sense," he wrote in a paper called "The Multiversity: Crucible of the New Working Class," he felt dubious about their political effect on the "established educational order":

> At best, they had no effect. But it is more likely that they had the effect of strengthening the existing system. How? First of all, the best of our people left the campus, enabling the existing university to function more smoothly, since the "troublemakers" were gone. Secondly, they gave liberal administrators the rhetoric, the analysis, and sometimes the manpower to co-opt their programs and establish elitist forms of "experimental" colleges inside of, although quarantined from, the existing educational system.[25]

Both Rossman and Davidson were probably stating conclusions that others had also come to, for after early 1967, it was virtually impossible to find SDS members or other movement radicals founding free universities. Davidson's remarks are also prophetic, for the free-university movement continued, in fact flourished, during the next several years, as it does today, although under different auspices: those of the National Student Association, student governments, or both, and sometimes under college administrators as well.

The entire tone was different—Davidson called it "liberal." At Notre Dame, for instance, the founders said that "the free university isn't rebelling—it's exploring." At the University of Houston, students urged the necessity for "reform" through a "demonstration project of a totally new approach to learning." The main theme was stated in Brooklyn College's brochure: to "give students a free learning experience." Or, as the students at Utah put it, to arrange a temporary way for the university to meet its problems. Thus, the new UCLA experimental-college founders (student editors and NSA members) declared their purpose "to complement" the college, not "compete" with it; and Whittier College students, with the announced approval of their president, who was concerned about gaps in the social-science curriculum, aimed "to help students get programs that are educational but not in the catalogue."[26]

By late 1967 and early 1968, the free-university movement, renamed "educational reform" and confined to that particular goal, was increasingly a legitimate activity, popularized and supported by the National Student Association, that received from the Ford Foundation in September, 1968, a grant of $305,000 for these purposes.[27] The second and larger wave of free universities was to produce "educational reform" in two interlocking ways: by channeling the energies of students into "constructive" study programs, administrators could at the same time fill in those ever-present gaps in the curriculum. Thus, the administration at the University of Iowa initiated a free university, making funds available to a student-faculty steering committee and arranging for some course credit. A university spokesman described the effort as an attempt "to provide an academic enterprise for the 'disaffected students' who were going through the motions because it's required of them."[28] President Howard R. Bowen's support of the Free University of Iowa might, except for one word, slip unnoticed into any number of free university catalogs:

> The purpose of the program would be to encourage thoughtful, timely, and relevant study and discussion of contemporary political, social, ethical and philosophic issues and to encourage *constructive* social service activities. [Italics added.]

On several campuses (University of New Mexico,[29] University of Utah, University of Notre Dame), student-faculty-administration committees were set up to supervise the new free universities. Early in 1969, a brief article in *College Management*, a trade journal for administrators, asked, "Why not benefit from the free universities?"

> It's easy enough to dismiss student-run free universities or experimental colleges with a superior smile. After all, how serious can you get about a course in Zen Basketball?
> But there's more to the free university movement than way-out subjects. There's often a genuine attempt to offer courses

that colleges and universities should be offering; and, if you keep an open mind and eye on the movement, you're quite likely to find that you can benefit from it.[30]

Using as example Dartmouth's experimental college, the article proposes the free university as a "bellwether" [sic] of students' interests to those who wish to revise or augment their curriculum. What further irony might one expect? What further example of "co-optation"? An instrument once conceived as useful for changing universities now appears recommended as a tool to be used by them for controlling change.

Even before 1969, the curricula of free universities had further changed from what we have just described. The proportion of political courses had diminished, few courses called for activities outside the classroom, and none for political or community organizing. What remains had typically the force of study groups or "clubs" on campus. Dartmouth's Experimental College, for example, provided a glossy printed catalog and somewhat glossier varieties of the nonacademic: "The Stock Market," "Contract Bridge," and "Gambling in the U.S." Political courses were limited to three of sixteen, then eight of twenty, including "The Development of Conservative Thought" and "Guerrilla Warfare." With enthusiastic support from the administration, courses were "sponsored" by campus groups or fraternities, "coordinated" by students who sometimes invited visiting lecturers, and held in fraternity lounges or homes of town residents. The issue was not change but a way of spending evenings informally engaged in "a provocative educational experience" with a novel mix of people.

We know of only two campuses, among hundreds where "late" free universities continue, on which students have consciously used the free-university idea to effect institutional change. In both cases, at the University of North Carolina and at Brown University, students were directly affected by the example set by San Francisco State's Experimental College. At North Carolina in the spring of 1967, student-government leaders organized thirty-two seminars (the Experimental College) limited to enrollments of twelve, "led" by faculty, graduate students, or chaplains.[31] At the same time, they launched a university-wide student evaluation of all courses. In August these students published a lengthy report of their work, including a preface charging the university with ignoring significant educational theory and developing passive nonintellectuals who cared only about getting through requirements to a degree. The academic style of the report, its meticulous and generally conservative use of statistics, its acknowledgment to two cooperative deans, and its concern with course organization and teaching style, suggest that North Carolina students were politically conscious of the necessity to convince the faculty of the need for change.[32]

The college-wide survey was hardly a credit to the faculty or the curriculum. The results were, in fact, "discouraging" for the reputation of the university in general, especially since "a majority of lecturers and teachers decided not to have their courses evaluated at all, thereby showing much less interest in how well they are communicating to their students." The report's conservative conclusions cautiously restate themes urged generally by the free-university movement. First, a tactful version of the usual charges of irrelevance: "educators need to pay greater attention to personal interest as a prime factor in motivating a student to learn." Second, labeled tentative and in need of more investigation: "teaching methods which promote active student participation" are superior to other methods. The founders conclude that the experimental college has functioned as a "laboratory" in which "neglected values" of higher education, especially the "independent learning ability" of students, could be tested. Were the powerful on campus interested, they might allow the experimental college to continue as a credit-granting (small) body that might hopefully, in some unspecified way, move the larger university toward reform.

The students at Brown University were more ambitious and more intrepid. In the fall of 1966, seventy of them planned an experimental college and then decided to use their chief energies, not in running it, but in pressing the college to adopt its design.[33] During the following three years, students worked "through peaceful means" to convince both the student body and the faculty of the necessity for change. They organized themselves into "teams" to talk with faculty individually, then reported their responses publicly in newsletters and "held weekly rallies, many of which drew more than 1,000 students." The result of their pressure—including an acknowledged "threat of a possible confrontation"—was the appointment by President Ray Heffner of a faculty committee which worked with student leaders to draw up and institute a "student-initiated curriculum" and a broad range of other reforms. Reminiscent of San Francisco State's "Styles of Thought," for example, "modes-of-thought" courses were arranged to replace traditional introductory surveys. Other aspects of the new program—the abolition of grades, requirements, and departmental majors—suggest that students are to have power independent of the faculty. As a student leader, Ira Magaziner put it, "Students will no longer have to take a badly taught course because it's required or because they need a good grade."

On large and small campuses, even in the current academic year, free universities continue to provide relief for students from lecture courses and traditional curricula. Their counterculture still fills their own catalogs more than those of their host institutions. At the staid University of Virginia, for example, fifty-five courses are announced in the fall, 1969, brochure of the experimental university.[34] For a fee of one dollar, any student may register in two of these, neither for grades nor credit, but for "learning as personal discovery." The courses range from the currently ubiquitous "Hermann Hesse" and "Modern Adult Fantasy" (i.e., Tolkien) to "The Editorials of Russell Baker," "The Dominating Non Artistic Artists," "Rock Music in Translation," and "Underground Komix,"; from "Introduction to Group Dynamics" to "Dynamic Christianity." There are as many activity-centered workshops—drama, poetry, silk-screening, dance, karate, surfing, chess—and two in bartending—as there are political courses: approximately fifteen of each. Politics of the right and left are both represented, local problems ("The South Since 1865") as well as Vietnam. Except for "Power Structure Research," political courses are reading and study groups. The sharp model of institutional change—fundamental to the vision of early SDS and the founders of San Francisco State's Experimental College and explicit in the rhetoric at least of all early free universities—has disappeared.

SERVING (CHANGING) THE CAMPUS

It is easy to dismiss the free-university movement as politically impotent. Like nonviolence in the civil-rights movement, setting a good example on the campus ("blackmailing the institution with quality") has not worked. Habit, self-interest, and power dominate the university as they do the wider society, in spite of rebellions, confrontations, or riots. The faculty and administration are in charge, and they intend to keep things that way. But the university is a different place from what it was in 1962 or 1965, and we would make two claims for the free-university movement. First, that it take major responsibility, through the rapid spread of counterculture, for the idea of student-centered curriculum. Second, that it take partial responsibility for raising hard questions about the elitism of universities that we expect will be central to campus struggles in the seventies.

A corrosive tone pervades a recent essay by Ford Foundation vice-president F. Champion Ward.[35] Remarking the "crisis" that has "strained the institutional fabric of American universities and colleges," Ward flays the backwardness of those institutions, their administrators' lack of imagination, their faculties' self-interest. His language is as sharp as that of student founders of early free universities. Though he dismisses them as "gypsy encampments . . . in the surrounding hills" and suggests that their "dissidents" are "so impatient for perfection that no finite amount of reform is likely to be enough for them," he asserts that "many students," who "may be half-baked" may also be "at least half right" in their criticism of the university:

> . . . most of the words which these students employ in saying what their education ought to be come straight from the lexicon of educational uplift with which all college catalogues begin and convocation talks conclude. . . . These students are asking questions of higher education which are directed to the relation between established disciplines and the courses of study and age-old questions of individual fulfillment and commitment, on the one hand, and the world's tensions and demands on the other.
>
> They do not wish to be processed or certified. (Some of them seem not even to want to be taught.)

Especially since "stakes for the Nation's intellectual life and social progress are very high," Ward urges that means be found, by "engaging both educators and students," to move toward "educational reform." "In the end," he concludes metaphorically, "the yeast" (gypsy encampments) and "the lump" (conventional university programs) "belong together." With irony, Ward suggests that "a mixture of courses, teaching and academic organization in which critical students appear to thrive is not beyond contrivance by serious educators. . . ."

Three pamphlets published by "serious educators" within the past two years also respond to student critics, first by flailing faculties, then by proposing reforms that summarize the chief features of the free-university movement. The mildest of these, a research monograph called *Undergraduate Curriculum Trends,* concludes that the student "should" become "the focal consideration in curricular planning."[36] The most recent of these, Lewis B. Mayhew's *Contemporary College Students and the Curriculum,* remarks the "growing evidence to suggest that many students are, in fact, creating an underground curriculum which makes sense to them but which would horrify their graduate-school-trained professors."[37] Mayhew's pamphlet and another by the Hazen Foundation, called *The Student in Higher Education,* are attempts to rationalize and hence legitimize the "underground curriculum" that we have discussed.[38] Both pamphlets begin by placing "the individual student, and not the abstract curricular concepts, at the center of the college experience" (Hazen, p. 12). The key to curriculum, as in free universities, would be the interest of students, or as the Hazen report puts it, "Discovering Knowledge." Colleges ought to facilitate "the development of the young adult personality," rather than promote vocational training for graduate or other professional schools. After all, the writers declare, "Learning is essentially discovery, and even though there is now very little of it in American higher education, we can find no reason why discovery should not be returned to the college years" (pp. 9–10).

In a university of discovery, requirements would vanish, also departments, attendance rules, grades, lectures, and teacher-dominated discussions. So, too, the notion of "objectivity" as an educational tool: "it is no longer possible," the Hazen group writes, to isolate "cognitive growth from moral growth and the general maturation of the person" (pp. 8–9). Instead, they call for an "ideological" or value-oriented curriculum, especially in the freshman year, "of critical importance because it is the time when the student's enthusiasm, curiosity, and willingness to work can be snuffed out or reinforced" (p. 45). Mayhew offers, as examples of new curriculum, a course focused on the question "What is the proper stance for a conscientious objector?"; or a literature course that might help students "expand their impulse lives"; or T-groups (p. 74).

A second significant curricular recommendation would integrate "classroom learning and meaningful service" (Hazen, p. 47). "We think it particularly important," the Hazen Committee writes (apparently without cynicism), "that before the volunteer era ends in complete disillusionment, colleges and universities give serious consideration to how volunteer service can be closely integrated with the educational experience" (p. 65). They and Mayhew both recommend courses that include "real life experiences" (Mayhew, p. 75), and suggest that colleges might give credit to students who "participate in many other social tasks, as teachers in schools, as workers with the poor, the handicapped, the sick, and also the prosperous and the successful—wherever there is material for observation and reflection and a chance to serve others" (Hazen, p. 47). Despite the gratuitous addition of "the prosperous and the successful," the proposal allows for such courses as those in community organizing notable in the early days of San Francisco State's Experimental College. The committee urges their proposals as a means to "preserve youthful idealism, refined and hardened, perhaps, by the fires of realism, but not burned out." More emphatically, they caution, the "preservation of youthful enthusiasm . . . may no longer be an option but a necessity" (Hazen, p. 7).

How is all this to happen? What kind of institution can hold students, without departments, with a campus that extends into cities and overseas? The Hazen Committee argues that every major American institution should found a "spin-off school . . . in some vague way affiliated with the multiversity" but enjoying the "freedom to experiment' (p. 60). That is, they are calling for legitimated free universities. Antioch College, often an innovator in such matters, has already instituted such "beachhead" colleges—called "beach fronts" by students somewhat skeptical of the "pick-up-the-driftwood" approach to learning. Mayhew doubts that such gadflies can further institutional change. He points to an early administrative failure in Texas and reviews San Francisco State's Experimental College as evidence of students' readiness for wholesale educational innovation and reform.

But both pamphlets and the ACE monograph view what Mayhew calls "unbridled faculty power" as the main block to change. Mayhew would send faculty to school again, to learn this time how to "concentrate" their "professionalization . . . on the needs and desires of undergraduate students" (p. 54). Admitting that the most effective teacher is another student, both pamphlets envision new kinds of teachers—called "facilitators" of learning experiences by the Hazen Committee and "organizers of experience rather than the prime provider of experiences" by Mayhew. The political alliance that emerges on campus from student-centered, faculty-challenging curricula links reform-minded undergraduates with administrators hip to change. Over against them huddle rigid faculties, committed only to their own disciplines and perquisites. It is an attractive picture to administrators, since it permits them not only to respond to legitimate student demands but to enlist students' energies in their own effort at change.

These proposals are realistic in another way. In 1962, writing in *The American College,* Nevitt Sanford worried about students ignoring their undergraduate experience. Now critics like Mayhew and the Hazen Committee point to the disaffected student both as a model for "autonomy and self-reliance" and as a threat to the continuation of campus life. They recognize that the student views himself not as a child to be taught but as a person to be dealt with—who has "interests" and can responsibly chart his own development, who has quite correctly asked for a "living, learning community" rather than a competitive assembly line. Thus, faculty and administrators both are warned to accede graciously to students' pressure for "democratization of rulemaking and enforcing on the college campus," since "it is undoubtedly going to take place in any event" (Hazen, p. 63). Refusing to allow students their wish to serve the campus and society —as they have shown themselves willing and able to do—will, in fact, lead students quite rightly to rebellion. Or, seen in a slightly different light, if the university doesn't find useful service for students, they will find it for themselves, and what they find may seem rebellious to their elders. Better, the reports advise, enlist students into change instead of being changed by them. The alternative, if colleges continue stifling the "intellectual goals and . . . service-oriented generosity" of students, is to face the consequences of their growing "cynicism." The Hazen report of January, 1968, in short, predicted the confrontations of that year and the next several as well.

How useful is educational reform for preserving, rather than serving, the campus? Will the recommendations we have been discussing accomplish what the policeman's billyclub and the threat of injunction have not? Such proposals may "keep the students happy" and very busy on elite campuses. One can imagine them spending full time organizing their courses, teaching themselves and other students, working on college-wide governing or curriculum committees, and, in fact, locked into similar institutional responsibilities that currently engage faculty and administrators. But there are a few loopholes in this vision, unacknowledged thus far. One is the concept of service itself, especially as it is related to self-determination; another the still open-ended questions of standards and admissions, generally avoided by those involved in educational reform.

If we return again to San Francisco State, we may recall that so long as the Experimental College functioned as a (culturally) lively but (politically) quiescent institution, so long as it made no demands on the host institution that might change the college population, there were no problems. Students might determine their own courses, without traditional grading procedures, and receive college credit. But demands from black and third-world students for self-determination, however similar to those already granted to white, middle-class students at the Experimental College—those were impossible for San Francisco State and the entire educational bureaucracy of California to deal with. Once the principle of self-determination is established, it is difficult to keep it from spreading. The principle, moreover, is both educational and political. Black and third-world leaders understood this clearly:

> The principle of self-determination is based upon the fact that we can no longer afford to allow the white man to control our lives in terms of the kind of education we get here at San Francisco State College. . . . We wish to take responsibility for all aspects of our lives. . . . The white establishment, the white Board of Trustees fear this. It threatens the financial interests which they represent. . . . They see clearly that once Third World people begin to get any kind of self-determination in any aspect of their lives it will ultimately mean for them a removal of their financial, political, and social control. It is people like this who politically manipulate masses of Third World people, keeping them unemployed and confined to a ghetto environment. The whole function of the state educational system is to produce human resources for the industries and businesses that the Board of Trustees represent.[39]

Even Hayakawa understood the reasons for the strike that paralyzed his campus:

> If we were dealing with hunger instead of education, you can imagine what would happen if we had a walled city in which the citizens had all the food they needed while outside there were hordes of starving people. We could not open the gates just a little to admit handfuls of the starving and expect the rest to remain patient outside.
>
> No.
>
> We would have to be prepared to open the gates wide and to admit everyone, or be prepared for a riot. That is the situation now with higher education.[40]

We repeat, once the principle of self-determination is established, it's hard to keep it from spreading. If educators will dismiss grading procedures and test scores, disparage current admissions practices as elitist, and call for a sharp reduction in the competitive atmosphere of educational institutions—as both Mayhew and the Hazen Committee do—on what basis are students to be admitted and to be graduated? And to which institutions? Who or what will decide whether a student should attend Brown or Rhode Island State; New York's City University or Manhattan Community College? San Francisco State or a junior college? Mayhew attempts a response by calling for a stratified definition of "excellence":

> It should be possible for an institution to aim at the education of second- or third-chance students, and to do so as excellently as does the institution which concentrates on the most highly talented potential academicians. It should be possible for a junior college to strive for excellence in the training of technicians without feeling inferior to the medical school. . . . [P. 55.]

On such hopes, it should have been possible to avoid confrontation at San Francisco State and at City University, but it wasn't.

In New York and elsewhere, the call for "open admissions" is a direct result of ideas about student-centered education and self-determination. Recall that the roots of the free-university movement lie not only in students' dissatisfaction with their education and campus lives but in their recognition of the significant relationship between the university and the society it serves. The Vietnam war clarified the curious, symbiotic relationship between the university and the warfare state. In particular, the concomitant institution of the draft (as we shall show in the following chapter) raised questions about the special class privileges of white middle-class students, reprieved from the rice paddies. The institution of educational innovations, currently in process at many elite institutions, will lead to further questions about standards, admissions, and whom the institutions serve. Self-determination is a dynamic principle. Set in motion by the ethic of service, now established as a legitimate element of college curriculum, the campus may once again become a base for activating and organizing communities. With more black and brown self-determined and self-confident students coming onto campuses, especially in cities, we expect that there will be many more San Francisco States in the decade ahead.

Notes

[1] Various "lists" of free universities can be found in the student press and other underground publications as far back as 1966 and in the mass media after late 1967. Usually, no attempt is made to distinguish, as we will here, between those organized as parallel institutions (on or near a campus and aimed toward educational reform of that campus) and those organized as separate institutions. We have, therefore, relied on no lists but on catalogs, the campus press, interviews, visits, and unpublished accounts written by participants.

In the summer of 1968, the National Student Association (NSA) made available a "directory" of approximately one hundred free universities, experimental colleges, free schools, and the like, prepared by Blair Hamilton from responses to questionnaires and a collection of catalogs. The directory warns readers of "many inaccuracies and conflicting statements." Again, in the same list are independent experimental colleges and on-campus free universities. The NSA list, nevertheless, provides a useful check against our own, since we have been selective rather than inclusive. Our research and a cautious use of the NSA list provides the following breakdown of ninety-six free universities founded (but not necessarily enduring) in the first four years of the movement: 1965, 5; 1966, 10; 1967, 35; 1968, 46.

[2] January, 1969, Vol. 4, No. 1, p. 45.

[3] We use the first printed version published in pamphlet form (New York, 1964) by Students for a Democratic Society. First printing (mimeographed) of 20,000 was dated August, 1962.

[4] This and other remarks of Nevitt Sanford are from his essay called "Higher Education as a Social Problem," in *The American College—A Psychological and Social Interpretation of Higher Learning* (New York, 1962), pp. 10–30.

[5] We quote from a mimeographed pamphlet by Steve Weissman, "Freedom and the University," distributed by Students for a Democratic Society.

[6] See "Free Speech Carols," a recording by the Free Speech Movement.

[7] New York, 1967. For additional documentation of this movement, see also Paul Jacobs and Saul Landau, *The New Radicals: A Report with Documents* (New York, 1966).

[8] This discussion is based on mimeographed reports which, so far as we know, remain unpublished, as well as on our own participation in discussions.

[9] UCLA *Bruin,* November 15, 1966.

[10] "The Experimental College at San Francisco State," in *Thought from the Education Reform Movement* (Mainly Catching Up): A Collection of Essays with editorial interventions gathered by . . . Rick Kean (published in 1969 by the National Student Association), pp. 43–56. Nixon's essay was originally a speech that, from internal evidence, can be dated the summer of 1967. When we quote him, we will cite page numbers within.

Our account of the Experiment College also relies on several other essays written by participants or observers, accounts in the student press, the mass media, catalogs, leaflets, as well as personal letters and private conversations.

One particularly useful source has been James Brann, formerly a reporter on *The Chronicle of Higher Education,* now writing a book about faculty. His early, full report on the EC appeared December 21, 1966. He has also supplied us with an unpublished manuscript on the history of San Francisco State's strike, written at the request of the National Commission on the Causes and Prevention of Violence, and then ignored by them.

[11] Begun in the summer of 1965, San Francisco's New School and the Free University of New York (FUNY) are not to be confused with the movement we are describing. Their distinctiveness is illuminating. First, they were organized chiefly by professors, rather than students, as separate, not parallel, institutions. Second, to defray expenses and/or pay teachers, both schools have charged fees ranging from seven to twenty-five dollars per course, with arrangements for "scholarships." Third, both schools were explicitly political in nature, though their particular purposes differed. FUNY is reminiscent of the secession one hundred years ago of students and faculty from the Lane Seminary to discuss "slavery without administration harassment" that resulted in the founding of Oberlin. FUNY's curriculum, primarily Marxist in orientation, drew attention to the university's absolute omission of such material. If a New Yorker wanted to study Marxist economics, or the "Theory and Practice of Radical Social Movements," he could not register at Columbia or NYU. Because of its location and its intellectual bravery, many big names—Conor Cruise O'Brien, John Gerassi, Staughton Lynd—were attracted to teaching at FUNY.

San Francisco's New School was organized to serve political activists in another way. In the summer of 1965, and for a brief period thereafter, the New School was affiliated with SDS. Its courses were organized as "projects" to produce pamphlets, films, papers, tapes, etc., "as decided by the students." In both schools, however, the curriculum included nonpolitical courses: at SFNS these were, like "Guerrilla Graphics," still to be useful to a political radical. At FUNY, these courses could be simply esoteric—"The Psychotic Experience as an Archetype of Paradise Lost," for example; or related to politics—"Contemporary Revolutionary Poetry" or "Nineteenth Century Russian Literature."

[12] Russell Bass with James Nixon and Ian Grand, "Some Notes on the Experimental College," unpublished paper available through NSA, 21 pp., dated October, 1967.

[13] See Roger Harrison and Richard L. Hopkins, "The Design of Cross-Cultural Training: An Alternative to the University Model," in *Thought* . . . , ed. Rick Kean, cited above. Kean says of this essay, originally published in 1967, "Although it very carefully claims to be dealing mainly with training for overseas work, it has a strange resonance for activist work here at home, too, and seems useful as a tool for planning work in any new culture," p. 220.

[14] Seventy such courses were taught in the spring of 1967 (Nixon, p. 53). The procedures whereby students might get official credit for Experimental College courses take up more than three large pages in the fall 1966 catalog; 250 of the 1,200 students who registered took that option.

[15] The funds were not difficult to come by, since the same group of stu-

dents controlled both the Associated Students and the EC—Jim Nixon had run for president and won in the spring of 1966—and since students had absolute control over a budget of $412,000 (1967–68), raised by a compulsory ten-dollar student activity fee. But because student funds had to be spread across such groups as *The Daily Gator;* football, basketball, and baseball teams; drama groups; community involvement; and downtown tutorial programs, the EC committed itself to foundation fund-raising and thenceforth some of its energies were siphoned off in that direction.

[16] The Black Power movement began in the Bay Area during the fall of 1966 (see the *Daily Californian,* October 27, 1966). By early 1967, the movement had absorbed the EC area called "Black Arts and Culture" into a Black Students Union that helped to organize the strike of 1968. The area called "Urban Communities and Change" was transformed in 1967 into a "Work-Study Project" in which college credit was available for six to nine hours per week of field work in a variety of projects in the Mission, Potrero Hill, or Bernal communities. Participants met weekly in small seminars organized by EC staff for evaluative discussion. In addition, there were monthly meetings of all participants in a given locale to share information and discuss the wider implications of their work.

[17] Brann, unpublished report, pp. 11–12.

[18] James Nixon writes of the blacks that they "used the experimental college and the freedom that was created by it to do their own stuff." (p. 49). Michael Rossman writes that the blacks "formed a cohesive block . . . working for their own needs." He adds that perhaps black and white students "will have to learn to work well separately—if even that is possible—before they can make a new try at working together. . . ." *Thought,* p. 111.

[19] Brann, unpublished report, p. 1.

[20] Brann, personal letter, November 23, 1969.

[21] We visited the Free University of Pennsylvania and conducted interviews with a group of its organizers and talked with others on campus. We have also used press accounts, catalogs, and mimeographed papers.

[22] Here and elsewhere, unless otherwise indicated, we are quoting from free university catalogs or leaflets.

[23] Anonymous unpublished essay, with extensive bibliography, on the origins of the Free University of Seattle.

[24] "Prospects for Radical Educational Reform Within the System," mimeographed pamphlet (NSA, n.d.), pp. 13, 15–16. Date probably late 1966 or early 1967.

[25] Davidson's essay, included in Kean's book, pp. 122ff., was widely circulated in the movement press from 1967 on. Another version of this essay, called "University Reform Revisited," was published in *The Educational Record* by the American Council on Education, Winter, 1967. Davidson proposed another model of educational insurgency: the organizing of a radical caucus inside a large lecture course to pressure a professor and his department to change texts, curriculum, and methodology, or at the very least to develop the radical consciousness of students inside the course who might engage in struggle with the professor and others.

[26] *Whittier Quaker Campus,* February 16, 1968.

[27] The NSA characteristically follows students' interests rather than initi-

ating them. As a "moderate" or "liberal" student organization, it serves to "legitimize" or popularize student-initiated demands or issues. Thus, in 1969, more than three years after the draft-resistance movement began, NSA announced its support. One year after SDS's workshops on the free university, in 1966 NSA held some of its own. A former staff member, Philip Wardell, has suggested a special motive for NSA's interest in free universities: ". . . the reform of higher education became the common denominator of the NSA staff that was hired (without their knowledge) to find alternative domestic funding to the Central Intelligence Agency." ("A Personal Bibliography on Higher Education," pamphlet dated November 15, 1967, and available through NSA.)

[28] *Daily Iowan,* January 26, 1968.

[29] An "early" free university in date, but a "late" model, New Mexico's was organized in 1966 by a NSA coordinator who worked first with the university's president, then with a group of faculty.

[30] January, 1969, Vol. 4, No. 1, p. 45.

[31] Ten of the thirty-two courses were political, including the ubiquitous "Basic Guerrilla Warfare" and "Conscientious Objection." But most of the others were strikingly academic, half of them literary: "Modern Literary Criticism," "The Earliest English Poetry," "Studies in Medieval Criticism," and the like. But of course the purpose of this particular experimental college had little to do with revising university curriculum as such.

[32] Perhaps that is why, though so much of the educational philosophy of San Francisco State's Experimental College is present, there is notable timidity about the use of undergraduates as teachers. Instead, the founders emphasize the freedom of undergraduates in small classes "organized" by relatively nonauthoritarian types of teachers. The 37-page report, including an appendix of statistics and questionnaires, was written by David Kiel and Terry Fowler.

[33] We rely on accounts of friends and a story by Philip W. Semas in *The Chronicle of Higher Education,* June 16, 1969.

[34] We are grateful to Tom Gardner, undergraduate student-council officer at the University of Virginia, for supplying us with materials and information.

[35] Washington *Post,* March 2, 1969.

[36] By Paul L. Dressel and Frances H. DeLisle, an American Council on Education monograph, published in 1969. For the period 1957–1967, the authors surveyed undergraduate curriculum "in a random sample of 322 institutions," and they found "remarkably little" changed. They reward with scorn the "tinkering" of faculties, and in a rare outburst, find "almost unbelievable" the "lack of major modification" in the curriculum. On second thought, they mark the "vested interests" of "faculty members and departments" and they are not optimistic about change.

[37] *Contemporary College Students and the Curriculum,* by Lewis B. Mayhew, is a Southern Regional Education Board monograph (No. 14), published in Atlanta, 1969, p. 77. Other citations will appear in the text.

[38] The Committee on the Student in Higher Education, appointed by the Hazen Foundation in early 1966 and reporting in January, 1968, published *The Student in Higher Education.* A most influential pamphlet, it is stocked in quantity by the National Student Association, which calls it essential read-

ing for liberal college faculty, administrators, and students. At least half of its authors are well known: Joseph F. Kauffman, Wisconsin dean (chairman); Joseph Katz of Stanford; Kenneth Keniston of Yale; Esther Raushenbush, former president of Sarah Lawrence; as well as a past president of NSA, Philip Sherburne. As a group, they probably represent the left wing of the educational establishment. Though the authors try to be tactful for the most part, one central chapter, pp. 28–41, describing current college practices, contains no sentence free of scathing irony or invective. Its bite is harsher than any free-university material we've seen.

Though Mayhew's pamphlet is distinctive, there is enough overlapping with the Hazen report to allow the two to be discussed together. Mayhew combines the ACE study's idea of a student-centered curriculum with the Hazen Committee's emphasis on the "developmental" function of undergraduate education. His general educational assumptions are similar to those of the Hazen Committee, though he is capable often of pushing those assumptions to a particularly sharp conclusion: he emphasizes, for example, the "enormously greater force" of "the student peer culture" for "important learning," and adds that "no one can really learn something until he has tried to teach it to someone else" (pp. 37–38). Other page citations will appear in the text.

[39] Roger Alvarado, age 25, one of the main spokesmen for the Third World Liberation Front, interviewed by James Brann, and quoted by him in his unpublished report, pp. 21–22.

[40] Statement to a congressional committee, February 3, 1969, quoted by Brann, *op. cit.,* pp. 110–11.

5

Draft Resistance

August 6, 1964, was a special day in Ruleville, Mississippi. The freedom school was reopening in a large community-center building. A folk singer, Barbara Dane, was scheduled to help the celebration; and movies about Martin Luther King, Jr., Gandhi, and others were to be shown that evening. The building was jammed when Barbara Dane began to sing at about five that evening; kids of all ages sat on every inch of floor space and dangled from the open windows; adults on their way home from work pressed in at the doors. Between two of Barbara's songs, one of the white freedom-school teachers asked whether anyone knew what was special about August 6. There were various guesses—the opening of freedom school receiving the most support. "There's something else," she said. "It was on August 6 that the United States dropped the first atomic bomb on the Japanese." And she gave a very brief lecture, comparing the black people of Mississippi to the yellow people destroyed by the bomb. Barbara Dane sang "Where Have All the Flowers Gone?" Later that night, we showed our films about King, Gandhi, and the lines between people and countries.

The Vietnam war was on the minds of many volunteers in Mississippi that summer; the Tonkin Bay incident and the subsequent air strikes against North Vietnamese coastal facilities took place in August. Most of us had been trained, as had, indeed, much of the leadership of the civil-rights movement, by pacifists schooled in the discipline of nonviolence. But for black Mississippians that summer, the war was a remote abstraction; for young men, the Army remained an escape from the state. As we discovered when we tried to raise funds for the Mississippi Freedom Democratic Party from professorial supporters of the Ban the Bomb movement, the connections between the war and civil rights seemed to many northerners academic if not sectarian.

But by the summer of 1965, black Mississippians were seeing in Oriental faces their own condition of oppression. In McComb we met a young black man named Joe Martin who had run off on a Freedom Labor Union mimeograph machine the first draft-resistance statement we had then seen:

Here are five reasons why Negroes should not be in any War fighting for America:

1. No Mississippi Negroes should be fighting in Vietnam for the White Man's freedom, until all the Negro people are free in Mississippi.

2. Negro boys should not honor the draft here in Mississippi. Mothers should encourage their sons not to go.

3. We will gain respect and dignity as a race only by forcing the United States government and the Mississippi government to come with guns, dogs, and trucks to take our sons away to fight and be killed protecting Miss., Ala., Ga., and La.

4. No one has a right to ask us to risk our lives and kill other Colored People in Santo Domingo and Vietnam, so that the White American can get richer. We will be looked upon as traitors by all the Colored People of the world if the Negro people continue to fight and die without a cause.

5. Last week a white soldier from New Jersey was discharged from the army because he refused to fight in Vietnam he went on a hunger strike. Negro boys can do the same thing. We can write and ask our sons if they know what they are fighting for. If he answers Freedom, tell him that's what we are fighting for here in Mississippi. And if he says Democracy, tell him the truth— we don't know anything about Communism, Socialism, and all that, but we do know that Negroes have caught hell here under this *American Democracy.*

Many of the older leaders of the local Freedom Democratic Party were displeased with the leaflet and the adverse publicity it had brought them in the Mississippi press. They were for banning it in the freedom schools. But elsewhere in Mississippi and through the North, the leaflet was picked up and reprinted, often in newspapers seeking to discredit the loyalty of the civil-rights movement, from which, presumably, it had come. And before the summer was out, a black private had, in fact, gone on a hunger strike to protest his assignment to Vietnam.

For those who felt racism first hand, who were conscious of its impact on their daily lives, it was like breathing to identify with those "poor folks in Vietnam" they saw on TV each night, pursued by familiar white, inscrutable faces. There wasn't anything particularly mysterious about the identification. The same questions, ages old, about persecution and irrational fears and hatreds could be turned by Mississippians onto Vietnamese lives.

Vietnam: A Poem
by Mrs. Ida Mae Lawrence of Rosedale, Mississippi

We say we love our country
We say other people love their
country
We said that all men are brothers.
What would we call the war
in Vietnam
Would we call that brotherly love
Does the word freedom have a meaning
Why do the history books say
America is the

Land of Liberty a Free Country,
Then why do all mens Negro and White fight
the Vietnam and Korea why cant we be Americans
as North and South regardless of
color
What does we have again
the Vietnams?
Why are we fighting them?
Who are really the enemy?
Are Vietnam the enemy or we
Americans enemies to ourselves,
If we are the same as Vietnams
Why should we fight them?

They are poor too.
They wants freedom.
They wants to redster to vote.
Maybe the people in the Vietnam
can't redster to vote
Just like us.

Mrs. Lawrence wrote her poem during the efforts to register black Delta voters in the summer of 1965. By that fall, the connections were drawn more brutally by the slogan, popular in northern demonstrations, "No Vietnamese Ever Called Me Nigger."

For whites, the connections between the civil-rights movement and the war were, at least at first, somewhat less visceral. Funds badly needed to combat poverty in Mississippi were even then being diverted to the war; the same congressional forces keeping southern blacks in poverty were also, and not by accident, deeply involved in promoting the war. Economic interest and power—in addition to racism—tied the war to the condition of black people in America. SDS, which had up to that time mainly concentrated on programs supporting the civil-rights struggle or on community organizing in northern poverty areas, turned in the spring of 1965 to the Vietnam war. At the March on Washington they organized in April of that year—the first of the large antiwar marches—Paul Potter, the president of SDS, spoke of the need to "name the system" responsible for Vietnam and Mississippi. Though he did not then name the system, the implications were clear enough for the 25,000 people, most of them students, who had turned out that day.

Young, white draft resisters were soon to find other connections to Mississippi. Tom Gardner, a southerner who had been a student at the University of Virginia, wrote in the fall of 1966, admittedly to allay his fears about the consequences of refusing to cooperate with the draft:

. . . I'm tired of that word "later." I'm tired of allowing my life to be ruled by a machine which I have no influence over. To quote Mrs. Fannie Lou Hamer, "All my life I've been sick and tired, and now I'm sick and tired of being sick and tired!" All of us have so many chains wrapped around us, we're slaves; but most of us are cringing inside those chains, trying to roll outselves into insignificant little balls of flesh so that we won't even be touched by the cold iron that surrounds us. Other people have been in that situation . . . some have stood up and pushed against the chains that bound them—with their whole bodies, with their feet, with their songs, with their lives. . . .[1]

Another college dropout heavily sentenced by the courts for noncooperation, James Taylor Rowland, also measured his courage by Mississippi standards. He wrote the following in a letter on August 12, 1966, just before he received his orders to report for induction:

Whenever a person undertakes the task of *really* protesting his government, not just marching around with a goddamn picket sign, but really protesting, he has to be mature enough to realize just what the consequences are likely to be. When Goodman, Chaney, and Schwerner were working in Mississippi in 1964, they realized what they were up against, but they went ahead. As it turns out, they lost their lives in the bargain. And so it is with all people who see the choices, who are free to make the choices, whose histories are not yet determinate. But, for all that I have lost, there is one thing I have gained, which can now never be taken away from me, and that is my self-respect. . . . Now I have no fear. I think the worst kind of fear, of dread, is the fear that you yourself will fail to act according to your conscience. . . .[2]

But beyond racism and economics, beyond the examples of determination and courage and conscience, Mississippi Summer and the civil-rights movement more generally had taught one lesson particularly well to the young people in its ranks: that nonviolence was the reasonable way for men to act on behalf of change, whatever the extremity of their circumstances. While not all participants in Mississippi Summer were agreed about the strategy of nonviolence, they had to abide by its use as a tactic. And it is fair to say that the participation in nonviolent acts turned the tactic for some into strategic or philosophic commitment. Few outside of the movement were respectful of or responsive to the rational determination of nonviolence: the government and the press often charged the civil-rights movement with "violence"; and, on the other hand, charged nonviolent individuals with "cowardice." It is only since the death of King and the concomitantly growing cynicism about nonviolence among young people who have seen Malcolm, the Mississippi three, two Kennedys, King, and now a score of Panthers all murdered—it is only now that adults and officialdom speak respectfully (and wishfully) of nonviolence.

But a whole generation of activists, by the middle of the sixties, had been turned on to nonviolence, even trained by its exponents in Mississippi to protect their heads and vulnerable bodily organs from serious injury during beatings. What was such a group to make of a national decision not only to send combat troops to Vietnam, but to bomb a largely rural country without a significant air force of its own, to bomb what industry it had, its power plants, railroads, bridges, trails, even its schools and hospitals?

As we have made clear in earlier chapters, the work of the civil-rights movement, of the early SDS and other parts of the student movement, even of the Peace Corps, depended on the belief that significant social change was possible through hard work, organizing, education, rational discussion, the spread of truthful information, and nonviolence. Even such difficult problems as racism and poverty might be solved, if some worked hard and others were willing. There was a fundamental belief, call it middle-class optimism perhaps, that institutions could be reconstructed, that people would be willing, at least, to allow their children to grow up without the hatreds that had corrupted them. There was a fundamental belief, at least among whites, that the U.S. government was no worse than most.

But the war changed all that. No doubt the failure of integration and the frustration of hopes generated by Mississippi Summer would have, by themselves, eroded that initial optimism. But the war hastened the process, perhaps immeasurably, not only because it was a war against people of color and not only because war itself contradicted the ideals of a generation devoted both to "service" and to nonviolence: but also because, in the form of the draft law, the war openly promoted class privilege in a manner visible not only to that same generation, but to anyone who cared to look.

In the spring of 1967, before the Selective Service law was due for renewal by Congress, a special Presidential commission submitted proposals for reforming the draft. The Marshall Commission was concerned to reduce inequities, increase efficiency, and generally streamline the operations of the Selective Service System, by then under considerable attack from all political quarters. The commission addressed itself to the deferment system, the order of call that decided which men ought to go first, and the organization of draft boards; it also felt constrained to answer a philosophical and political challenge being put to the draft. The question was a unique one that flowed directly from the unpopularity of the Vietnam war. Could a man legitimately claim his abhorrence for that war as reason for refusing to fight? Could a serious moral and/or political objection to this particular war grant a man the right to "serve" in some alternative manner rather than in the paddies of Vietnam?

The 1940 draft law included a provision that permitted "conscientious objectors" to perform alternative civilian service or noncombatant service in the military rather than carry a gun. But there were two conditions: the provision was limited to men who "by reason of religious training and belief are opposed to war in any form." In deciding the Seeger case on March 8, 1965, the Supreme Court broke into one of the two limitations: men of deep and fundamental beliefs equivalent to but not identifiable as religious conviction might qualify for c.o. status. But the applicant still had to claim aversion to *all* wars. By 1967, a sufficient number of people—civil libertarians, church leaders, as well as draft resisters—had begun to argue that men should have the right to claim aversion to a particular war.

The Marshall Commission's response to this argument no doubt represented a consensus among those in the government, for they rejected it swiftly and clearly. The majority felt

> that a legal recognition of selective pacifism could be disruptive to the morale and effectiveness of the armed forces. A determination of the justness or unjustness of any war could only be made within the context of that war itself. Forcing upon the individual the necessity of making that distinction—which would be the practical effect of taking away the government's obligation of making it for him—could put a burden heretofore unknown on the man in uniform and even on the brink of combat, with results that could be disastrous to him, to his unit, and to the entire military tradition.[3]

In short, the commission argued that resisters who claimed the obligation or duty not to serve in the military represented a threat to constituted authority and to the political stability of the society.

Paradoxically, however, Erik Erikson, one of the country's most notable authorities on youth, had argued a few months earlier that resistance was a form of service. In a memorandum prepared for a conference on the draft held at the University of Chicago in December, 1966 (and attended by Marshall Commission staff), Erikson named "three legitimate areas in which youth can feel its energies activated or at least not misspent in organized service at this time." The first, he said, is in responding to a clear national emergency (which did not seem likely to arise); the second, in providing voluntary humanitarian service, like that in the Peace Corps. The last, which Erikson thought might seem "remote to the middle-aged middle class" in evidence at the conference, is "service in movements of civil disobedience. . . ." We admire the insight and Erikson's elaboration:

> . . . any aggravated and seemingly corrupt alliance of government (and especially the military) with advancing technology will necessarily lead to a new kind of rebellion which, in fighting "super machines" of all kinds, can only fight by refusing services. What once was loudly voiced dissent must, where there is no way of being heard, become noncooperation.[4]

Erikson's audience—college administrators and educators, federal officials, military personnel, and manpower specialists—were interested in youth as a natural resource. The conference, after all, had been organized to focus on the draft and on proposed forms of "national service." What were such adults to make of Erikson's suggestion that youth's withholding (military) services might itself constitute a form of "service." If it seemed quixotic to the Chicago audience and to members of the Marshall Commission, the insight characterized the new antiwar movement of the young. Clearly, they viewed the war as a "corrupt alliance of government (and especially the military) with advancing technology." Clearly, too, whatever else draft resistance might be, it was obviously to begin with a withholding of services. Erikson's insight will be useful, once we have described the movement's history, to explain both the strengths and limitations of the draft-resistance movement.

Until 1965, at least, opposition to the draft had been primarily an individual and usually a private matter. Some young men had concluded in difficult loneliness that they could not participate in a war that violated their sense of justice or humanity. A very few had decided that they would not cooperate with the draft. More had sought to achieve "conscientious-objector" status within the Selective Service System. Organizations like the American Friends Service Committee and the Central Committee for Conscientious Objectors maintained c.o. counseling services. But they were generally careful to distinguish between aiding an individual conscientiously opposed to war to gain his rights as an objector and actually *encouraging* men to oppose the draft, or so much as to take the legal step of applying for c.o. status. Gene Keyes and David Mitchell had tried, as early as 1963, to organize groups of draft resisters, but very few responded to them. Even as late as 1966, young people continued to debate the legitimacy of applying for c.o. status, and certainly few people publicly urged others not to go.

Late in 1965, Students for a Democratic Society printed and distributed widely a brief "Guide to C.O.," which suggested that the acquisition of c.o. status was legitimate and might be obtained by men hitherto barred by the law's rather narrow provisions. But even in SDS the idea of *organizing* men to oppose the draft seemed an extreme step, which might bring down on them the force of federal repression; and though proposals for a draft-resistance program had been discussed, they had never been accepted. In October, 1965, at the height of furor caused by nationwide antiwar demonstrations, the national secretary of SDS, Paul Booth, issued a statement challenging the President to permit young Americans to "build instead of burn." We propose, Booth wrote,

> that he test the young people of America: if they had a free choice, would they want to burn and torture in Vietnam or to build a democracy at home and overseas? There is only one way to make that choice real: let us see what happens if service to democracy is made grounds for exemption from the military draft. I predict that almost every member of my generation would choose to build, not to burn; to teach, not to torture; to help, not to kill. . . . Until the President agrees to our proposal, we have only one choice: we do in conscience object, utterly and wholeheartedly, to this war.[5]

Booth's statement was attacked by some members of SDS as a trap through which all young men might be forced to serve, in one manner or another, an increasingly repulsive and repressive American government. Nevertheless, the statement, combined with rumors inflated by the news media that SDS intended to press an antidraft campaign, swelled the organization's membership. Clearly the statements expressed by Booth, demanding that all young men be allowed to conscientiously object to the Vietnam war, rang a responsive note among many students. The idea of "service to democracy" rather than service in war continued to have wide appeal, even among those deeply opposed to American policy in Vietnam.

Antipathy toward the Selective Service System was fed by its own behavior. When antiwar demonstrators in Ann Arbor sat in, on October 15, 1965, at a local draft board's office, the Michigan state director of Selective Service decided to use the system to punish through reclassification those who had sat in. Congressmen and columnists reacted in outrage. The SSS officials persisted until their arguments were rejected, more than a year later, by the courts. And of course similar demonstrations proliferated. At the same time, another pattern of action and reaction began to function. Late in 1965, General Hershey asserted that students would probably have to be drafted to fill quotas enlarged by the expected Vietnam buildup, and hence that rank in class would be used as one criterion for determining who would go and who would be allowed to stay in college. Protesting the university's cooperation with Selective Service—they were sending class rank to draft boards—hundreds of students at the University of Chicago in the spring of 1966 sat in at their administration building for three days. That demonstration helped to spark a series of similar protests on campuses throughout the country, which continued right up until summer vacation.[6]

If the controversy over ranking proved something of a mirage, and if students reacted in self-interest, it was all not without its usefulness to the movement. Students had not, in fact, been drafted nor was it likely that they would be. General Hershey's "threat" had been an empty one designed perhaps to frighten students into "working harder," but mainly to encourage enlistments among some who might feel inadequate at college. The invention of ranking as a means for deciding who ought to be "saved" and who sent off to Vietnam served a different purpose from General Hershey's. It helped to clarify for some students the inequities of the draft system that had traditionally served to benefit them. It proposed to separate them from their fraternity brothers, even as they were all separated from those "brothers" who had not made it into the university at all. Not surprisingly, therefore, the demand began to be heard at some of the antiranking demonstrations that students reject the privilege of their 2-S deferments altogether. And though few could respond definitively, the discussion of privilege was thus begun on many campuses. In New Haven, for example, a small group of young men met most of the summer to consider the special responsibility of college men in the antiwar movement.

Late in the summer of 1966, a number of young people from various parts of the country who had been meeting in such small groups to talk about the draft gathered in Des Moines to discuss the possibility of *organizing* resistance to it. As they had in their separate groups, they talked for several days and nights without stop. The atmosphere was tense, comparable perhaps to nothing since Mississippi, where many of them had served. Perhaps because they had known Mississippi—its sense of community in siege—they understood how different was draft resistance. Selective Service separated and isolated individuals: each one of them had, in fact, to deal with a separate draft board. How could you hold people together when they were being classified by different boards at different times in different ways? Could one force draft boards to take groups? Did one want to do that anyway? In fact, no one really knew what the limits of legal opposition to the draft were, nor what sorts of "illegal" actions the government might choose to prosecute. It was true enough that in the past few people had been jailed for urging young men not to join the military. But what if one organized men to say that they would not go to Vietnam *if* they were drafted? Or to say that they would not go at all *if* they were called—was that illegal? Would the government tolerate such organizing?

No one could answer those questions. Only one fact seemed clear: in the South, a white volunteer might get fifteen days in jail; draft penalties were for up to five years.

The talk dragged on, slow, soul-searching, painful. What would your parents think? Your girl friend? Your teachers? Would you have financial support if there were legal difficulties? Or could you manage it alone, especially if you had a group of other young men in your city or on your campus who would be making similar decisions, needing similar support? What were the best tactics, locally and nationally? Should there be organized a large-scale act of civil disobedience or small, local communities of resisters? How many months might it take to organize a group? How many months would it take you to decide?

One of the first "We Won't Go" groups declared themselves publicly at the University of Chicago just before the December conference we have referred to earlier in this chapter. Thirty-two men, almost all students, had taken several months to come to a goup decision about how to organize their resistance to the draft. They announced their position in the Chicago *Maroon* at the same time that they decided to hold a conference to counter the one being sponsored by the university. The purpose of the conference, announced by Tom Gushurst, chairman of the afternoon sessions, was personal and political:

> This conference is about those who would not, and will not go. There are many ways to not go. Today we will consider some of these on the admittedly biased assumption that those who will not go are completely justified. I know that you will listen, knowing that the questions, dilemmas, and frustrations that will concern us today are not matters which are of greatest concern to scholars and politicians, but matters of most concern to the young men who are tired of attending rallies in Madison Square Garden to End the War Now, men who are tired of marching down Fifth Avenue, men tired of hearing their President say, "Forgive them for they know not what they do."[7]

In spite of short notice and only two weeks of preliminary organization, the newly emerged group was able to gather speakers and attract a local and national audience of 500.

The "We Won't Go" conference may help us summarize the level of draft-resistance activity in the winter of 1966–67. It was one of the first occasions on which a *group* of men declared in public that they would refuse to cooperate with the draft. The conference served to heighten their resolve, though it did not add immediately to their numbers. The afternoon's speakers consisted of historian Staughton Lynd and a number of resisters. While Lynd's report on the development of the French resistance to the Algerian war suggested that the American movement was at a very early stage, the model provided general encouragement. Still more élan emerged from the separate stories of three resisters: Jeff Segal and David Mitchell, even then heading for prison, described their isolated struggles with draft boards, the FBI, and the courts; John Sumrall, a black organizer for CORE from Quitman, Mississippi, came not to describe his case but to express "the feeling of some of the people in Mississippi about why they don't want to fight in Vietnam." Segal and Mitchell emphasized two points: they'd do it all again—it was worth resisting; and their loneliness—how much better, therefore, to be a "group." Sumrall's presence suggested, however misleadingly, that the draft-resistance movement might someday be other than a movement among middle-class white men.

That evening, workshops for those young men attending the conference proved sobering. Discussions focused on the technicalities of getting over the border into Canada or on penalties after imprisonment for draft refusal. Could a noncooperator ever become a lawyer? Or run for Congress? Can you travel out of Canada once you get status as a landed immigrant? Few people talked of the political significance—or lack of it—involved in going to Canada; fewer of their responsibility to the antiwar movement or to the Vietnamese. The thirty-two We Won't Go signers were admired by other students, and a few more young men signed the pledge, but most were not ready for that kind of commitment and the sacrifices it implied. It seemed clear that the months of serious discussion that had preceded the conference would be necessary again and again for each group of resisters.

During the spring of 1967, however, after a number of men had been sentenced to jail under a recent harsh law against draft-card burning, a group of We Won't Go students at Cornell University proposed calling young men together to burn their cards during a massive antiwar demonstration planned for April 15 in New York. Their pledge was a conditional one: if 500 agreed to burn their cards, then all would; if 500 did not, then none would be obligated. By April 14 it was clear that the goal of 500 had not been reached, and that evening many of the young men who had signed the pledge, as well as others who were hanging fire or actively opposed, met in New York to decide whether the card burning should go forward in any case. Some argued that if only the 120 signers were to proceed, the act would be politically insignificant, that an act of symbolic witness was not worth the sacrifice of one's freedom. Others, however, felt

that even primarily symbolic acts might communicate the seriousness of opposition to the war among young Americans. Like whites
going to Mississippi in 1964, or the Peace Corps volunteers going
into the *campo* of Colombia, the collective burning of draft cards,
they argued, would provide a dramatic symbol that could not be
ignored. The debate was not, of course, finally resolved, but a decision was eventually made that if fifty agreed, the card burning would
be carried out. When Bruce Dancis of Cornell asked for a count,
fifty-seven people raised their hands. But the following day, as it
turned out, some 200 young men and women participated in burning
about 175 cards in the Sheep Meadow of Central Park, as parents
wept, photographers shoved, Paul Goodman admired, and FBI
agents scrambled for the charred bits.

Martin Jezer, one of the participants in that act, has recounted
the personal history that led him to it. A liberal, white college graduate, he had entered graduate work in journalism, partly because he
wanted to write and partly to avoid the Army. A trip to Hazard, Kentucky, he writes, "had a decisive impact on my life. For the first time,
and firsthand, I identified with the struggles of the oppressed. But
though shaken, I was still in the liberal bag. The only hope, I thought,
was for massive federal aid." In 1964 he campaigned for Lyndon
Johnson, but after the Gulf of Tonkin incident, became more and
more fully involved in the antiwar movement, writing letters, participating in peace parades, picketing, vigiling, getting arrested in sit-
downs in New York. He was one of the first to sign up for April 15,
determined to burn his card whether or not the required 500 was
achieved. "Not to have burned a draft card April 15 would have been
tantamount to living in Boston in 1773 and not to have dumped tea
in Boston harbor." He saw the act as the culmination of his education:

> Burning my draft card was a recognition that I had finally learned
> something. But that I decided to commit what the U.S. govern-
> ment considers a heinous crime is due to a large degree to those
> responsible for my education. They instilled in me a sense of
> values, principle, and morality. They taught me that we were a
> peace-loving democracy, and I believed them. The education
> of Martin Jezer is the realization that if this *is* to be a peace-
> loving democracy, functioning on principled, moral values, it is
> for us, for me, to make it so.[8]

We quote Martin Jezer as characteristic of those who burned their cards that day. Once again, on a combination of idealism and bravado, the draft-resistance movement took another step. The act of mass card burning helped anneal its participants into new and reactivated groups when they returned to Chicago and Ithaca and Boston and elsewhere. The original We Won't Go groups had virtually exhausted their energies in endless worry about whether their actions would send them to jail. These new resisters had crossed that threshold and could energetically begin to organize others. By burning those bits of cardboard, they had stepped out of their protected status as students, ministerial candidates, or even 4-F rejectees to lay some still-unmeasured part of their own lives in the scale against the war. They felt, resister after resister reported, "free." It had been only a card, but it had defined their relationship to a government they could not respect, much less obey. "The draft card," Tom Cornell has written, "became the symbol *par excellence* of involuntary servitude for the works of death, and the symbol of moral and intellectual suffocation. It deserved to be burned."[9]

But others were not convinced about the political value of card burning: it did not communicate clearly enough, they charged, either with draft boards or with people around you. Another tactic, the mass turning in of draft cards, was invented, the first date announced for October 16, 1967, a few days before a scheduled demonstration against the Pentagon. All over the country, in Los Angeles, Seattle, Philadelphia, Yellow Springs, Chicago, wherever resisters gathered in even the smallest groups, young men went out to persuade, urge, even shame their friends to declare openly their rejection of the war by turning in their cards. On October 16, about one thousand registration and classification cards were turned in to ministers, professors, and writers at dignified and impressive ceremonies, many of them in churches. Most of the cards were brought to Washington, where they were collected by a group of adult supporters of the resistance movement, and then left with the Justice Department by a contingent led by Mitchell Goodman, Dr. Benjamin Spock, and the Reverend William Sloane Coffin.

By the fall of 1967, the groups of resisters had (somewhat grandiloquently) named themselves "The Resistance." They were a loose network of some two dozen groups, perhaps six of which were of significant size and activity, but without national organization, center, or agreed upon core of leadership. Yet a series of national days of card turn-ins produced about 2,500 cards by the following spring. At that time, moreover, Louis Harris predicted on the basis of polls that "between 20 and 30 percent of the college groups called up for service in the next few months will be seriously contemplating whether or not to refuse to serve." The activists, Harris added, "do not represent anything approaching a majority of students in college today. But in the aggregate they come to well over 100,000 or a potential of over 70,000 draft resisters. . . . If even as many as 25,000 choose to go to prison or one of the other courses of refusing to serve, the size of the crisis will exceed any this nation has ever faced before in terms of resistance to the draft."[10] Though most of the men who turned in their cards have not yet been prosecuted, an increasing number—something on the order of one thousand at this writing—have been sent to prison, and the rate of prosecution has increased as the war has dragged on.

Even as The Resistance gained both notoriety and numbers, its members began disappearing into federal prisons for from two to five years, depending on the humanity of the particular judges. The idea of prison had already sent thousands to Canada and more into the Army itself. For resisters who had committed themselves to the idea of prison, it was part of the "price" one had to pay in order to be "free" someday to continue one's resistance. As Dennis Riordan put it to us before he went to prison, he wanted to be able to spend the rest of his life in the movement: what, therefore, was the sacrifice of a few years right now?

But the idea of prison may be different from its reality. Can one say that it was worthwhile for the individual and for his future relationship to movements for social change? Does going to prison constitute a useful "service"? Three different accounts illustrate the range of responses collected by Alice Lynd two years ago. James Taylor Rowland, after a month in prison, could remark with relative optimism:

Prison has given me a chance to solidify, as no other experience could, my politics. I know why Joseph Vissarionovich Dzhugashvili chose the name Stalin—steel; I, too, feel like steel. I'm not bitter, just determined. I know how to live, how to make a living, within the system, and yet at the same time work to destroy the system, and replace it with a system built for men, not for profit. That is my perspective. . . .[11]

Francis Galt, on the other hand, according to his wife, "found it was impossible to cope with prison in terms of 'why he was there' soon after arriving." Nor could Galt believe, later, in the political efficacy of his act. He wrote to a friend six months before he was granted parole: "It should have become evident to me that, given the particular structure, attitude, and inaccessibility of our government, my noncooperation would have no practical effect whatsoever, and that even this would not serve totally to divorce me from the roots of the circumstances I deplored."[12] David Mitchell, one of the first draft resisters, had been in prison for about six months when he wrote in response to a request from Alice Lynd:

> I have nothing to write for her. You can tell her that it is hell. Maybe I should write for her, but I can't! I never pretended it was "otherwise" before coming and, as then, I would still do what I did on the basis of my own integrity and in a striving and with a hope for effect and change. I would probably, though, reconsider the "jail" question, but then I always had that question as an open one in my mind to the last and still do. But also, now I question even more whether jail adds any mileage to the position or struggle, and other alternatives leaving me active although possibly removed, could. And then—as I said—jail is hell.[13]

The question—was it worthwhile?—is obviously impossible to answer in general terms. Though there is no comparative collection of their views to draw from, we expect that the bulk of resisters who have gone to prison since 1968 would not respond very differently. We know that resisters have planned lengthy study programs, that others have been writing fiction and poetry, as well as diary-length letters. We know that in prison some have refused to cooperate, and others have tried using their organizing skills. It is probably premature to summarize the effect of prison on these resisters, just as it is impossible to predict their future relationship to movements for social change.

But there is a second question more amenable to analysis. Was the act of going to prison worthwhile politically? Did it convince others to go and do likewise, did it lead to other "movement"? To answer these questions, we should like to turn to Erikson's equation of resistance with service.

At the very least, resisters would "serve," as Erikson suggested, by withholding service to the military, thus reducing by that little its destructive capacity. In dedicating themselves to the goal of ameliorating the misery of Vietnamese, investing their personal resources of time, energy, and life, the resisters were working well within the traditions of service. At the same time, to be sure, non-cooperation was a political act, just as most forms of service, from Mississippi to free universities and to the Peace Corps, involved a "political" dimension. Mississippi Summer was, of course, an overt challenge to the white power structure of the state and finally of the national Democratic party. Peace Corps officialdom itself has spoken of the Corps's mission to bring about change, even "revolutionary" change. The willingness of the resisters to accept hardship, obloquy, and prison for the sake of their ideals expressed both the ethic of service and the political strategy of draft resistance. Denying the privilege of draft deferments or exemptions, they wished, as one resister put it, to persuade their fellow Americans to their point of view by the "eloquence of the act."

The eloquence of such civil disobedience, acknowledged even by those who have opposed draft resistance,[14] has been one source of the movement's strength. It has placed on many young men a moral compulsion to take the future in their own hands and stand on principle. In their ceremonies the resisters, like evangelists, have challenged men faced with the hell of Vietnam to step forward, decide for non-cooperation, put their draft cards away from them, and embrace the community of resistance. The religious quality of their appeal grew in effectiveness as the war deepened, and especially among the college students who were effectively "safe" from the draft. That the young men accepting prison were almost entirely the sons of white, middle-class parents was another source of the political strength of the movement. Draft resistance could be seen, in this regard, as an attempt to make pursuit of the war too costly in domestic political terms; in effect, it said to the policy-makers, "If you go forward, it will be only over our lives and freedom." "The Resistance Strategy," a paper prepared by The Resistance for a card turn-in scheduled for April 3, 1968, and widely adopted by other groups that spring, defined the position:

> If large numbers of people—both draft and non-draft age—were to confront the government in this way [i.e., by turning in cards or pledging to "counsel, aid, abet" resistance] . . . then it would be possible to place the administration in a position of inflexibility, where any of the responses available to it has a high political cost. If we are arrested, tremors will be felt where our potential power is, throughout the middle class community . . . since our parents, relatives and friends—as well as those college professors, professionals, and clergymen who publicly declare their complicity with us—are strategically placed in the society, we can expect by our collective act to move the American conscience and hasten the end of the war.

The vision of thousands of such men filling the nation's prisons was a distressing one to parents, politicians, and commentators. In the spring of 1968, for example, just before President Johnson "abdicated," Walter Lippmann wrote:

> The country is increasingly against the war because the Johnson Administration is acting on the unexamined assumption that men can be drafted for war whenever the government decides to wage it. This is a huge fallacy which ignores the lessons of experience. . . . The President is confronted with the resistance, open or passive, of the whole military generation, their teachers, their friends, their families. The attempt to fight a distant war by conscription is producing a demoralization which threatens the very security of the Nation.[15]

No doubt, this spreading of resistance, most of which did not take the overt forms of turning in or burning draft cards, was at least one influence affecting the President's decisions to retire, halt the bombing of North Vietnam, and at least begin the talk in Paris.[16]

The politics of resistance might be described as an eloquent *plea,* only in some limited sense a "demand" (dramatized by the willingness of those making it to accept the consequence of prison) to the administration to turn away from "error." It was neither open rebellion against those in power, nor against the institutions which invested them with power. Staughton Lynd has carefully delineated the intermediate position "between reform and revolution" of such nonviolent obstructive disobedience:

> Without yet seeking to overthrow the government, resisters declare their determination to overthrow a given policy or complex of institutions by refusing to obey them or permit them to function. The resister does not rely on the electoral process or the courts to bring about the change he seeks, but he leaves open the possibility that these conventional institutions can adapt themselves to changes brought about by more direct means.

This intermediate, restrained, not-yet-revolutionary politics is the corollary, in Erikson's equation of resistance and service, to the willingness of young men to place their own lives and futures in the balance. For service is not, as we have suggested, a revolutionary ethic. But it should be clear that if the balance does not swing toward change, people who have committed so much of themselves into it will, at some point, begin trying to overthrow the balance itself. And as resisters have increasingly spoken of the need for "revolutionary change in the United States," that would seem to be the direction in which their movement is headed.

Notes

[1] Alice Lynd, ed., *We Won't Go: Personal Accounts of War Objectors* (Boston, 1968), p. 7.

[2] *Ibid.,* pp. 48–49.

[3] National Advisory Commission on Selective Service, *In Pursuit of Equity: Who Serves When Not All Serve* (Washington: Government Printing Office, 1967).

[4] In Sol Tax, ed., *The Draft* (Chicago, 1967), pp. 280–82.

[5] In *Guide to Conscientious Objection,* distributed by Students for a Democratic Society.

[6] At Chicago, the students withdrew from the administration building, after prolonged and fruitless negotiations, as a gesture of good faith, and in hope that the administration would take some action. The administration did: in characteristic academic fashion, it established a committee to study the problem, and it called a conference on the broader issues of the draft. It was to this conference that the Erikson memorandum we have mentioned was addressed.

[7] Quoted by Paul Lauter, Richard Flacks, and Florence Howe, "The Draft: Reform or Resistance?" *Liberation,* January, 1967, p. 34.

[8] Lynd, *op. cit.,* pp. 222–23.

[9] *Ibid.,* p. 37.

[10] Harris Poll, Boston *Globe,* May 16, 1968.

[11] Lynd, *op. cit.,* p. 51.

[12] *Ibid.,* pp. 61, 62.

[13] *Ibid.,* p. 108.

[14] Harris Poll, *op. cit.*

[15] Washington *Post,* March 24, 1968.

[16] No doubt the atmosphere of resistance among the young also affected the McCarthy campaign. One of Senator McCarthy's youthful staff members said, in a comment widely quoted by his fund-raisers, "For us this is a last chance. If we don't win here, it means Canada or jail." Though many McCarthy people openly supported resisters, it is clear that their use of youth effectively swallowed up much of the political energy generated by resistance activities and finally dissipated it in the frustration and discouragement of Chicago. Almost two years later, the Vietnam Moratorium, an antiwar coalition held together by former McCarthy people, seems once again headed for a repetition of that history. Its leadership is split between those moving toward congressional elections and those wishing to organize another round of nonviolent civil disobedience against the draft.

6

The Law and the Young

PARADISE OR PARADOX

Young Americans are generally accounted the most fortunate in the world. They have more money, more mobility, more education than their parents, who struggled through and out of the Great Depression, ever dreamed of. The statistics are, indeed, impressive. In 1968, eighteen- to twenty-four-year-old Americans spent upwards of $40 billion, a sum that omits money spent on the young by friends and relatives. The Bureau of Labor Statistics reported that in 1960–61 the clothing bill for women 18–24 ran 20% higher than for women 25–64; for young men the bill was 9.5% higher.[1] It has been estimated that teen-age girls spend some $2 billion on clothing during the 60-day back-to-school whirl in August and September. Girls nine to thirteen years old are the *major* purchasers of phonograph records. And in California alone, about one million minors drive automobiles.[2] Three times the percentage of men and more than twice the percentage of women had graduated from college in 1967 as in 1947. At least for young males with B.A.'s, salaries between 1960 and 1968 rose an average of 45%. Statistics do not, of course, even begin to convey the privileges most middle-class, white youths share: travel, space to live and grow, books, records, and pot.

But over against these statistics are others, less rosy. Over

40,000 young Americans have been killed and some 300,000 wounded in the Vietnam war. Estimates are that suicide rates among students are 50% higher than for Americans generally; in one year some 90,000 students might threaten suicide, 9,000 make an attempt and 1,000 succeed.[3] According to the Children's Bureau of the Department of Health, Education and Welfare, *one* out of every *six* boys will be hauled into juvenile court on delinquency charges before he is eighteen years old.[4] Lisa Aversa Richette, a former assistant district attorney in Philadelphia specializing in juvenile cases, estimates that as many as 90% of all young people have committed acts for which they might be brought before juvenile authorities.[5] According to the report of the U.S. Senate's Subcommittee on Juvenile Delinquency, "from a half to two-thirds of all criminal and delinquent acts are never reflected in official crime statistics or records of any type."[6] The report points out that arrests of youths under eighteen increased by 54% between 1960 and 1965, while the population of that age group increased by only 17%. Some of the additional arrests may be the result of more formal reporting by the police; but we have seen figures which suggest that the chances of a young American being arrested by the time he is twenty-one are three in five! Nor are these increases in arrests limited to "high crime areas," as they are called. In suburban communities during 1967 over a third of offenders were "children under eighteen."[7]

Finally, jobs are *not,* in fact, easy for young people to get. The unemployment rate for American youth, higher than in any other industrialized country in the world, has generally run about *three times* the national average.[8] For young whites, the rate has ranged in the last few years between 11% and 15%; among young blacks, unemployment rose from 22.7% in 1960 to 30.4% in 1968.[9] According to a Labor Department spokesman, "There has been very little improvement for teen-agers as compared to adult workers the last few years."[10] The Nixon administration has even proposed *lowering* the minimum wage for youth in order to reduce unemployment.

The statistics report paradoxical conditions: better jobs, more unemployment; lots of spending money, lots of arrests; longer schooling, deeper discontent. Some people are inclined to explain these contradictions as the result of ingratitude and laziness among youth who have never been hungry or ill-housed or who, if they have, now expect the government to hand comfort to them on a mattress.

Others suggest that young people have been led astray by the prophets of indulgence and permissiveness—Dr. Spock, Paul Goodman, Abbie Hoffman. And others argue that there remain unfortunate dislocations in American society: we haven't yet found the best ways of employing all our youth, of making their education fully relevant, of ensuring that laws are enforced with an even hand and without police "overreaction." Still, these people continue, our directions are correct; time, technology, and proper leadership will resolve whatever difficulties exist.

There is yet another way of looking at the contradictions between the rosy picture of affluent young Americans and the rather bloodier and smokier picture of young Americans at war in Vietnam, Chicago, Berkeley, and in their home towns. It is a picture more often painted by the young themselves. It goes like this: the affluence is real enough—though more limited to white, middle-class America than we care to admit (and with sexual stratification that qualifies the canvas for women). But the price of affluence is acquiescence in the system—which means being willing to give up one's freedom young:

> But it isn't a free country. You can't drop out of school because you'd be drafted, and you have to study certain things to get a degree, and you have to have a degree to make it, and you have to make it to get what you want, and you can't even decide what you want, because it's all programmed into you beforehand. You can *say* whatever you want, but you won't be heard because the media control that, but if you do manage to be heard, the people won't like it, because the people have been told what to like. And if they don't like you, they might even kill you, because the government endorses killing by exemplification.[11]

At least one prominent political figure, Mayor John Lindsay of New York, has been able to see the United States through the eyes of the young. Addressing a group of Princeton undergraduates, he said:

> The frustration of the sophomore alienated from his university by its size and impersonality is not very much different from the resentment of the ghetto youth who is alienated from his city because its opportunities and rewards are foreclosed to him. Both suffer the malady of powerlessness—powerlessness in the face of huge, authoritarian institutions that routinely cause fundamental dislocations in the lives of the people they affect each day.[12]

Both the student who doesn't feel free and the mayor who talks of "powerlessness" understand that the "problem" of youth is a political as well as a psychological one. Do U.S. social institutions function to fulfill or to control the lives of young people? Which side are they on? In the chapters that follow, we shall examine the school and the draft, two institutions in charge of youth; and then two groups of young people, blacks and women, particularly afflicted by institutional control. In this chapter we will look first at the frightening statistics of youthful offenders arrested, and at the "juvenile crime wave" they supposedly imply; at the "rectification" procedures for the young; then at the "marijuana war"; before returning to the central question about the relationship between institutions and the young. For the confrontation between youth and the law is the most naked and immediate test of institutional purpose.

THE CRIME OF YOUTH

Arrest records do not by themselves tell very much. They may indicate that more crimes are being committed, or they may indicate that police are enforcing certain laws more zealously. In New Haven, Connecticut, for example, a long-standing ban of fireworks was ignored for many years, but in 1968 police decided to enforce the prohibition during a popular local holiday. Result: a vast increase in violations of fireworks statutes. Again, in California, arrests for drug use have soared from 18,188 in 1961 to 33,622 in 1966, 61,792 in 1967, and 43,304 for the first six months of 1968! At that rate of increase, drug arrests in California might reach half a million by 1970 and nearly one million by 1972.[13] Needless to say, drug use has grown rapidly in California as elsewhere. But *convictions* of adults (only adult records are made public) have steadily fallen, from 40% in 1961 to 35% in 1964, all the way down to 29% in 1966 and 26% in 1967. At the same time, indictments and convictions of federal narcotics agents for perjury in trials of accused narcotics users has steadily risen.[14] Thus the statistics might indicate not only that more people smoke marijuana in California (of the 61,792 drug arrests in 1967, 37,514 were for marijuana offenses), but that more cops are more determined to bust more "dope fiends" more often. We will turn later to the intensive use of police in the drug war; it is useful first to look more closely at other "offenses" for which young people can be, and are, arrested.

Edgar Z. Friedenberg once pointed out that there used to be only two classes in the United States who could be in violation of the law simply by being where they were—blacks and youths. Blacks, by sitting in the front of the bus, urinating in the "white" lavatory, swimming at the "white" beach, were, prior to the Public Accommodations Law and court decision, subject to arrest. But it still falls on youths, who can be arrested simply for being out of school (truancy), being away from home (running away), or just being out of their houses after a certain hour (violation of curfew). Curfews are particularly intriguing. The law in Taneytown, Maryland, a small country community, reads: "It shall be unlawful for any child under the age of 19 to be or remain in and upon any of the streets . . . stores or other public places . . . in Taneytown after eleven P.M." Thus young men old enough to die in Vietnam are not old enough to congregate with their buddies in Taneytown after eleven o'clock. Some businesses enforce private curfews: in Baltimore, an ice-cream store in a white, working-class neighborhood refuses to serve minors after nine P.M. Such laws are enforced with zeal when town and city fathers perceive a "rising tide of teen-age lawlessness." In Chicago, during the first six months of 1965, "10,660 teen-agers were arrested for violations of a curfew that, one youth lamented, would be 'martial law' if applied to adults."[15] Beyond that, young people can be sent to juvenile court by parents as "incorrigible," by school officials as "disruptive," or by nearly anyone as "potentially dangerous to themselves or others." Once in juvenile court, a young person can be packed off to the functional equivalent of prison simply for refusing to discuss his case with police or the judge; until recently, juveniles had *no protection* under the law against self-incrimination, and could thus be trapped between self-conviction and uncooperative behavior—either leading to "training school." In practice, a somewhat less blatant form of this dilemma still remains.

Aside from the distinctively juvenile "crimes" mentioned above, young people are subject to considerable harassment if they insist upon unconventional behavior, dress, or especially hair. The stories of conflict between youths and authorities over hair are by now legion, and every person has his own favorite repertoire. Two years ago the Wyoming Senate tacked a provision onto a constitutional amendment lowering the voting age to nineteen. The provision asserted that to be eligible to vote, men of nineteen or twenty must have haircuts that conformed to military standards! There might be something laughable about such fervor, were it not that Wyoming draft boards are taking nineteen- and twenty-year-old men to fight a war they have never had the chance even to vote about; and that Wyoming is notorious among young people for violating their civil and human rights if they are, for example, picked up while hitch-hiking. But there is little to laugh at when police systematically raid, arrest, assault, and brutalize "hippies," like those who congregate in Philadelphia's Rittenhouse Square. On June 17 and July 15, 1967, the police carried out mass arrests in the square, sweeping up all observable flower children and various non-hippie observers who protested the arrests. After being questioned for several hours, all those taken into custody were released. Intermittent harassment continued until the hippies, aided by the American Civil Liberties Union, sought—of all things—an injunction in federal court to stop verbal and physical abuse by police and park guards. The latter, it came out in the hearings, were under orders to harass hippies. Police had participated in repeated interrogations in a small guardhouse at one end of the square, during which the young people were sometimes slapped around, and always questioned about their views on Communism, dope, homosexuality, the war. Lisa Aversa Richette, who describes the incidents in some detail, tells about

> Patrick Hughes, one of the plaintiffs, [who] testified that on one occasion earlier in the spring the policeman interrogating him in the guardhouse smacked him in the face. When Hughes did nothing, the policeman asked, "You won't even throw up your hands, will you?"
>
> Hughes' testimony continued. "And I said, 'No, I won't. It would be ridiculous.' He said, 'Why, you're a punk,' and I got smacked again. And I said, 'Now, you have four friends outside the door with sticks. I am not throwing up my hands to you or anyone else in this guardhouse.'"[16]

This confrontation had, at least along the broad and staid walks of Rittenhouse Square, a happy ending, for the hippies were vindicated by the judge, and the police withdrew—perhaps to redirect their attacks, the following winter, against black high-school students. Other such confrontations of nonconformist youths and police have had no happy endings at all, from the battle of Sunset Strip, back in 1966, to the battle of Tompkins Square on Memorial Day, 1967, to the battle of Boston Common in the summer of 1968, to the battle of Berkeley People's Park in the spring of 1969. If anything, each of these incidents has shown heightened conflict, more intense police violence, and finally more readiness of youth to fight back.

A relatively less publicized series of events in Montgomery County, a well-to-do Maryland suburb of Washington, D.C., illustrates that cycle. During the 1967–68 school year a group of young people, calling themselves Compeers, Inc., began to establish an "exchange" program between white Montgomery County high-school students and blacks from inner-city Washington. The project, which had considerable support from liberals in the adult community, was designed to provide tutorial aid to the blacks and some "cross-cultural" experience for the whites. The director of the program, J. Brinton Dillingham, who had worked as a probation officer in Montgomery County as well as for VISTA, believed in the need to involve county youth in creative programs. After the program had run for a while, the organizers of Compeers thought that suburban young people needed, in addition to a chance to help others, a center for themselves, where they might obtain such services as draft counseling and where they could print underground papers, leaflets, or simply hang out.

Quickly, Freedom House, Compeers' center in the plushy suburban community of Bethesda, became a local hangout, then a scandal. At first, attention centered on a pamphlet, "Wanted: A Humane Education," written by a high-school student and circulated widely through the county. Seriously distressed by the pamphlet, by high-school underground papers, and by other outbreaks of "student unrest," teachers, administrators, and the school board were pressed by the "Student Alliance" for school reform. But when few changes were forthcoming, and more alienated and disenchanted students began to frequent Freedom House, right-wing publicists in the county accused it of involvement with SDS, and clashes between the police and young people at the house began to escalate.

At about the same time, the Washington *Free Press,* a local underground paper, was having its troubles with local authorities, some of whom wanted it prosecuted for "sedition," others for "obscenity." Young people, including some frequenters of Freedom House, were arrested for selling or distributing the *Free Press,* among them the director of Compeers, Brint Dillingham, who sold the paper in front of the police station as a test case. Editions of the paper were seized; printers in the area refused to run it and even "lost" mock-ups. The *Free Press,* in turn, ran stories and editorials blasting the local power structure, a cartoon showing a particularly hostile judge masturbating, and finally sued police chiefs in the District of Columbia, Montgomery County, and elsewhere for restraining its press freedom.

In the spring of 1969, when Freedom House youths attempted to bring their complaints to the Montgomery County Council, the Washington *Post* reported that "ashtrays and other objects were removed from the hearing chamber and hallways of the County Office Building before the young people arrived. The building was sealed off by police, and detectives photographed those who came to the meeting."[17] A month later, in May, the council was willing to listen without such elaborate "security precautions." They heard the young accuse police of "blackmailing" drug suspects to inform on others in exchange for escaping possible prosecution, and of "traffic arrests allegedly based on the unorthodox dress of young drivers." A student at Walt Whitman High School told "how six county policemen searched Freedom House without a warrant. When we later objected to this, I was told that if I ever trespassed on neighboring properties, I would be shot," the student reported. Council members privately admitted the justice of the young people's complaints, but the battle was hardly over.[18]

A month later the director of Compeers was convicted of violating obscenity statutes for his token sale of the *Free Press.* Police continued to prevent frequenters of Freedom House from using a public parking lot across the street, and young people retaliated by smearing black paint over meters and cars in the lot. Finally, late in June, Compeers, Inc., was evicted from its Freedom House, and the old furniture in it was turned over to the county trash removers for disposal. Newspapers, taking their cue from local authorities, headlined the story "Hippie Colony Is Evicted from Bethesda House."[19] Thus, in the short space of a year and a half, Compeers, Inc., had been transformed—at least in the eyes of adult beholders—from a project of youthful service to needs of others and their own, through an effort at "student power," into a "hippie colony."

Though a single series of incidents, the year-long battle between Freedom House and Montgomery County typifies the clash of young people with authorities. The Washington *Free Press* provided a major focus: its harassment by adults and its subsequent defense by the young is not merely symbolic. Like other underground papers through the country, the *Free Press* visibly embodied the counter-culture of the young.[20] Adults, antagonized by other embodiments of youth culture at Freedom House, "odd" styles of dress and hair, claimed indignantly that the "virus" of such behavioral infection might be transmitted to other impressionable young people in the community. It is possible to dismiss the scene as a tempest in a tea-pot: who cares about such embodiments as underground papers, hair, and clothes? But the police, judges, and adult vigilantes adopted the stance of righteous defense of their children; and the young defenders stood up for their culture and its manifestations, the *Free Press* and Freedom House. Thus life styles and politics coalesced as suburban and theoretically forward-looking adults spoke the rhetoric and practiced the persecution characteristic of the right wing against an "enemy"; and nonpolitical, "hippie" youths organized themselves in defense.

YOUTH RECTIFICATION

Juvenile courts were begun by reformers, notably Jane Addams in Chicago, in order to free young people from the burden of adult criminal courts. Directed toward punishment rather than rehabilitation, criminal courts had evolved elaborate technicalities for evidence, testimony, and appeals which, often as not, lost the man in the procedures of the case. The reformers expected that by providing an informal atmosphere in which a judge might act as a kindly parent and dispense with legal red tape, the interests of rehabilitating an individual young person would be served. Keeping the procedures secret would shield young people, reformers anticipated, from futures blighted by public notoriety. They assumed, of course, that the judge, a "lover of children," might specialize not in procedural juris-prudence, but in sympathy and an understanding of the needs of particular children and their families. They also assumed that the judge would be well supplied with information about cases from dis-passionate and reasonable sources, probation officers, social work-ers, psychologists. Perhaps most important of all, they assumed that juvenile courts would lead toward opportunities for rehabilitation, whether at home under the supervision of a case worker or in camps, foster homes, or centers especially designed for the purpose of aiding young people.

The reformers probably also believed that those who might be caught up in juvenile court and those in charge of them shared social values. Certainly, they could hardly have imagined fundamental divisions between young people and officialdom, let alone that the juvenile courtroom would become a contest between adversaries, with the system pitted against the kid and the kid against the system. The reformers, of course, might have known better. Jane Addams in particular had observed the way in which U.S. institutions, from the schoolhouse to the poorhouse, attempted to impose alien values on their charges. Her sensitivity to the inherent dignity of the values of the poor and the oppressed distinguished her approach to social work. She and other early reformers would have been horrified to discover that juvenile courts have not simply strayed from their original prescriptions, but have become far more sinister institutions than the adult courts they were meant to replace.

In the first place, almost every assumption about juvenile-court judges and their use of information and rehabilitative facilities has proved false. A *U.S. News & World Report* survey indicates that three-quarters of all juvenile-court judges spent one-quarter or less of their time on youth cases. A third of the judges had *no* probation officers, and five-sixths lacked regularly available psychologists or psychiatrists.[21] Court dockets are so crowded that in Chicago, the birthplace of the juvenile-court concept, family cases average fifteen minutes each, while in California, where one case is completed every three minutes, a juvenile court devotes no more than twenty minutes, on the average, to each case.[22] Since the Supreme Court ruled that juvenile defendants have the right to counsel, the twenty-three dep-uty public defenders in Los Angeles County (where some 12,000 cases are now heard yearly) averaged 838 cases during the fiscal year ending June 30, 1968; that permitted a maximum of perhaps twenty-eight minutes for out-of-court consultation between lawyer, juvenile, and family.[23]

Before young people get to court, moreover, they are held in abominable places. Between 83% *(U.S. News)* and 93% (Philadelphia *Evening Bulletin,* May 20, 1968) of counties in the United States lack detention facilities other than regular jails for minors. (The discrepancy in the figures is explained, incidentally, by whether or not one counts the jaillike "juvenile receiving centers" that some states have established—often in old prisons.) Whether in regular jails or in juvenile lock-ups, young people are subjected to the usual array of prison horrors: forcible homosexuality, sadistic keepers, gross overcrowding. The list goes on and on, and every study of every juvenile system has added its gruesome particulars, from homosexual attacks in the sheriffs' vans[24] to incarceration of paranoids with regular prisoners. Jails aside, truly rehabilitative facilities for juveniles are in notoriously short supply. Thus, young people who are held specifically on the ground that they will receive psychiatric treatment often receive no treatment whatsoever: they are simply held.[25] Psychiatric clinics often reject cases as "uninteresting" for research or training, particularly from among poor people who don't always keep appointments with regularity. Such children often find their way into detention centers, simply because no one has any other way of handling them. Lisa Aversa Richette's book is filled with such stories, and with the harshest condemnation of juvenile facilities. It is therefore not surprising, as she points out, that "The FBI's 1967 *Uniform Crime Reports* shows that of *all* young offenders under twenty released from institutions in 1963, 70% have committed new crimes for which they have been arrested, many as adults."[26] So much for rehabilitation!

However inadequate the personnel of the court, however destructive the court's facilities, these are enlightened and adequate compared with the court's procedures. Until 1967, when the U.S. Supreme Court decided *In re Gault,* juveniles had no right to legal counsel at hearings, no right to confront accusers or cross-examine witnesses, and not even the right to remain silent in court. Instead of nonlegal informality producing rehabilitation and understanding, as the reformers had hoped, "there is evidence," Judge Abe Fortas wrote for the majority in an earlier case, "that the child receives the worst of both worlds; that he gets neither the protections accorded to adults nor the solicitous care and regenerative treatment postulated for children."[27]

The case of fifteen-year-old Gerald Francis Gault, which the Supreme Court used to provide some legal protection for young people, illustrates the autocratic workings of the juvenile system. In the summer of 1964 one of the Gaults' neighbors, who had been receiving obscene telephone calls, thought she recognized Gerald's voice. Knowing that he had been before a juvenile court (because he had been with another boy who had snatched a purse), she called his probation officer. Within hours, and without his parents' knowledge, the boy was picked up and taken to the detention center. What transpired in court the next morning no one will know precisely, for in accord with juvenile procedure, no records were kept. It is clear that the neighbor did not appear, for the only people there were Gault and his parents, the probation officer, and the judge. From later accounts, we know that the probation officer repeated the neighbor's story, the judge sharply questioned Gerald, and he admitted something—whether holding the phone while another boy spoke or actually using obscenity himself remains obscure. The judge ended the proceeding by announcing that he would make up his mind what to do with Gerald in a few days; meanwhile, he would stay in detention. When Mrs. Gault returned to court a few days later, she arrived again without a lawyer. No one had told her she and her son would need— or could even have—one. Well, said the judge, he had reviewed Gerald's record (a secret file, open only to the court's officials, but not to the juvenile, his parents, or counsel), and he felt that it would be best for the boy were he sent to the state's "training" school for an indefinite period. His confinement might last, the judge explained, till age twenty-one—for six years. Thus fifteen-year-old Gerald received a term of up to six years allegedly for the purpose of "bettering himself," whereas an adult committing a similar "crime" might be punished by a fine of fifty dollars and two months in prison.[28] When Mrs. Gault tried to appeal the ruling in Arizona courts, she discovered that the law provided no appeals from juvenile-court decisions. Nor indeed until the U.S. Supreme Court accepted and decided the case had there been much hope that juvenile-court cases would be considered by them.

The Supreme Court's decision in the Gault case has, in theory, assured minors some basic rights in court. But these remain sharply limited. In the first place, the court left untouched a whole series of legal rights held by adults, but not by minors. Thus, the Maryland Appeals Court declared, on December 7, 1968, that juveniles are not entitled to jury trials, let alone to trial by their peers, nor to ask that their trials be moved to another jurisdiction, that witnesses be separated, nor even to ask for a new trial. Judge Thomas B. Finan wrote, with the kind of perverse logic characteristic of those wishing to maintain the juvenile-court system, that the Supreme Court "certainly stopped short of insisting that built-in protections afforded minors in juvenile proceedings be discarded, and that they be tried in all cases like adults." What "built-in protections" had been afforded sixteen-year-old Dennis P. Fletcher, accused of fire-bombing a grocery store during racial disturbances in Cambridge, Maryland, remain obscure, since he was incarcerated in the Maryland Training School for Boys for up to five years just as surely—though perhaps not so securely, since he escaped—as an adult in the penitentiary.

In the second place, theoretical rights have not always been translated into court practice. In Washington, D.C., for example, relatively few juvenile defendants or their parents actually avail themselves of counsel: the image of an informal proceeding remains, and either parents can't afford a lawyer (or don't wish to plead poverty to get a public defender), or they fear to antagonize the judge by retaining one. In New York, on the other hand, where up to 96% of young people appearing in court do have lawyers, the press of extra legal work has led to as many as a third of the cases being handled "outside court."[29] And no one will ever know what deals are worked out "for," or at the expense of, those minors who are defendants. Many juvenile judges have retained their paternalistic styles, and appeals from what might be judicial error or prejudice are difficult, expensive, frustrating, and hence rare. In Los Angeles County up to 1966 Superior Court officers had recorded fewer than five appeals from the some 3,000 minors committed to custody each year.[30] The number has grown somewhat, but on no scale comparable to adult rates.

Finally there remain, relatively untouched by judicial review, the practices by which young people are snared by the elaborate mechanisms of the juvenile-court system. They can be "referred" by hostile teachers or principals, overworked social workers, distraught or angry parents. And though such referrals must now contain clearly stated charges, they remain relatively easy ways of "taking care of" (with all the ambiguities implicit in that phrase) "difficult" or often simply different young people.

Most important, the sentencing power of the judge (who is also jury and often prosecutor as well) remains unimpaired, and often effectively unappealable. In theory, of course, juvenile courts do not impose sentences, but provide "opportunities" for rehabilitation, terms of institutional confinement for a young person's "own good." We have already examined the reality of "rehabilitation." When one comes upon (in the cases of minors sent over to adult criminal courts) ten-year terms for stealing a bicycle, or fifteen years to a seventeen-year-old for setting an old school ablaze, or four years for stealing a marking pen—one wonders whose good is being served. Federal judges have recently taken to giving minors who violate draft laws— "for their own good"—indefinite zero- to six-year sentences under the Youth Corrections Act instead of the definite one, two, or up to five years (or the common term of two or three years) mandated by the Selective Service law. The judges' theory is that a draft resister might be "reformed" by the possibility of a sentence shorter than six long years. Thus, what is for a young person's "own good" comes to be his surrender of political principles strong enough to have led him to jail. It is a rare juvenile authority willing "to respect the stubborn dignity behind the refusal of these children to accept us as allies in their turbulent struggle for survival and identity."[31]

Mrs. Richette is speaking of black ghetto children. But her observation clearly pertains not only to them but to the increasing numbers of young people who find themselves in juvenile court primarily because their values and life style are antithetical to those of their parents, their school, and the business-oriented middle-class culture against which they are in rebellion. Even before the recently additional strains of generational and cultural conflict, the juvenile-court system had degenerated, every serious study contends, into little more than a dumping ground for young "social problems." Mrs. Richette, one of the few people connected with the system to have written extensively about it, summarizes her view of it:

> Rhetoric and high-sounding phrases aside, the best that juvenile courts are doing is exactly—and only—what the adult

criminal courts have done with children since time immemorial: locking them up in jails. While mouthing the language of the reformers, the juvenile court has become, in many cases, the legal strong arm of the community. And the kids know the score. [pp. 294–95.]

These are strong words, but in a sense the condemnation is inadequate. Nowadays, millions of young people share values in some degree hostile to those enshrined in American law; most of these young people—smoking pot, demonstrating, making love, hooking classes, beating curfew, driving fast, liberating food—violate laws or rules or regulations or customs for which they might, at any time, be pulled into the juvenile bureaucracy. Under such circumstances, a system permitting adults casual and petty "referrals" of young people into murky, paternalistic procedures smothered by rhetoric about the "best interests of the child" and leading to self-righteous or vindictive sentences—for they are sentences the judge pronounces—such a system is guaranteed not merely to produce abuses but to become a ready-made contrivance for repression. And, as Mrs. Richette comments, "the kids know the score." That is to say, they correctly see that the juvenile-court system serves the interests of society in containing and coercing them *not* in spite of, but in many respects by means of its very abusive character. As one young writer put it in the underground Los Angeles *Free Press* (March 21, 1969), the fundamental procedures of the juvenile-court system "deny justice to vast numbers of juveniles in the courts, but do so WITHIN THE LAW."

The inadequacy of proposed reforms is rooted precisely in the failure to see how a "flawed" system may serve dominant interests in society. Like the President's Task Force on Juvenile Delinquency, Mrs. Richette, for example, suggests a combination of adult volunteer efforts and an elaborated "Juvenile Justice System" that adds to the courts a "Youth Services Bureau" and a variety of rehabilitative services. What she does not begin to suggest is where, in a society which she charges with gross failure to deal with open abuses in the present system, the will and the cash may be found to energize an even more extensive and expensive system. Or how this new, more involved bureaucracy will be informed any less with the spirit of coercion that now seems to characterize relations between institutions and young people. If, as she says, "control and punishment, not treatment and rehabilitation, are what the public *really* demands" (p. 15), can she imagine that tales of woe or appeals to voluntarism will change that fundamental demand—particularly now, as the calls mount in the press and in Congress for control over youth? The truth of the matter, as we have already suggested, is that any system dependent on the goodwill of bureaucrats or the good intentions of volunteers will come to be dominated by the fundamental mandate of society—for "control and punishment." Thus it is not simple neglect, not the shrugs of "good Germans," not even the paternalism or hostility of some judges or policemen or probation officers that has created the disaster of juvenile courts. It is the growing need of American society to coerce and control its youth.

THE MARIJUANA WAR

Nowhere does the control of youth become more clear than in connection with marijuana—grass, Mary Jane, or pot, as it is popularly called, *cannabis,* as the scientists term it. We offer a few basic facts: Marijuana is a relatively mild hallucinogen, not a narcotic like heroin; smoking or eating it will make most people "high"; its possession, let alone its use, is illegal. Marijuana has been known for thousands of years. Once it was smoked in the United States mostly by poor people. Today, especially among the young, it use has skyrocketed, and so have arrests of its smokers. Little or no hard scientific evidence has been produced to show distinctly harmful effects of the normal use of pot. Why, then, the increasing hysteria about marijuana and the severe punishments for its young smokers? Is the hysteria about pot proportional to the danger of its use—to young people and to society generally? Or is the marijuana war another manifestation of strong and angry currents in adult society?

A favorite rallying cry of students during massive drug raids on campus in the spring of 1969 was "We all use dope." That seems to be a slight, though by no means wild, exaggeration. Some college officials estimate that 50 to 60 percent of their students use drugs of some sort on an irregular basis.[32] Another *Times* survey found students and observers who estimated that "up to 85% of the students at various colleges and universities have tried marijuana at least once."[33] And still a third *Times* story said that taking drugs, especially marijuana, "has reached the point where its open use, even in [New York City public] school buildings, is steadily growing." The story also reported that "of 30 student leaders in the city's schools, more than one-half said they smoked marijuana occasionally, and the remainder had friends who did."[34] At the giant Woodstock rock festival in August, 1969, reporters and police calculated that 90% or more of the almost half-million young people attending were smoking grass. The police gave up arresting them because, said one state trooper, there wasn't enough jail room in Sullivan or the four surrounding counties to hold them all. Across the country, Dr. Joel Fort, a San Francisco psychiatrist who has specialized in drug problems, reported in 1968 that "Surveys I have conducted over the past year show that in one large urban school district 18 percent of 7th grade boys and 12 percent of the girls have used marijuana. In the 12th grade, 41 percent of the boys and 43 percent of the girls have used the drug, the majority with some regularity." Fort "conservatively" estimates that five million Americans use pot.[35] In one sense, the precise number of young people using pot is not central to our argument. The chant— "We all use dope"—and the fact that young people don't turn in users point to the wide acceptance that smoking marijuana has among youth. This is significant, for it has meant that as pot busts have spread, the nonusers have largely found themselves siding with the prosecuted—and, from their perspective, often persecuted—users. Nonusers have perceived the attack as in some sense directed at them, too.

The huge increase in drug, and especially, marijuana, use has been accompanied by steadily escalating legal threats. The federal penalties for illegal use or possession are two to ten years for the first offense, five to twenty for the second, and ten to forty for any others. For sale, even of pot, the federal law *requires* a *minimum* sentence of five to twenty years for a first offense. Only recently, on May 19, 1969, the U.S. Supreme Court unanimously held key sections of the 1937 federal Marijuana Tax Act to be unconstitutional, essentially because anyone who (as the law required) paid the marijuana transfer tax (except for a few scientists or drug firms approved by federal authorities) would be known to authorities and subject to local and state prosecution. The court held that such a procedure violated the constitutional guarantee against self-incrimination in the case of Dr. Timothy Leary, who had been sentenced in a Texas court to five to thirty years in jail and a $30,000 fine for transporting what was presumed to be illegally imported marijuana without having paid the transfer tax of $100 an ounce. Older federal laws which effectively do not differentiate between marijuana and physically addictive narcotics like opium and cocaine, and which still impose a mandatory five-year minimum sentence for sale, remain on the books. And so, of course, do a variety of state and local laws banning possession, "transfer" (which can mean either selling or giving), or even being present where pot is smoked. Many of these laws are exemplary in their harshness: the State of Washington mandates a twenty-year minimum sentence for selling marijuana to a minor;[36] while Georgia, not to be outdone, can impose the death penalty for selling to minors.[37]

With such harsh laws enforceable and increasingly enforced, the list of legal "horror stories" lengthens. That list includes Samuel Williams, a thirty-two-year-old Seattle black man, given twenty years for selling a single joint (marijuana cigarette) to a sixteen-year-old boy for one dollar; Lee Otis Johnson, twenty-nine, a Houston field secretary for SNCC, much arrested by local authorities for his political activities, finally given thirty years for sale of pot to a narcotics agent; Matthew Culmore, a nineteen-year-old student at San Diego State College, previously convicted of possessing LSD, given sixteen years for possession of a few bags of marijuana. And other, more complex stories: A thirty-one-year-old Detroit "hippie," Larry Belcher, had written for the local underground paper a column that contradicted the Narcotics Bureau's pamphlets on pot. For selling five dollars' worth of seeds to an informer, his bail was set at $45,000, a sum that kept him in jail for four months awaiting trial. His 20–30-year sentence named him as a "habitual criminal" on the basis of a record which showed one conviction for unarmed robbery when very young and an arrest not leading even to trial for being in a house where marijuana was being smoked. Belcher's case was widely seen as a symbolic attack on the whole Detroit hippie community. In another case, Candy Barr, the Texas stripper, who had served three years of a fifteen-year sentence for a first offense of possessing marijuana in 1959, was rearrested in 1968 and bail set at $25,000. A Texas news columnist compared her bail with the few thousands of dollars normally required of persons accused of anything from burglary and robbery to murder and rape. One might also have compared that bail with the $5,000 or so set on top traffickers in hard drugs arrested in Washington, D.C. In still another case, Jimmie Johnson, one of the few "hippies" of Prince George's County, Virginia, was given twenty years (with ten suspended on condition he stay out of trouble) for possession after the sheriff had arranged for one of Jimmie's fellow high-school seniors to buy marijuana through him for $200 worth of marked bills. Johnson was no pusher, the sheriff admitted; he had occasionally sold a bag or two in the past. But he was one of the few oddballs in a conservative, rural county. We include a generous sample of cases[38] because among many young people they constitute a kind of "honor roll" of casualties in the "marijuana war" they see as increasingly fought between themselves and the "narcs." Young experts can cite chapter and verse of such harsh decisions with the ease and completeness that others lay out Red Sox batting statistics. There is no question, moreover, that in at least some if not all of these cases the law, even on its own terms, is being applied with ferocity and with an eye toward politics at least as much as justice or rehabilitation. Indeed, in one recent case, a ten-year mandatory sentence for a second offense of possession, a U.S. Court of Appeals held the penalty violated the constitutional provision against "cruel and unusual punishment."[39] If such punishment for a hard-drug addict is "cruel and unusual," what would one expect young people to make of other cases cited?

Of course, arrests for drug use, especially for marijuana and more especially of young people, have soared. For the period 1960–1967 arrests of those under eighteen have increased 63.9% generally; arrests for drug-law violations have increased 778.3%.[40] From 1966 to 1967 alone arrests of *minors* for possession or use of drugs leaped 131.4% in cities, 222% in suburbs, and even 132.5% in rural areas.[41] Federal narcotics arrests were up 48% in 1968 over 1967, FBI reports showed drug arrests up 60%, and states reported rises in 1968 ranging from 23% in New York to 400% in New Jersey.[42] The National Student Association, whose Drug Studies program keeps tabs on such matters, estimated in December, 1968, that 1968 drug-arrest rates were up over 1967 by 800%. For example, in 1967, nearly 11,000 juveniles (under eighteen, not twenty-one) were arrested in California on marijuana charges; in the first six months of 1968, 10,000 had been arrested.[43] A few months later, NSA had collected information on 6,684 drug arrests in the two months between December 1, 1968, and February 1, 1969 (they estimated that the total national figure had been some ten times that). Of their two-month total, 5,510 were for marijuana; and of those, only 343 were of persons over twenty-five. Similarly, in 1967 almost half of those arrested by state and local authorities for drug-law violations were under twenty-one.[44] And the trend continues: after a series of raids on college campuses, New York State police estimated—or, it might be more accurate to say, promised—that arrests in 1969 would be up 400% over 1967, perhaps to make up for the very modest 23% rise in 1968.[45] All told, a writer in the conservative *National Review* estimated in January, 1968, that some 10,000 individuals are in prison on marijuana charges, many of them young people without previous criminal records.

It is thus clear enough, whatever else is true about the matter, that drug-law enforcement agencies have, as they themselves say, been carrying on an escalating war against marijuana, and that young people have provided the vast bulk of the casualties in this war. In the past, the primary victims of stiff enforcement of marijuana laws have been blacks, among whom the use of the drug was relatively widespread. Now, as increasing numbers of white and middle-class youth are caught in wider-flung drug-enforcement nets, some state legislatures, including those of Illinois, Nebraska, Oregon, and North Dakota, have recently considered (though not often passed) bills to reduce penalties for first-offense possession of marijuana from the usual 2–10-year felony to a misdemeanor carrying perhaps six months in prison. But other states—Pennsylvania, Maine, and Rhode Island, for example—have been considering bills to *increase* penalties both for possession and transfer. Recent legislation has sought to attack "pushers" and to develop means for compulsory "rehabilitation" of users. But both approaches are, unfortunately, open to the same kind of selective, politically inspired, and hysterical application as previous laws. In New Mexico, for example, where the use of marijuana and other, similar substances anteceded the white man, new laws recently lowered penalties for first-offense users of pot, but increased terms and fines for "pushers." Since anyone who gives another a joint, or even, presumably, a puff or two at a pipe can be construed a "pusher," the definition can be used by local lawmen to come down hard on "troublemakers."[46]

A more striking instance of abuses inherent in new drug laws occurs in Maryland's recently passed (April, 1969) "Comprehensive
Drug Abuse Control and Rehabilitation Act." The act establishes a
Drug Abuse Authority to conduct research and education programs
and to establish facilities to treat "addicts." Its major provision establishes a procedure by which "drug addicts" can be incarcerated in
facilities established by the authority for *up to seven years.* The substances to be controlled include marijuana as well as hard drugs, and
an "addict" is defined as any "person exhibiting the symptoms of drug
addiction" or, more loosely, somebody "in imminent danger of becoming an addict." Since "addiction" includes "physical and psychological dependence," as a writer in the Johns Hopkins University
News-Letter pointed out, "it is easy to see that, relying on the old saw
that marijuana use leads to heroin addiction, any user of marijuana is
in imminent danger of becoming an addict."[47] In a manner reminiscent of juvenile law, the new Maryland drug law empowers not
only public authorities but "anyone residing in the same house as an
addict," including parents, relatives, or even college dormitory
mates, to "apply for an order certifying such person to the care and
custody of the authority." Upon such application, a judge may issue
an order directing the alleged "addict" to appear before him to determine whether or not he shall be sent for medical examination; if he
does not appear, a warrant may be issued. If he is judged an "addict"
by the Drug Abuse Authority, the judge may refer him for treatment
or, if he seems unlikely to report, may incarcerate him for up to seven
years so that he can be "rehabilitated." All of this may be done without benefit of jury. When the Maryland law was signed, a similar "rehabilitation" program of New York State's Narcotic Addiction Control Commission had just been widely attacked by judges, lawyers,
doctors, and addicts themselves as medically inadequate, unpro-
fessional, prisonlike, violent, and probably contrary to the constitutional rights of those committed.[48] Again, under recent federal law,
an "addict" *charged,* but not convicted, with certain crimes can be
committed for lengthy treatment. The Maryland bill may thus be typical of drug laws to come. Yet so dubious did it seem that the presidents of every major Maryland college and university signed an open
letter to the governor asking for a commission to review all laws per-
taining to drugs.

As if to underscore the potential dangers in the bill, some two months after its passage, a Baltimore County Circuit Court judge sent a nineteen-year-old Catonsville Community College student, with excellent character witnesses, off to jail for four years for selling five dollars' worth of hashish (a marijuana derivative) to an undercover police cadet. In passing sentence, Judge W. Albert Menchine said, according to the Baltimore *Sun* (June 23, 1969), "that in his 11½ years on the bench, he had seen the crime rate climb ever upward and that he had decided that marijuana, of which hashish is a derivative, was at least psychologically addictive." It is thus clear that even casual marijuana users, under the new Maryland law, could be sentenced for seven years. Past experience suggests, moreover, that in the hands of troubled parents and teachers, or angry police and judges, or even sympathetic counselors, such a law may become a club with which to keep recalcitrant or rebellious young people in line—or to send them away.

As the marijuana war has escalated, as the horror stories have spread among young people, and individual arrests have mounted, mass arrests have recently become common occurrences. In New York State during the spring of 1969, police raided the State University Center at Stony Brook (for the second time in fifteen months), Long Island University's Southampton campus, C. W. Post College, Dutchess Community College, and Bard College (for the second time in thirteen months). Similar raids occurred in the space of a month or so that same spring at Monmouth College in New Jersey, at Johns Hopkins University and Catonsville Community College in Maryland, at the University of Georgia—and so across the nation. The raids have had the flavor of old gangbuster days: undercover agents, sometimes police cadets, disguised as students; massive concentrations of police (at Stony Brook in 1968, 198 policemen arrested thirty-eight students) swooping onto campuses in the wee morning hours or at dawn; students led off to paddywagons, hands manacled behind their backs; coincidence in at least the timing of the raids with scheduled hearings by, in New York, state legislative committees. They have also had touches not from the gangbusters' script: massive student protests; attempts to prevent arrested students from being carted off; sit-downs in front of police cars; police use of tear gas and chemical Mace; and increasing questions among students about the university administration's "complicity" in the busts.

Similarly, during the spring and summer of 1967, the Washing-

ton, D.C., Narcotics Squad spent about 70% of its working hours investigating drug use by the District's hippie community. Two separate four-month investigations, complete with undercover agents
hanging around Dupont Circle, culminated in the bust of thirty-one
persons, most under twenty-five and including three juveniles. The
arrests led to fifteen marijuana charges, six for LSD, three for being
present in an illegal establishment, five for unauthorized use of a car,
but only two for heroin violations. In previous years, the Narcotics
Squad had concentrated on hard drugs, and especially pushers, who
were often connected with crime syndicates. After the August bust of
the hippies, in the course of which their house had been ripped apart,
presumably in search of contraband, individuals and newspapers in
Washington questioned the allocation of so much of the Narcotics
Squad's time to pursuing young users instead of organized pushers
of narcotics.[49] Why, it was asked, were there at least nine separate investigations involving hippies in 1967, but only one of heroin traffic.
The effective answer had been supplied a few months before by
D.C. Judge Halleck after a similar mass arrest (in which fifteen of the
twenty-five arrested were charged simply with being where others
were smoking pot): the action was meant, said the judge, "to show
these long-haired ne'er-do-wells that society will not tolerate their
conduct."[50]

In truth, however, large-scale raids on young pot users have
mostly succeeded in bringing sharp protests both from the students
themselves and from some college administrators. After the New
York State raids, an extensive *New York Times* report by Richard
Severo made the following observations:

Many students feel that the raids are selective and reflect
the legal and moral attitudes of certain law-enforcement officials.
They contend that several colleges where drugs are openly used
have not been raided. [These might have included Columbia University, where, earlier in the year, the son of a prominent New
Jersey politician had died of a drug overdose.]

Some of the campus raids appeared to reflect an intensified
interest on the part of the state police to enforce drug laws,
spurred by a directive from Governor Rockefeller last year. . . .

The on-campus raids are apparently not always aimed at
pushers. At Stony Brook, the last raid netted thirteen freshmen.

Student sources there say the major pushers on campus have not been touched.

The raids have apparently had little effect on drug traffic.

Characteristically, the *Times* report indicates, only four of the thirty-six people arrested at Bard in 1968 pleaded guilty, while charges against the others were dropped. Nevertheless, the boys among the thirty students arrested in the second Bard raid quickly had their long hair shorn by jailers, before they were bailed out later on the same day they were arrested. And even in federal areas of law enforcement, where agencies generally boast that 96.3% of arrests lead to conviction, only 43% (1,701 of 3,930) of those arrested on drug charges were actually convicted in 1968.[51]

The doubtful effectiveness of such raids, the newly found and often politically motivated zeal for enforcing drug laws, the apparent focus on minors who use grass—all of these have produced among young people a cynicism about drug laws and their enforcement. Such attitudes have been further fostered by the widespread scandals involving "narcs." We have already cited cases of perjury for which former and present narcotics agents have been indicted. Since April, 1968, when the Federal Bureau of Narcotics and the Bureau of Drug Abuse Control were combined, forty agents have resigned for cause. Attorney General Ramsey Clark said that an investigation begun in August, 1967, indicated "significant corruption." The forty agents represented almost 10% of the *total* of agents and supervisory personnel in the entire new Federal Bureau of Narcotics and Dangerous Drugs. Their cases have mainly involved sale of drugs, perjury, and other similar activities. In at least one case, over one million dollars changed hands.[52] One young friend summarized the matter casually to us: "Well," he said, "it just goes to show that the narcs are the Mafia." And even congressmen have been singularly unimpressed with the "glittering generalities" of the federal drug-control administrators' claims for their agency's effectiveness.

But perphaps what has most exasperated young people is that even as prosecutions for marijuana have risen, evidence suggesting its relative harmlessness has also been accumulating. Those who believe pot dangerous charge that it leads to the use of hard drugs and produces dependency, failure of physical coordination, and deleterious social and intellectual effects. In 1965, for example, Donald E. Miller, chief counsel of what was then the U.S. Bureau of Narcotics, summarized much of the conventional wisdom about marijuana. "There is often," Miller wrote, "a clear pattern of graduation from marijuana to the stronger addictive opiates"; and he cited a number of studies showing that heroin addicts had first used pot.[53] But the chief of the World Health Organization's drug-dependence unit, who opposed legalization of marijuana on the grounds that it produces psychological dependence, "rejected the view that marijuana leads to the use of more dangerous narcotics." To deduce from statistics showing that heroin users began with marijuana, he continued, "that marijuana leads to heroin is 'wildly spurious reasoning' because of the unknown but 'obviously very great' number of marijuana users who have never gone on to heroin."[54]

While there is general agreement that marijuana is not physically addictive,[55] "pyschological dependence" has been cited as a remaining reason for not legalizing or encouraging its use. At a spectacular Boston test case, however, Dr. Nicholas Malleson, chief of the University of London's Student Health Service, responded to the phrase thus:

> All that means is "I want." There's absolutely nothing wrong with that, my dear sir. After all, I am psychologically dependent on gin and my wife, although I am not absolutely certain in which order.[56]

Similarly, Dr. James L. Goddard, former commissioner of the Food and Drug Administration, said, to the almost instantaneous accompaniment of congressional condemnation, that he didn't consider marijuana to be more dangerous than alcohol.

Nevertheless, Miller and others also warned of the dangerous "effect of the drug on the performance of complex tasks and particularly the operation of motor vehicles." One Wolff—a favorite source of the chief counsel—"says that numerous traffic accidents in Mexico and Cuba are attributed to the drug." Unfortunately for that idea, a study done by the Washington State Motor Vehicle Department showed that of a possible 405 errors, unintoxicated people averaged 84.46 errors while the same people after getting high on marijuana made 84.49 errors. After having two drinks, instead of two joints, however, the same people made 97.44 errors, an increase of about 15%[57] Studies of students have similarly indicated that academic performance of users and nonusers is indistinguishable. One professor, Robert Hogan of Johns Hopkins University, who favors drug raids on college dorms and believes that "heads are losers," did find that those he called "principled nonusers" "showed no clearly defined academic preferences, and were responsible and rule-abiding. However, they also tended to be rigid, conventional, and narrow in their interests." Users, he found, "tended to major in the humanities and social sciences, and could be generally described as socially poised, open to experience, and concerned with the feelings of others. On the other hand, they also tended to be impulsive, pleasure-seeking, and somewhat rebellious." In the fall of 1969, Hogan additionally reported that users tended to do *better* academically. Other studies have also suggested that they were more likely to be involved in politics.[58] Such identification of politically active or rebellious students and drug users tends to suggest a political motivation among the forces pursuing the marijuana war. At any rate, Dr. Sidney Cohen, director of Narcotic Addiction and Drug Abuse studies of the National Institute of Mental Health, which is coordinating a large number of studies of marijuana, summed up the situation by saying that little or none of the evidence so far developed indicated that short-term use of marijuana is physically or psychologically harmful.[59]

It is not our intention here to argue the case for legalizing marijuana, or to contend that it is absolutely harmless. Pot is an intoxicant; no doubt, some people will abuse it. There are those—probably few in America now—for whom that is sufficient cause to ban its use. And then there are those, ourselves included, who prefer vodka and activism, or who feel that grass removes people from political struggles. But these considerations aside, the point of the evidence we have collected is that the response to marijuana by authorities and the public in the United States is clearly in excess of the dangers the drug presents either to individual users or to society in general. Moreover, this "overreaction"—to use a recently popular word—has grown even more widespread and brutal as the evidence of marijuana's relative harmlessness has accumulated. And thus we return to the question with which we began: how to explain the "overreaction," or is "overreaction" itself a conveniently extenuating term?

Let us sharpen the emotional content of the issue by listening to questions as young people put them. What kind of society strikes bargains with the tobacco industry about how short, how small, and how long-delayed warnings of the cancer-producing properties of cigarettes might be? How does grass compare with nicotine as a menace to public health and welfare? Or how is it that the same government which so energetically enforces marijuana laws and helps spray foreign fields of grass permits big pharmaceutical firms to market badly tested substances, like thalidomide and cyclamates (or even the Pill), which may be far more dangerous than pot?[60] Or consider six million alcoholics, cirrhosis of the liver as America's sixth leading cause of death, the alcoholic brain damage which produces 20% of those in state mental hospitals, the minimum of 50% of the 53,000 highway deaths and 2,500,000 serious injuries annually associated with drinking.[61] What sort of society leaves that disaster area to Alcoholics Anonymous and similar voluntary agencies, yet spends millions of public dollars and mobilizes thousands of public servants to sweep up Washington hippies or Stony Brook freshmen? In 1966 many of the most respected professionals dealing with drug problems were predicting that "the severity of the marijuana laws against possession should be sharply reduced within the next few years . . . and legal repression at the user level seems likely to be markedly reduced in the not too distant future."[62] How could they be so wrong? Or here are the words of a former officer of the National Student Association, now editor of *Moderator* magazine:

Students find marijuana no more—probably less—dangerous than alcohol. This is their own overwhelming personal experience. This is the consistent finding of medical journals. This is the finding of the recent President's Task Force on Narcotics and Drug Abuse. Why are the legal penalties so absurdly high? Why should marijuana be illegal at all? Why should the Federal Narcotics Bureau continue to spread its threadbare scare campaign? Why did they recently assure that marijuana legislation was "secured" under the protection of an international treaty? Why have they expanded their activities on campus when they have been singularly ineffective in stopping traffic and use of clearly more dangerous drugs like heroin? Why is the Food and Drug Administration talking of plans to more than double (from 200 to 500) the number of their agents, trained by the Federal

Narcotics Bureau? Why are college administrators standing idly by watching the violations of student civil liberties? Why is there every indication of a major national campaign to involve college administrators in the detection of student drug use and, thereby, undermine the foundation of the entire educational process? Why? Why? These are the questions of the students.[63]

And that was in 1967.

A few social scientists and others have tried to deal with such questions rather than with the interesting, but to young people finally maddening, concern about why some students use drugs. The question for young people isn't why they use grass but why adults react so strongly to the fact of their smoking. Joel Fort suggests that "the real marijuana problem is the law and its fanatical enforcement. Police, bureaucrats, politicians, and the mass media define the drug for society as being far more interesting, important, and desirable than it actually is." Thus, Fort continues:

When we discuss and react to marijuana, we respond to a symbol of the chasm between young and old, between open and closed minds, between libertarian and authoritarian mentalities. Politicians have loved the subject: the more one succeeds in foisting the marijuana menace on the public, the less one needs to talk about alcohol, racism, poverty, war, and other far more serious matters, the discussion of which in any depth might result in loss of votes, decreased income, or worst of all, unpopularity. The drug laws have an important scapegoating and anti-intellectual function in our society, being used to attack youth and other minorities, dissent, and nonconformity.[64]

In short, in Fort's view, the "marijuana problem" is a political dodge.

Michael E. Brown, a Queens College sociologist, sees the marijuana war in the context of a more general persecution of hippies. Young and disobedient, the hippies dangerously "challenge our sentiments," at once questioning received customs—from dietary and healing practices to living arrangements and land use—and tempting others to "drop out" of "straight" life. Their culture, with its emphasis on immediate experience, drugs, and sexual liberation, can be portrayed as a "heresy" and the hippies themselves as "dirty," psychologically misfit, naïve if not subversive. They thus become appropriate scapegoats for public and private harassment, designed to frighten, control, and perhaps finally to destroy them, or—as Brown does not suggest—to convert them. Brown proposes, with deliberate exaggeration, that the process by which the hippies become first a scorned symbol, largely created by the mass media, then the subject of official physical attack (as in San Francisco, Philadelphia, New York's Tompkins Square), then the object of private, vigilante action, parallels the process by which German Jews were subjected to a "final solution." The comparison is, as he says, an "exercise in overestimation." There can be little question, on the other hand, that "social, cultural, and political resources have been mobilized so as to bring a group of individuals into line and to prevent others from refusing to toe the line. Those are the consequences, regardless of the original intentions of the agencies involved." Effectively, media, juvenile and social agencies, psychiatric clinics, drug-control agencies (newly centralized at the federal level), local police and school administrators, and political leaders have joined in what Brown calls a loosely articulated "control conglomerate," which views hippie drug users less as citizens who must be accorded civil and political rights than as objects of scorn against whom violent impulses—from hair-cutting to head-beating—may be enacted. The overestimation thus has uncomfortable grains of truth.[65]

Joseph R. Gusfield, chairman of the Sociology Department at the University of California's San Diego campus, presents a comparable view, though he uses the analogy of alcohol. He points out that the temperance campaign against alcohol was "closely related to the immigration of Irish Catholics and German Lutherans," and it "became a politically significant focus for the conflicts between Protestant and Catholic, rural and urban, native and immigrant, middle class and lower class in American society. . . ."[66] Gusfield sees the issue of drugs in similar terms. One indication, he argues, that

criminal sanctions are largely symbolic is the severity and hostility of the treatment of drug users. The length and mandatory character of criminal sentences testify to an excessive zeal toward drug clients, absent in the treatment of clients of gamblers, prostitutes, and abortionists. The continued use of heavy criminal sanctions . . . is further evidence that policy makers are more interested in expressing disapproval of drug use than in controlling it effectively.

For treating drug users as criminals is not effective either in stopping the spread of drug use or in "curing" individual users. "This severe treatment of the drug user," Gusfield maintains, "must be seen in the light of the fact that issues of drug addiction become entangled with society's orientation toward the disadvantaged and toward youth."[67] As another writer has suggested, "The real issue of marijuana is ethical and political, touching the 'core of cultural values.'"[68]

Like the saloon, the hippie pad has become a battleground of a larger social and political struggle. The marijuana war is a channel, partly real in itself, partly carrying heavy symbolic overtones, through which cultural values are challenged and defended, as the battle for control continues.

Notes

[1] *Fortune* magazine, special issue on youth, 79 (January, 1969), p. 75.

[2] *Youthquake* (New York: Cowles Publications, 1968), pp. 93, 10.

[3] See Nat Hentoff, "Youth—the Oppressed Majority," *Playboy*, 14 (September, 1967), p. 192. Hentoff reports that the co-director of the Los Angeles Suicide Prevention Center thinks the last figure conservative.

[4] President's Commission on Law Enforcement and Administration of Justice, *The Challenge of Crime in a Free Society* (Washington, D.C.: U.S. Government Printing Office, 1967), p. 55.

[5] *The Throwaway Children* (Philadelphia & New York: J. B. Lippincott Co., 1969), p. 8.

[6] Report of Subcommittee to Investigate Juvenile Delinquency in the United States, 90th Congress, 1st session, Report #823, November 30, 1967, p. 2.

[7] Richette, *op. cit.*, p. 9.

[8] See *The New York Times*, November 5, 1967.

[9] See *The New York Times*, September 3, 1966, and November 8, 1969.

[10] Quoted in *The New York Times*, February 12, 1969.

[11] James S. Kunen, a Columbia student, "Why We're Against the Biggees," *The Atlantic*, 222 (October, 1968), p. 65.

[12] Quoted in Hentoff, *op. cit.*, p. 136.

[13] Press statement by Charles Hollander, director, Drug Studies, U.S. National Student Association, December 18, 1968; figures cited from California Department of Criminal Statistics.

[14] See, for example, Washington *Post*, July 25, 1969, which reports the indictments of two agents and three former agents for perjury in Los Angeles, and below, p. 171.

[15] Peter Myerson, *The Young Americans*, quoted in Hentoff, *op. cit.*, p. 138.

[16] Richette, *op. cit.*, pp. 273–76.

[17] Washington *Post*, May 11, 1969.

[18] *Ibid.*

[19] Baltimore *Sun*, June 25, 1969.

[20] Persecution by local officials of underground papers has become so bad that *The Wall Street Journal* ran a summary of incidents (July 7, 1969). These included a police raid on the Dallas *Notes*, during which two tons of newspapers, four typewriters, a camera, and an enlarger, among other things, were stolen; two obscenity convictions of the Milwaukee *Kaleidoscope's* editor; arrests of members of Atlanta's *Great Speckled Bird*, despite a federal court decision that it is not obscene. In all, the Underground Press Service said that twenty-three of its subscriber papers had been harassed by "spurious charges designed to shut them down." See also *The Repress*, I (July, 1969), p. 3.

[21]"Crisis in Juvenile Courts," *U.S. News & World Report,* 66 (March 26, 1969), pp. 62–64.

[22]Ruth Gossland, *Juvenile Rights in Court—1968 California Family Edition* (Los Angeles, 1968); *U.S. News, op. cit.*

[23]Gossland, *op. cit.*

[24]Richette, *op. cit.*, p. 114.

[25]Judge David L. Bazalon, "Justice for Juveniles," *The New Republic* (April 22, 1967).

[26]Richette, *op. cit.*, p. 293.

[27] The case in question involved Morris Kent, age sixteen, who had been given 30 to 90 years in adult criminal court for housebreaking, theft, and rape, although he had been acquitted of rape on the grounds of temporary insanity. The court found that one reason Kent had been sent to adult court was that the juvenile-court judge had recognized that he was disturbed but had no facilities to treat him. See Bazalon, op. cit., and Kent *v.* U.S., 383 U.S. 541.

[28]See Richette, *op. cit.*, pp. 298–302, and the Supreme Court record of *In Re Gault* 387 U.S. 1.

[29]*U.S. News, op. cit.*

[30]Gossland, *op. cit.*

[31]Richette, *op. cit.*, p. 154.

[32]"Campus Narcotics Raids Stir Protests," in *The New York Times,* May 31, 1969.

[33]"Columbia Students Call Use of Marijuana Widespread and Open," in *The New York Times,* March 8, 1969.

[34]"Drug Use Rises in City's High Schools," in *The New York Times,* March 10, 1969.

[35]Joel Fort, "Marijuana: The Real Problems and the Responsibilities of the Professions in Solving Them," printed by the National Student Association, 1968.

[36]See "Drugs and the Law," *New Republic,* 159 (November 30, 1968), p. 11.

[37]See *Time,* September 29, 1967.

[38]See, for these and other such stories, "Drugs and the Law," *New Republic,* 159 (November 30, 1968); "Playboy Forum," *Playboy* (June, 1969), p. 72; "Texas Justice vs. Candy Barr," *Playboy* (June, 1969), pp. 65–66; *The Marijuana Review,* 1 (June–August, 1969).

[39]U.S. Court of Appeals for the District of Columbia, 12/13/68.

[40]1967 FBI Uniform Crime Reports, p. 118.

[41]Richette, *op. cit.*, p. 7.

[42]See Presentation by Bureau of Narcotics and Dangerous Drugs to Subcommittee on Departments of State, Justice, and Commerce, of Committee on Appropriations, House of Representatives, 91st Congress, 1st session, April 23, 1969 (Washington: Government Printing office, 1969), pp. 936, 952–53. And *Drug Law Bulletin,* I (May, 1969), p. 3.

[43]Press statement, December 18, 1968, by Charles Hollander, director, Drug Studies, for NSA, and Executive Committee member, National Coordinating Council on Drug Abuse, Education, and Information.

[44] 1967 FBI Uniform Crime Reports, p. 32.

[45] *The New York Times,* May 31, 1969.

[46] See *The Marijuana Review,* I (June–August, 1969), p. 4.

[47] *News-Letter,* May 9, 1969.

[48] *The New York Times,* April 21, 1969.

[49] See Carl Bernstein, "Hippie Dope Raids Plotted Last Spring," in the Washington *Post,* August 19, 1967.

[50] Washington *Post,* May, 21, 1967.

[51] See Hearings Before Subcommittee of the Committee on Appropriations on Department of State, Justice, etc., John J. Rooney, chairman, House of Representatives, 91st Congress, 1st session, Pt. 1 (Washington, D.C.: Government Printing Office, 1969), p. 972.

[52] Rooney Committee Hearings, *op. cit.,* pp. 983–85.

[53] Miller's article is conveniently printed in Charles Hollander, ed., *Student Drug Involvement* (Washington, D.C.: National Student Association, 1967), pp. 135–45.

[54] *The New York Times,* January 22, 1969. Miller's credibility on such matters is further strained by his rather selective interpretation of evidence. He claims, for example, that a 1966 "report of the Subcommittee on Narcotic Addiction of the New York Medical Society found that the prohibition against marijuana clearly should be maintained." He omits from his version of that report, what is quoted elsewhere in the Hollander volume by Allen Ginsberg: "There is no evidence that marijuana use is associated with crimes of violence in the United States . . . marijuana is not a narcotic nor is it addicting . . . New York State should take the lead in attempting to mitigate the stringent federal laws in regard to marijuana possession."

[55] See, for example, "Drug Dependence: Its Significance and Characteristics," *Bulletin of the World Health Organization* (1965): "There is, in consequence, no characteristic abstinence syndrome when use of the drug is discontinued. . . ." Quoted by Allen Ginsberg, "Fact Sheet: A Small Anthology of Footnotes on Marijuana," in Charles Hollander, ed., *Student Drug Involvement,* p. 12.

[56] See reports in *Time* (September 29, 1967) and *Newsweek* (October 2, 1967).

[57] Interestingly, when *The New York Times* ran a very brief story about the study, the headline did not call attention to the fact that marijuana smokers erred no more than nonsmokers (though the study had been started to test an earlier claim that persons arrested for marijuana had 39% more accidents than other drivers); rather, the *Times'* headline read: "Marijuana Is Found Safer for Drivers Than Alcohol"—a small comfort. In another series of experiments carried out at the Boston University School of Medicine, scientists concluded that smoking pot did not affect the subjects' capacities for sustained attention, and that while "cognitive function" and "muscular coordination" decreased among those who had seldom or never smoked, experienced users improved their performances on both counts after smoking. See *Drug Law Bulletin,* I (May, 1969), p. 3.

[58] For example, in a study conducted by Michigan State Representative Dale Warner's Committee on Public Health and Narcotics. See *Drug Law*

Bulletin, I (May, 1969), p. 3. The Michigan study also indicated that the academic performance of users and nonusers was indistinguishable. Dr. Hogan's conclusions were presented to the spring, 1969, meeting of the Eastern Psychological Association and summarized in the Johns Hopkins *News-Letter,* May 2, 1969. These conclusions are corroborated by the finding of Dr. Richard Brotman of the New York Medical College. His study of the long-term results of marijuana so far indicates that students who use it over four or five years show no apparent effects. It was also true, however, that another group of students who smoked grass showed decreased concern with academic work and greater involvement with the civil-rights and antiwar movements.

[59] *Drug Law Bulletin,* I (May, 1969), p. 3. Similar testimony has come from England, in the form of the Wootton Report, prepared for the British government by a subcommittee of the Home Office which included the superintendent of Scotland Yard, a magistrate, and a professor of psychiatry, among others. The report called for an end to imprisonment for possession of or small-scale
British Home Secretary.

[60] See, for example, *The New York Times* of July 29 and August 15, 1969, which expose the supposed prison-testing program of new drugs as little more than a hit-and-miss operation of hardly any scientific validity and of doubtful legality.

[61] See Joel Fort, "Marijuana: The Real Problems," *op. cit.*

[62] William H. McClothlin, "Toward a Rational View of Hallucinogenic Drugs," paper distributed at National Association of Student Personnel Administration Drug Education Conference, November 7–8, 1966.

[63] Philip Wardell, "Introduction," *Student Drug Involvement, op. cit.,* pp. 2–3.

[64] Fort, "Marijuana: The Real Problems," *op. cit.*

[65] Michael E. Brown, "Condemnation and Persecution: Social Control and the Closing of Alternatives," unpublished typescript.

[66] Thus victory or defeat in the limited issue of Prohibition came to symbolize the relative status and power of the opposing cultures. Because the dominant Protestant culture attempted to define a political issue in terms of morality and public health, it was "not until after Repeal that chronic alcoholism became defined as illness" rather than as sin and deviation.

[67] "On Legislating Morals: The Symbolic Process of Deviant Designation," *Drug Law Bulletin,* I (May, 1969), pp. 16–18.

[68] Bennett Berger, Denver *Post,* April 19, 1968, quoted in Michael Brown, *op. cit.*

7

Channeling:
Manhood and Manpower

In the spring of 1967, two governmental commission reports, three or four books, and a large number of essays in the student and general press documented and debated the absurdities and inequities of the Selective Service System.[1] Some of these proposed extensive reforms, others the abolition of the draft and its replacement with a volunteer army. But few bothered to consider why the draft had become a hot political issue: the Vietnam war. That war, more than most in U.S history, was even then unpopular with many who did not oppose it, or who continued to defend the conduct of it. Yet the administration had been able to wage the war without serious political challenge, in part because of the power to conscript. A year later, debates in Congress about manpower needs in Vietnam illustrated how the draft had functioned to bypass legislative restraints on the President's power to make war. The congressmen talked, in 1968, not of the draft's imperfections, indeed not of the draft at all, but demanded that they be "consulted" *this* time before men were sent to Vietnam.

But 1967's debate about the draft served chiefly to reveal the Selective Service as an inequitable and irrational institution. Bruce K. Chapman's *The Wrong Man in Uniform* documented the great variation, from state to state, in the proportion of men who were classified 4-F or who were, for a variety of reasons, deferred altogether. In one state, married men were vulnerable, elsewhere they were not. Peace Corps volunteers were deferred in New York, but drafted in Kansas. Illinois gave special consideration to mortuary trainees, but Alabama did not. The system as a whole creaked with age, inbreeding, and inefficiency. Draft-board members, the Marshall Commission report showed, were all male, mostly veterans and white-collar workers or businessmen, and virtually all white—only 1.3 percent were then black. Twenty-two percent of all draft-board members were over seventy years old; the average age was fifty-eight. Although Congress intended Selective Service to be controlled by civilians, its top officials were and still are heavily military in orientation and training.

The system had even then begun to stumble over its own manipulations. Early in the spring of 1966, General Lewis B. Hershey, director of the draft, had claimed that the 1-A pool would be exhausted shortly, and that therefore some students would have to lose their deferments. Draft boards began demanding reports on class standings, and hundreds of thousands of students rushed to take the Selective Service Qualification Test. Some were reclassified; thousands enlisted; thousands more engaged in antidraft and "antiranking" sit-ins. But no manpower crisis did appear; by June, 1966, it was clear that Selective Service had simply overestimated its needs by more than a third! According to Chapman, that crisis was the result of the temporary loss in the bureaucratic "pipeline" of 100,000 men classified 1-A. The episode seemed to confirm the charges that Selective Service, with its inefficient decentralized system, created enormous uncertainty and unnecessary anxiety for millions.

In significant measure, criticism of the Selective Service System as a bungling institution, perhaps in need of skilled engineers and computerization, missed the point. The "flaws" of the draft were not accidental, but designed by its administrators as necessary to its effective operation. Although the truth of this observation was never easy to argue, a document began to circulate early in 1967 on campuses throughout the United States that provided unquestionable evidence.[2] Neither a manifesto nor a call to arms, but rather an official publication of the Selective Service System, the "Channeling Memo," as it came to be called, helped transform diffuse discontent with an embarrassingly "flawed" system into critical analysis of the system's goals and procedures. Written in the bland, inflated style of bureaucrats justifying the wisdom of their procedures and the value of their successes (there is not one mention of failure), the author or authors were clearly unaware that they might be revealing relatively well-kept secrets about the draft and the United States. Even to people with few illusions about the faltering decency of the "American way," the memo seemed at first improbable except as satire. "Channeling" was, however, part of the "Selective Service Orientation Kit," a set of papers used by the Selective Service System to explain its procedures to new employees and local board members and to persuade congressmen of its effectiveness. Hence perhaps its fatuous, self-congratulatory tone, its patriotic fervor turned to self-righteous manipulation.

Within a year, the original document was quietly withdrawn and, for a time, was available only through the student press. For the Selective Service System, which has now issued a rewritten version, the first Channeling Memo has become a piece of nonhistory. The original is, therefore, an essential document. Not only is it the best (and most authoritative) description of the draft at work, it is also a classic definition of the social control of young people, whether that technique is called "channeling," "tracking," or "placement counseling." Since it is this chapter's purpose to provide a detailed analysis of channeling, we print the original document as it appeared under the date of 1965. (The version we have is on buff paper, unsigned except with a date, and with "GPO [Government Printing Office] 899–125" in tiny print on the last page.)

CHANNELING

One of the major products of the Selective Service classification process is the channeling of manpower into many endeavors, occupations, and activities that are in the national interest. This function is a counterpart and amplification of the System's responsibility to deliver manpower to the armed forces in such a manner as to reduce to a minimum any adverse effect upon the national health, safety, interest, and progress. By identifying and applying this process intelligently, the System is able not only to minimize any adverse effect but to exert an effect beneficial to the national health, safety, and interest.

The line dividing the primary function of armed forces manpower procurement from the process of channeling manpower into civilian support is often finely drawn. The process of channeling by not taking men from certain activities who are otherwise liable for service, or by giving deferment to qualified men in certain occupations, is actual procurement by inducement of manpower for civilian activities which are manifestly in the national interest.

While the best known purpose of Selective Service is to procure manpower for the armed forces, a variety of related processes take place outside delivery of manpower to the active armed forces. Many of these may be put under the heading of "channeling manpower." Many young men would not have pursued a higher education if there had not been a program of student deferment. Many young scientists, engineers, tool and die makers, and other possessors of scarce skills would not remain in their jobs in the defense effort if it were not for a program of occupational deferments. Even though the salary of a teacher has historically been meager, many young men remain in that job, seeking the reward of a deferment. The process of channeling manpower by deferment is entitled to much credit for the large number of graduate students in technical fields and for the fact that there is not a greater shortage of teachers, engineers, and other scientists working in activities which are essential to the national interest.

More than ten years ago, it became evident that something additional had to be done to permit and encourage development of young scientists and trained people in all fields. A million and a half registrants are now deferred as students. One reason the Nation is not in shorter supply of engineers today is that they were among the students deferred by Selective Service in previous years. Similarly, Selective Service student deferments reduced what otherwise would have developed into more serious shortages in teaching, medicine, dentistry, and every field requiring advanced study. The System has also induced needed people to remain in these professions and in industry engaged in defense activities or in the support of national health, safety, or interest.

The opportunity to enhance the national well being by

inducing more registrants to participate in fields which relate directly to the national interest came about as a consequence, soon after the close of the Korean episode, of the knowledge within the System that there was enough registrant personnel to allow stringent deferment practices employed during war time to be relaxed or tightened as the situation might require. Circumstances had become favorable to induce registrants, by the attraction of deferment, to matriculate in schools and pursue subjects in which there was beginning to be a national shortage of personnel. These were particularly in the engineering, scientific, and teaching professions.

This was coupled with a growing public recognition that the complexities of future wars would diminish further the distinction between what constitutes military service in uniform and a comparable contribution to the national interest out of uniform. Wars have always been conducted in various ways but appreciation of this fact and its relationship to preparation for war has never been so sharp in the public mind as it is now becoming. The meaning of the word "service," with its former restricted application to the armed forces, is certain to become widened much more in the future. This brings with it the ever increasing problem of how to control effectively the service of individuals who are not in the armed forces.

In the Selective Service System the term "deferment" has been used millions of times to describe the method and means used to attract to the kind of service considered to be most important, the individuals who were not compelled to do it. The club of induction has been used to drive out of areas considered to be less important to the areas of greater importance in which deferments were given, the individuals who did not or could not participate in activities which were considered essential to the defense of the Nation. The Selective Service System anticipates further evolution in this area. It is promoting the process by the granting of deferments in liberal numbers where the national need clearly would benefit.

Soon after Sputnik I was launched it became popular to reappraise critically our educational, scientific, and technicological [sic] inventory. Many deplored our shortage of scientific and technical personnel, inadequacies of our schools, and shortage of teachers. Since any analysis having any connection with manpower and its relation to the Nation's survival vitally involves the

Selective Service System, it is well to point out that for quite some time the System had been following a policy of deferring instructors who were engaged in the teaching of mathematics and physical and biological sciences. It is appropriate also to recall the System's previously invoked practice of deferring students to prepare themselves for work in some essential activity and the established program of deferring engineers, scientists, and other critically skilled persons who were working in essential fields.

The Congress, in enacting the Universal Military Training and Service legislation declared that adequate provisions for national security required maximum effort in the fields of scientific research and development, and the fullest possible utilization of the Nation's technicological [sic], scientific, and other critical manpower resources. To give effect to this philosophy, the classifying boards of the Selective Service System defer registrants determined by them to be necessary in the national health, safety, or interest. This is accomplished on the basis of evidence of record in each individual case. No group deferments are permitted. Deferments are granted, however, in a realistic atmosphere so that the fullest effect of channeling will be felt, rather than be terminated by military service at too early a time.

Registrants and their employers are encouraged and required to make available to the classifying authorities detailed evidence as to the occupations and activities in which the registrants are engaged. It is not necessary for any registrant to specifically request deferment, but his selective service file must contain sufficient current evidence on which can be based a proper determination as to whether he should remain where he is or be made available for service. Since occupational deferments are granted for no more than one year at a time, a process of periodically receiving current information and repeated review assures that every deferred registrant continues to contribute to the overall national good. This reminds him of the basis for his deferment. The skills as well as the activities are periodically reevaluated. A critical skill that is not employed in an essential activity does not qualify for deferment.

Patriotism is defined as "devotion to the welfare of one's country." It has been interpreted to mean many different things. Men have always been exhorted to do their duty. But what that duty is depends upon a variety of variables, most important being the nature of the threat to national welfare and the capacity and opportunity of the individual. Take, for example, the boy who saved the Netherlands by plugging the dike with his finger.

At the time of the American Revolution the patriot was the so called "embattled farmer" who joined General Washington to fight the British. The concept that patriotism is best exemplified by service in uniform has always been under some degree of challenge, but never to the extent that it is today. In today's complicated warfare when the man in uniform may be suffering far less than the civilians at home, patriotism must be interpreted far more broadly than ever before.

This is not a new thought, but it has had new emphasis since the development of nuclear and rocket warfare. Educators, scientists, engineers, and their professional organizations, during the last ten years particularly, have been convincing the American public that for the mentally qualified man there is a special order of patriotism other than service in uniform—that for the man having the capacity, dedicated service as a civilian in such fields, as engineering, the sciences, and teaching constitute the ultimate in their expression of patriotism. A large segment of the American public has been convinced that this is true.

It is in this atmosphere that the young man registers at age 18 and pressure begins to force his choice. He does not have the inhibitions that a philosophy of universal service in uniform would engender. The door is open for him as a student to qualify if capable in a skill badly needed by his nation. He has many choices and he is prodded to make a decision.

The psychological effect of this circumstantial climate depends upon the individual, his sense of good citizenship, his love of country and its way of life. He can obtain a sense of well being and satisfaction that he is doing as a civilian what will help his country most. This process encourages him to put forth his best effort and removes to some degree the stigma that has been attached to being out of uniform.

In the less patriotic and more selfish individual it engenders a sense of fear, uncertainty, and dissatisfaction which motivates him, nevertheless, in the same direction. He complains of the uncertainty which he must endure; he would like to be able to do as he pleases; he would appreciate a certain future with no prospect of military service or civilian contribution, but he complies with the needs of the national health, safety, or interest —or is denied deferment.

Throughout his career as a student, the pressure—the threat of loss of deferment—continues. It continues with equal intensity after graduation. His local board requires periodic reports to find out what he is up to. He is impelled to pursue his skill rather than embark upon some less important enterprise and is encouraged to apply his skill in an essential activity in the national interest. The loss of deferred status is the consequence for the individual who has acquired the skill and either does not use it or uses it in a nonessential activity.

The psychology of granting wide choice under pressure to take action is the American or indirect way of achieving what is done by direction in foreign countries where choice is not permitted. Here, choice is limited but not denied, and it is fundamental that an individual generally applies himself better to something he has decided to do rather than something he has been told to do.

The effects of channeling are manifested among student physicians. They are deferred to complete their education through school and internship. This permits them to serve in the armed forces in their skills rather than in an unskilled capacity as enlisted men.

The device of pressurized guidance, or channeling, is employed on Standby Reservists of which more than 2½ million have been referred by all services for availability determinations. The appeal to the Reservist who knows he is subject to recall to active duty unless he is determined to be unavailable is virtually identical to that extended to other registrants.

The psychological impact of being rejected for service in uniform is severe. The earlier this occurs in a young man's life, the sooner the beneficial effects of pressured motivation by the Selective Service System are lost. He is labeled unwanted. His patriotism is not desired. Once the label of "rejectee" is upon him all efforts at guidance by persuasion are futile. If he attempts to enlist at 17 or 18 and is rejected, then he receives virtually none of the impulsion the System is capable of giving him. If he makes no effort to enlist and as a result is not rejected until delivered for examination by the Selective Service System at about age 23, he has felt some of the pressure but thereafter is a free agent.

This contributed to establishment of a new classification of

I-Y (registrant qualified for military service only in time of war or national emergency). That classification reminds the registrant of his ultimate qualification to serve and preserves some of the benefit of what we call channeling. Without it or any other similar method of categorizing men in degrees of acceptability, men rejected for military service would be left with the under-standing that they are unfit to defend their country, even in war time.

An unprejudiced choice between alternative routes in civilian skills can be offered only by an agency which is not a user of manpower and is, therefore, not a competitor. In the absence of such an agency, bright young men would be importuned with bounties and pirated like potential college football players until eventually a system of arbitration would have to be established.

From the individual's viewpoint, he is standing in a room which has been made uncomfortably warm. Several doors are open, but they all lead to various forms of recognized, patriotic service to the Nation. Some accept the alternatives gladly—some with reluctance. The consequence is approximately the same.

The so called Doctor Draft was set up during the Korean episode to insure sufficient physicians, dentists, and veteri-narians in the armed forces as officers. The objective of that law was to exert sufficient pressure to furnish an incentive for appli-cation for commission. However, the indirect effect was to in-duce many physicians, dentists, and veterinarians to specialize in areas of medical personnel shortages and to seek outlets for their skills in areas of greatest demand and national need rather than of greatest financial return.

Selective Service processes do not compel people by edict as in foreign systems to enter pursuits having to do with essen-tiality and progress. They go because they know that by going they will be deferred.

The application of direct methods to effect the policy of every man doing his duty in support of national interest involves considerably more capacity than the current use of indirection as a method of allocation of personnel. The problem, however, of what is every man's duty when each individual case is ap-proached is not simple. The question of whether he can do one duty better than another is a problem of considerable proportions and the complications of logistics in attempting to control parts of an operation without controlling all of it (in other words, to control allocation of personnel without controlling where people eat, where they live, and how they are to be transported) adds to the administrative difficulties of direct administration. The organization necessary to make the decisions, even poor decisions, would, of necessity, extract a large segment of population from productive work. If the members of the organization are conceived to be reasonably qualified to exercise judgment and control over skilled personnel, the impact of their withdrawal from war production work would be severe. The number of decisions would extend into billions.

A quarter billion classification actions were needed in World War II for the comparatively limited function of the Selective Service System at that time. Deciding what people should do, rather than letting them do something of national importance of their own choosing, introduces many problems that are at least partially avoided when indirect methods, the kind currently invoked by the Selective Service System, are used.

Delivery of manpower for induction, the process of providing a few thousand men with transportation to a reception center, is not much of an administrative or financial challenge. It is in dealing with the other millions of registrants that the System is heavily occupied, developing more effective human beings in the national interest. If there is to be any survival after disaster, it will take people, and not machines, to restore the Nation.

July 1, 1965
GPO 899-125

There it is—the lives of American men could not be better described. Are you in a state of perpetual worry about military service? Do you feel yourself pushed into a way of life against which your deeper impulses rebel? Would you rather be a poet than a graduate student in English, an organizer in the ghetto than a law student? Would you like to lumberjack or bum around Europe or "tune in and drop out" or just be free this year? Your anxieties and frustrations are not accidental; U.S. government policy, as interpreted by General Hershey, creates them. And if you happen to rub your eyes and ask, "Tell me, again, what exactly are our objections to totalitarian collectivism?" the answer is really very simple: the American way is the "indirect way."

Understandably, an initial reaction to the Channeling Memorandum has often been disbelief, even about its authenticity as an official government document. Once convinced, at least by the official Government Printing Office number, older people often say, "But that's only Selective Service—what else would you expect from them?" Though that response reveals the disrepute into which the draft has fallen, such cynicism is both too easy and too shallow. The response underestimates the role of Selective Service in the lives of young Americans—it's "membership cards" are the only ones every male over eighteen is supposed to carry; and it ignores the power of so universal an institution. We would agree with the unknown writers of the Channeling Memo that their work "is entitled to much credit. . . ." For an institution that dominates many lives and profoundly affects other institutions of a society may come to symbolize the innermost quality of that society itself.

"Channeling" is, in the first place, an accurate description of how Selective Service operates. One problem for the manpower channeler and a major reason for a system of *selective* rather than universal military service is, oddly enough, a surplus commodity: young men. Each year now 1,800,000 men turn draft age; by 1974 the figure will reach 2,100,000. The military cannot absorb all of them even if it wanted to (which, by and large, it does not). Thomas D. Morris, Assistant Secretary of Defense for Manpower, testified at a House Armed Services Committee hearing in June of 1966 that "in 1958, 70% of men reaching age twenty-six had seen military service; in 1962, 58% of those reaching age twenty-six had served; today the figure is about 46%." Even with the escalation of the Vietnam war, the military could use the 60% of men who turn nineteen in any one year and who meet its highly flexible physical, mental, and moral standards, *only if it took no one from any other age group.* For instance, from July 1, 1965, to June 30, 1966, during one period of the Vietnam buildup, about 1,090,000 men entered the military (exclusive of officers), a figure almost identical to the 60% of the 1,800,000 nineteen-year-olds whom the Army's examination stations would classify, given today's semiwartime standards, as acceptable. The question thus becomes, to use the language of the Marshall Commission Report, "who serves when not all serve?" Channeling's answer has been that those who are students, or whose occupations are deemed critical to the national interest—scientists, technicians in war industries, certain teachers—remain; the rest go, unless they find other readily provided channels, like the Reserves or the National Guard.

The system of channeling manpower satisfies a second mission with which Selective Service sees itself charged: making sure that the economic life of the nation continues and develops as usual whatever the immediate military manpower needs. In the past, Selective Service, together with a clutch of government and semi-public agencies and business representatives, promulgated a set of guidelines which local boards used to determine occupational deferments.[3] These guidelines and the practice of deferring college students have assured American industry, and especially those large and influential sectors which General Eisenhower described as the "military-industrial complex," of a steady supply of trained manpower. Even in the event of large-scale mobilization, industries would be assured sufficient manpower to continue business with minimum disruption. Seen thus, channeling resembles a form of federally operated business insurance.

Operationally, channeling has succeeded in drawing even more sharply the lines of class in the United States. White, upper-middle-class sons of professional and managerial families, who could afford to remain in college and graduate school, have often avoided military service altogether or, at the very least, qualified for officers' posts when their means of evasion had run out. Assistant Secretary Morris has said that as of 1964 only "40% of the college graduates had served, compared to 60% of the college dropouts, 57% of the high school graduates and 50% of the non-high-school graduates." And only 25% of the men who go on to graduate school serve at all. But even these figures badly understate the far greater disparity, among men considered physically and mentally fit for military service, between those who graduate from college and those who fail to complete high school.[4] There are other lines sharply drawn by channeling. Sons of men in specialized trades can follow their fathers as apprentices into unions and thus into deferrable jobs as electricians, construction craftsmen, or tool-and-die makers. But the high-school graduate who wants to tinker with cars; the college student from a rural family who thinks he might like to try a career in sales; the kid who just doesn't know what he wants to do and thinks that a year of trying a few things would help him decide; or the student committed to social change who wants to organize welfare recipients—these will receive the President's "Greetings." As for black Americans, there are in Vietnam's rice paddies twice as many proportionately as in the American population; only the bitter fact that many young blacks were rejected from the Army because of inadequate education or poor health has kept the proportion from being four to one.

By the time the draft law came up for renewal in mid-1967, two factors urged the President and Congress toward some action. Hostility toward the draft had kept pace with the war's increasing unpopularity, and channeling's way of sending mainly the sons of the poor to war had come to be seen as anything but accidental. Some of the stir about the character of draft boards succeeded in forcing the retirement of overage members and the addition of token Negroes. The new law and subsequent rulings by the Executive branch seemed to be a serious attempt to prevent the parleying of yearly deferments into permanent exemptions. Though Congress ensured automatic deferment to all undergraduates (and thus eliminated the punitive power of Selective Service to draft those at the bottom of a class), for example, the law appeared to open the way for an end to deferments of graduate students and those in essential industries. The new law also attempted other means to ensure that eligible men would go: for example, the permanent barring of fatherhood deferments to men who from then on took student deferments. In February 1968, after a long and agonized delay, the National Security Council did indeed announce an "end" to graduate-school deferments and suspension of the List of Critical Skills and Occupations, on the basis of which local boards had granted occupational deferments. The Channeling Memo was withdrawn, and it began to look as if the concept itself might be doomed.

But that proved far from true. Many of those who had previously been channeled into graduate study were now rechanneled into teaching, especially in urban areas where shortages of teachers were critical and schools intensely eager to hire men. In New York City, for example, the Board of Education received 61,029 applications for teacher's licenses during the 1967–68 school year, 20,000 more than the year before. Most of the new applicants were draft-age men, and a large proportion of them sons of white, middle-class families. Eighty-five percent of the participants in short-term teacher-training programs in New York City were also men under twenty-six. Consequently, the board processed some 12,000 applications for draft deferment in 1968.[5] Other men were granted deferments at the request of universities, which claimed them as necessary (cheap) labor for staffing freshman courses. Those who could afford to be channeled into college were deferred, as before; occupational deferments continued to be given by local boards with little change, but even more local iconoclasm. Even graduate-school deferments continued to be granted. The practice of calling for induction the oldest men first (starting from age twenty-six), responsible for the uncertainty and the frantic search for deferment through eight youthful years, remained as usual one of channeling's primary means of control. In short, though slightly streamlined, slightly hidden, slightly more attuned to "social needs" (teaching) rather than the business demands of industry, channeling had not fundamentally been changed. Nothing could obscure the fact either that the war continued or that those killing and dying in Vietnam were draftees.

Even as these reforms were being introduced at the beginning of the 1968 Presidential campaign, therefore, the candidates were issuing proposals for further change. And in its early months, the Nixon administration produced a new rationale for revising the draft. Though the lottery's novelty temporarily obscured its significance, the new rationale suggested changes that would, in effect, support precisely the same interests which the Selective Service System had always served. The irony could not be more evident. In early April, 1969, the Department of Defense let it be known that it had prepared legislation to institute a lottery system and to call younger men first. The plan was later presented to Congress by President Nixon and hurried through with little considered debate and, as it turned out, little consultation with Selective Service officials about its numerous bugs. The main reason offered by the Pentagon in April for its new willingness to support draft reform was, according to a story obviously inspired by sources inside the Department of Defense, to "avoid the calling into service of an undue proportion of college graduates. . . ."[6] In fiscal 1967–68 only 5% of all drafted men were college graduates; during the first half of fiscal 1968–69, the proportion had risen to 16%. According to the same news story, the Pentagon feared that the figure would rise to 33%

later in 1969–70—or about 85,000 college graduates annually. Drafting an increasing percentage of college graduates is a possibility, the story continues, that "the Pentagon regards as imposing an unfair burden on the college-graduate group."

A greater irony could hardly be imagined than that the Selective Service System, consistently unfair to the poor and the noncollegiate, should now be altered because it threatened to be "unfair" to college graduates. To be sure, this rationale, however politically apt, was somewhat disingenuous. For the military has not only preferred more malleable nineteen-year-olds, but it has recently had excessive trouble with some college intellectuals. Thus its own preferences in fact meshed with the desires of the powerful segment of American society that sends its children to college. The result was the lottery of December 1, 1969.

Like other "reforms" of the draft, the lottery changed far less than its promoters claimed. The system of deferments on which channeling is based remains. A man can still escape the draft if he can afford to step from deferment to deferment, undergraduate to graduate to occupation. The lottery system was touted as considerably reducing the uncertainty from which men suffered by making it clear that those among the first third of the numbers chosen would most likely be selected and that those in the last third would most likely escape. In fact, the lottery *increases* what the Channeling Memo calls "the pressure—the threat of loss of deferment" on those men in the first and middle thirds. For they must either stay in colleges or find jobs that will defer them—or prepare at once for Vietnam. Moreover, the lottery mechanism seems not even to have conferred some degree of immunity upon men in the last third of the drawing, since it is now clear that some boards and some states (because of the peculiar machinery by which local boards report month to month on how many men are available) will run through most or the entire list of 366 birthdays. Most important of all, any man whose number comes up during the year of his eligibility will continue to be eligible up to age twenty-six; he will enter the pool of draftable men at any time that he may lose his deferment. He will be, even as others were before the lottery, subject to the "club of induction" for seven years. He will be channeled no differently from all those who have gone before him. Thus, the main impact of the "reform" seems what the Pentagon thought desirable back in April, 1969: by ending the practice of drafting older men first, to reduce the proportion of college graduates drafted at all.[7]

But channeling would not be different even were every physically fit man from a well-to-do, college-oriented family to be drafted, and the burdens of military service to fall, like Los Angeles smog, on rich and poor, clever and ignorant alike. Our objections to channeling do not arise simply from its inequities, nor are they based on its procedures. We object to the fact that it has been permitted to work at all. Channeling tells us a great deal about the class-bound, authoritarian United States and about the war between the young and the old.

The Channeling Memorandum provided two infuriating insights for young people: first, they saw a repulsive view of American social ideals; and second, they felt the indignity of the draft to their own persons and lives. One sentence perhaps more than any other summed up the memo's message: "The psychology of granting wide choice under pressure to take action is the American or indirect way of achieving what is done by direction in foreign countries where choice is not permitted." It is, of course, naïve of young people to regard any nation-state, including their own, as unique in goals or virtues. But young Americans have been, no less than in the older and happier days about which we hear, just so naïve. They had seen their country's role in the world as that of a disinterested and benign policeman —a view still encouraged by official rhetoric. And they had believed that American domestic institutions were organized to foster creative individuality. Their experience of these institutions—in school, with the police, and with the draft board—may have suggested, as we are suggesting, something different. But on the whole, it was possible to attribute the failures of institutions, or of the society, to eliminate blotches like racism, to accidents of history or defects of personality.

Even Carl Oglesby, while president of SDS in 1965, asserted: "I deeply believe in my country as much as President Johnson says he does." Oglesby said that his objective was to get the United States "to stop practicing things, all over the world, that are contrary to its greatness, contrary to what Thomas Jefferson believed, contrary to what the American Revolution was all about. I believe America has become warped by a few powerful government people who fundamentally do not believe in or practice the ideas upon which our country was founded."[8]

To be sure, within a couple of years Oglesby had developed a rather different analysis: "The scope of American commerce now being global, the scope of the federal government must also be global. . . . Imperialism is the national public concomitant of private commercial expansionism; big business makes big government, and multinational business globalizes it. And as business and government cooperate to rationalize and dominate the world political economy, chanting 'peace, law, order' just as the old Romans did, so they cooperate to rationalize and dominate the domestic political economy. The ultimate demand is for nothing short of total order, total control—the total state of the total world. . . . The totalitarian society is the logical interior of the imperialist state."[9] Many young people began politically where Oglesby began. For them it was a unique and startling experience to be told in an official government manual that the only distinction between America and "foreign" totalitarian societies was our "indirect way," and that the "flaws" of the draft were, in fact, policy. One major ingredient in changing the thinking of young people about the role of the United States in the world was the role of channeling in their lives.

As other elements of the Selective Service System have been illuminated, the draft's alleged "flaws" have been more clearly revealed as policy. Kenneth M. Dolbeare and James W. Davis, Jr., recently published an extensive study of the system's 4,100 local boards, complaints about which have usually been blamed on the system's inefficiency.[10] Dolbeare and Davis use as title General Hershey's characterization of draft boards as *Little Groups of Neighbors,* and their study bears out what many young registrants instinctively believed about their boards—precious little neighborliness to be found there. Contrary to General Hershey's assertions, the authors find that local boards "are by and large not 'neighbors' in any representative sense, they are *not* in contact with registrants, they are *not* known or widely trusted by local citizens. . . ." Local boards, with discretionary powers, they conclude, may be a "principal reason for public *disapproval* of conscription." Yet of course the system of local boards has survived repeated attacks. Why, then, the authors query, do local boards seem likely to endure?

The backgrounds and attitudes of board members provide much of the explanation. The Marshall Commission Report showed, for example, that most draft-board members are professionals, managers, or proprietors, aside from being male, white, and past fifty, if not sixty or seventy. Only 9 percent said they were blue-collar workers (though about half the males employed in the United States have blue-collar jobs), and only 1.3 percent were black (though blacks constitute about 11 percent of the population and an ever higher proportion of the active armed forces). The authors of *Little Groups of Neighbors* also suggest that board members display some enthusiasm for using the draft to reinforce community norms regarding regular employment and marriage, not to speak of protest and "patriotism." In short, local draft boards, far from representing a cross-section of the community in class, race, sex, attitudes, or age, are drawn from, and express the priorities of, what has come to be called the local "power structure." Seen thus, their unrepresentativeness and often—especially from the point of view of young people—arbitrary procedures are no accident, no series of flaws. Rather, according to Dolbeare and Davis, the implications of all these findings are clear: "Local boards cannot be the source of public acceptance of conscription, for local boards are neither known nor approved—and not even the knowledgeable people approve of their discretionary powers. But local boards *may* be the price of acquiescence from that politically powerful segment of the middle class that itself mans and controls the local boards. In this case, of course, the local-board system boils down to a cynical grant of power to the middle class to draft the sons of the working class in the least visible manner possible."

Not only is the draft thus "class conscious," but the fundamental assumption of "channeling" *is* authoritarian: that the state has the right, and indeed the duty, to organize and arrange the lives of individuals "in the national interest." As the Channeling Memo maintains, "This brings with it the ever increasing problem of how to control effectively the service of individuals who are not in the armed forces." Or, as General Hershey said on another occasion, "We have a deferment to encourage somebody to do something that the nation wants. In other words, there's no point in deferring people to do nothing or to prepare themselves for something that the nation doesn't need."[11] But further, the Channeling Memo identifies the "national interest" primarily with the preparation for and making of war: "The club of induction has been used to drive out of areas considered to be less important to the areas of greater importance in which deferments were given, the individuals who did not or could not participate in activities which were considered essential to the defense of the Nation."

In the process of fulfilling this predominant national interest, some other presumed national goals might be subverted: "Even though the salary of a teacher has historically been meager, many young men remain in that job, seeking the reward of a deferment." General Hershey is fond of pointing out that from 1949–50 to 1961–62 the number of teachers increased by 750,000, and the proportion of men among them from 29% to 37%.[12] "I know of no dramatic increase in pay or other attraction," he told the House Armed Services Committee, "to account for this increase, especially among men." The availability of deferments had "some influence," he suggested. Indeed, we will never know what contribution Selective Service has made in helping keep teachers' salaries low and in maintaining the low status of the profession by funneling channeled labor into it; nor the effects on the morale of the young teacher forced by government policy to see his job as a haven for dodging the draft. It is obviously true—though Selective Service perhaps exaggerates—that channeling has worked to keep men in school, to "drive" them into work related to national defense or into jobs whose pay and working conditions could not have been attractive without the bait of deferment. In these respects channeling has "succeeded." Yet the cost of such success has been disenchantment, cynicism, a fostering not of a sense of duty or service, let alone patriotism—about which the Channeling Memo likes to speak—but of a mentality of evasion. Without encouraging men to evade the draft, channeling could not work.

Even if one argued that the Channeling Memo might be regarded as a useful corrective to misplaced idealism, that argument would explode into further anger. Young people knew, let us say, that American society was not really what they had read about in civics texts; they were ready to give up whatever childish illusions still remained in their heads and hearts. But few or no young Americans knew the means or the extent to which their own lives were controlled and manipulated. In that discovery lay the outrage. College students and others had once viewed achieving a deferment as a triumph over the system—American individuality and ingenuity at work. Now their work had to be understood simply as their performance of the system's script. Evasion, it turned out, was mostly compliance. And some aspects of the compliance, furthermore, caught the college student in ironies guaranteed to inflame his impotent rage. He realized that the deferment of a college student meant, more than likely, that his place in the draft quota would be taken by someone less privileged and possibly black. Thus, while he sallied forth from college to demonstrate for the rights of blacks, he was, by remaining a student, cooperating with a system which produced a death rate among blacks in Vietnam double or more their proportion in the population. On the other hand, dropping out of college did little to change the system either, for the college dropout would be driven up the channel into the Army or, for a specially conscientious minority, down the even narrower channel to jail, or out of the system into exile. It rapidly became clear that you *could not* by any means "beat" the system within its own terms.

Nor did it leave you alone in privacy. It demanded some sacrifice of conscience or of self-interest. You could avoid conscience or rationalize interest, but you could not hide from channeling. Thus, many young people who might otherwise have pursued private desires found unavoidable a "confrontation" with the draft and the war it supported. They did not, in this light, seek out the Pentagon to "confront" it. The "warmakers" sought them out, even in the most private recesses of their college rooms. And increasing numbers have decided, thus confronted and hemmed in by channeling, that their only recourse was to challenge the system itself, in jail or out, to work for fundamental, radical change in U.S. society. Here, for example, is Tom Gardner's account of why the "probable threat of induction," should he drop out of college, made him do just that. He offers three reasons: first, the example of a "best friend"; second, the moral integrity of noncooperators; and then, "The third factor, probably the decisive one, was my strong personal resentment and rebellion against the idea of some distant group of old men presuming to control my life. I grew up believing in democracy and the sanctity of the individual conscience—you know, Thomas Paine, Jefferson, Adams, Thoreau, Jesus Christ, etc. (or, by antithetical example, Adolph Eichmann)—and it was just too late for all those old people who taught me those things to reverse themselves and tell me: 'Forget all that conscience stuff, don't think, just follow orders—kill, kill,

kill!' Not only was I so much of a Christian, American, 'democrat' that I wouldn't let them order me to kill a stranger, but I also didn't think that they should be able to force me to go to college."[13]

The language of the Channeling Memo, moreover, reinforced similar discoveries about other institutions. It pictured young men as "products" of the draft's "processes" of delivering manpower. Its passive constructions—like "considered essential"—removed to a remote and unseen authority the fundamental decisions affecting men's lives. The language revealed a reality parodied earlier in some of the slogans and songs produced by the Berkeley Free Speech Movement: "I am a student: do not fold, spindle, or mutilate." Universities have come under increasing criticism, even from their own faculties, for treating students precisely as products to be processed for the market. As we will indicate in chapters that follow, the idea of channeling clarified the operation of similar systems of control and processing that characterize other institutions that affect young people.

The Channeling Memo has also become a social touchstone against which young people are measuring the character of institutions controlling their lives. Students' response to a recently proposed Berkeley Academic Plan provides a case in point. Designed chiefly by science and engineering professors and administrators, who excluded students from decision-making processes, the plan proposes to manipulate requirements and counseling in order to reduce the number of students majoring in social studies and humanities and increase enrollments in science and engineering programs. Responding to the plan, the students quote first from the (revised) Channeling Memo: "Selective Service processes do not compel people by edict as in foreign systems to enter pursuits having to do with essentiality and progress. They go because they know that by going they will be deferred." Then the students comment about "one of the major philosophies behind the policy of student and occupational deferments":

. . . to force people to comply with a given conception of the society or with a given governmental desire while still maintaining the impression that free choice and full freedom obtain. It is obvious that by making certain choices more difficult to implement than others, people other than those of extremely strong will can be made to cooperate with the defined social interests.

The Academic Plan serves the same purpose. . . . In truth, the Academic Plan nowhere states that the individual student is to be limited in his free choice. It merely insures that not too many of those individuals will be able to exercise it. Spurious definitions of free choice, indeed, abound in the literature of mass administration.[14]

The draft, and its system of channeling, have by themselves been major concerns of young people in America. But perhaps as important, they have enforced immediately and personally a perspective on other American institutions. They have cast a hard light on schools, courts, and marriage, and in that light young Americans have increasingly come to see such institutions as coercive, class-biased, and manipulative. Thus, if the draft has supplied the manpower for America's war on Vietnam, it has also supplied the impetus for the student movement's attack on American institutions.

Notes

[1] Burke Marshall, et al., *In Pursuit of Equity: Who Serves When Not All Serve?* Report of the President's National Advisory Commission on Selective Service (Washington: U.S. Government Printing Office, 1967). Mark Clark, et al., *Civilian Advisory Panel on Military Manpower Procurement Report to the Committee on Armed Services* (Washington, D.C.: U.S. Government Printing Office, 1967). Bruce K. Chapman, *The Wrong Man in Uniform* (New York, 1966). Jean Carper, *Bitter Greetings* (New York, 1967). We published (with Richard Flacks) two essays that spring, some of which we draw on here: "Draft Reform and Draft Resistance," *Liberation*, March, 1967; and "The Draft: Dodging the Issues," *The New York Review of Books*, April 6, 1967.

[2] The first public revelation of the existence and character of this memorandum was by Peter Henig in "On the Manpower Channelers," *New Left Notes*, January 20, 1967.

[3] The basic guidelines were set out in a "List of Currently Critical Occupations," issued by the Secretary of Labor, and a "List of Currently Essential Activities," issued by the Secretary of Commerce. Both lists were compiled after consultation with the Interagency Advisory Committee on Essential Activities and Critical Occupations, on which Selective Service was represented, and which consulted with professional and private organizations. For fuller details, see Leslie S. Rothenberg, *The Draft and You* (New York: Anchor Books, 1968), pp. 165–68.

[4] Secretary Morris' figures are not corrected for factors like physical and mental fitness. The vast majority of men who did not complete high school did not serve because they were rejected for physical or mental deficiencies; some significant proportion of them actually wished to enter military service, often to escape their lives of poverty. On the other hand, the rejection rate for mental or physical defects among college graduates is much lower: it is very likely that most of the 60% of college graduates who did not serve in the military were qualified but managed to avoid the draft through deferments. Precise figures are difficult to acquire, but estimates can be made on the basis of studies like those of Bernard D. Karpinos, statistics in Selective Service reports, and available profiles of high-school and college graduates. See, for example, Sol Tax, ed., *The Draft* (Chicago, 1967), pp. 35–53, 312–13. Secretary Morris' figures also do not reveal the proportions of men assigned to combat as distinct from those assigned to jobs requiring the kinds of skills or contacts developed in college.

[5] *The New York Times*, January 7, 1969.

[6] See Charles W. Corddry, "Draft-Law Revisions Sought Now," in the Baltimore *Sun*, April 9, 1969.

[7] One sidelight of the drawing helped to underscore the fundamental indifference of the Selective Service System, however brushed up, to the lives of young people. Seventeen days in December were among the first 30% of those chosen; and days in November and October were similarly drawn disproportionately. A University of Michigan astronomer has calculated that

the chances of the drawing having come out this way if it were truly random was 100,000 to 1. What appears to have happened was that capsules for January were put in the drawing bowl first, February second, and so on up to December. Then the capsules were mixed—but not very well. And the result is that men born in December find themselves much more vulnerable than men born in January.

[8]Quoted in Chandler Brossard, "The Draft 'Resisters' in 1965," *Look,* December 28, 1965, p. 16.

[9]Carl Oglesby, *Containment and Change* (New York, 1967), p. 160.

[10]*Little Groups of Neighbors: The Selective Service System* (Chicago, 1968). A useful summary of part of this book is contained in *Trans-Action,* VI (March, 1969), pp. 34–37, 51.

[11]On the WBZ, Boston, radio program "Contact," March 27, 1968, quoted in *The Resistance,* April 3–15, 1968, p. 4.

[12]The proportion of male high-school teachers had leaped by 1966 to 54%, a statistic for which women may someday show their gratitude to General Hershey, since teaching is one of the few careers nominally open to women.

[13]Quoted in *We Won't Go,* ed. Alice Lynd (Boston, 1968), p. 5.

[14]Student Committee to Research the Academic Plan, "The Berkeley Academic Plan: A Critical Analysis," *The Daily Californian Weekly Magazine,* Vol. 4 (May 6, 1969), pp. 7–10.

8

Schools in America— The Making of Jet Pilots

The plane wrote another word: SPEED . . .
"How high you reckon he is?" Bigger asked.
"I don't know. Maybe a hundred miles; maybe a thousand."
"I could fly one of them things if I had a chance," Bigger mumbled
reflectively, as though talking to himself.
Gus pulled down the corners of his lips, stepped out from the wall,
squared his shoulders, doffed his cap, bowed low and spoke with mock
deference:
"Yessuh."
"You go to hell," Bigger said, smiling.
"Yessuh," Gus said again.
"I could fly a plane if I had a chance," Bigger said.
"If you wasn't black and if you had some money and if they'd let
you go to that aviation school, you could fly a plane," Gus said.
For a moment Bigger contemplated all the "ifs" that Gus had
mentioned. Then both boys broke into hard laughter, looking at each
other through squinted eyes.

Richard Wright, *Native Son*

"If you could be any of these things you wanted, which would you want to be?" When sociologist James S. Coleman asked that question of a cross-section of high-school students, almost a third (31.6 percent) of the boys said they wanted to be jet pilots. The only category to score higher was "nationally famous athlete," a perfectly reasonable result, since the most glamorous kids in high school are often athletes.[1] Coleman and others have taken these figures as evidence of the "failure of the schools," since the vocational areas "that students identified as relevant are not shared by the conventional educational process."[2] But one might with equal justice conclude that the students are remarkably well tuned in to schools in the United States; that the jet pilot, streaking over the Vietnamese countryside, is the logical, magnetic consummation of American education, as well as of American technology. In this chapter, we wish to explore these images—the frustrated yearnings of Bigger and Gus, the aspirations of young people today and how schools ironically fulfill them: and whether the unwritten history of American education is embodied in villages like My Lai and in the terrible skies of Vietnam.

SUCCESS OR FAILURE

In American education, the name of the game is crisis. There has hardly been a time in the last 150 years when Americans were not being told that the schools were at a turning point, confronted with a crucial challenge, or entering an era of new importance. At the same time, they have forever been at the edge of failure. Indeed, one major enterprise of educators in every generation has been analyzing that failure and proposing new sets of remedies. In the 1840's, industrialization, urbanization, and immigration produced conflict and dislocation in most cities of the North. Educational innovators envisioned public high schools as the means for unifying and civilizing communities, as well as promoting economic growth and social mobility. According to Joseph White, fourth secretary of the Massachusetts Board of Education, in the high schools:

> The children of the rich and poor, of the honored and the unknown, meet together on common ground. Their pursuits, their aims and aspirations are one. No distinctions find place, but such as talent and industry and good conduct create. In the competitions, the defeats, and the successes of the schoolroom, they meet each other as they are to meet in the broader fields of life before them; they are taught to distinguish between the essential and true, and the fractious and false, in character and condition. . . . Thus a vast and mutual benefit is the result. Thus, and only thus, can the rising generation be best prepared for the duties and responsibilities of citizenship in a free commonwealth. No foundation will be laid in our social life for the brazen walls of caste; and our political life, which is but the outgrowth of the social, will pulsate in harmony with it, and so be kept true to the grand ideals of the fathers and founders of the republic.[3]

Thus, the aspirations of mid-nineteenth-century America are to be fulfilled by the schoolroom.

Similarly, Sputnik launched a cry, in the 1950's, for a new high-school curriculum to save the national honor and restore military superiority. Vice-Admiral Hyman Rickover and President James Bryant Conant of Harvard proposed more rigorous mathematics and science courses, better preparation of teachers, and special attention to the "gifted." Schools all over the land hung the slogan "Quality Education" from their flagstaffs.

In the 1960's, the focus of agitation shifted to the "disadvantaged" student, and the byword became "equality of educational opportunity." No major school system is without some special project for the children of the poor. Nor has there been any shortage of federally sponsored programs: Head Start, Follow-through, Upward Bound, NDEA Institutes, Model Cities colloquia, Titles I–IV. During the single fiscal year ending June, 1967, the federal government alone provided over one billion dollars, supposedly for educating poor children under Title I of the Elementary and Secondary Education Act. Another $100 million was authorized under Title III for experimental and model programs, many of which could be directed to the problems of the "disadvantaged." Private foundations have invested very heavily in educational innovation. And during the last year or more, dozens of books each have offered new hopes and desires to straining educational bureaucracies and a public impatient to solve the continuing and deepening "crisis."

There are a few common threads in these diverse and sometimes contradictory efforts: that the schools play crucial roles in achieving transcendent national goals, and especially in breaking the "cycle" of ignorance, joblessness, and poverty; and that the educational system has, for the most part, been failing to achieve these objectives. The goals and assumptions to which most writers on education, the Congress, and the bulk of Americans would subscribe have been stated, for example, by the Committee for Economic Development, a very influential organization of financial and corporate executives:

The well-being of individual citizens, the integrity of the nation's social institutions, the strength of the economy, and the long-term national security depend on the effectiveness of the schools. Unless schooling keeps pace with the large demands that will be made on it in the years ahead, the American people will not achieve their personal, community, and national goals. A free society must always depend on the capacity of its schools to provide the kind of education that produces rational, responsible, and effective citizens.[4]

If these are, indeed, the goals of our educational system, it has surely failed, especially in the urban ghetto. Long lines of statistics bear witness to the fact that schools in Harlem, Watts, the District of Columbia, do not impart even the most basic skills to their pupils. Nearly 81 percent of sixth-grade Harlem pupils score below grade level in reading comprehension, 77.5 percent in word knowledge, 83.3 percent in arithmetic. Often these poor and black children are two or three years behind in achievement scores,[5] and in the years since Kenneth Clark publicized these statistics, the situation has not materially improved. But, of course, defective schools are not confined to the ghettos. In the Elementary and Secondary Education Act of 1965 the failures of the schools are noted, with somewhat more down-to-earth insights about the objectives of the educational system than those posited by the Committee for Economic Development:

> A national problem . . . is reflected in draft rejection rates because of educational deficiencies. It is evidenced by the employment and manpower retraining problems aggravated by the fact that there are over 8 million adults who have completed less than 5 years of school. It is seen in the 20% unemployment rate of our 18 to 24 year olds.[6]

Surely, the proposers of the 1965 ESEA seem to be saying, that if the schools fail to prepare men for the Army and for industry, they have failed altogether.

This litany over the failure of the schools is repeated in almost every new book on the subject. Mario Fantini and Gerald Weinstein, who have had much to do with shaping the Ford Foundation's broad program of educational support, cite Kenneth Clark and the ESEA in their *The Disadvantaged: Challenge to Education.* They add their own variations on the theme: the schools have not only failed the poor and the black, but they have not taught "adult maturity" or necessary skills to many children from comfortable, middle-class homes.

. . . it becomes all too clear that our education has been severely deficient in achieving its purpose, quantitatively and qualitatively. Yet education is the only institution upon which we, as a nation, can rely to provide us with a population which has a significant proportion of truly democratic, socially oriented, dedicated adults who will contribute to our country's welfare.[7]

Thus Fantini and Weinstein join their hopes to those of Joseph White a hundred years ago, to those of the Committee for Economic Development, to those of the Elementary and Secondary Education Act. And they devote their 455 pages to strategies for helping educators achieve these presumed—and traditional—objectives.

But are the schools "failures"? If they do not accomplish the goals which educators have laid out for them, it may well be that all they need—as the CED, Congress, and Fantini and Weinstein urge— is more money, more innovation, more machines, more specialization. It may also be, however, that the stated goals of American education are false and irrelevant ones, that their grand rhetoric clouds the character and social objectives of the schools. A review of the alleged "failures" of the Selective Service System—the uncertainty it engendered, its unfairness, its apparently arbitrary and harebrained procedures—reveals features built in because they have been *necessary* to its channeling function. (See Chapter 7.) Looking at what the schools *do* rather than at what they should or might do may tell a similar story. What if the apparent "failures" of the American educational system have served necessary functions in American society? Perhaps the schools, like almost all other American institutions, have been terribly, indeed horrifyingly, successful.

Such a proposition may seem shocking, if not downright perverse, since Americans have traditionally believed in the virtues of schooling as much as in motherhood or a balanced budget. The black and Jewish communities in New York City continue to quarrel bitterly about the control of education, yet they agree about the fundamental importance of keeping children in schools. Recently, however, observing conditions in Harlem, Kenneth Clark suggested that schools function in a manner precisely contrary to their acclaimed ideals:

. . . American public schools have become significant instruments in the blocking of economic mobility and in the intensification of class distinctions rather than fulfilling their historic function of facilitating such mobility.

In effect, the public schools have become captives of a middle class who have failed to use them to aid others also to move into the middle class—it might even be possible to interpret the role of the controlling middle class as that of using the public schools to block further mobility.[8]

Although Clark's analysis of the present situation is accurate, he accepts too readily the historical claims, rather than the performance, of American education.

Michael B. Katz has compared in some detail such historical claims with what the schools really accomplished. Those promoting high schools in the nineteenth century presented them as mechanisms for achieving social mobility and economic development, for democratizing society, for eliminating class distinctions, and for producing, as Fantini and Weinstein put it more than a century later, "truly democratic, socially oriented, dedicated adults who will contribute to our country's welfare." In fact, however, as Katz shows, the innovation called high schools produced none of these goals. Few poor and working-class children actually attended, and before very long, those who did were channeled off into vocational programs "more suitable to their interests and capacities." The pressure for schools originated in response to economic growth, and there is little evidence to demonstrate that continued industrial development depended in any sense on the expansion of education. So much for democratization, mobility, and development.

This is not to say that the public educational system had *no* functions. On the contrary, some of its achievements seem to have been inversely related to the claims made for it. For the middle-class children who made up the bulk of high-school students, schools helped to maintain their status and position in the community. Schools were an entrée for boys into business (though they taught little of major importance to enterprise) and for girls into teaching. And teaching, as Katz says, "was undoubtedly the most attractive vocational goal for the middle-class girl who wanted to earn some money because all the other occupations populated by large numbers of females were manual, arduous, and decidedly lower-class."[9] The public high school also served middle-class parents, because "they could spread among the population at large the [fiscal] burden of educating their children."[10] Thus, far from pulling down "the brazen walls of caste," as Joseph White had asserted, the high schools reinforced them.

Though the schools did not function to the advantage of poor and working-class children, they did not ignore them. Katz quotes a contributor to the *Massachusetts Teacher* who explained the value of education to business: "the habit of prompt action in the performance of the duty required of the boy, by the teacher at school, becomes in the man of business confirmed; thus system and order characterize the employment of the day laborer."[11] And a Lowell manufacturer, one H. Bartlett, insisted, Katz writes, that

> Workers with more education possessed "a higher and better state of morals, [were] more orderly and respectful in their deportment, and more ready to comply with the wholesome and necessary regulations of an establishment." Perhaps most important, "in times of agitation, on account of some changes in regulations or wages, I have always looked to the most intelligent, best educated and the most moral for support." . . . The educated, in short, were seen as company men.[12]

In their conscious attempt to impose personal habits of restraint, self-control, diligence, promptness, and sobriety on their students, particularly those from "loose," "shiftless" (or disadvantaged) backgrounds, school men served the desires of business for a disciplined and acquiescent work force. In this sense, too, schools served the dominant interests of the middle-class business community; and, not surprisingly, such businessmen and industrialists were among the major promoters of school reforms.

This history is important, for it contradicts the easy assumptions we have usually made about the uniform virtues of schooling. And it suggests that earlier "failings" in the educational system can better be understood as contradictions between the professed objectives of educators—their ideology—and the real social and economic forces to which the educational system was in fact responding. Such forces continue to operate: a recent Harris poll shows that 62 percent of parents questioned thought that in school "maintaining discipline is more important than student self-inquiry."[13] A *Life* reporter, commenting on the study, wrote that "the parents in the *Life* poll know exactly what *they* want from the schools: 'Teach the kids to understand our existing values,' they say; 'disipline them to conform. . . . They think the schools should keep the children passive and disciplined, and provide them with the tools that lead to college and a job."[14] We wish, therefore, to turn to some of the salient features of our educational system today, and to see whether its organization, curriculum, and methods continue, not to "fail," but to succeed in serving these by now traditional objectives.

TRACKING CLASSES

In 1927 many Americans were troubled about their society. Morals seemed to be disintegrating, crime increasing. Indeed, some felt there was a "legal bias in favor of the criminal." He "is petted and pampered and protected to a degree which makes the punishment of crime relatively rare." Educators were quick to rise to this social crisis. They urged their fellow Americans to look to the schools to train citizens not to "set themselves against the state." After all, there was "no other organized force which aims primarily at citizenship and at the same time represents the state." Schools could, moreover, satisfy the demands of industry for "the type of help that knows something, that has social graces arising from extended social experience" of the sort provided by high schools. There was one problem, however: how to keep the children *in* school? Many dropped out because their main experience in the classroom was one of frustration. A new way of organizing schools had to be found that would not forever be confronting those most in need of schooling with failure, that might more fully "individualize" their instruction so as more efficiently to prepare children for the kinds of jobs they would get. The way was "ability grouping."

> Ability grouping in the junior high school is to be defined as the classification of the pupils of the school into groups which, within reasonable limits, are homogeneous in ability to perform the kind of task which confronts those pupils in the classroom. It is not a social segregation. It is not a caste stratification. It is not an attempt to point out those who are worth while and those who are not. It is not a move to separate the leaders from the followers.[15]

Despite the best intentions of its promoters, ability grouping—or tracking, or streaming, as it is variously called—has unfortunately become all that they asserted it would not. What it has *not* been is either a means of keeping children in school or of improving their performance while they attend.

In Washington, D.C., for example, where an elaborate track system reached far down into the elementary schools, 54 percent of the classes of 1965 and 1966 dropped out before graduation. The most extensive and careful study of ability grouping, moreover, concludes "that ability grouping, *per se,* produces no improvement in achievement for any ability level and, as an administrative device, has little merit."[16] The study indicates further that children may learn better in strongly heterogeneous groups. Arthur W. Foshay, who wrote the Foreword, suggests also that evidence from Sweden and England "raises the dark possibility that ability grouping functions . . . as selective deprivation."[17] Tracking may actually *prevent* children from learning, the study indicates, because "teachers generally underestimate the capability of pupils in lower track classes, expect less of them, and consequently the pupils learn less."[18] None of this is surprising, since teachers generally concentrate on students who respond. Buy why, then, if tracking has not succeeded in keeping most kids in school and has succeeded in creating for those lower-tracked kids the "self-fulfilling prophecy" that they won't learn anything in school—why, then, has it persisted for more than forty years?

In the first place, tracking is with respect to schools what channeling is with respect to the draft. Its function is identical, namely, the control of manpower "in the National Interest." In democratic societies like that of the United States, individuals are encouraged to believe that opportunities for social advancement are unlimited; such beliefs are part of the national mythos, and also necessary to encourage young people to achieve and get ahead. Yet opportunities are, in fact, limited. Not everyone with the talent can, for example, become a scientist, industrial manager, engineer, or even a college professor; the economy has greater needs for technologists, technicians, white-collar workers, not to speak of men on production lines. It has been estimated that industry demands five semiprofessionals and technicians to enable every professional to function.[19] There must be "valves" which can help to control the flow of manpower into the economy. "Tracking" is one of those important valves; it helps ensure that the American work force is not "overeducated" (as has been the case, for example, in India, where there are far too few jobs "suitable" for college graduates). It also helps to ensure that unpopular industries, like the Army, or less prestigious occupations, like sanitation worker, are supplied with manpower.

Indeed, sociologist Theodore Caplow has argued that:

> the principal device for the limitation of occupational choice is the education system. It does this in two ways: first, by forcing the student who embarks upon a long course of training to renounce other careers which also require extensive training; second, by excluding from training and eventually from the occupations themselves those students who lack either the intellectual qualities (such as intelligence, docility, aptitude) or the social characteristics (such as ethnic background, wealth, appropriate conduct, previous education) which happen to be required.[20]

Tracking is one of the educational system's major techniques for thrusting forward students with the necessary qualities of school-measured intelligence, docility, background, and the rest; and for channeling the others into "appropriate" slots. James Bryant Conant is quite explicit about this practice. "I submit," he writes in *Slums and Suburbs,* "that in a heavily urbanized and industrialized free society, the educational experiences of youth should fit their subsequent employment." Accomplishing this goal in cities is difficult, Conant continues, given the limitations of guidance personnel and parental indifference; therefore, "the system of rigid tracks may be the only workable solution to a mammoth guidance problem."[21]

The "valves" of ability grouping, some economists complain,[22] have become sticky, and have slowed economic growth by limiting the flow of students with middling talent and motivation, particularly from under-class backgrounds. In fact, however, from another point of view one might argue that the valves have been operating effectively to limit the competition of the children of white, middle-class parents who, on the whole, have controlled the schools.[23] In New York City in 1967, for example, nonwhites, the vast majority poor, made up 40 percent of the high-school population; they constituted about 36 percent of students in the "academic" high schools and about 60 percent of those tracked into "vocational" high schools. In the Bronx High School of Science and in Brooklyn Tech, elite institutions for which students must qualify by examination, "nonwhites" totaled only 7 and 12 percent of the students, respectively. But the real effects of tracking can better be seen in what happens to students in the academic high schools. A majority of blacks and Puerto Ricans fill lower tracks, which lead them—if they stay at all—to "general" rather than "academic" diplomas. Only 18 percent of academic-high-school graduates were black or Puerto Rican (though they were, as we said, 36 percent of student population); and only one-fifth of that 18 percent went on to college, as compared with 63 percent of whites who graduated. In other words, only 7 percent of the graduates of New York's academic high schools who went on to college were black or Puerto Rican. The rest, for the most part tracked into non-college-preparatory programs, left school with what amounted to a ticket into the Army.[24]

The statistics for Washington, D.C., are even more striking, in part because figures are available on the basis of income as well as race and ethnic background. In the nation's capital, where in 1966 91 percent of the students were black, 84 percent of those black children were in schools *without any honors track.* In areas with a median income of $3,872 a year, 85 percent of the children were in basic or general tracks, neither college-bound; while in areas where the income was $10,374 or better, only 8 percent of the children were in the general track, and in such areas there was *no basic track at all.* Theoretically, tracking ranks students according to their ability to achieve. Yet Washington's statistics suggest that the children of the poor have less than one-tenth of the ability of the children of the well-to-do—an obvious absurdity. Indeed, tracking in Washington was more than absurd: in 1967 Federal Judge J. Skelly Wright declared that the system unconstitutionally discriminated against poor and black children and ordered it abolished.[25] But although it has officially been disbanded in the District's schools, it lingers on subtly in placement and curriculum, and more openly in the way teachers teach.

If one studies the means by which students are selected into tracks, one discovers a further layer of discrimination against the children of the poor. It is on the basis of reading scores, IQ, and other standard achievement tests—as well as teachers' recommendations

—that children are determined "slow" or "superior." Yet Herbert Kohl reports that he was able to help his students raise their reading scores from one to three years, within a period of months, simply by teaching them how to take tests. Middle-class children, Kohl points out, learn about tests early in their school careers; indeed, "a predominantly white school located less than a mile down Madison Avenue [from Kohl's Harlem school] even gave after-school voluntary classes in test preparation." But in the Harlem schools it was "against the rules" to provide copies of old tests so that the teachers could help their pupils prepare for them; Kohl had to obtain such copies from friends who taught in white, middle-class schools, where back files were kept and made available.[26] Recent studies have suggested, moreover, that the content of "standardized" tests conforms to the life experience and norms of white, middle-class children, thereby discriminating in still another manner against able children of poor or black parents.

Thus, just as the establishment of high schools in the nineteenth century promoted the interests of middle-class parents, so ability grouping has become an elaborate mechanism for insuring those same interests. In this respect the track system has joined with "the ordinary operations of educational institutions," which, deliberate discrimination aside, by themselves tend to deny poor and working-class children equal opportunities for social mobility. Experienced teachers transfer out of schools in poorer neighborhoods, seeking better-paying and less exacting assignments.[27] Schools develop studied institutional defenses of secrecy and professional mystification against criticism or even inquiry by lower-class parents. But they are, of course, much more responsive to wealthier parents, who often control P-TA's and school boards and who, in any case, schoolteachers and administrators emulate. Thus, as sociologist Howard Becker has written, "the schools, organized in terms of one of the subcultures [that of the middle class] of a heterogeneous society, tend to operate in such a way that members of subordinate groups of differing culture do not get their fair share of educational opportunity, and thus of opportunity for social mobility."[28] Which is an elaborate way of saying that schools institutionalize and maintain privilege in America.

But statistics and abstractions may obscure the lives of children trapped in what has been called "programmed retardation." A group of New York City parents, whose allegedly "difficult" children have been tracked into the "600" schools, has begun to prepare a suit to challenge the compulsory-attendance law. While the state has the right to make laws for the health, welfare, or safety of children, they claim, it has no right to subject children to a system that deprives and injures them. Their point is that tracking is not simply a neutral "valve" to control manpower flow, as our initial image might at first have suggested. Rather, tracking harms some children, depriving those we call "deprived," making them less capable, less able to reach, let alone to use, the instruments of power in U.S. society. In the light of tracking, schools become for such children not the means of democratization and liberation, but of oppression.

On the other hand, tracking is also one means of controlling middle-class students. Selective Service's "channeling" system benefits the young man who can afford to go to college, and whose culture supports both higher education and avoiding the draft if he can. Channeling helps him, however, only so long as he lives up to the draft board's standards of behavior and work. Just as the "threat of loss of deferment" drives draft registrants into college or jobs in the "National Interest," so the threat of losing privileged status within the school system drives students to fulfill upper-track, college-bound requirements. In a school in which students are tracked from, say, 12–1 down to 12–34, demotion not only would threaten a student's social position, but his entire future life. Having a child placed in a lower track is a stigma for a college-oriented family, as every principal faced with angry parents pushing to have their children in the "best" classes will testify. Moreover, entry into prestige colleges, or even into college at all, normally depends upon track and other measures of school status. Thus, though the threat, like that of channeling in the past, has been largely unspoken, it continues to push students to behave and achieve as required.

These operations of tracking and channeling (and of racial segregation, for which tracking is often an administrative substitute)[29] help to explain why, contrary to popular American mythology, this society has more and more rapidly become stratified, structured by class. Increasingly, Americans follow the occupations of their fathers or, at any rate, enter occupations of roughly the same prestige and income.[30] Level of education—which must be distinguished both from what a student has learned and from how competent he might be—is a major determinant of what kind of job he can get.[31] The more education attained, on the whole, the better the job; and, of course, the more prestigious the college, the better too. There is a direct correlation between a student's social and economic class and the likelihood that he will enter *or* graduate from college. A recent study by the Carnegie Commission on Higher Education found that children from families whose income is above the national median have *three* times the chance of getting into college that children from families below the median have. And only 7 percent of college students come from families in the bottom quarter of national income.[32] "The passage from school to college, in fact, seems to depend more upon socialization, life experience, and opportunity than upon intellective factors."[33] The track system provides a formal basis for translating these class-based factors into academic criteria for separating those students who will drop out; from those whose diplomas will not admit them to college; from those who will be able to enter only two-year or junior colleges; from the lucky few in the honors classes who will go on to elite institutions and to graduate or professional schools. Thus while tracking may assure the "failure" of under-class students, as a system it allows the schools to "succeed" in serving middle-class interests by preparing their children to fill the technological and professional needs of corporate society.

In several cities during the past few years, as the contradictions between systems of tracking and the rhetoric of social mobility have become especially apparent, some groups have begun to pressure for the abolition of tracking and, others in the meantime, for "open" admissions to colleges. It is clear enough to students and their parents that there are fewer jobs available for young men who have not completed high school or who have emerged from "basic" or other lower tracks. Jobs requiring no secondary education have decreased 25 percent in the past ten years; and white-collar workers, who made up 15 percent of the work force in 1900 and 28.5 percent in 1940, will make up about 48 percent in 1970. Schools with tracking systems have not been particularly responsive to a job market changed by automation and "upgrading" (an economists' term for saying that you now need more educational credentials to get the same level of job). Manpower specialists, often writing under the auspices of major foundations, have therefore called on school systems to change their practice so that their products will suit a modernizing industrial economy.[34] But of course, the pressure to maintain a system segregated by class has not abated.

The clash between those upholding tracking and those wishing to end it has taken particularly dramatic forms in several cities. In Washington, D.C., for example, tracking was a primary issue in the battle over former Superintendent Carl Hansen's job. In New York City, the issue of whom the schools will serve has been fought in terms of community control. Experiments designed to make schools more responsive to the needs of blacks and Puerto Ricans by giving them direct control over the education of their children through the creation of community school boards have been funded by the Ford Foundation and supported by politicians, including Mayor Lindsay and Governor Rockefeller, sensitive to the changing needs of large industry. In opposition to community-controlled decentralization, the New York Teachers' Union and the bulk of the white, middle-class electorate correctly understand the demand for community control as a demand that the schools help, rather than prevent, the children of poor blacks and Puerto Ricans from competing with their own children. Jewish teachers remember their battle against WASPs and Irish Catholics entrenched in the schools before them. Odd alliances between the Ford Foundation and the Ocean Hill-Brownsville local board, on the one hand, and liberal Jewish and conservative Italian communities, on the other, as well as the bitterness of the struggle in New York City suggest how fundamental are the social and economic stakes at issue in the control of schools.

The issue is also powerful and divisive for higher education. Encouraged by U.S. society to believe that young people can rise to the top, whatever their race or class, blacks, Chicanos, Puerto Ricans with new conscious pride, and some working-class white students are beginning to press into colleges. Higher education in the United States has had to manage an elaborate and delicate technique for diverting many of these students from goals toward which they have been taught to aspire, but which a stratified society cannot have them all reach. "Cooling" them "out," the term openly used in higher education and now beginning to become as familiar to students as "channeling," means that certain students are deliberately and secretively discouraged from aspirations middle-class youth take for granted. Working-class students are tracked into second-class or "junior" colleges, "cooled out" and counseled into substitute curricula (a medical technician's program rather than a premedical course), or, if they get to a university, programmed for failure in large "required" courses.[35]

California's three-tiered system of higher education has provided an important model for other states: the "top" eighth of high-school graduates may be admitted to the university system, the "top" third to the state colleges; the rest are relegated to what one writer has described as "those fancied-up super high schools, the local two-year community colleges.'"[36] Factors closely related to race and economic class—students' high-school track, grades, and College Board scores—determine placement into a particular level of higher education, though the fees students pay are relatively similar wherever they may go in the state.[37] Like tracking in high schools, state-subsidized higher education channels students into distinctly inequitable systems. In Maryland, for example, the average per-pupil expenditure during fiscal year 1966 was $802 in community colleges, $1,221 in the state colleges, and $1,724 (excluding research funds) in the University of Maryland.[38] Another significant discriminatory index is the relative teaching load of faculties: at the University of Maryland, an English professor teaches three courses, at state colleges four, and at community colleges five. Theoretically, at least, university students are taught by professors with better credentials, higher salaries, and lighter teaching loads than at state or community colleges. It is not surprising, therefore, as Todd Gitlin has put it, that from the university campuses come "high professionals and managers for the great corporations. At the bottom, the two-year junior colleges take on all comers, and process them into clerks, punch-card operators, foremen—the dregs of the white-collar labor force."[39]

But it is not only that the student attending a junior college will have far less public money spent on his education than the student attending Berkeley, Michigan, or the University of Maryland. It is rather that tracking at public colleges also functions to benefit the children of the rich at the expense of the children of the poor. Patricia Cayo Sexton has stated the case: "in general the more money a student's parents make, the more money will be spent on his education, despite some efforts at public 'compensatory' expenditures for the disadvantaged."[40] In New York City, for example, tuition-free colleges with "'high standards' . . . have . . . subsidized many middle-income students and virtually excluded most impoverished ethnic groups." "Low college tuition," Mrs. Sexton writes, "offers few opportunities to lower-income students if entrance 'standards' are too high to hurdle." Significantly, her statistics bear out the relationship between income and admission: at the University of Michigan, only 25 percent of the fathers of entering freshmen had less than a college education, only 4.8 percent less than a high-school diploma; consequently, only 1.8 percent of the students were from families with incomes under $4,000.[41] The circular process is obvious: just as the economic class of a student's family determines his admission to a particular college or university in the first place, so does his placement at that college determine his future. Indeed, economy is destiny![42] Given the process of "upgrading" jobs, one might find suitable the image of a squirrel in a circular cage: the faster he runs, the more firmly does he remain bound to his position. While the admission of working-class students to community colleges may seem to be serving their desire for upward mobility, in fact it may barely be keeping the lid on potentially explosive campuses.

For demonstrations throughout the nation during the spring of 1969 arose from students' increasing awareness that tracking, and its methods of cheating and controlling the poor, has been translated into new campus forms. Demands for "open admissions" of black and third-world students, prominent first at San Francisco State College, attempt to strike at the heart of the tracking system by effectively negating the streaming process of earlier school years. Students at State, at City College in New York, and elsewhere, in lengthy strikes and demonstrations, have first paralyzed the institution, then divided it irrevocably on principles similar to those we have described with relation to schools. In the official catalog of San Francisco State, a passage claims that the curriculum ought to satisfy "existing student interests" and "the technical and professional manpower requirements of the State."[43] As we proposed in a previous chapter, interests of students and those of manpower specialists often diverge fundamentally: they are obviously most divergent with respect to working-class students' aspirations for the alleged room at the top and industry's needs for a highly differentiated work force.[44]

Can the track system survive this new, better-informed, and

deeply outraged onslaught of college students? The "valves" of tracking in high school may be sticky, at once denying both reasonable opportunity to poor and black students as well as better-trained manpower to industry. But the demand for dividing the work force by some tracking mechanism remains. To be sure, it doesn't much matter, at least abstractly, to the corporation manager just *who* fills what slots—so long as young people are channeled and trained to fill them. In this respect, the need for a class-based track system diminishes. But a particular John D. Executive—not to speak of Jack Salesman—wants to maintain *his* privilege for *his* kids. Thus the pressure to maintain the present social and class divisions has hardly diminished. Colleges are, on the one hand, pressed from below by poor, black, and radical students to end discriminatory admissions practices. On the other hand, they are pressed from above by politicians, trustees, and contributors to "maintain standards," not to "capitulate to the demands of demonstrators."[45] Implicitly, they are of course urged to maintain the present system of class and economic privilege embodied in those "standards."

In March, 1969, Rutgers University agreed to an "open admissions" policy for disadvantaged students from the three cities in which its campuses are located. Almost at once, opposition to the program developed in the New Jersey legislature, partly because the plan would reduce the number of students not from those lucky three cities able to enter the state university. Similarly, an announcement by New York City's Board of Higher Education that it would attempt to implement an "open admissions policy" by 1970 was greeted with opposition by key state legislators.[46] More sensitive to the complexities of New York City's educational politics, a conservative Democratic candidate for mayor in 1969, Mario A. Procaccino, "hoped" that money could be found so that all city youths would have access to "free education," but warned "against any lowering of academic standards at the university." The New York City plan by no means envisaged an end to tracking. As initially presented, it pictured only 19 percent of graduating high-school seniors entering the senior colleges, some 26 percent going on to community colleges, and another 20 percent or more being channeled into "educational skills centers," where, presumably, they would be trained to fill vacancies in low-paying hospital, teaching-aid, and clerical positions.

The revised plan now being implemented considerably increased the proportion of high-school graduates entering senior colleges. But more ingeniously, it changed the standard of admission to the senior colleges from high-school grade-point average alone, adding as an alternative criterion a student's rank in his high-school class. Thus the student from ghetto schools, where grade-point averages are notoriously low, will be able to enter one of the senior colleges by finishing in the top half or so of his class. The competition for places in the city's colleges will thus be increased even for middle-class students, since the compromise tries to placate white, middle-class advocates of "standards" by saying to them that their children can be admitted to a senior college if they maintain high standards. At the same time, the compromise attempts to placate ghetto residents by opening the senior colleges to more of their children—those, on the whole, perhaps, with middle-class aspirations. What the plan does, rather neatly, is to turn a threatening racial and ethnic crisis into a division of students by class; it is precisely such school-maintained divisions which Americans have in the past chosen not to contest.

New York City's response to the pressure for open admissions and an end to tracking seems a likely harbinger. It shifts part of the burden of tracking upward to "education beyond high school," now available for "all who want it," and held out as a carrot for disaffected minorities. The plan expands Upward Bound and SEEK programs to permit more individuals of "high potential but weak background" to flow into higher educational streams. In short, it places the valves higher in the educational system and lets them function a bit more freely. It places the needs of the economy for a screened, differentiated, and controllable work force somewhat above the wishes of white middle-class parents that the schools perpetuate their privilege.[47] But it by no means destroys the mechanisms by which schools have maintained class privilege. Now students will be separated—according to grades and class standing—into senior college, community college, and "other" categories. Not surprisingly: for the systems of tracking are so closely tied to those who control American education and to the inner qualities of American schools (to which we must now turn), that it is hard to imagine their replacement altogether—certainly not by a system which would permit children to develop according to their own needs and abilities.

THE TEXTBOOK WORLD

At the end of the 1920's, Bessie Louise Pierce of the University of Chicago ironically reviewed current "civic attitudes" expressed by U.S. school textbook writers:

> Judging from the evidence accumulated in history textbooks, those countries are indeed fortunate, not only in material, but in spiritual matters who fall under the jurisdiction and protection of the United States. Cuba, "pest-ridden" and rescued from "chaos" in three years, was given law, order, and cleanliness by American officials. "To the amazement of the world," after this brief period, American "troops were withdrawn leaving Cubans to win their own place among the world's free people." Although the Platt Amendment somewhat limits Cuban freedom, Long confesses, yet it assures the Cubans a "security from rebellion at home and from enemies abroad."
>
> Under the protection of the United States, "though disturbed at times by temporary upheavals," Cuba, Fite believes, "has had on the whole a happy history."[48]

Those were, one might think, days of Babbittry, messianic nationalism, and self-congratulatory attitudes among Americans. But so far as school texts are concerned, things have changed very little for generations of students. Commenting recently on textbooks' basic inaccuracy, their inability to confront significant problems, and their failure to help students understand useful concepts, two designers of social-studies curricula sum up the prevailing qualities of books today:

> It is instructive to look at topics such as "Cuba" in modern elementary school social studies texts. Pre-Castro Cuba is usually presented as a happy republic which was originally set "free" from Spain by the United States. Reforms guaranteed in the Cuban constitution (e.g., "Women have the right to vote") are commonly presented as facts rather than as legal fictions. Little is said of the poverty among great masses of people. Nothing is said of the ruthless Batista dictatorship.[49]

In short, to the extent that an American's understanding of Cuba is shaped by the textbooks he is given to read in school, he will be uninformed, misled, inclined to view the role of the United States as benevolent and unimpeachable. And to the extent that such "understanding" helps shape political attitudes, those attitudes will be suspicious if not hostile toward the Cuban revolution, self-serving, and inclined to support at least the legitimacy of all U.S. interventions.

Closer to home even than ninety miles, we came across a new elementary-school social-studies text on the desk of a principal in a Washington, D.C., school, 98 percent of whose students are black. Clearly meant for an urban market, the chapters each deal with a U.S. city: Pittsburgh, Chicago, Detroit, Atlanta. We stopped to read about Atlanta: It is now, we learned, the hub of southern industry as it once had been the hub of the cotton trade; the cotton gin had worked a revolution in the production of clothing; George Washington Carver had made significant contributions to American agriculture. But nowhere in the account of Atlanta, the cotton trade, and southern life, was there a single mention of slavery! Zero. It was as if the cotton had grown itself in the green, green fields.

The omission from school texts of materials about blacks—or the insertion of stereotyped and even racist content—is by now notorious, and we will have more to say about it in Chapter 9. Similar neglect or distortion of the role of women has hardly been noticed (but see Chapter 10). In fact, one cannot name a social or controversial issue, a minority group, a historical conflict—communism, poverty, the Civil War, labor history—that school texts do not either misrepresent or omit from consideration. A well-known American historian, William L. Neumann, has described, for example, the paradoxical approach promoters of courses on communism have taken:

The combined N.E.A.-American Legion publication for teachers urges "an honest, realistic" comparison of democratic and Communist systems; the Catholic Education Association advises selection of reading materials for "factual accuracy and objectivity" . . . while a California board of education warns against teaching "a canned line of propaganda" and urges instead that students "formulate reliable value judgments through careful scrutinization" of undistorted information. . . . But in teaching about Communism the schools are reminded that the conclusions are already firmly agreed upon and that discussions can have only one acceptable ending. The American Legion resolution urges the teaching of "the elements that comprise the communist system and why they are evil." A California course outline expects it to develop in students "a permanent antipathy to all schemes which are foreign to the values which they hold to be absolute." The Catholic guide warns that Communist literature should not be made "too readily available" and urges that "indiscriminate reading of Communist literature" without teacher supervision and criticism should be discouraged.[50]

Neumann concludes that "courses about Communism are thus intended to involve an objective study of 'sin.'" In this way, anticommunism becomes a fundamental element in the American school curriculum.

At the same time, textbooks ignore or distort class conflicts in American society. A friend born and raised on the West Coast told us that when he first visited Chicago he was eager to see Haymarket Square, because it had been prominent in the city's early labor struggles, about which he had read in a novel. He asked his host, a high-school-aged cousin from a working-class family, if he could show him how to get to the square. The response was, "What do you want to go there for? There's nothing but some restaurants and old stores." The cousin had never read in his Chicago school texts of the Haymarket trial, the McCormick strike, the Knights of Labor, nor of Governor Altgeld. Which is not surprising: the 1962 edition of *The Story of the American Nation* devotes four paragraphs to the DEW (Distant Early Warning) line but never mentions Eugene Debs or Norman Thomas, let alone A. J. Muste. Another text mentions the 1937 sit-down strikes, but tells neither their location nor their connection with the automobile industry.[51] Just as black people have, on the whole, been deprived of their past, so young working-class men and women have no conceptions even of those events of the last hundred years that have helped determine how they lived, and where.

To be sure, the grosser "failings" of earlier texts—the "happy darky," the "yellow peril," the "secret combines" of workingmen—have been edited out. But the subtler stereotypes, the less obvious omissions and distortions with which such absurdities have been replaced, once more raise the question of whether "failure" is an apt description. Mrs. Pierce suggested forty years ago that textbooks revealed what "the American people want their children to remember" (p. 256). She might have added "and to ignore." Indeed, Jules Henry has argued that the omissions and misrepresentations in textbooks do not reveal the ignorance or incompetence of their authors; these are, rather, central to their true function: "By leaving out and distorting information, textbooks strive for the goal of stupidity. . . . The world is presented to children and adolescents in such a way as to prevent them from getting from school the information necessary to enable them to form an intelligent opinion about the world."[52] Such "stupidity," Henry argues, serves a social function, that of incapacitating children from putting our "complicated and specialized" culture together in their own heads in their own way. They are rather at the mercy of adults who organize the flow of history or the structures of society into patterns that maintain or serve their own special interests. Generating hostility to Cuba and support for American intervention in the Dominican Republic or Guatemala is easier if Americans believe that the United States in general and in the past "has done more for world advancement than any other nation."[53] In order to maintain white supremacy and institutional racism, it is useful that whites and blacks picture Negroes as capable only of performing menial tasks or providing entertainment. In order to uphold state police power, it is helpful that historical precedents of the illegitimate use of such power be hidden: how might people react to directives to "support their local police" if they could recollect that the police have historically been used to destroy new organizations and popular attempts to change society? The corollary of "those who do not understand history are doomed to repeat it" is that those who are deprived of history will be its victims. In this light, the question one must ask of textbooks (and later of the classroom atmosphere) is not how and why they "fail" to be useful, to engage students, to provide dependable information. Rather, one must inquire what functions their very "stupidities" serve.

With respect to English texts, that question is both particularly pertinent and difficult to answer. An extraordinarily detailed study of such texts, published in 1963 by James J. Lynch and Bertrand Evans,[54] documents their faults: vulgar content, omissions, irrelevant organization, ignorant and condescending editing. Lynch and Evans point out, for example, that in ninth-grade anthologies Ogden Nash appears twenty-two times, as compared with Walt Whitman's ten; that in tenth-grade anthologies, Sara Teasdale appears more often than Whitman; and that Tennyson, Masefield, Kipling, and Housman are the only English poets who appear frequently enough to list in statistical tables; that in eleventh-grade anthologies, which concentrate on American writers, Sara Teasdale appears thirty-seven times and Dorothy Parker twelve, but William Carlos Williams, and e. e. cummings, among others—whose poems we have often found to be highly successful with eleventh-grade students—appear too infrequently to enter the statistical tables. Or, again, instead of Shakespeare in ninth-grade readers, we find such "hit" plays as *Sorry, Wrong Number, This Bull Ate Nutmeg,* and *Juliet in Pigtails.* Or in one volume, said to include *David Copperfield,* only the first twenty-two chapters of the novel are reprinted, altered in places beyond recognition and without any indication that such bowdlerizing has taken place. Twenty percent of all material in anthologies is altered in some way, usually without indication of omissions or alterations; even Wordsworth's "Intimations" ode is presented in abridged form. Perhaps the supreme example of editorial "failure" is illustrated by a comparison of the text of Blake's "The Tiger" with an anthologized version (italics indicate alterations):

Blake's Text	*Anthology Text*
Tiger! Tiger! burning bright	Tiger, Tiger, burning bright
In the forests of the night,	In the *forest* of the night,
What immortal hand or eye	What immortal hand or eye
Could frame thy fearful symmetry?	*Framed* thy fearful symmetry?
In what distant deeps or skies	In what distant deeps or skies
Burnt the fire of thine eyes?	*Burned that* fire *within* thine eyes?
On what wings dare he aspire?	On what wings *dared* he aspire?
What the hand dare seize the fire?	What the hand *dared* seize the fire?

Such editing reflects not only incompetence, but a condescending attempt to simplify either by smoothing out alleged linguistic "abnormalities," or predigesting the material for the "children." In either case, of course, students are not allowed to learn that language reflects a living development nor that ideas may be debatable, even contradictory. Neumann traces a similar pattern in history texts that characteristically omit the controversial and emphasize consensus:

The average American high school history now excludes almost everything which might suggest that the evolution of this society has been anything but a smooth progression from colonial times to the triumph of the democratic way of life in the present. The United States becomes a make-believe land, populated by men who have freed themselves from the weaknesses of mankind. Differences over politics, economics or race never reach a point where they are not adequately adjusted by the triumph of one political party every four years in the struggle for the presidency. Only in the outside world of foreign nations and alien ideologies do differences develop which plague America.[55]

On the whole, the evidence Lynch and Evans have compiled similarly suggests that English texts are not so much inept or inconsequential as they are manipulative, deliberately discouraging intellectual and critical inquiry, substituting for it, in fact, bland pap. Lynch and Evans complain, for example, that substituting miscellaneous nonfiction, much of it by athletes, explorers, newspapermen, for "literary pieces" turns reading books into "a kind of junior *Reader's Digest*" (p. 78). But they do not seem to see, as one of the teachers they quote has suggested, that that is the point: " 'Reading in snatches prevents true learning. The complete piece of work of one author often gives a truer picture of the period than excerpts from the works of many authors. . . . The anthology conditions the pupils to *The Reader's Digest*'" (p. 515). The director of composition for a community college explained to us his preference for a freshman text consisting of many brief excerpts from essays, some of them quite serious and literary: with the excerpts, he said, you don't have to worry about the students getting involved in content, so you can concentrate on syntax and rhetoric. Beyond that recipe for keeping students from learning to write, we discover from Lynch and Evans that most high-school texts draw stories from the *Saturday Evening Post* and *Collier's,* supplemented by *Woman's Day* and *Calling All Girls* (p. 38). Training students to become uncritical readers of sentimental and simplistic short fiction and essays prepares them for mass consumption of popular magazines and for easy acceptance of such stereotypes as they purvey.

Dismayed by curricula both nonliterary in quality and trivial in content, critics like Lynch and Evans propose returning to the established classics. But to offer a choice between Milton and Teen-Topics is itself part of the problem of the English curriculum, rather than a solution, since either deprives students of the significant and serious literature currently being written in response to the problems, conflicts, aspirations, pains, and joys of the world into which he is growing. Further, the choice deprives students of an opportunity to discover their own language as an elevated and precise instrument for conveying complex ideas and feelings. Serious contemporary literature, of course, often deals with issues taboo in school—sex, race, religion—and its language challenges the ordinary limitations of teachers. Thus it is suspect, dangerous. Milton and Shakespeare, oddly, just like *The Reader's Digest* and *Calling All Girls,* are safer, perhaps just because they are more remote in language and culture from young Americans (as they were not, of course, for young Englishmen of the seventeenth century).

Needless to say, textbooks do not by themselves shape the perceptions and attitudes of students, nor has this modest sampling and brief analysis plumbed their effects. But it is worth pausing for another moment to consider the following description, from a widely used fourth-grade reader, of the Pequot Indian tribe's extermination by American Army Captain John Mason:

His little army attacked in the morning before it was light and took the Pequots by surprise. The soldiers broke down the stockade with their axes, rushed inside, and set fire to the wigwams. They killed nearly all the braves, squaws, and children, and burned their corn and other food. There were no Pequots left to make more trouble. When the other Indian tribes saw what good fighters the white men were, they kept the peace for many years.

"I wish I were a man and had been there," thought Robert.[56]

Readers can obviously decide for themselves the connections between the lesson taught to children about relations between whites and people of color, about violence and about manliness—and the barbarities of the Vietnam war. We wish only to suggest, as an introduction to the next section, that schools are organized and conducted in ways calculated to reinforce similar lessons for Americans.

THE RULE OF SCHOOLS

Among the terms that settled the series of teachers' strikes in New York during the fall of 1968 was the extension for forty-five minutes of a specific number of schooldays. Union and school administration agreed that the students would thereby "make up" time lost during the strike; and, not incidentally, the teachers would make up in overtime for lost pay. Many students, unappreciative of the opportunity afforded them in the schools, took to the streets instead to demonstrate their displeasure. One New York City policeman, talking with a reporter during the demonstrations, expressed his anger with the students. He had followed the difficult negotiations which had led at long last to a settlement, "and now he saw these hundreds of kids proving to him that they were more interested in rampaging through the streets than going back to school 'to get an education.'"[57] A few moments later, the cops charged the students—and the reporter (Joe Pilati)—clubbing whomever they could catch. "It is safe to assume," the injured reporter wrote, "that the cops knew nothing of the real resentment which the 'overtime' provisions of the settlement generated in students who understood just how little of 'an education' they had gotten in their schools before the strike. . . ." This scene—angry students, baffled and brutal police, sympathetic bystanders who get their noses broken—was repeated across the land in 1968 and 1969. By 1970, truancy had become so widespread in New York City's high schools that attendance rates had sunk to their lowest levels since 1900.[58]

In a certain sense, it is a scene appropriate to schools in America. For since the compulsory-education acts were passed, many students have been kept in school, not merely for an extra forty-five minutes a day, but for years, by the police power of the state. Like Joe Pilati's policeman, Americans have on the whole thought that was good, even those who admitted the experience as disagreeable. At the same time, there does at first seem something incongruous about policing kids into school: just what can they learn if they are kept there by clubs and cops? Our answer to that question is that students can learn precisely what the schools wish to teach. And in many respects, *what* the American educational system is designed to teach is conveyed by *how* the students are kept in school and treated there, rather than by the curriculum alone.

Teaching, whatever the presumed subject matter, conveys more than algebra or Shakespeare's plays or history. Whether or not they are conscious of their role, teachers carry into the hearts and minds of students the cultural imperatives of U.S. society (and when they deviate, they usually get fired). It is the schools' function to inculcate desired patterns of behavior, desired aspirations and attitudes: the formal term is "socialization." Since the church is no longer a potent institution, the family undependable, the schools have become the chief socializers of young people. In an essay fundamental to understanding the social function of schools, Jules Henry points out that "it is *not* primarily the message (let us say, the arithmetic or the spelling) that constitutes the most important subject matter to be learned, but the noise! The most significant cultural learnings—primarily the cultural drives—are communicated as *noise.*"[59] *Noise* is Henry's graphic term for a school's rules, the character of its cafeterias, corridors, and classrooms.

Noise includes "the competitiveness of the students, the quality of the teacher's voice ('I remember exactly how she sounded when she told me to sit down') . . . the shuffling of the children's feet" (p. 289). Noise includes, we would add, the silence of all but the teacher's voice in the classroom. Our experiences in Mississippi convinced us of the reality of Henry's theory: we practiced conducting nonauthoritarian classrooms; we taught students rather than subject matter. In fact, we were arranging for the presence—to use Henry's term—of different kinds of cultural "noise," those that might promote students' independence, activity, and growth. We described in Chapter 2 the way in which the initiators of freedom schools (and in Chapter 4, the organizers of free universities) set about deliberately to change the atmosphere and teaching methods as well as the curriculum of educational institutions. They were conscious of the fact that such matters as needing a white card to walk through the halls of a school building teach students perhaps something more memorable than mathematical formulae they may have rote-learned for a particular quiz. Countless experiences, observations, and activities, many of them below the ordinary level of consciousness, wear, as it were, grooves of habit into us, down which thenceforth we normally travel. Indeed it may take a considerable wrench—maybe a Mississippi experience—to force us out of such grooves. In the pages that follow, we will argue that the "noise" of schools is designed to furrow habitual patterns of response particularly inimical to the development of children into free, humane, and intelligent adults.

Every public school has its rules. For the most part they consist of additional "commandments": thou shalt not wear mini-skirts or dashikis; remember thy hair, to keep it short; thou shalt not smoke; thou shalt not distribute unauthorized publications; honor the front door, it is not for student use. Not all schools insist upon all such rules; some have others. Some enforce them by having vice-principals play sheriff; others have elaborate systems of supervised student courts. But the distinctions are less notable than the underlying similarities and the basic functions of such rules.

They are generally imposed upon students, on grounds varying from tradition to the immaturity of teen-agers. They are also quite arbitrary; it is hard to see why long hair or African dress might threaten the "learning climate" of one school but not another. Or why it is reasonable to allow faculty special places to smoke, while denying that privilege (or right) to students not many years their juniors (and old enough to die in war, as well as of cancer). The student who wonders "Why can't we go in the front door?" at the Bronx High School of Science expresses the same question we asked twenty years ago in different buildings. Meaningless traditions persist. Or are they "meaningless"?

All these rules appear trivial and, it would seem, unnecessary. It might, indeed, seem easier for schools to give most of them up rather than suffer the disputes required to keep them. For example, in Boston, the black students' demands to be allowed to wear African dress and organize their own student union were resisted stoutly on the grounds that permitting blacks to depart from traditional dress patterns would encourage white students to ask for the elimination of shirts and ties. So it did: some whites joined the protests by burning their ties, and before things were done the School Committee asked for a National Guard alert. A reaction, one might think, a bit out of keeping with issues of cloaks and cravats. Is public life in Boston the better for its schoolchildren having worn ties?

But no particular rule is, in fact, the issue. Particular rules and the processes of enforcement are vehicles which a school uses to transmit its "noise" to students. The message is perfectly clear: students must submit to being controlled and remaining in their place as dependents. Searching students' lockers, patrolling their open-stalled bathrooms, demanding their I.D. cards in the hallways, have little to do with a school's academic objectives, but are vital to instilling the required sorts of behavior. In this respect the school cafeteria teaches a good deal more than its classrooms, and the methods developed for cafeteria "teaching" reveal, just as class-room methods do, the character of the lessons to be taught.

> A whistle, used in conjunction with the microphone, may be used to signal students to their seats before daily announcements. If blown more than several times during the period the whistle will become ineffective. . . . Be sure the cafeteria clock is syn-chronized with the school master clock. . . . One administrator, assigned to handle chronic problem cases, should pass through the cafeteria daily, to help set a proper tone. . . .
>
> Every day must have a similar pattern from start to finish, consistent with a prearranged organizational plan. Entering the cafeteria is the first phase of the pattern. Students should form an orderly line and wait to pick up their food. Immediately have those who attempt to sneak ahead, push, or create a disturbance go to the end of the line. Do not hesitate! Act at once and the days to come will be automatically easier, once students rec-ognize that poor conduct will be dealt with firmly.[60]

Educators may disagree about whether the techniques of using the whistle, raising the voice, establishing a "manners table," in-specting for cleanliness, are inimical or essential to creating a "learn-ing climate" in the school. But the point is less the influence of the cafeteria on the "climate" outside it, than the lessons (habits) en-forced by the cafeteria experience itself. The quotation above and others we do not include suggest that the cafeteria is but one bat-tlefield of a steady war between the school staff and the students, and that what students have to learn, above anything else, is who has the power and who must obey.

That lesson has become increasingly hard to teach in today's schools, bestirred by the rise of black pride and power, by a mood of protest and doubt, and by the manifest contradiction between schools' ostensible aims and their real lessons. Policemen are now a common sight in many ghetto schools, sometimes in each hallway. "Security guards" now patrol the buildings of most high schools in New York City, and some cities have armed such guards. In a Denver junior high school, each classroom last year was graced with a blue-coat for the space of two weeks. In middle-class schools, however, the lessons of power and obedience can be taught by "indirect" methods, since getting into a good college matters to students and/

or their parents. They are vulnerable to threats—that their misbehavior will mark them as "undesirable college material." If they fail to heed warnings, they are subject to punishment—reports to colleges—that others will view as threats.

Colleges, it is clear enough, are interested in the patterns of behavior of students applying for admission. During 1969 the American Council on Education, a trade association of colleges and universities, began to prepare a profile of "protest-prone" students, which might aid admissions officers to identify and exclude potential "troublemakers" from their campuses.[61] College personnel had already been informally at work at such exclusionary policies without the council's computers. At Oberlin, for example, two students newly appointed to the admissions committee discovered annotations, made by an administrative interviewer, on the religious, sexual, and political inclinations of applicants. Among the comments was one like this:

> Here's a classic case. A National Liberation Front member. Every cliché at his grasp. Very difficult to pin down. Never a straightforward answer. Outspoken. Very factual in approach. Active in all movements. Instead of answering a question in his own words, he refers to a quote or a study or actual history. He doesn't show me much. It's an R [for reject] all the way.[62]

The University of Chicago had a similar scandal about two years ago. It doesn't take much, of course, for the word to get around to anxious high-school students that any sort of trivial rule violation, distributing underground papers, or wearing long hair or "hippie" clothes may spell doom to his chances at Oberlin or Chicago or other prestigious colleges.

In this regard the triviality of the rules is their source of strength. A lively student can hardly help running afoul of some now and again, talking instead of listening, dressing to please herself instead of the counselor. And, as Edgar Friedenberg has pointed out, in an essay on hair well known to young people:

> Trivial regulation is more damaging to one's sense of one's own dignity, and to the belief, essential to any democracy, that one *does* have inalienable rights, than gross regulation is. The real function of petty regulations like these is to convince youth that

it has no rights at all that anybody is *obligated* to respect, even trivial ones. And this, after all, is what many—I think most—American adults believe.[63]

When we went to school, uniform dress regulations in the form of white shirts or middies and dark skirts or trousers were required of us in an effort to enforce the illusion of equality. Rich and poor attended that junior high school in Brooklyn. Shouldn't they at least seem to be "equal"? Because the requirement depended on one's parents' ability to buy particular forms of shirts, skirts, and trousers, the result, as one might expect, was fraudulent except from a distance. And yet the rule prevailed, long after we had grown up, and may yet prevail. We raise this matter of dress regulations because we have heard adults say recently that if we left it to students, they'd all dress alike, regardless of economic class, regardless even of sex. The voluntary uniform would, of course, take the form of jeans, denim shirts or thick sweaters, at least at the moment. But the point is neither uniformity nor style: it is rather control. Young people have few ways to define themselves, since they do not have "work identities." They have, in fact, what most of the fuss in schools is about— clothes, hair, voices, manners.

A recent documentary film by Frederick Wiseman call *High School* sketches the enforcement of school rules that establishes the functional relationship between adults and students. We found the film a searing indictment. Rather than describe it, however, we choose to quote from a report by Fred Hechinger, educational editor of *The New York Times:*

. . . none of the teachers and administrators mean to insult the children—it is just that they do by virtue of a frightening gap between the two worlds. The intended—and effective—message is clearly that, if this gap is so wide in the placid, all-white middle-class setting, what must it be in the more volatile ghetto?

What are the values taught in the school? A bedraggled boy, who maintains that he is being punished for an offense he did not commit and that the teacher refused to hear his side of the story, is told by the dean of discipline to prove that he is a man by taking the punishment, especially since it is only an hour's detention.

When the boy, closer to tears than anger, finally agrees to

"take it" under protest, he is told: "It's time you showed a little character."

"Thoughts for the day" are presented like remnants of Victorian primers. . . .

In a dreary counseling session, a bright young thing is endlessly lectured for having "insulted" the school by wearing a short dress to a formal dance.

. . . There is a strange mixture of authoritarianism ("Don't you talk, you just listen," says the dean), blanket suspicion (in the manner students are asked to show their program cards in the hallway) and pseudo-psychology. . . .

Mr. Wiseman denies that he filmed anything that seemed extraordinarily bad, adding that he cut out much that was worse. Nor does the reaction to the film by many educators and parents indicate that they disapprove of the school. . . . After a Boston showing, Mr. Wiseman said, many parents and teachers praised the school's efforts at inculcating values and respect.[64]

Mr. Hechinger, a moderate and at times conservative critic, comes away from the film feeling that the school is an "obsolete container for modern youth." But the parents and teachers understand, it would appear, better than Mr. Hechinger that in humiliating, containing, insulting the students, the school does the job our society has established for it. That is the meaning of the "noise" to which students are steadily subjected and which Mr. Wiseman's soundtrack has faithfully reproduced.

One might argue that the classroom, not the cafeteria, hallway, or principal's office, is most important. We would agree, but only with a clear understanding of context: what can be achieved in a classroom depends in large measure on the context of school and community. The lessons of freedom ring hollow in a prison, just as do the tales of affluent America in the ghetto. It is not simply that two or three relatively "free" classrooms do not change the character of a particular school or of a school system; it is also damnably difficult even for the most well-meaning and well-trained young teacher to conduct a "free" classroom in most public schools. For the "noise" of schools forces itself into classrooms: far from countervailing that "noise," classrooms by and large explicitly reinforce it.

Recent studies document the internal character of classrooms. We quote at length from a two-year study of the Washington, D.C., school system, conducted by a team of more than a hundred researchers under the direction of A. Harry Passow of Teachers' College, Columbia University. We choose as typical of their book-length report a description of the language-arts program that in Washington, D.C., takes up much of the grade-school day:

> The striking characteristic of these classrooms was the quiet and orderliness that was everywhere apparent. . . . The bulk of the child's day seemed to be spent in a "read and recite" mode. . . . The child spent most of his day paying the closest possible attention to his teacher, following her directions, responding to her questions, and obeying her rules. The children were not encouraged to talk to one another, either formally or informally—indeed, the principal technical criticism the observers had of the language program was that it did not seem to deal with speech. And the sad fact is that in spite of all this, *the children don't really learn to read,* as the test surveys have repeatedly shown. . . .
>
> This comment is typical of many others made by the observers: "In the three grades visited the children were told what to do, how to do it, and were expected to unquestioningly follow the teachers' directions. The children sang when instructed to do so, chorused responses when given recognized signals, and worked on written assignments, copying exercises from the chalkboard. The children spent most of the day writing at their desks, rarely speaking except in chorus. No one argued, disagreed, or questioned anything. At no time when I was in the room did any child ask a question."
>
> The many observations that made this same point lead to the conclusion that *children* in the elementary schools visited by this task force *were having abundant opportunities to overlearn passive conformity.* When the teacher has all the ideas, gives all the directions, handles all the materials, and admonishes the children to sit still and not talk—if they do not rebel or withdraw completely—most children respond with an unquestioning acceptance of the teacher's rulings on all matters.[65] [Italics supplied.]

In short, while Washington's schools fail to teach their mainly black students to read, they succeed in teaching "passive conformity"—

or withdrawal and rebellion. The "noise" of the classroom tells students to be silent, unexpressive, uncreative, docile, and perhaps "unteachable" as well.

Many anecdotes might illustrate similar classrooms. Bernard Asbell described, several years ago, a teacher who viewed himself as a policeman in his sixth-grade classroom, and who made the following comments about his students loudly, in their presence:

> "How do you get them interested when they don't *want* to get interested?" The teacher went on. "Like in art. I put something on the board, some kind of design, and tell them to copy it, except to change it a little so it will be original. They just look at me. They don't understand. They don't try to understand, so what can I do?"[66]

The content of such an "art" lesson is sufficiently stupefying, a "failure." But the "noise" transmitted by its very triviality, by the teacher's comments, by the two-by-four club lying conspicuously across his desk conveys even more precisely the teacher's contempt, and his expectation that the students will not or cannot learn. That is the crucial lesson. The school system judges, and it finds the *children* wanting. The major function of schools, Dan W. Dodson of the New York University Education School writes, has been to "take all the children of the community and teach them their place in the power order." They are taught in such a way, he continues, that "all will understand their failures are their own, rather than those of the system. Otherwise they would rebel and blow the system apart."[67]

Dodson's comment joins the school experience of ghetto youth, described by Passow's team and by Asbell, to experiences of the white, middle-class students described in John Holt's *How Children Fail*. Holt maintains that the primary emotion experienced by children in school is fear, primarily of failure, and his book documents the elaborate techniques students devise to evade the moments in which they must perform or stand revealed as "stupid." It is, of course, the steady experience of black children to be told, directly or by the "noise" of the school (and of the society), that they are stupid and unworthy. What Holt shows is that the same message lurks in every middle-class schoolroom, that the whole thrust of the school experience is designed to force children to internalize the school's judgement of them. Every year the demand to "do well" presses into earlier and earlier grades: make Bronx Science, make Harvard, achieve, achieve. And there is only one way to "do well": figure out what the teachers want and give it to them. "Doing well" thus becomes a function of a kind of cunning obedience, detached in most students from their real interests and real impulses.

And the schools recognize this. They operate on a theory of infant damnation: children are dangerous primitives, backsliders, they must learn the teachers' catechisms. Only then will they be reassured of their worth, rewarded with grades and a place in the honors track. They need not ask if their achievements are worthwhile, if what they have learned is of interest or of use. The school certifies that. The only question to ask is whether the work has been done. And for the others, those who have not learned to play by the teachers' rules, the school certifies to them that *they* are failures, "difficult," "disruptive," "culturally deprived," that their boredom arises from *their* ignorance, their irritation from *their* stupidity.

Two specific examples illustrate the effects and the causes of characteristic classroom methods. Here is Peter Schrag's transcription of a lesson in a Boston school:

Q. Did we win the revolution, Foote?
A. Yes.
Q. Of course we did. . . . So then we had to establish a plan of government that was called what?
A. The Constitution.
Q. I'll hit you in the head. (Hands are up.)
A. The Articles of Confederation.
Q. What were they?
A. Our first plan of government.
Q. Why did we drop it? (Confusion.) What was the matter with the Articles of Confederation?
A. They weren't strong enough.
Q. What happened at the meeting to alter or change the Articles?
A. They decided to drop them and make a new plan.
Q. There were two main weaknesses in the Articles. What were they?
A. They could make laws, but couldn't enforce them.
Q. It's the same in the cafeteria. If there weren't any teachers there, if Mr. Walsh wasn't there with his whistle, there'd be bed-

Iam. . . . We need rules, not laissez-faire. Now open your books
to the section about the three branches of government. What are
they?
    A. (All students in unison) Executive, legislative, and judicial.
    Q. Say it again.
    A. Executive, legislative, and judicial.[68]

In a Baltimore high-school English class, a teacher asked what
the author of an essay thought of Helen Keller. Students gave many
answers—"intelligent," "creative," "hard-working"—but the teacher
responded to none, simply called on other students, until one of
them said, "He thinks she's courageous." "Yes," the teacher said,
"courageous." The student had pushed the one true button (on
her lesson plan). No one stopped to argue that, at least by implication, Helen Keller had also been described as intelligent, creative,
hard-working. The students accepted the announcement of the correct answer as a signal that they were to move on to the next question. There was, in fact, never any discussion, but rather a series of
guesses, some relatively random, to the teacher's series of questions, prepared especially carefully for visitors she knew would be
there. No student, perhaps because of the visitors, ever asked a
question independently of the teacher's catechism. And the teacher
never paused even for a minute to respond to several interesting and
and a few outlandish "answers." She was equally unresponsive to all
but the answers she had written down in her plan.

The ostensible subjects in these examples are different, history
and government in one case and a writer in the other. But the real
lessons are identical. These have to do with the forms of behavior
teachers will approve. To begin with, they asked "closed" questions.
That is, they asked questions the single answers to which were already in their heads. The students are thereby taught day after day,
whatever the supposed subject, that knowledge consists of tidbits of
information prepackaged by authorities, the teacher or the textbook.
Their job, the approved behavior, is to memorize or to guess these
tidbits, to give the teachers the answers they want.

The years of our own schooling have accustomed most of us to
a mode of closed question and answer, to endless sessions of recitation, to short-answer quizzes. We tend to accept the dullness and
shallowness of such classrooms as natural, the "order" they enforce
as necessary. We forget that only within the last century have chil-

dren been subject to so much formal schooling, and that only more recently has education been uniformly identified, as in College Board and other "achievement" examinations, with the formal possession of defined bits of information and the manipulation of certain abstract concepts. Until recently, most young people were not in high schools. They learned in and from their work, rather than by rote or in order to please a teacher. As John Holt has shown, moreover, children in general learn more useful skills and information during their preschool years and in the time they spend outside of school through their school years than they do in the classroom. And their methods are, by and large, trial-and-error, or experiment, or question-asking. As adults accepting closed questions and classrooms as normal, we fail to view them functionally, to ask what the repetition of such procedures for years and years accomplishes. Our general failure to imagine alternatives, even when we hate what school has been for us and for our children, is a measure of the school system's success in limiting and controlling us. We have accepted the right of schools to make us behave like frightened parrots, to make us feel guilty that we are bored with endless terms of triviality and repetition, to stifle whatever we might feel and think in dread that we might displease the teacher. Even the simplest alternatives reveal to us the extent to which schools have helped make us absurd.

A teacher can, for example, ask "open" questions, that is, questions for which there is no answer already established in her head. She might ask about the poem "Do you like it? Why?" or "How does it make you feel?" Or she might ask, "Would you have preferred to live under the Articles of Confederation or the Constitution?" or "Had you been present at the meeting to evaluate the Articles of Confederation, what would you have said?" Such questions do not test the ability of the student to conform to preestablished patterns of behavior in an either/or world. Instead they indicate the teacher's interest in the student's own ideas, they provide an opportunity for the student not only to express himself, to explore his own feelings and assumptions, and to discover that these are important, but to learn how thought processes are rooted in assumptions. The "closed" question asserts the unimportance of the student, the absolute character of authority, and the need for the student to accept and obey that authority if he is to be judged "successful." To be sure, "open" questions are frightening; they lead almost anywhere, certainly into territory which the teacher cannot have charted in advance, perhaps into problems her teachers' guides and supervisors have never laid out for her. "Open" questions can lead straight to the students' passions, to argument and excitation. And if classroom control is at a premium, they are therefore dangerous. Much safer to make the kids give back the answer you want, that your authority can assert is, wholly and completely, correct.

Conformity to authority is, however, only one of the objectives of closed classroom methods. The hands waving in Schrag's class indicate that a second result is to stimulate competitiveness. One of Jules Henry's observations helps illustrate how children are trained into this style of behavior. When his observer entered an elementary-school classroom, the teacher asked sweetly, "Which one of you nice, polite boys would like to take [the observer's] coat and hang it up?" All hands went up. The teacher might simply have said, "Johnny, please hang up Mr. X's coat." In either case she can choose only one child, but she operates to demand a ritualized response, in which children obediently enter into the competition for her preference. Even if they are not chosen, they have at least communicated their desire to please her; obviously, any child who does not raise his hand is guilty of an act of hostility toward the teacher, a form of emotional treason in the world of the classroom. "It is only natural," Henry continues, "that when the teacher next asks, 'Now who will tell what we have been doing?' and 'Who would like to tell the answer to the next problem?' there should appear 'a large and agitated forest of hands,' for failure to raise the hand could be interpreted only as an act of aggression." So trained, children do not have to be told to compete, or that competition is a form of behavior approved by the school. Moreover, they soon internalize that value, however alien competitiveness might have been to their own culture or family, or to their preferences as individuals. Indeed, as Henry concludes:

In a society where competition for the basic cultural goods is a pivot of action, people cannot be taught to love one another, for those who do cannot compete with one another, except in play. It thus becomes necessary for the school, without appearing to do so, to teach children how to hate, without appearing to do so, for our culture cannot tolerate the idea that babes should hate each other. How does the school accomplish this ambiguity? Obviously through competition itself. . . .[69]

Thus, by the time we enter the kind of classroom Schrag describes, it has become second nature for us to press forward in our seats, hands waving frantically at any sign of faltering by a fellow student. Or we have been taught that our failure to join in the hand-raising assault is a confession of our own inadequacy, of our stupidity or deprivation. Either way, the school traps us into *its* norms, into the pattern of behavior society demands.

Once again, the alternatives are not readily apparent to us, precisely because we have, as Americans, been so thoroughly imbued with the ideology and practice of conforming "individualism." The alternative is not the "groupiness" (as Henry calls it) which all the uniform hand-raising or Schrag's choral rendition of the divisions of American government promote. Nor is it the contrived and manipulated catechismlike "discussions" by which a teacher can "guide" his students into accepting his ideas and his rules. But genuine processes of collective decision-making can be built around projects in which a class is engaged, particularly after discussions based on "open" questions. For open discussion leads students into areas of shared curiosity—what if we were at the convention called to rewrite the Articles of Confederation? What would all the different people there be trying to accomplish? What interests would have to be reckoned with? What did the slaveholders want? Would you want a strong central government? In working out, or in playing out, such a scenario, the classroom becomes a place "to plan and carry out activities in pursuit of shared goals," and thus it becomes, in some sense, a "voluntary association of learners."[70] In short, it is conceivable for students to work together in a classroom for the mutual benefit and enlightenment of all. But not, obviously, if the very point of classroom activity is to isolate students in mutual competition in which each is wholly dependent upon the teacher for satisfaction and approval.

We have suggested that the emotional fuel driving students into the sorts of conformity and competition we have described is fear. But that is only part of the story. Fear is, as it were, the school's emotion; it is pushed into children, in turn pushing out of them, at least in school, the myriad feelings with which they engage other experiences. Or, to put it another way, the feelings that students have are ruled irrelevant to their studies. A teacher asks about the content or structure of a poem, but not about the feelings it generates in the student reading it. Freshmen in college twist their sentences into grotesques to avoid the word "I"—they have been told, they explain, to avoid that word because their feelings and attitudes are unimportant. The class returns from a trip: the teacher asks what it is they saw and why the pieces of old paper are "significant." The guessing game is on, the hands waving with a "better" answer. But the children are not asked what struck them as interesting, or silly, or awesome; or what they want to know about it all. "We all know the policeman is our friend, don't we, class?" What happens is that the "successful" student, the one who will make it in the tracks laid out for him by the school system, learns to dissociate his own feelings from the work he must accomplish in order to make it. Boredom is as irrelevant as joy, passion as unnecessary as hope. The only question is: can you do the tasks assigned, learn the formulae, recall the words, respond when called, pass the tests, fly the plane, drop the bombs.

In the beginning we wrote of the jet-fighter pilot. Consider him once again. One of the most highly trained men in history, he is something of an engineer, a technician, a geographer. Possessed of at least a college education or its equivalent, he is also as well conditioned as a pro-football quarterback. As a tactician he is Johnny Unitas, cool in the blitz of enemy fire.

He has been channeled into his exclusive seat in the sky, far from the dark jungle slogging of Bigger and Gus. He has passed his tests, learned the formulae, recalled the words, responded when called, done the tasks assigned. And now in splendid isolation he possesses what few men ever do: the almost uncontested power of death. He has been taught that that power defends Freedom. He understands his job is to separate the unseen enemy from the good Vietnamese below, whom we could and would help to build up their country. We have always done so for people in need, the textbooks have informed him. And if the ferocity of his weapons should raise doubts, he has always the flat fact of doing his job to fall back on. He has his orders. Meanwhile, he is part of the best damn fighting team on Yankee Station, and all the other guys think and feel like he does—if they feel at all.

Chris Koch interviewed one of the first American pilots to be captured by the North Vietnamese, Captain Robert Daughtrey, whose

F-105D "Thunderchief" had been shot down on August 2, 1965. "I asked him," Koch wrote:

> what he felt about killing people and destroying things. He said he'd never thought about it. Then he added, "I never thought I'd be shot at." We asked him why he thought he'd been sent to bomb North Vietnam, and he replied: "Well, I guess the war escalated and they sent me. I'm not a politician. I'm a military man. An army is built on discipline. You just follow orders." He said he had not been given any political education in the air force. "It was just another job, like working in a factory." . . . Daughtrey seems to feel that if he maintains his pleasant disposition and does what he is told to do, nothing serious can ever happen to him. "When I get out of this I think I'd make a fine salesman for Sears, Roebuck." He did not express any strong emotional attachment to anything except flying. When we asked if he had any message for his wife and three children he said, "No, just tell my dad I'm all right. He'll pass the message along."[71]

The last scene of Wiseman's film, *High School,* consists of a faculty meeting in which the principal is reading a letter from a former student, now stationed aboard the USS *Okinawa* off the coast of Vietnam. He is writing to say that his insurance money should be used to establish a scholarship for some kid like himself; it is quite possible that he won't come back, for he is being dropped behind the demilitarized zone into North Vietnamese territory. His family has asked him, he writes to the principal, "'Don't you value life, are you crazy?' But I also value lives in South Vietnam and in the Free World." "You understand," he concludes, "I am only a body doing a job." "To me," the principal says through her barely restrained tears, "it means that we are very successful at Northeast High School."

When one looks at the system of U.S. education, at its structure, its textbooks, the conditioning processes of its halls and classrooms, one can come to no other conclusion, we think, than that men like Captain Daughtrey and the unknown Northeast graduate—only "a body doing a job"—are its perfect products, and the Vietnam war its supreme testimony to success. Were U.S. schools not successful in the tasks we have outlined, a war almost everyone in this country now claims to hate would not—after six years of barbarism—still be pursued with unexampled ferocity.

If schools have been "successful," the task of educational reformers is far different from their conceptions. For remedying the system does not involve the simple tonics of money or the reeducation of teachers that turns them into "facilitator" or "change agent." It involves, rather, changing the fundamental tasks which this society demands of its schools. So long as these remain the separation of people and the perpetuation of privilege, the cultivation of social stupidity, the inculcation of conformity and competitiveness, and the dissociation of feelings and ideas from the performance of technical functions, tinkering will not do. The educational system is, finally, a reflection of the values of the society itself. And a society devoted to war and profit will always create schools equally dedicated to those goals.

Notes

[1] J. S. Coleman, "Social Climates in High School," *Cooperative Research Monograph 4* (Washington, D.C., Office of Education, U.S. Department of Health, Education and Welfare), pp. 11–12.

[2] Mario D. Fantini and Gerald Weinstein, *The Disadvantaged: Challenge to Education* (New York, 1968), p. 163.

[3] *The 28th Report of the Massachusetts Board of Education,* pp. 83–84. Quoted in Michael B. Katz, *The Irony of Early School Reform* (Cambridge, 1968), pp. 44–45.

[4] "Innovation in Education: New Directions for the American School," a statement by the Research and Policy Committee, July, 1968, pp. 9, 10.

[5] Kenneth Clark, *Dark Ghetto* (New York, 1965), pp. 120–21.

[6] *"Elementary and Secondary Education Act of 1965,"* Report #143, House of Representatives, 89th Congress.

[7] Fantini, *op. cit.,* pp. 172–73.

[8] Kenneth Clark, in a paper for a conference sponsored by the U.S. Commission on Civil Rights in November, 1967.

[9] Katz, *op. cit.,* p. 91.

[10] *Ibid.,* p. 92.

[11] *Ibid.,* p. 87.

[12] *Ibid.,* p. 88.

[13] *Life,* 66 (May 16, 1969), p. 29.

[14] Bayard Hooper, "The Task Is to Learn What Learning Is For," *Life,* 66 (May 16, 1969), pp. 34, 39.

[15] All quotations from Heber Hinds Ryan and Philpine Crecelius, *Ability Grouping in the Junior High School* (New York, 1927), pp. 1–10.

[16] Miriam L. Goldberg, et al., *The Effects of Ability Grouping* (New York, 1966), p. 163. "Differences in achievement growth over the two-grade span," the authors found, "did not support the common wisdom that narrowing the ability range or separating the extreme groups from the intermediate groups enables teachers to be more effective in raising the pupils' achievement level. . . . On the contrary, although the achievement differences among patterns of varying ability range were small, overall observed increments tended to favor the *broad range"* (p. 160). See also Joseph Justman, "Ability Grouping—What Good Is It?" *The Urban Review,* 2 (February, 1967), pp. 2–3: ". . . homogeneous grouping is not a panacea for educational ills. . . . Grouping by itself, without curricular modification as a concomitant, will not give rise to the desired outcome of improved pupil performance." Unfortunately, no one has shown, either, that grouping with "curricular modifications" would make real differences, or just what "curricular modifications" there might be that would not, for example, straitjacket and limit "slow learners."

[17] The *Times* of London reported in August, 1966, on a set of samples being taken by the British Foundation for Educational Research: "Most of the

existing research of streaming [tracking] has come to the conclusion that children get better results in unstreamed schools. One notable piece of work was that of J. C. Daniels (1961). Dr. Daniels compared academic progress in two streamed and two unstreamed schools in detail. He reported that progress in English and arithmetic was more rapid for all children in unstreamed schools, but particularly for the weakest children. These findings have not been seriously challenged by later research.

"Dr. J. W. B. Douglass examined the school careers of 5,000 children in the Medical Research unit's permanent sample. He showed that although children in higher streams all made good progress, the IQ's of children in lower streams actually deteriorated during the latter years of primary school. The deterioration was most marked in children of working class background. Dr. Douglass' general conclusion was that streaming by ability tends to reinforce the process of social selection. The initial act of streaming was, in Dr. Douglass' view, heavily influenced by social and nonacademic factors."

[18]Goldberg, *op. cit.,* p. 165. The study "reinforces the conclusion that what pupils learn is at least as much a function of what teachers teach and expect of them as it is a function of pupil attitudes, self-percepts, or, within limits, even tested intellectual ability" (p. 164). See, in this regard, Robert A. Rosenthal, *Pygmalion in the Classroom* (Cambridge, 1968). Rosenthal relates the results of an experiment in which teachers were told that certain of their students were revealed through "tests" as having superior, though hidden, ability. Though the students were not, in fact, special, they began to perform better, apparently in response to teachers' special ministrations.

[19]See, for example, Maryland Council for Higher Education, *Master Plan for Higher Education in Maryland* (Baltimore, 1968), p. 2–36.

[20]Theodore Caplow, *The Sociology of Work* (Minneapolis, 1954), p. 216.

[21]*Slums and Suburbs* (New York: McGraw-Hill, 1961), pp. 40, 66. Conant's comments on tracking help explain some of the mistrust felt by black communities for liberal educational reformers. He writes: "In short, my recommendation in both my senior high report and my junior high report still stands. In these subjects [English, social studies, mathematics, science—in short, in all the academic curriculum] there ought to be subject-by-subject grouping in three groups—fairly small top and bottom groups and a large middle group. Such an arrangement may well isolate Negroes in some schools in the bottom group, but surely there will be considerable mixing in the large middle group if not in the top group. Moreover, with an integrated staff and with frank discussions of the problem I should think a workable solution might be arrived at in good faith" (p. 64). What is one to say in the face of such naïve optimism?

[22]See, for example, John Vaizey and Michael Debeauvais, "Economic Aspects of Educational Development," in *Education, Economy, and Society,* ed. A. H. Halsey, Jean Floud, and C. H. Anderson (Glencoe, 1961), p. 43.

[23]See, for example, Patricia Cayo Sexton, *Education and Income* (New York, 1962), pp. 228, 234.

[24]These figures were obtained by Columbia University SDS from the records of the N.Y.C. Board of Education through the office of the Reverend Milton Galamison, then a member of the board.

[25]The figures cited in this paragraph are contained in the briefs filed by the plaintiff in Hobson *vs.* Hansen, the case decided by Judge Wright. . . .

Hansen's own description of Washington's track system, printed in the November, 1960, *Atlantic Monthly,* is worth quoting at length.

Honors Level: ". . . To protect the quality of instruction, the honors curriculum is selective. A student is enrolled in this curriculum only if he has demonstrated ability to do superior work by his previous grades, testing, and by teacher judgment. . . ."

Regular College Preparatory: "While this program is designed as preparatory for college, it offers excellent general background for able students not planning college careers. If I could be, or wanted to be, fully authoritarian on this point, I would require every capable pupil, college-bound or not, to choose this or the honors curriculum. The intellectual development most needed for general citizenship can best be obtained through study of the great and significant disciplines taught at a demanding and invigorating level. Many capable students are underachieving, and maximum persuasion, short of authoritative controls, should be used to motivate them to move up to the more difficult but richer curriculums."

General Curriculum: ". . . cafeteria-type election of subjects with bargain-basement rummaging for good grades at reduced prices."

Basic Curriculum: ". . . This curriculum is for the academically delayed high school student, as indicated by standardized test scores in reading and math, academic grades and teacher opinion. Teacher opinion is of first importance. . . . The two objectives of this curriculum are to upgrade the academic achievement of retarded pupils and provide education for those whose innate endowments, so far as they are reflected in performance, limit the range and difficulty of learning. . . ."

Small wonder passions in the black community ran rather high against the superintendent.

[26] See Herbert Kohl, *36 Children* (New York, 1968), p. 178.

[27] In forty schools in New York City with more than 90 percent black and Puerto Rican enrollment, for example, 46.8 percent of the teachers had three years or less of experience, compared with a quarter of the teachers in similar schools with predominant white enrollment. In Washington, where the median income is under $4,000, about 46 percent of the teachers are "temporary"—that is, they cannot, for one reason or another, achieve permanent certification.

[28] Howard S. Becker, "Schools and Systems of Stratification," *Education, Economy, and Society, op. cit.,* p. 103. See also August Hollingshead's classic study, *Elmtown's Youth* (New York, 1949), which describes how schools give rewards to students based on their families' class position.

[29] Because assignment to track reflects so closely class and racial factors, it is still not unusual to observe in theoretically "integrated" schools predominantly white "advanced" classes and predominantly (more often, all) black "slower" classes.

[30] See, for example, J. W. Bennett and Melvin M. Tumin, *Social Life* (New York, 1949), p. 587. In his massive study, *Wealth and Power in America,* Gabriel Kolko shows that despite the New Deal and higher levels of government spending on welfare, there has been no change in basic distribution of income and wealth in the United States since 1910.

[31] See, for example, Patricia Cayo Sexton, *The American School* (Englewood Cliffs, N.J., 1967), p. 51: "There is, in fact, an absence of evidence that

the most able in performance of jobs or other real-life tasks are selected or produced by the standards set and training offered by higher education. Employers often hire from among the degree elite because of the prestige rather than the superior training or job performance skill attached to a college degree."

[32] See *Chronicle of Higher Education,* December 9. 1968.

[33] Bruce K. Eckland, "Social Class and College Graduation: Some Misconceptions Corrected," *American Journal of Sociology,* 70 (July, 1964), p. 36.

[34] See, for example, John Vaizey and Michael Debeauvais, "Economic Aspects of Educational Development," *Education, Economy, and Society, op. cit.,* pp. 38–39, 43.

[35] See, for example, Burton R. Clark, "The 'Cooling-Out' Function in Higher Education," *American Journal of Sociology,* LXV (May, 1960): "In summary, the cooling-out process in higher education is one whereby systematic discrepancy between aspiration and avenue is covered over and stress for the individual and the system is minimized. The provision of readily available alternative achievements in itself is an important device for alleviating the stress consequent on failure and so preventing anomic and deviant behavior. The general result of cooling-out processes is that society can continue to encourage maximum effort without major disturbance from unfulfilled promises and expectations.

"For an organization and its agents one dilemma of a cooling-out role is that it must be kept reasonably away from public scrutiny and not clearly perceived or understood by prospective clientele. Should it become obvious, the organization's ability to perform it would be impaired. If high school seniors and their families were to define the junior college as a place which diverts college-bound students, a probable consequence would be a turning-away from the junior college and increased pressure for admission to the four-year colleges and universities that are otherwise protected to some degree. This would, of course, render superfluous the part now played by the junior college in the division of labor among colleges."

[36] Kingsley Widmer, "Why Colleges Blew Up," *The Nation,* 208 (2/24/69), p. 238.

[37] Bowdoin College recently eliminated College Board scores as an entrance requirement. Richard M. Moll, the director of admissions, explained that "there is a widespread feeling and convincing evidence today that standardized aptitude and achievement tests cannot escape cultural bias and that they thereby work in favor of the more advantaged elements of our society, while handicapping others." *The Chronicle of Higher Education,* February 2, 1970, p. 1.

[38] *Master Plan for Higher Education in Maryland,* p. 2–19.

[39] "On the Line at S. F. State," *Mayday.* (now *Hard Times*), 18 (February 10–17, 1969).

[40] *The American School,* p. 54.

[41] *Ibid.,* p. 52.

[42] Race is obviously also a factor of exclusion: even the most casual observation of campuses in Maryland bears out the same kind of racial divisions

that Mrs. Sexton documents for other states. Indeed, so few blacks attend the university that it is under orders from the U.S. Office of Education to implement a plan for integration.

[43]Todd Gitlin called this passage to our attention in his "On the Line at S. F. State."

[44]See above, pp. 214–15.

[45]See, for example, Leonard Buder, "On Open Admissions," *The New York Times,* July 11, 1969.

[46]See "Open Admissions in City U. Opposed by Albany Chiefs," *The New York Times,* July 11, 1969.

[47]In their pamphlet, "The Political Economy of Youth," John and Margaret Rowntree argue that the schools are fully rationalized by "market-profit principles." "When education becomes seen as an 'investment in human capital' and the school becomes a factory producing workers and technologists, the rationalization of the purposes of schooling shifts from that of serving nonmarket or social class interests to serving the market or economic class interests. It therefore ceases serving individual capitalists and their families only to begin serving the capitalists as a class (or capitalism as a system). The invasion of the school by the market brings the class struggle into the schools. . . . This process results from the development of mass educational systems to replace their elite-serving predecessors." "The Political Economy of Youth" (Detroit: Radical Education Project), p. 21.

What the Rowntrees describe is certainly the trend, but we would contend that the schools continue to serve mixed social and economic functions; indeed, that the conflicts within and about them are in some large measure a reflection of that mix.

[48]Bessie Louise Pierce, *Civic Attitudes in American School Textbooks* (Chicago, 1930), p. 93. The quotations are from various school texts.

[49]Donald W. Oliver and James P. Shaver, *Teaching Public Issues in the High School* (Boston, 1966), p. 28.

[50]William L. Neumann, "Teaching Communism in American High Schools," unpublished typescript, used by permission.

[51]William L. Neumann, "Make-Believe History for Maturing Minds," unpublished typescript, used by permission.

[52]Jules Henry, "Education for Stupidity," *The New York Review of Books,* X (May 9, 1968), pp. 25–26.

[53]Quoted in Pierce, *Civic Attitudes,* p. 110.

[54]*High School English Textbooks: A Critical Examination* (Boston, 1963).

[55]Neumann, "Make-Believe History," *op. cit.*

[56]Harold B. Clifford, *Exploring New England,* New Unified Social Studies (Chicago: Follett Publishing Company, 1961). Noam Chomsky called this passage to our attention: he found it in his own child's textbook in Lexington, Massachusetts.

[57]Joe Pilati, "'New York's Finest' Like Chicago's Worst," *The Village Voice,* December 5, 1968, p. 56.

[58]Michael Stern, "Truancy Overwhelms the Truant Officers Here," *The New York Times,* February 2, 1970.

[59] "Golden Rule Days: American Schoolrooms," *Culture Against Man* (New York, 1963), p. 290.

[60] Joel T. Santoro, "Control and Discipline in School Cafeterias," *The Clearing House*, 1965; reproduced by *This Magazine Is About Schools*, I (Winter, 1967), end pages.

[61] See Paul Lauter, "The ACE Menace," *The New York Review of Books*, XIII (October 9, 1969), pp. 59–60, and "ACE: Defender of the Educational Faith," *Antioch Review*, XXIX (Fall, 1969), pp. 287–303.

[62] *The New York Times*, March 16, 1969.

[63] "Contemptuous Hairdressers: Ceremonies of Humiliation in School," *This Magazine Is About Schools*, I (August, 1966), p. 14.

[64] *The New York Times*, March 23, 1969.

[65] A. Harry Passow, et al., *Toward Creating a Model Urban School System: A Study of the Washington, D.C., Public Schools* (New York: Teachers College, Columbia, 1967), pp. 275–77.

[66] Bernard Asbell, "Not Like Other Children," *Redbook*, October, 1963.

[67] Quoted by Patricia Cayo Sexton, *The American School*, p. 32.

[68] Peter Schrag, *Village School Downtown* (Boston, 1967), p. 95.

[69] *Culture Against Man*, pp. 293–95.

[70] Herbert A. Thelen, "Some Classroom Quiddities for People-Oriented Teachers," *Journal of Applied Behavioral Science*, 3 (July–September, 1965), pp. 270–85. The article bears out many of our own observations about "closed" and "open" questions and classrooms.

[71] Reported in *I. F. Stone's Weekly*, XIII (October 11, 1965), p. 3. A similar response was reported in a CBS television interview with an F-100 pilot, who had been dropping napalm. The pilot said that it had "bothered" him at first, but then it became "only a job" and was "sort of impersonal."

9

The White Problem
for Black Youth

JL: No, I was jus' sayin' jus' suppose there is a God, would he be white or black?
LARRY: He'd be white, man.
JL: Why?
LARRY: Why? I'll tell you why. Cause the average whitey out here got everything, you dig? And the nigger ain't got shit, y'know? Y'unnerstan'? So—um—for—in order for that to happen, you know it ain't no black God that's doin' that bullshit.

—From an interview with Larry L., a supposedly inarticulate black, fifteen-year-old gang member. Quoted by William Labov in his "The Logic of Non-Standard English."

In 1969 the American Red Cross set out to rebuild the Mississippi Gulf Coast, devastated by Hurricane Camille. New and used clothing and other relief supplies flowed into communities, and special forces arrived to begin replacing destroyed housing. Tarpaper shacks put up quickly for blacks allowed them an excellent view of foundations being dug for new ranch homes—to be filled by their white employers. Why did black people receive secondhand clothing, while whites expected and got fresh goods? Why weren't ranch houses built for all? The Red Cross blandly disclaimed charges of discrimination: regular policy, after all, dictated that disaster victims be restored to "normalcy." Red Cross officials were merely doing their jobs, offering aid to people in proportion to their previous standards of living. No offense meant. And if the tarpaper shacks were not much better than previous dwellings, certainly the secondhand clothing was plentiful. Certainly no racism was involved: where would the black people be if there hadn't been a hurricane?

The incident is hardly unique, for there have been other hurricanes and similar disasters, though this time, leaders of the black community testified about their dissatisfaction before a U.S. Senate Public Works subcommittee, and the entire story was reported in *The New York Times*.[1] Thus we can point to the blatant perpetuation, even by a "relief" organization, of long-standing class and racial privileges.[2]

In many of these chapters we have presented detailed statistics to demonstrate, for example, class discrimination in schools or inequities in the draft laws. The oppression of black people in the United States might be graphed similarly: from infant-mortality rates often double those of whites to unemployment rates almost triple; from the fact that a decade and a half after the Supreme Court ruled school segregation unconstitutional, over three-quarters of black children attend segregated and inferior schools, to the fact that while 30.5 percent of the membership in the laborers' union are black, only 1.6 percent of the carpenters', 3.7 percent of the painters', and 0.2 percent of the plumbers' are. One could list grim statistics for income, poor housing, disease, or report stories of continued discrimination, not to speak of assault and assassination by white police and vigilantes. By now, such statistics and such stories fill dozens of books, voluminous reports by the U.S. Commission on Civil Rights, by the Kerner Commission, by almost every American newspaper and magazine in survey after survey. The realities, if not known, are at least public information; yet change is not merely slow—it is often nonexistent. In its last report, the Kerner Commission warned that we were becoming a country of two nations, increasingly separate and *unequal.*

One might theorize that white Americans have been surfeited by these facts and figures, by the continuing horror of life in the ghetto—just as they have been by the televised brutality of the war on Vietnam. But that is, we think, a superficial explanation. It is not, on the whole, that white America has turned wearily from black reality; rather, racism so pervades U.S. institutions that individual Americans can contribute to its maintenance without ever being conscious of their roles. Like the German railroad workers who shunted boxcars full of Jews onto concentration-camp sidings, ordinary Americans have screened themselves from the results of daily, commonplace actions, their assumptions about housing, law, school, even their charities like the Red Cross. Thus, as the Gallup poll of July 22, 1967, discovered, "only 1 out of 100 whites believes, or admits to believing, that Negroes are treated "badly." Seventy-five percent believe that "Negroes are treated the same as whites."[3]

"Institutional racism" is an increasingly popular term that, like "black power," may evoke fearful and agitated responses. It means something rather simple: that discrimination and bigotry are built into the laws and customs by which Americans conduct business, courts, government, schools, even philanthropy. Whether or not individual Red Cross officials are racist is beside the point. When they follow their operations manual and their orders, they perform acts which are "objectively" racist—that is, acts which perpetuate the results and maintain the values of a society stratified by racism. Nor need the writers of a manual be "subjectively" racists—that is, they need not hate niggers or even feel subtle prejudice against Negroes. They merely have to do what seems right and fair to most Americans. And thus they remain, to use Eldridge Cleaver's key distinction, part of the problem instead of part of the solution, since what has seemed right and fair to Americans has, in fact, often been a settled form of racism: either "winning the West" from the Indians or "separate-but-equal" facilities of the neighborhood schools. Institutions are racist if their daily processes and their "objective" effects promulgate inequities for black people, quite regardless of the "subjective" states of mind of participating white individuals. The lives of black people in the United States are "ghettoized" by institutional racism.

To make the concept palpable, we will begin with the ghetto itself. No one, it is said, except an occasional evil slumlord, wants to perpetuate segregated housing, yet new public housing projects continue to be built smack in the middle of black ghettos rather than on fresh tracts of land in suburbia or even in white parts of cities. The official reasons offered: to maintain neighborhood stability and compatibility and to insure access for black people. Recently, Judge Richard B. Austin found the Chicago Housing Authority guilty of racial discrimination in its selection of building sites and in its assignments of tenants, and ordered the CHA to build 75 percent of its new low-income apartments in white areas. In most cities' fringes and suburbs, however, zoning restrictions prevent the erection of apartments or of inexpensive houses on small lots that might permit black people from the inner city to escape ghetto rat-traps—and, equally important, to gain access to new jobs opening outside the city. According to the New York Regional Planning Association, families earning less than $15,000 annually—90 percent of those people in the area—cannot afford to live in the suburban communities that surround New York City. At the same time, industry has been moving out of the city at an accelerating pace. Between 1952 and 1966, only 111,000 out of 888,000 new jobs in the New York region were gained by the city. Between 1960 and 1965, the nonwhite population of New York City rose by 500,000. During the same period, in Oyster Bay, a Long Island community about an hour's drive from the city, the nonwhite population dropped from 4,600 to 3,000, while the white population rose from 309,000 to 348,000. Nearby, war plants and aircraft manufacturers offer draft-deferrable jobs to those who can reach them.[4] Similarly, International Harvester has been planning on the grounds of modernization to move a major Chicago plant to the distant suburbs, into which its substantial corps of black workers cannot follow. The same story can be told for every city.

The traditional justification for zoning restrictions may sound reasonable: to prevent overcrowding of schools, raising of taxes for services, to preserve the character of the neighborhood, its light and trees . . . and cleanliness. Indeed, a Negro physician or investment counselor may even have integrated a community. After all, racially restrictive covenants (until recently insisted upon by the Federal Housing Authority to "preserve" property values) have been ruled legally unenforceable. And if banks "hesitate" to float mortgages for most Negroes, is it not merely that most are bad risks, likely to lose their jobs? The real culprits, like the few evil slumlords, are a few vicious realtors who refuse to show "white" housing to black people, unless they are "blockbusting."[5] Though we hardly condone their manipulation of fear and racism for quick profits, slumlords and realtors are convenient scapegoats, visible signs only of more pervasive racist institutions. Segregated housing is maintained chiefly by zoning restrictions that function in the name of preserving neighborhoods and by mortgage practices that function in the name of good banking. Together zoning and banking operate as effectively as the old restrictive covenants to exclude black people, especially if they are nonprofessional, working-class, or poor.

More blatant than housing are institutional features of welfare and antipoverty programs. A report of the National Nutrition Survey, issued early in 1969, called food aid for the poor inadequate, effectively substantiating charges that black people in Mississippi and elsewhere were slowly starving. Regulations for such food programs hold that counties must choose between free distribution of surplus federal foodstuffs (restricted in quantity and to particular items) and the food-stamp program. No matter the hunger, a county cannot have both programs. It took President Johnson's good-hearted, liberal

Secretary of Agriculture years to figure out why, when a county switched from the free-food program to the food stamps, the number of users diminished sharply: there were black families too poor to buy the food stamps.[6]

At the same time, the Agriculture Department, established to aid farmers, not consumers, was providing crop "loans" to big planters. In 1961 Senator Eastland, whose plantation in the Mississippi Delta was paying three dollars a day to cotton pickers, received a federal "loan" of $140,299.65 (and in 1962, another of $393,514.79); such loans do not have to be repaid, for unsold cotton becomes government surplus. Agricultural price-support programs have, needless to say, become notorious for buying up foodstuffs or paying farmers *not* to plant, thus institutionalizing procedures that effectively contribute to the hunger of black children in the South.

In the North, another governmental arm—in this case the progressive New York State government—hired 120 additional "employment" workers at a cost of one million dollars a year to enforce a mandate that able-bodied welfare recipients report every two weeks for possible work. Once again, a regulation functions indirectly to affirm primitive ideas about "lazy nigras." The million dollars annually expended will directly affect fewer than one in a hundred people receiving payments, the bulk of them blacks or Puerto Ricans in New York City. What it mainly does is take funds away from those who need them and, by pushing more people into the menial labor market, restrict even further the chances of unskilled blacks finding work.[7]

Nowhere is racism more institutionalized than in law-enforcement agencies, from police departments through the courts and prisons. The recent murders of Black Panthers may have shocked whites unaware of the typical treatment blacks are subject to in the ghetto, even by black policemen. They are, after all, doing their job, following the rules or customs. We quote from Judge George William Crockett of Detroit's Recorder's Court, explaining why he released almost all in a group of 142 blacks arrested after a white policeman was shot to death in a ghetto:

"You see," say Judge Crockett, "the U.S. Constitution is violated day in and day out by the police, by prosecutors and by judges. . . . It has become a habit, and because of the racism that runs all through the administration of justice, especially criminal justice, black people have been the worst victims. . . . In that 'New Bethel Incident' I broke the habit. I saw that the constitutional rights of all those people had been violated, so I did what I was supposed to do. I applied basic law and the police and the press got upset about it. . . . Sure, a policeman had been killed and another one had been wounded and good police work probably would have turned up the prime suspects. But can anyone imagine the police invading an all-white church and rounding up everybody in sight and bussing them to a wholesale lock-up in a police garage? Can anyone imagine a group of white people being held incommunicado for six or seven hours, and white women and children being locked up all night when there wasn't the slightest evidence that they'd been involved in any crime? But you see these were 142 black people and the police have been doing all these things to black people all the time, and judges have been letting them get away with it."[8]

Needless to say, these illustrations could be multiplied. We could add supporting details about charity, housing codes, the court system, or investigate the job market, sales practices, and road-building to uncover the perpetuation of racism and the disabilities it has imposed on black people. We offer examples to provide a context within which black children grow up and thus to serve as an introduction to our major concern in this chapter: the educational system. We will argue that educators and psychologists, no less than Red Cross officials, bankers, and policemen, function inside institutions that express and promulgate racism in U.S. society.

One major basis of the Supreme Court's 1954 decision outlawing segregated schools was the clear evidence that black children were not learning in them. Substantiating the court's view of segregated schools as inherently unequal were the findings of educational psychologists that black students scored two years or more behind national norms in basic subjects like arithmetic and reading. The decision launched a drive, gradually accelerated during the sixties, to integrate American schools. Not only was integration morally right and the law of the land, educators insisted, it was also the key to assuring that black children improved their test scores.

That view was apparently substantiated in later years by studies, like that of James Coleman,[9] which seemed to show that blacks integrated with substantial numbers of middle-class white students scored better than their brothers and sisters undergoing segregated education (though not, of course, as well as the whites). No one quite knew why. Some attributed it to peer-group influences: white students, taught good school habits at home, impressed these on the blacks. Others suggested that teachers in predominantly white schools expected more of their pupils—and got it. Some talked of the "rub-off" or "leavening" effects of the whites! We recall a prominent liberal activist explaining privately to us that if sufficient numbers of white children could only be attracted back to the 98 percent black school in his neighborhood—say, up to 10 or 15 percent whites—then the schools educational problems would be solved. Others challenged Coleman's findings, asserting that his methods exaggerated the effects he described. But by the time this controversy was seriously joined in 1967, it had become largely academic for two reasons. First, integration just wasn't happening; especially in big cities, schools were more segregated than ever. And second, fewer and fewer black people were dedicated to integration.

In the Deep South, "massive resistance" to orders to desegregate white and "colored" school systems was replaced by general foot-dragging and pleas for time to prevent "chaos." In the North, however, where schools are now no more integrated than in the South, there were officially no white or black schools, but only "neighborhood" schools. When a school district's boundaries changed as blacks moved into neighborhoods, the new arrangement was said to prevent "overcrowding." If two elementary schools, one white and one black, fed the same junior high school, and if blacks were "gaining," why then another junior high would be built . . . further out in the white area. The reasoning: why build a new facility in a deteriorating neighborhood, perhaps one slated for "renewal"? Temporary, portable classrooms would then do if the old black school were "overcrowded."[10] And if you believed that such maneuvers were carried out, for the most part, by conscious racists, you have only to encounter their genuine surprise when government investigators explain to them that they are running, and perpetuating, segregated and unequal systems. Some northern communities have begun working out desegregation plans (to the accompaniment of complaints that public bussing is too expensive and time consuming), but federal officials have all but given up on the big cities. We have already noted the brute fact of residential segregation. There is also the political reality that when, in 1965, federal officials tried to cut off funds from Chicago's highly segregated schools, Mayor Daley interceded with the President, and funds have continued ever since—along with the increasing segregation of the schools.

Even at the university level, despite the widely publicized early struggles over the admission of James Meredith and Autherine Lucy, in 1969 fewer than 2 percent of the students in the nation's major state universities were black. A study of the one hundred members of the National Association of State Universities and Land Grant Colleges, which enroll about 30 percent of all college students, showed that apart from the eighteen predominantly black state universities, only two others enroll more than 5 percent black students. Nearly half the blacks in mostly white schools were freshmen in 1969, while probably less than one percent of students receiving degrees from such universities in 1968 were black. Indeed, there were more foreign students enrolled in them than American Negroes.[11] These figures have effectively been known to university administrators for years; they were a result, administrators usually explain, not of discrimination but of the maintenance of "standards"—about which we have written in Chapter 8.

But factors other than "standards" account for at least part of the segregation of colleges in Maryland. In 1963 a long debate about the location of a new campus for the University of Maryland designed to serve metropolitan Baltimore was concluded with the decision to build west of the Baltimore Beltway in the county rather than in the center city's inner-harbor area. The Beltway location, it was argued, would be cheaper, since state land was available; and it would be more convenient for students who could reach the campus by driving from "all over" Baltimore County, which rings the city like a horseshoe. A white horseshoe, it should be added: Baltimore County (Vice-President Agnew was its executive) is almost entirely white. Though one city busline passes only seven-tenths of a mile from the campus, public transportation being what it is in Baltimore, the decision to place the college in the county effectively decreased its proportion of black students. The bus trip from the city can take more than two hours. In its fourth year of operation, perhaps 3 percent of the student population is black. While that proportion exceeds the national average, it hardly reflects the Baltimore city population of students, more than half of whom are black.

We do not believe that most of those who made the decision to build in the county are subjectively racist; we know a number of these people, and believe that they express sincere desire for equal educational opportunity. Indeed, the judgment that more money might be available for educational purposes if less were needed for building and land may, in the long run, prove a correct one. Meanwhile, however, one short-term effect of the decision—accompanied by a minimum "C" average for admissions and early failures to recruit in the city—have produced an institution which is simply not part of the solution. Nor is it at all clear that it can become part of the solution, given location and the elite role assigned to the university in the Maryland Master Plan for Higher Education. During the controversy over the site, for example, a Baltimore politician suggested with apparent seriousness that a "driver's license" be one criterion for admissions, for, he explained, students who could afford to drive to college generally did better in it.

Most school systems and most campuses still function in 1970 as segregated institutions. Many have failed even to effect token integration. When integration did not occur in the decade following the 1954 Supreme Court ruling, black people began to develop suspicions about its fundamental motives and assumptions. It was not simply disappointment about hundred-year-old hopes. It was not only the cynical knowledge that white people could flaunt the law of the land and get away with it. That black people knew. The push for integration among blacks ironically taught them how racist white society really was. For the price of integration, it gradually became clear, was surrender of black identity: in sociological terms, assimilation. It was a price that many Negro parents would have been willing to pay, following thus in the somewhat mythic footsteps of the Irish, the Jews, and the Italians before them. They might have been willing even if integration "on an individual basis in a society that makes this increasingly possible for the fortunate" might have meant "an exodus of the talented tenth from the black community, with the consequent decimation of the ranks of potential leaders whose commitment to the whole community could help set their people free."[12] But even on these terms, the option of integration, as we have suggested earlier in the chapter, was never really open to blacks. The white community simply didn't want it—one need only point to the rapid development of white suburban rings around northern cities. Institutional racism was stronger than both white liberals and blacks willing to assimilate. Only CORE spoke of integrating whites into black schools or of the contribution blacks could make to the education of white students. The lesson was a hard one for blacks to learn, even blacks inured to the hypocricies of white racism. Black militants view the failure of integration as a necessary step in the process of developing black consciousness. For assimilation really meant death of the person and the race; instead of disappearing into the culture of U.S. middle-class whites, black people have turned to their own blackness. And even some white liberals, still dreaming of integration as a long-range goal, have realized that its usefulness as a tactic for improving the school performance of black children has vanished.

Educators were prepared with another answer: compensatory education. As soon as the first black students had been accepted into white classrooms, teachers discovered that they were not as "well prepared" as their new schoolmates. Aside from being less tractable to the somewhat compulsive discipline of most elementary schools, black students did not respond to the usual reading and arithmetic lessons nearly so well. They did not recognize zoo animals in the picture books, talked all "wrong"—when they talked at all—didn't seem very keen on schooling altogether, fell further behind with each grade. Clearly, there was something lacking in their backgrounds, the educators decided, deficiencies that had to be made up. And thus the compensatory programs were launched with "cultural enrichment": smaller children were taken to visit the zoo, the farms and suburbs in which stories in their readers were set, while their elder brothers and sisters were carted to the ballet, Shakespeare, and museums under the aegis of fancy-sounding projects like "Higher Horizons." These were, everyone recognized, only a scattering of candies to the hungry. More careful, well-researched, pointed programs were needed; large sums from Congress were required; a theory of "intervention" in the normal educational and family life of the black student had to be elaborated; and the more flagrant abuses of the school system had to be ended.

Among the most obvious abuses were the lily-white textbooks. The most notable feature about the Negro in school texts used up till the late sixties was his absence. A 1961 study for the Anti-Defamation League of B'nai B'rith showed that only six of twenty-four popular school texts mentioned the names of one or more black Americans. Of the six, "one refers solely to a baseball player and one solely to two prizefighters."[13] Even the illustrations, the study demonstrates, convey the invisibility of blacks from textbook consciousness. The eight American histories examined included no photographs of black and white Americans together; only one of the eight world histories contained interracial photographs: Ralph Bunche with Eleanor Roosevelt and Trygve Lie and Bunche with David Ben-Gurion.[14] The Dick and Jane family, as it is hardly necessary to repeat, were white, their neat suburban kitchens cleanly swept, their lawns suitably kept (by the invisible Negro maids and gardeners?). When we began a project in a 98-percent-black Washington, D.C., school in 1967—a school that had been a "colored" school even before integration—its bookroom contained a total of a dozen books with brown faces: new books, used just one term, not enough for any whole class, and still the same old Dick and Jane, now in brownface.

But silence on blacks (and other minorities) is probably preferable to the content of typical texts. One junior-high civics book examined in the Anti-Defamation League study tells its readers, "Very likely it is best that people of different races should not be forced to live where the differences between them might cause unpleasantness." Another presents a map, with cartooned figures to show what various groups have contributed to the United States:

> The English are given credit for "law and order," the Irish as "public servants," the Germans for orchestras and mid-western farming. The three depictions of Negroes, all placed in the South, show them picking cotton, singing spirituals, and driving a wagonload of tobacco.[15]

Another text, *History of a Free People,* still widely in use in 1969, proposes that students write a composition comparing the Ku Klux Klan with the underground resistance to the Nazis during World War II or to the vigilantes of the American past.

Needless to say, publishers have in the last few years rushed "multi-ethnic" readers into print, even some with settings and stories which poor and working-class black children might recognize. It remains true, however—and we shall return below to the significance of this—that black children in textbooks speak quite differently from most black children. Nor is the published history of Negroes in America consonant with black reality. In the spring, 1969, issue of *The School Review,* Professor Mark M. Krug of the University of Chicago exposed the inadequacy and distortion of school history texts. Almost every high-school and college text avoids discussing slavery as a moral issue, Krug points out, nor, indeed, as the irreducible canker at the center of the Civil War. Perhaps, he suggests, publishers wish to avoid losing southern markets, sensitive to harsh treatment of their "peculiar institution," but more likely authors wish to draw out of the Civil War a suitable civics lesson: namely, the desirability of national consensus. Thus, the writers of history texts attribute the war to "a breakdown of the democratic process" caused by the "failure of the moderate majority" and, on both sides, the domination of "extremists." Similarly, texts retain gross distortions of Reconstruction, often deploring the "Radicals" who harassed supposedly well-meaning Andrew Johnson and, in one case, characterizing the Reconstruction governments in which southern blacks participated as "perhaps the most corrupt and extravagant governments ever known in an English-speaking land." For corruption, one might think first of the 1850's, when most members of the Illinois state legislature were involved in financial manipulations over the construction of the Illinois Central Railroad. Or later of the notorious Tweed Ring's looting of New York City's treasury. In short, it would be remarkable were black students, their parents, and other sympathetic adults not to find school texts irrelevant or deplorable, "gross," as students say, or simply racist.

But even before the brown faces and urban landscapes began to appear between covers or the "hip" Nat and Lil readers on shelves,[16] the major compensatory programs had been devised. For high-school-age students, these were named SEEK, Talent Search, and Upward Bound; for preschoolers, Head Start.

Upward Bound was conceived with enviable simplicity in accord with one of the poverty program's fundamental dogmas: that education is the key to breaking the poverty cycle. Obviously the public schools were failing to move substantial numbers of students from poor and working-class families into college. Denied college, such students were denied the training and credentials necessary to enter the mainstream of American life—that is, the American economy—from which poverty had so long held them. Given the realities of public-school education, and the reluctance of colleges to alter their admissions requirements, the problem was clear enough: what do you have to do with (or to) poor, "deprived" high-school students so that they may enter and get through college? The answer was Upward Bound, described in one of its earlier brochures as a "pre-college preparatory program designed to generate the skills and motivation necessary for success in education beyond high school among young people from low-income backgrounds and inadequate secondary school preparation."[17]

For all its simplicity, the original objectives within the Office of Economic Opportunity for Upward Bound were ambitious ones. Since the schools did not seem capable of rapid change, even with all the money pumping into them from the Office of Education, Upward Bound would be established as a kind of parallel school system, a free university of the poor, or the Mississippi freedom schools beautified and writ large. Deprived of needed care in schools, students would come to Upward Bound and there find real learning experiences in the subjects school had failed to teach—and real attention to their own problems. During summers they would live outside their deprived environments on pleasant college campuses, studying in small groups with inspired instructors, offered in addition tutors and counselors eager to serve, and granted opportunities to paint or act, write poetry, study chemistry, or build boats, and with it all paid ten dollars a week—for school! Upward Bound would become their true, their only, alma mater, offering a new spirit of group identity, caring for their health, helping them through family crises, finding them places in college. They would, unfortunately, have to remain in their high schools, but their spirits as students would be tied to Upward Bound. More than that, unlike the schools, Upward Bound would penetrate the barriers at home and in the community to educational advancement. It would work in harmony with the rest of the poverty program, involving parents, community councils, local citizens from poor communities; Urban Progress Centers would become tutor-study centers; education of the young would become a community priority.

At the same time, and as if changing the student and the community were not sufficiently ambitious projects, Upward Bound would not ignore the schools. Half of Upward Bound's teachers, recruited from regular teaching staffs, would discover that disadvantaged kids are teachable; and that as teachers they could—indeed, would have to—break loose from traditional classroom techniques. When in the fall they returned to their regular jobs, therefore, their experiences would provoke a "ripple effect," helping create a new climate of innovation and hope along the dingy corridors of ghetto schools.

Like many parts of the poverty program, Upward Bound settled down in a year or two to slightly less lofty goals: teaching the skills and motivations supposed to be necessary for college. Most programs have, in fact, concentrated on the first of these, proposing as goals, to take one example, increasing students' "reading speed and comprehension," "vocabulary and facility in verbal expression," "auditory and visual perceptual skills," "mathematical skills," "ability to think critically," and other "skills essential to academic success, such as using the library, taking exams, and studying efficiently." The Indiana State University program, from which we have been quoting, included "tachistoscopic training" in more rapid perception of letters and numerals; a course in study habits; "Language Arts," which applied to spelling, grammar, usage, and vocabulary "the basic technique of 'test-teach-test-teach-test' to the point of mastery" (or misery), and which used poetry "as a means of changing pace . . . providing a contrast in course content . . . [and] for choral reading" and music, in which "the students were given frequent occasions to exercise by standing, flexing the muscles of their bodies, and executing all drills and exercises with a full voice not unlike that required in military training situations."[18]

While the approach of the Indiana State program is more explicitly behaviorist than most, it is also fair to add that all programs were more filled with lovingkindness than tachistoscopic training might imply. But from the first there was conflict about underlying assumptions. Upward Bound's public-relations booklet proclaimed that the program

> aims to turn these youngsters around. . . . It seeks to rescue the youngster whose brains and ability may be lost to society, or worse yet, be directed against society, unless he can be motivated to apply his talents and energies constructively.

"Rescue," "lost," "constructively"—the words of religious social work seep through the prose. We "rescue" a student from high school and send him "constructively" to college. Over against them, we heard the words (unknown to the pamphlet's writers) of the popular civil-rights song, distinctly "improper" in syntax and pronunciation: "Ain't gonna let nobody turn me roun', turn me roun', turn me roun'. . . ." What did "turn . . . around" mean? Grow less hostile to school? Recognize the institution as your friend? In Mississippi, when you sang that song, you were refusing to give up the struggle for freedom, you were refusing to be a good nigger or a passive acceptor of racism and racist institutions. You were promising to be disobedient to immoral rules that would control you.

Inside Upward Bound, as teachers, and later as consultants, we argued the paradox in 1967 and 1968. Why convince students that institutions hostile to their race and class were "friendly" when, in fact, students had to divest themselves of race and class in order to be acceptable, to "make it" in college? Why, in other words, send black students acceptingly into a new educational prison even as you were, at least by implication, condemning their current ones? Upward Bound, conceived as a program outside the system and critical of it, might provide black students with "space" to flex their muscles and brains: to be themselves, black women and men, instead of carbon copies. Most early programs we knew firsthand suggested (and early Washington staff members agreed) that the way to change the system was to enlist Upward Bound teachers and students in the struggle. Black students could be taught the truth about the schools, their class and racial status in U.S. society; and on the strength of this knowledge—as in Mississippi freedom schools—students would be motivated to work for change even as they made their way through college. Teachers, drawn into the program and changed by their participation in it, would return to their high schools or colleges also equipped to work for change, or at the very least, to support those students. The idea is not implausible, were schools not so deeply committed to social control, were racism not so deeply implanted in us all and in our institutions, were economic inequities not so intransigent.

Even more immediate practical problems plagued those organizing programs to activate political consciousness. Such programs may not at first (nor ever) produce students who speak standard English or evince gratitude. Test scores may not be altered quickly enough, say, in the course of one summer, to appease those impatient for real signs that money has been well invested. From the start, there were pressures on Upward Bound to show evidence of success in the form first of before-and-after test scores, and later in the form of a low dropout rate from college. One additional practical problem had to do with tone: how could programs send hundreds, then thousands of rebellious or bumptious students into colleges? Would such students pass enough courses even to be allowed to stay? Would thirty Upward Bound students, from a single two-year program, spread out through nearly as many colleges, find the strength, separated as they were, to endure, let alone fight, the system?

Some of our questions, though useful for this chapter, were rendered rhetorical for Upward Bound. National staff members who had been discreet about their visionary goals for the tiny program found themselves by 1968 not only pressed from above to produce visible "results" but at the same time incapable of finding local staff below them to organize programs emphasizing activism and political consciousness. The bulk of staff were local high-school and college teachers, who, without special training, could only continue to do what they had been doing. Thus, while early Upward Bound directives called for the selection of a strong proportion of "high risks"—students with very poor grades and possibly with disciplinary records—after 1968, the emphasis is on signs of achievement and malleability. The original notion that those students who reacted negatively to high schools might indeed be among the most creative one could attempt to "turn around" and into college disappeared in a sea of rationalizations about the need for blacks to receive "proper training" in skills, period.

We had heard these arguments expressed at various Upward Bound conferences in 1967 and by members of the program we participated in. "We're responsible," one teacher said, "for giving these boys and girls what they need to be self-sufficient in our society." They have to be helped to hold a job, another added, "by accepting or learning some middle-class values." And as still another said, "We've got to fit them to the real world; if you deny that, you deny the name you give the program." Upward Bound—and its title is undeniably prophetic—thus becomes not a visionary scheme for changing racist institutions but a means to fit more youngsters into them. We return to the language of the public-relations booklet:

> . . . to turn these youngsters around . . . finding a way to boost the
> deflated self-esteem of the impoverished youngster. Convincing

him of his own personal worth and ability to succeed *despite the deprivation of his background* is the key that releases the student to develop his potential. [Italics ours.]

The deprivation of his background: how do you teach a student whom you view in this light? What must he learn? "We all know," Upward Bound staff members were fond of saying, that "what black students need to complete high school and enter college is mostly irrelevant to their lives." "The curriculum," some went further, is "irrelevant even to the lives of middle-class students." But there is a difference between them. The Indiana State program's booklet puts it explicitly, though we have heard the same analysis everywhere. Black students "were highly likely to be missing" two things that were "required" presumably of all students for success in school: a firmly fixed goal for attainment in the future and the capacity to defer the need for immediate gratification for the sake of attaining that future goal.

We will not here outline the procedures recommended for teaching students to delay gratification—an unsophisticated version of baiting mazes with cheese. Nor will we do more than name as bald racism the stereotypes of immediate versus delayed gratification as it is currently used in the jargon of psychologists and educators. The message to all students, though we are concerned with blacks here, is clear enough: do what you are told now, swallow the nasty or useless lesson, and you will receive your just reward—admission to college. Alone, or with regard to whites, this might be insipid pedagogy. Combined with the element named by the Indiana writers and fundamental to Upward Bound's general strategy as "intervening in the life situation" of ghetto youth, the notion of "deprivation" becomes explicitly racist.

Why *deprivation of his background?* What does that conjure up? Vague slurs against his parents' poverty? Or his genetic structure? Why not name the system that has controlled the lives of black people? Why emphasize "his background"? And how is it possible for a student (or a teacher) to separate his "background" from his "self," his personal being, his esteem, his motivation? Scrutinized, the idea is an awkward one for educators to maintain, unless they admit frankly that they want the student to disassociate himself from "his background," and thus, in the words of the Indiana program again, "form a reasonably self-consistent and compatible structure within the context of the student's on-going life situation." That is, if the student is moved onto a campus ("intervention in the life situation"), the educational theory assumes that the act "protects nascent attitudes or feelings about goals and goal-directed behavior." In plain language, the student has to be taught to turn his back on his black and/or lower-class "background" and become an assimilated member of a campus society. Only thus can he allegedly break the cycle of poverty with which he has been unluckily afflicted. At the same time, the notion of a deprived background also forces students to internalize the deficiencies of a racist society and, even further, to declare themselves part of its racist institutions on the campus. We prefer the frankness of a New Jersey program director who announced once at a meeting that he says to students, "Look, it's all a matter of test-taking. We'll teach you to take tests and you can do what you like in college." At least there is no attempt either to do social work among those of "deprived backgrounds" or to recruit blacks blinded by the system into its service.

Identical theories about deprived backgrounds and similar strategies of intervention inform Head Start, from the first a larger, more costly, and more respected program than Upward Bound.[19] Educational theorists—notably Martin Deutsch—had observed that poor and working-class black children were not "prepared" for school as were middle-class children. Thus, they fell immediately behind. Why not, the logic asked, provide black youngsters with a "Head Start" before school began? Initially, summer programs were organized, but when these produced no notable results, year- and summer-long preschool Head Starts were begun.

From the outset, the programs were drawn in two directions, different more in appearances and tone than in reality. Traditionalists, regardless of race, saw the extra year as an opportunity for starting children on what they would have to learn in school: standing on line for the bathroom, recognizing the letters, wiping their noses, learning the numbers, obedience. For them, preschool meant a well-disciplined, orderly room and results that one could test and measure. On the other side, many nursery-school teachers, amateurs, and educational innovators tried to build their programs around free play, free form, and new learning experiences for the children. The new experiences, Deborah Meier pointed out, were of two types:

(1) good and consistent examples of politeness, middle-class articulation, vocabulary, and neatness; and (2) a planned program to introduce the children through experiences, games, drills, etc., to various habits, manners, skills, and language arts already familiar to the middle-class child entering kindergarten. They will play house and, as they do so, learn how to set the table, say "please pass the butter," answer the door or phone politely, etc.[20]

More rarely, where Head Start was the result of local effort, as in the Child Development Group of Mississippi, the program involved significant numbers of parents and people from the community as staff members. It thus did manage to channel at least some federal funds into the black community. And it provided a happy ground for educational psychologists anxious to test out theories.

What it didn't do was work. A long and detailed study by the Westinghouse Learning Corporation, released in early 1969, only confirmed what was already clear to observers: that children who emerged from Head Start might begin slightly ahead of other black or poor children, but within a year or two at most their performances were indistinguishable. And there was no reason to believe that by the fifth year of school the achievement levels of these black children, for all of Head Start, would not once again be two years behind national norms. The Westinghouse report has been attacked, it is true, but mainly because of its failure to consider the program's side effects on local communities. To judge by the attack mounted by Mississippi officials against the Child Development Group and its successors, these effects may have been substantial. But the basic finding only confirms earlier evaluations of other compensatory education funded under Title I of the Elementary and Secondary Education Act: intervention programs like Head Start do not significantly improve black children's achievement scores.

Considerably before the Westinghouse study, some criticisms of Head Start had effected the beginnings of yet another compensatory program and a cluster of proposals for earlier intervention. Those who believed that the effects of Head Start were real, but "lost" in school, began to develop "Follow Through" projects in a handful of ghetto schools during 1968–69. Much more vocal were those who asserted that intervention in the child's fourth or fifth year came "too late." Daniel Patrick Moynihan, the President's urban-affairs adviser, known for his negative view of the Negro family structure, urged on the administration a commitment not only to Head Start but to the entire "first five years of life." This commitment, *The New York Times* reported, "stems in part from the belief that one trouble with Head Start is that children may have been so badly damaged in infancy by poor nutrition and lower-class circumstances that Head Start cannot make much difference."[21] The groundwork for earlier intervention had been already laid. Bettye M. Caldwell, for example, wrote in 1967 that

> the research literature of the last decade dealing with social-class differences has made abundantly clear that all parents are not qualified to provide even the basic essentials of physical and psychological care to their children. . . . There is, *perhaps unfortunately,* no literacy test for motherhood.[22] [Italics ours.]

Her solution? "Educationally oriented day care for culturally deprived children between six months and three years of age." Children would be removed to such centers during the day, "hopefully [to] prevent the deceleration in rate of development which seems to occur in many deprived children around the age of two to three years." It is only a short step from here to Bruno Bettelheim's proposal to remove all ghetto children to kibbutz-like compounds, where they can be properly brought up without the infections of ghetto life.[23]

The psychologists and educators prepared to destroy Negro family life in the name of rectifying the school performance of black children seem to confuse effects and causes. They locate the child's difficulties in himself or his parents, rather than in the racist institutions which control his life. Their programs calling for earlier and earlier intervention assume that black families and especially black mothers do not provide an adequate educational environment for their children. In practice, as Joan and Stephen Baratz have pointed out, educators have thus provided another explanation for the low achievement of blacks in schools, one that eliminates some, if not all, of their culpability. If one intervenes at six months, why not at three, or at one, or before birth or conception? The Baratzes conclude: "the deficit model of Head Start forces the interventionist closer and closer to the moment of conception and to the possibility of genetic determination of the behavior now attributed to a negative environment."[24]

And that, of course, is where Arthur Jensen has arrived. In response to the mounting evidence that compensatory and interventionist programs were ineffective, he produced a huge document, published by the *Harvard Educational Review*, suggesting that the problem lay, finally, not in poor ghetto environments or inadequate black mothers. It might also be, he argued, that American blacks were genetically inferior—not, to be sure, because, as older southern racists had maintained, God willed it so, but because they had been bred by slavemasters for brawn rather than brains, and then steadily deselected by the kind of world in which they had to live.[25] Conservative columnists and politicians seized upon Jensen: at last the scientific proof that took them off the hook. "Allus said ya cain't edjicate 'em." And liberals hurried to the defense of more, bigger, and better interventions.

But when we are faced with the choices of doing what has failed, only more so ("Follow Through"); destroying the normal patterns of child-rearing and family life among black people (Caldwell, Bettelheim); or accepting the racist scientism that declares blacks mentally inferior (Jensen)—it is time to call a halt, time to stop looking for the mote in the eyes of the children and their families, and to begin scrutinizing the psychologists, the educators, and their institutions. That is precisely what a group of linguists and young psychologists, led by William A. Stewart, Joan and Stephen Baratz, and William Labov, has begun to do.[26] In a series of papers, only recently beginning to see print, they have attacked the theory and "evidence" behind compensatory and interventionist programs.

The initial premise of all interventionists, from Upward Bound directors down to Bruno Bettelheim, is that black children are, if not defective, at least deficient. In particular, they are verbally "impoverished," because their environments are thin, empty of objects worthy of discussion, and because their mothers do not talk much to them, or only in half-formed sentences. Thus black children speak poorly, in incomplete, incorrect sentences; their vocabulary is limited; they are, thus, typically characterized as unable to respond to simple instructions or to follow thoughts logically. In a pamphlet called "Principles and Practices in Compensatory Education," widely circulated around the Chicago school system, Professor Paul A. Witty cites Robert Havighurst, the University of Chicago educator, to the effect that "disadvantaged" children have "family characteristics resulting from living in homes in which language facilities and general experiences are meager and limited. . . . "[27] Or to provide another example, in a popular pamphlet issued by the New Jersey Community Action Training Institute, John Henry Martin, a busy educational bureaucrat, asserts that "by the age of five, there is a wide difference in the vocabulary and complexity of speech of children of poverty and their middle-income counterparts."[28] The educators are, of course, simply relaying to the general public the "findings" of psychologists like Martin Deutsch, Carl Bereiter, Arthur Jensen, and others.[29] Unfortunately, as William Labov has pointed out,

> these notions are based upon the work of educational psychologists who know very little about language and even less about Negro children. The concept of verbal deprivation has no basis in social reality: in fact, Negro children in the urban ghettos receive a great deal of verbal stimulation, hear more well-formed sentences than middle-class children, and participate fully in a highly verbal culture; they have the same basic vocabulary, possess the same capacity for conceptual learning, and use the same logic as anyone else who learns to speak and understand English.[30]

Labov goes on to examine each of the assumptions of the verbal-deprivation theorists—that black children are nonverbal, monosyllabic, withdrawn; that middle-class speech is a richer, more flexible code; that blacks speak an ungrammatical, deficient form of English; and that they are incapable of logical discourse. Citing detailed evidence drawn from his own work with black children in central Harlem, and from the linguistic analyses of Stewart, Baratz, and others, Labov proceeds to puncture each of these assumptions. He reports, for example, on a succession of interviews between a black researcher, from the Harlem community, and an eight-year-old black boy. In the first interviews, formally structured, despite the relative closeness of the relationship between interviewer and child, the boy is indeed monosyllabic, withdrawn, almost suspiciously "stupid" in his widely separated responses. But then four changes are introduced into the interview situations: the interviewer sits down on the floor with the child, Leon, brings him a bag of potato chips, thus making it a kind of party, invites another eight-year-old friend, and introduces taboo words and taboo ideas, thus overcoming the child's suspicion of the microphone and setting. And suddenly Leon is an excited and quite normally verbal child, as anyone who observed him at play in his community would have known him to be. The point, Labov observes, is

> that the social situation is the most powerful determinant of verbal behavior and that an adult must enter into the right social relation with a child if he wants to find out what a child can do: this is just what many teachers cannot do.

Nor is it what the verbal-deprivation theorists have done; they have judged children deficient on the basis of formal interviews or children's often fearful and defensive reactions to white, middle-class, organized classrooms. They have not credited their own or others' ears in discovering the verbal lives of ghettos. As we know from Mississippi, from our own teaching, experience, and friendships, from the epigraph to this chapter, black language is colorful, precise, sharper than foamy middle-class speech, consistent, and logical— a dialect different from but hardly inferior to middle-class-white English.

A series of experiments and papers by Joan Baratz and William A. Stewart demonstrates that the black child's "language does not represent a pathology, a failure to learn the rules of a linguistic system, but rather . . . the fact that he has learned some different, equally highly structured, highly complex rules of language behavior." Baratz, for example, adapted a technique often used to cite black children's supposed lack of verbal skills: asking them to repeat standard English sentences read to them. She used two groups, one of black speakers of nonstandard English, and the other white speakers of standard, and she asked them to repeat sentences, some of which were standard, others nonstandard. White children found it as difficult to repeat nonstandard sentences as blacks to repeat standard ones; and blacks were as successful in repeating nonstandard as whites in repeating standard. Thus, to declare black children verbally deficient on the basis of their inability to repeat standard-English sentences is to reveal only the cultural bias of the experimenter, perhaps his racism as well, and probably his ignorance of linguistic theory. For he is testing neither children's capacity to use language nor their intelligence, but rather their ability to handle a dialect not their own.[31]

The significance of the linguistic evidence which Stewart, Labov, and the Baratzes have brought into focus for us can hardly be exaggerated. For if they are correct in asserting—as the evidence overwhelmingly testifies that they are—that black children are quite verbal, that their language, while different from standard, white, middle-class speech, is by no means deficient, either in imagery or in logic, then the foundations upon which the ever-more baroque and expensive interventionist programs are erected must disintegrate. As do the racial-inferiority spooks of Jensen. The supposed linguistic inferiority of black children becomes a function not of inferior environment or heredity, but an artifact created by imposing on black children the white, middle-class standards of the white, middle-class educators and psychologists themselves. Not understanding the language, the depth, the nature of black, and lower- and working-class culture, the interventionists assume that blacks are to be treated as defective whites. Like other kinds of interventionists, they would bring to the struggling blacks the benefits of white man's culture and language; all he must do is surrender his own. And thus they created programs, as the Baratzes put it, "designed (1) to destroy an already functionally adequate system of behavior because it is viewed as pathological and (2) to impose a system of behavior without recognizing the existence of a functionally adequate system of behavior already in place (thus it is comparable to attempting to pour water into an already wine-filled pitcher)."[32] In this spirit, Americans have brought civilization into every corner of the globe and every hamlet in Vietnam.

The assumption that "white is right" creates institutions to prove and to maintain that assumption. It is not merely that the interventionists calculated incorrectly, that Head Start failed because its goal was to "correct a deficit that simply does not exist."[33] More fundamentally, language has its roots at the very core of individual personality and of group culture. There is no marvel to equal the process by which the brain absorbs the extraordinarily complex set of linguistic rules governing our speech. And language persists. We recall the Chicano organizer Corky Gonzales, speaking of the Mexican-American's Spanish: it is like the land, hidden and despoiled, but it remains and returns. William Stewart suggests that African patterns still exist in nonstandard Negro dialects. And Michele Russell, a young black professor of literature, talks of black language as secretive, shifting, ambiguous, like slave songs, because of the demands of "survival."[34] To "correct" a child's language, is to "correct" him, for he is not separate from it. To stigmatize a child's language as "wrong," as teachers do day in and out, is to stigmatize him and his people. To devote massive programs and the early years of school to wiping out his language is to attempt to wipe him out, the black real him, that is. If kids defensively withdraw or strike out in rebellion, shall we be surprised? For they are in a machine that grinds everyone to white, middle-class dimensions or proves the superiority of such standards by spitting them out as rejects, defective goods.

In this light we can understand how not only the ordinary operations of school, but even the programs supposedly set out to help black kids, in fact injure them. For, to borrow Labov's indignant view,

> Bereiter and Engelmann, Deutsch and Jensen are giving teachers a ready-made, theoretical base for the prejudice they already feel against the lower-class Negro child and his language. When they hear him say "I don't want none" or "They mine," they will be hearing through the bias provided by the verbal deprivation theory: not an English dialect different from theirs, but the primitive mentality of the savage mind.[35]

Like the Red Cross's notions of "normalcy" we described at the outset, like the theories upholding black integration into white schools and culture, the deprivation hypothesis, erected presumably to help blacks, branches into a means of institutionalizing racism. It is not, we must repeat, that men like Deutsch and Bereiter are "subjectively" apologists for racism any more than the "rub-off"-theory integrationists were; it is rather that the unchallenged assumptions at the heart of their work—and especially their pose of scientific objectivity—produce objectively racist results.

The demands for black-community control over black schools and for black studies arose dialectically as integration and intervention programs failed. Such demands are in the first place a call for an end to the racist control over the education of black people that extends in an unbroken line from the first slave ships to the white-marble buildings of the Office of Economic Opportunity and the Office of Education. They are also injunctions that education be responsive to the problems and needs of the black community, that it become a process not of expunging blackness, but of discovering, understanding, and celebrating it.

Blackness, Vincent Harding has proposed,

> meant the beginning, for some, of a profound search for roots, roots to let them stand firmly in the midst of the constant struggle, roots to feed long-felt but scarcely comprehended inner thirsts for meaning, authenticity, and life. Blackness meant, too, an increasing sense of solidarity with colonized and broken colored peoples across the globe whose movement for new life and new control had quickened black Americans and in turn been strengthened by our struggle.[36]

For many white and especially some Negro faculty members, administrators, and professionals, such yearnings and aspirations seemed vague, romantic, half-baked. They would lead to programs, it was warned, that would neglect academic principles, ignore standards and the accumulated knowledge of scholars. Worse, black studies would become a retreat for Negro students unwilling or unable to compete, a "pork-chop" haven used by universities cheaply to push through black students whom they had been pressured to admit, but for whom they had no programs. Andrew Brimmer, a Negro governor of the Federal Reserve Board and an overseer of Harvard University, criticized black students' concern with the "blackman's cultural image":

> They should have no illusions about the extent to which they are likely to acquire in "black studies" programs the mental discipline, technical skills, and rigorous training in problem-solving that they will so desperately need in their future careers.[37]

Stressing that Negroes are now getting ahead more rapidly than whites, Brimmer called for greater effort to be "concentrated on the improvement of technical competence, the acquisition of marketable skills and the enhancement of their ability to compete in an economy of expanding opportunities." Similarly, John W. Blassingame, writing in *The American Scholar,* asserted that Negro students should "study business practices, high finance, labor law and practices, judicial procedures, consumer practices and the communications media. Armed with this knowledge, blacks would know which of the inter-locking corporations to boycott or buy stock in to bring about a mean-ingful change in their economic position." If such critics are correct, black studies, though conceived by blacks, could emerge as much a cheat as white-organized integration or intervention programs.

Judge George William Crockett, Jr., provides some insight to the need for black consciousness, even, or particularly, among profes-sionals:

> "I'm a *black* judge," he says, "and I never allow myself to forget that fact. If I did, I'd be lost. See, you can't grow up in a racist society then get a chance to serve on a judicial bench and not be conscious that you're black. I don't care what some other black judges say, you just can't do it. You're always aware that you're not white, you're *black*. Now some people will say that such a consciousness should be suppressed when you're elec-ted to the bench. But the law doesn't say that you've got to for-get your race. It says that you're not to let race influence your judicial decisions. And I don't. I just insist that every defendant, white or black, who comes before me be given a *fair* trial, a *proper* trial. And during that trial my feelings about race are never used *against* anyone. But by feelings about race have been, and will continue to be, used to right some of the wrongs that have been committed against black people."[38]

Judge Crockett thus makes explicit that his ability to function as a judge determined to right wrongs done to black people is rooted in his black consciousness. And that is fundamentally the theory of black studies. Students must be made aware and proud of them-selves as blacks so that they can apply their skills to the liberation of all black people. Or, to use the words of Malcolm X: "We are creat-ing a generation of black young people who will know what they want, and they will create a generation who will know how to get what they want."

Black studies implies, in some large measure, the rejection of traditional career patterns espoused by Brimmer, and thus of the professionally oriented curricula of most colleges. "Young people are no longer satisfied," says L. F. Griffin, president of the Afro

Association at Harvard, "with just pulling down their bundle, and that goes for whites as well as blacks."[39] Such students are prepared to refuse what one has called "the white man's benevolent offer of a 32nd vice niggership at General Motors,"[40] not out of some abstract spirit of self-sacrifice. Rather they have begun to understand institutional racism in the United States, and thus learning what the white boys learn, taking on the same jobs and the same coloration, is for them "to learn how to support and administer the political structure and economic system that subjugates and manipulates black people in every social sphere."[41] What they have to learn, black students say, is not how to get ahead in the system, but how to change it.

Changing it requires, first of all, changing their own consciousness, unindoctrinating, "decolonizing" their minds. Schools, the operations of intervention and compensatory programs, the actions of racist institutions, have subjected blacks as well as whites to the "white-is-right" viewpoint, to the white view of what is appropriate for study, of what is "objective" and what is propagandistic. Thus, for black students, work for social revolution must be preceded by an "internalized revolution":

> It is the necessary function of knocking out old psychic structures, and the creation of new images. This process of black "re-socialization"—which students have spearheaded for the past decade—is creating a new consciousness of self and political awareness of the socio-political and economic institution that perpetuates the dual caste-class oppression of black people in America.[42]

One part of black-studies programs is devoted to such ends. A course at the University of Chicago, its instructor explains, is "a survey of institutional racism":

> I look at schools, welfare politics and the social services in terms of their racist impact. I am trying to teach people how to take apart institutions and eliminate their built-in biases.[43]

Far from becoming cake walks, courses dealing with institutional racism—as this chapter has only suggested—carry the student into a number of academic disciplines and insist that he develop analytic skills. Or perhaps to redefine separated disciplines like economics and political science as political economy. Courses in black history are designed to correct long-perpetuated myths, as well as to view America from a perspective seldom represented in textbooks. Black-literature courses examine ignored writers as well as develop a critical perspective that does not view works of art as remote, permanent things of beauty, but as actively engaged in shaping and evoking consciousness. Other parts of black-studies programs develop the sources of black culture, pride, and strength: the history and arts of Africa and of the Caribbean, the cohesiveness and vigor of black life in America, as well as its problems.

What students are seeking in black studies, we would suggest, is not an evasion of reality, but an understanding of it and the development of tools to grapple with it. Malcolm X Liberation University, opened in the fall of 1969 in Durham, North Carolina, carries the logic of independent black-studies programs one step further into a separate institution. But its goals are not different from those articulated by blacks at other institutions. Director Howard L. Fuller explains that Malcolm X University "will provide a framework within which black education can become relevant to the needs of the black community and the struggle for black liberation. This is a nation-building school. . . . " Though the graduates will receive no formal degrees, they will, as Malcolm had hoped, "be black people who know what they're doing."[44] These students and others soon to emerge from black-studies programs will, we think, begin to redefine the United States and its institutions from the black perspective of those whom such institutions have oppressed. And they will begin to bring into being for black people in the United States a society in which they need not choose between subservience and assimilation, but in which they can be equal as well as distinctive. Thus the answer to institutional racism, black studies leads us to believe, is neither integration nor intervention, but the institutions organized for black solidarity and black revolution.

Notes

[1] Jon Nordheimer, "Status and Storm Relief," in *The New York Times,* January 12, 1970. Nordheimer suggests that the anger of the blacks was directed "not at racial bigotry as much as it was at class distinctions." That would be an accurate observation except for the fact that in many parts of the United States blacks make up a substantial part of the working class and almost wholly the "under" or "lower" class—i.e., those without regular jobs or salable skills. Thus, in practice, class discrimination and racism can become almost indistinguishable. Another way of putting the point is that blacks are discriminated against both as working- or under-class people and as blacks— but the point can get to be academic.

[2] Though we write chiefly about blacks here, most of what we say may be applied with ease to other people of color in the United States.

[3] Cited in Frank Joyce, "An Analysis of American Racism" (Boston: New England Free Press).

[4] For these and other details, see David K. Shipler, "Zoning Laws Face a Growing Attack by Rights Groups," in *The New York Times,* December 14, 1969.

[5] For a detailed account of the effects and mechanisms of "blockbusting" and similar real-estate practices, and of white flight from blacks, see Douglas Connah, Jr., "Blockbusting in Baltimore: Less Blatant and Rapacious," Baltimore *Sunday Sun,* January 26, 1969.

[6] See Homer Bigart, "Hunger in America: Mississippi Delta," in *The New York Times,* February 18, 1969. Bigart points out that in Mississippi Delta counties the infant-mortality rate among blacks was 72.7 per 1,000 in 1965; maternal death rate was 25.1. Such outrageous statistics are directly related to nutrition.

[7] See Francis X. Clines, "State to Implement a Disputed Law Requiring Able-Bodied Welfare Recipients to Work," in *The New York Times,* December 14, 1969. Clines reports the concern of New York City's human-resources administrator that the law could require hundreds of thousands of people, including welfare mothers, to report every two weeks instead of remaining at home with their families.

[8] Charles L. Sanders, "Detroit's Rebel Judge Crockett," *Ebony,* XXIV (August, 1969), pp. 116, 118.

[9] James S. Coleman, *Equality of Educational Opportunity* (Washington, D.C.: U.S. Government Printing Office, 1966).

[10] See Roy Reed, "School Segregation—Northern Style," in *The New York Times,* February 23, 1969.

[11] See John Egerton, *State Universities and Black Americans* (Washington: National Association of State Universities and Land Grant Colleges, 1969).

[12] DeVere E. Pentony, "The Case for Black Studies," in David A. Hughes, ed., *From a Black Perspective* (New York, 1970), pp. 212–13.

[13] Lloyd Marcus, *The Treatment of Minorities in Secondary School Textbooks* (New York, 1961), p. 44.

[14] *Ibid.*, p. 47.

[15] *Ibid.*, p. 45.

[16] For example *The Hip Reader* (Brooklyn: Book-Lab, Inc., 1969) was prepared by two psychologists for inner-city "nonreaders." Full of "duke, juke, Luke, uke" rhymes, and conventional school morality, they are being touted as able to improve reading scores by as much as a year or two. An excerpt suggests how tuned in they are to ghetto life: "Mat the Cat from 46th Street and Dan the Rat were now good pals. They dug Jane and June who were their wives. Dot and Tom, Ed and Gus, also in the mob, were their pals. Luke the Duke, Rube the Dude, cute Lil and fat Gil were in the mob, too.

"Now they all had jobs, some in the shop, some in a bus, and some in a store. One was a cop.

"They had a juke box in the shop. Each Sunday they had a dance. No one was now on dope, or wine, or rum. All were dudes in the good life."

Perhaps it is irreverent to wonder what jobs they had in a bus.

[17] From the beginning Upward Bound attempted to be integrated; in 1966, about half the 20,000 students were black and a third white. The others were Puerto Ricans, Chicanos, Indians, Chinese. Nevertheless, the ideology of the program arose out of cultural-deprivation theories largely rooted in research on black people.

[18] Quotations from "Upward Bound: War on Talent Waste at Indiana State University," a special issue of *The Teachers College Journal,* XXXVIII (January, 1967).

[19] The differences between the two programs may tell us something of the fundamental pessimism characteristic of many apparently enlightened educators who count as "lost" those vast numbers of students in poor schools beyond first grade.

[20] "Head Start or Dead End?", in *Poverty: Views from the Left,* eds. Jeremy Larner and Irving Howe (New York, 1968), pp. 133–34.

[21] Robert B. Semple, Jr., "White House and Advisers Stand by Report Critical of Head Start Program," In *The New York Times,* April 27, 1968.

[22] "What Is the Optimal Learning Environment for the Young Child?" in *American Journal of Orthopsychiatry,* XXXVII (1967), pp. 16, 17.

[23] *The New York Times,* March 17, 1969.

[24] "Early Childhood Intervention: The Social Science Base of Institutional Racism," in *Harvard Educational Review* (Winter, 1970).

[25] "How Much Can We Boost IQ and Scholastic Achievement?" in *Harvard Educational Review,* XXXIX (1969), pp. 1–123.

[26] These works include, in addition to the Baratz article mentioned above, the following: William Labov and Clarence Robins, "A Note on the Relation of Reading Failure to Peer-Group Status in Urban Ghettos," in *Teachers College Record,* LXX (1969); William Labov, "The Logic of Non-Standard English," in *Georgetown Monograph Series on Languages and Linguistics,* #22 (1969), pp. 1–43; William A. Stewart, "Urban Negro Speech: Sociolinguistic Factors Affecting English Teaching," in W. Shuy, ed., in *Social Dialects and Language Learning* (Champaign, Ill., 1964); William A. Stewart, "Historical

and Structural Bases for the Recognition of Negro Dialect," *Georgetown Monograph Series on Lanuages and Linguistics,* #22 (1969), pp. 239–47, and "Sociopolitical Issues in the Linguistic Treatment of Negro Dialect," in *Georgetown Monograph,* #22 (1969), pp. 215–23; Joan C. Baratz, "A Bi-Dialectal Test for Determining Language Proficiency," typescript; Joan C. and Stephen S. Baratz, "The Social Pathology Model: Historical Bases for Psychology's Denial of the Existence of Negro Culture," APA paper, Washington, D.C., 1969; "Urban Education: A Cultural Solution," typescript. The most complete bibliography of the subject is contained in the Baratzes' *Harvard Educational Review* article.

[27] "The Educability of Undereducated Americans," in "Principles and Practices in Compensatory Education," offprinted from the Sixty-Sixth Yearbook of the National Society for the Study of Education (Chicago, 1967), p. 67. Later Witty explains how "studies show that educationally retarded and 'disadvantaged' pupils," between whom, interestingly, he does not distinguish, "often have meager or narrow interests" (p. 79).

[28] "A Model Program for Educationally Deprived Children" (Trenton, New Jersey, 1968), p. 2.

[29] These positions are developed in the following works, among others: Jane B. Raph, "Language and Speech Defects in Culturally Disadvantaged Children: Implications for the Speech Clinician," *Journal of Speech and Hearing Disorders,* 32 (1967), pp. 203–15; Carl Bereiter, "Academic Instruction and Preschool Children," *Language Programs for the Disadvantaged, NTCE Task Force Report,* ed. Corbin and Crosby (Champaign, Ill.: NCTE, 1965); Carl Bereiter, et al., "An Academically Oriented Pre-School for Culturally Deprived Children," in Fred M. Hechinger, ed., *Pre-School Education Today* (New York, 1966), pp. 105–37; Carl Bereiter and Siegfried Engelmann, *Teaching Disadvantaged Children in the Preschool* (Englewood Cliffs, N.J., 1966); Martin Deutsch, et al., *The Disadvantaged Child* (New York, 1967); Martin Deutsch, Irwin Katz, and Arthur Jensen, eds., *Social Class, Race, and Psychological Development* (New York, 1968).

[30] "The Logic of Non-Standard English," *op. cit.*

[31] "A Bi-Dialectal Test for Determining Language Proficiency," *op. cit.*

[32] "Early Childhood Intervention," *op. cit.*

[33] *Ibid.*

[34] "Some Notes Toward a Radical Course in Black Literature," in *The Radical Teacher,* eds. Florence Howe and Paul Lauter, #2 (December 30, 1969), p. 1.

[35] "The Logic of Non-Standard English," *op. cit.*

[36] "Black Students and the 'Impossible Revolution,' " *Ebony,* XXIV (August, 1969), pp. 141–42.

[37] Joseph R. Slevin, "Black Studies Called Career Peril," Baltimore *Sun,* July 4, 1969.

[38] Charles L. Sander, "Detroit's Rebel Judge Crockett," *Ebony,* XXIV (August, 1969), p. 118.

[39] Steven V. Roberts, "Black Studies Aims Symbolic and Real," in *The New York Times,* May 15, 1969.

[40] Quoted in Harding, "Black Students and the 'Impossible Revolution,' " *op. cit.,* p. 143.

[41] James Turner, "Black Students and Their Changing Perspective," *Ebony,* XXIV (August, 1969), p. 137.

[42] Turner, "Black Students," *op. cit.,* p. 135.

[43] Roberts, "Black Studies Aims," *op. cit.*

[44] James T. Wooten, "Malcolm X University to Open in Durham as Militants'.School," in *The New York Times,* October 28, 1969.

10

The Female Majority

*The whole education of women ought to be relative
to men, to please them, to educate them when young,
to care for them when grown, to counsel them, and
to make life sweet and agreeable to them.*
—Jean Jacques Rousseau, Emile

*Feminine instincts are characterized by caring qualities,
concern for beauty and form, reverence for life, empathy
in human relations, and a demand that men be better than
they are.*

*—Charles De Carlo, shortly after
replacing Esther Raushenbush as
president of Sara Lawrence College*

In 1969, an eleven-year-old black girl, flown with her Alabama family for a week's vacation in New York City, was asked what she wanted to be when she grew up. Her answer was predictably "an airline stewardess"; like her fictional older brother, three or four decades earlier, Sweet Pea Anderson wanted a vocation in the sky; unlike him, however, she knew her place as a female. Since Bigger's day, racial integration among the staffs of the big jets has occurred, but their sexual stratification remains absolute: men fly; women look pretty, serve drinks, keep house.[1]

By and large, women have been content with that arrangement. Stewardesses have asked only that they may continue to serve past a marriage and the fading of their beauty. Sweet Pea might have been more socially ambitious; she might have said that she wanted to be a teacher, an editor, or a social worker, but she could not have said that she wanted to be a flier (just as most college women do not "want" to be engineers or lawyers), not if she was also a healthy, normal young American girl. Sexual lines in the United States are (and are likely to remain) more rigid than racial lines.

For better or worse, moreover, the battle to free women, beginning again after nearly forty dormant years, once more depends for symbol and sustenance on the black revolution. The analogue is a complex one and confusing, but worthy of review, especially since both women and blacks receive special treatment from U.S. institutions.[2] If one focuses only on the myth of inferiority, whether the victim is black or female hardly matters—the description is identical: inferiors are stupid or lazy or wicked, or all three. Social and economic institutions that support racism—the schools and the job market—also oppress women. And in the United States, both for blacks and women, the dominator-persecutor has typically been a white male, though his relationship to his victim may be different in each case. John Stuart Mill, who posed the analogy one hundred years ago, differentiated "forced" slaves from women, whom he characterized as "willing" ones. He distinguished also between the methods of masters who relied on "fear" and those "masters" who were husbands: "Men do not want solely the obedience of women, they want their sentiments." And hence, Mill wrote, "they turned the whole force of education to effect their purpose."[3]

Some who scorn the analogue altogether argue that most women hardly suffer even at the hands of the harshest husbands the forms of slavery that blacks have known; and that most of the women who still endure extreme economic hardship are not the white college students or professionals who have been among the most outspoken supporters of women's "liberation" but black working women (25 percent of whom in 1966 were domestics) and welfare mothers. Others point to the enormous power of women as consumers: consider, they say, that women are responsible for upwards of two-thirds of national domestic spending. On the other hand, current graphs of wages, arranged by race and sex, indicate that black men have taken the second place usually occupied by white women, now pushed down to third. (Of course, black women are still in fourth place.) Especially if one considers the proportion of black males in the population as against the proportion of black and white women, it is clear that racial barriers to employment are not as severe as sexual ones. The nation's "first black woman congressman" (as Shirley Chisholm prefers to be called) "had to fight doubly hard," and harder because of her sex than her race.[4]

It is impossible to say in 1970, for example, that particular professions are restricted—though they remain unbalanced—racially. Black males are courted as students, searched for as professors, and highly desired as professionals generally. They are, in fact, receiving what is justly due to their race—preferential treatment—in a belated effort to repair hundreds of years of injustice and injury. No department chairman in a "liberal" college or university would dare to say, "We have too many blacks in this department." Yet we know chairmen to have remarked, and in the presence of women who remained silent, "We have too many women already." While employment opportunities for black professionals continue to rise both in black institutions of higher education and in others eager for integration, no similar pattern prevails for women. The trend for at least two decades has in fact been the reverse: the proportion of women on faculties of women's colleges has sharply declined (as much as 27 percent in twenty-nine years, for example), and in the last several years most women college presidents (in nondenominational colleges) have been replaced by men. As for coeducational colleges and universities, every statistic points to discrimination on the one hand and, instead of the active faculty recruitment we now observe with regard to blacks, an active process of discouragement, on the other. In contrast to the rising expectations at least of black men, women, whatever their color, have been on their way down or back to slavery.

Perhaps the word is too harsh or crude for a culture built on deception and false expectations—"the American way is the indirect way"—on convincing young girls, whatever their opportunities for education, that their "place" is no different from that of their ancestors hundreds of years ago. Girls marry later than their great-great-grandmothers, and they live longer, and if they're middle or upper class, their education is not very different from their husbands'. But they spend anachronistic lives as full-time housekeepers, wives, and mothers. Unlike the recently angry or rebellious black man, moreover, women are the twentieth century's mythic happy slave, their lives paradigms of "service" to family and society.

But surely, the skeptics persist, women have not been subject to the gun and the rope, to the lynch mob, to the daily oppression of the cop on his beat. Given a chance, in fact, the chivalric policeman is women's friend. The brutalization of women, black and white, is less public than that of the black male. Though rape is increasingly commonplace (up 14 percent between 1967 and 1968), it is not a political crime. Even more rapidly increasing rates of physical assault have led young women to courses in karate and other forms of self-defense. Nor do women have control over their bodies in more fundamental respects, as, for example, whether or not they shall bear unwanted children. Even the most "liberal" abortion laws (in Washington, D.C., and Maryland) subject women to the decisions of psychiatrists, gynecologists, hospital boards, and lawyers, the vast bulk of them men. Even under these "liberal" laws women are forced into the humiliation of explaining how bearing a child might be injurious to "mental health" or physical well-being. Outside the law, the cost of abortion is at least $600 to $1,000, for those who can afford careful practitioners, and a high risk of infection for those who cannot. Almost a million women a year become "criminals" when they choose to control their own bodies.

There are also more subtle forms of oppression. The working woman at a liberation meeting who says, "If my husband knew I was here, he'd be sore. He thinks women ought to stay out of politics—and away from each other. I told him I was going to do some shopping." Or the middle-class woman unhappy but submissive about her husband's decision that it would be cheaper for him if she stayed home in the suburbs rather than worked in town. Or even the woman professor refusing to assume administrative responsibility, but accepting the task of taking notes: "I can't chair a meeting—men are much better at that sort of thing." Or perhaps most painful of all, the bright young girl who isn't sent to college because it's more important that her brother go. To be sure, the low expectations of women themselves are as essential to their subjection as more obvious external factors of discrimination in employment. It is no "accident," no anachronism, that our culture "channels" women not only into subordinate roles but into willing acceptance of their own subordination. Here, of course, the black analogue is obvious: for several centuries institutions from slavery itself to segregation to welfare have maintained the myth of black "inferiority"; now, in a single generation, the idea of black pride or "power" has overthrown these myths—at least among blacks. Attitudes among whites may not have changed in the last decade and a half, but that is not the point. People have to fight for their own freedom; no one can get it for anyone else. And women will have to learn, as black people have learned, to rediscover themselves as people.

But the black analogy is thoroughly misleading if women expect that their "liberation" can be accomplished as "readily" as that of blacks, however incomplete that liberation remains and however hard the struggle thus far. For educated women are "choosing" to stay at home or think about "jobs" for themselves rather than "careers," or to place their careers second to their husbands'. They accept jobs that pay them less than men for the same work; they accept jobs for which they are overqualified; they accept menial work; or they simply disappear from the statistics of the unemployed into the tasks of housekeeping. By and large, they do not complain; they certainly have not yet begun to organize collectively; the women's liberation movement notwithstanding, women are years, maybe longer, behind blacks even in feeling solidarity with each other.

The problem of "liberation" for women, moreover, is complicated by factors that are not present at all for blacks or other U.S. minorities: first, the institution of marriage and the family is an intransigent, basic fact of our culture, and women therefore can hardly consider separatism as a rational "solution," even as a temporary one. Though their history has been mostly repressed and denied to them, women cannot claim a separate historical culture or language, as U.S. blacks can. A study of the history or language and literature of women only reveals how inextricably they have been tied by men to men. Second, and paradoxically most difficult of all, women constitute not a minority but a majority. Hence, they are far more threatening, potentially, to males and to male-dominated institutions than any minority group. The truth is plain enough: it is perfectly understandable that men, on practical grounds alone, would oppose any potent move to demystify the notion of sexual stratification. For in U.S. society, there are just so many jobs: to open them equitably to women would mean that ordinary males would have to compete not only with each other but also with extraordinary as well as ordinary females. Such competition, given the additional element of marriage as an institution, would undoubtedly prove demoralizing and disruptive to a society that depends on women's keeping their places as the true silent majority.

NATURE OR NURTURE

Few young people are taught to believe in the genetic inferiority of black people, and most educated adults were embarrassed by Arthur Jensen's reopening of the biological discussion. If the question of race has been won by the scientific evidence of environmentalists, we ought to remember that most of the world's population, including ancient civilizations in the Orient and elsewhere, are nonwhite. In other words, it's rather difficult to maintain the biological inferiority of U.S. citizens of color with the evidence of three-fourths of the world out there to contradict such chauvinism. But women have never had the advantage of separatism. Discussions of their alleged genetic inferiority continue to rest only on belief.

Plato and Aristotle illustrate the two poles: the revolutionary believer in equality between the sexes and the traditional believer in the inferiority of women. Plato writes in *The Republic* that "There is no occupation concerned with the management of social affairs which belongs either to woman or to man, as such. Natural gifts are to be found here and there in both creatures alike; and every occupation is open to both, so far as their natures are concerned." He concludes, therefore, that "we shall not have one education for men and another for women, precisely because the nature to be taken in hand is the same." When he describes roles for women, he allows them "their full share with men" in all areas of life, "whether they stay at home or go out to war." He continues, "Such conduct will not be unwomanly, but all for the best and in accordance with the natural partnership of the sexes." Obviously, Plato's beliefs have not only not prevailed; they are hardly known today.

To read Aristotle on the same subject is to note how little a student may learn from a teacher. Aristotle believed that women were not only inferior to men intellectually, but emotionally and morally as well. His key statements appear in the *Politics:*

> We may thus conclude that it is a general law that there should be naturally ruling elements and elements naturally ruled. . . . The rule of the freeman over the slave is one kind of rule; that of the male over the female another. . . . The slave is entirely without the faculty of deliberation; the female indeed possesses it, but in a form which remains inconclusive. . . . It is thus clear that while moral goodness is a quality of all the per-

sons mentioned, the fact still remains that temperance—and similarly fortitude and justice—are not, as Socrates held, the same in a woman as they are in a man.

Aristotle thus offers no education to women. Or if we think of her in a category close to the slave's, only such education as will make her more useful to her master.

On the basis of observation and logic, two men in an ancient civilization came to different conclusions about women's nature. The fallibility of those conclusions notwithstanding, their significance lies in their application. For beliefs about the nature of woman inevitably control her nurture. A belief in capability will allow that destiny. But the tradition rooted in Aristotle and the Old Testament, rationalized by the Church fathers, and given modern dress by Freud and his followers, settled the question of female inferiority for the next two thousand years.

Western myths of the genesis of woman bind her dependently to man. Athena springs full-born from the brain of Zeus; Eve, from Adam's rib, as his "helpmeet." The Hebrew myth is explicitly hostile to woman: she is responsible for the loss of Paradise, objectively the source of man's punishment as well as her own. Expulsion from Eden brings forth explicit commandments about the hierarchical relationship between man and woman. Adam is warned never again to hearken "unto the voice of thy wife. . . ." Eve is told:

I will greatly multiply thy sorrow and thy conception; in sorrow thou shalt bring forth children; and thy desire shall be to thy husband, and he shall rule over thee.

When Milton turned his hand to writing a Christian epic, he hardened the hierarchy to begin with so that in *Paradise Lost* God speaks only to Adam, and Adam tells Eve just enough to keep her powerless and (dis)contented. She is, after all, not a "whole" person, but out of Adam's rib. As Milton characterizes the pair, they are

Not equal, as their sex not equal seemed;
For contemplation he and valour formed,
For softness she and sweet attractive grace;
He for God only, she for God in him.
                    [*Paradise Lost,* IV, II. 296–99]

While Milton announces that "true authority" rests "in men," recent versions are subtler.

In Freud's terms, the rib from which Eve was made deprived her of a penis, which is an exceedingly unhappy loss for her, and one for which she makes men suffer when she can. When woman is good, she is content with her second place; when she is bad—discontented or rebellious—she is a "castrating bitch." The theory that serves to locate sexuality in the phallus, conveniently for men, thereby denies woman her own independent sexuality. If sexuality also represents life, work, and such traits as aggressiveness and curiosity, she is denied all that as well. A female Freudian, Helene Deutsch, outdoes the master by equating "femininity" with "passivity" and "masculinity" with "activity," since these are "fundamental identities . . . in all known cultures and races. . . ." If a woman is "not entirely content with her own constitution," Dr. Deutsch writes, "the expression of this dissatisfaction, combined with attempts to remedy it, result in woman's masculinity complex.'"[5] Thus psychoanalysis denies woman, as Simone de Beauvoir has said, all choice. Her role as wife and mother is ascribed as compensation for her loss of penis.

It is not merely that psychoanalytic belief has replaced religious belief in our time; it is rather that such theories as Freud's are dangerous because of their association with biblical myth. Though most of us are not religious fundamentalists, the myths of a culture die hard, if at all. Myths are not "proofs" of anything but the status quo—they offer physical explanations of social conditions or social expectations. In other words, we can understand the story of the rib in the Old Testament as an attempt to explain the already established social inferiority of women. The social condition preceded the myth as well as the writing of the myth. Since the myth expresses a belief, not necessarily a truth, the condition of Eve's inferiority is possibly reversible—that is, if one were to think about changing social conditions rather than perpetuating them. But when, on the other hand, allegedly scientific theories are made of myth, they become totally irreversible. Freud claims to be describing ultimate or innate physical reality translated into psychological terms. According to Freudians, women are as Freud made them, in a biblical image. As we have said, myths die hard, if at all.

And apparently not at the hands of logic or reason. One hundred years ago John Stuart Mill proposed an agnostic view of the nature of women that still seems to us eminently reasonable today:

Standing on the ground of common sense and the constitution of the human mind, I deny that anyone knows, or can know, the nature of the two sexes, as long as they have only been seen in their present relation to one another. If men had ever been found in society without women, or women without men, or if there had been a society of men and women in which the women were not under the control of the men, something might have been positively known about the mental and moral differences which may be inherent in the nature of each. What is now called the nature of women is an eminently artificial thing—the result of forced repression in some directions, unnatural stimulation in others. It may be asserted without scruple, that no other class of dependents have had their character so entirely distorted from its natural proportions by their relation with their masters. . . .

Though Mill asks for agnosticism on the subject of woman's nature, he is, of course, assuming, as Plato did, that woman is potentially man's equal. He believes in her natural capacity and urges that environmental factors—"forced repression" and "unnatural stimulation"—account for her condition of subjection. If marriage keeps women at home managing households and rearing children, it is the institution's need, not woman's biological destiny. The differences in "nature" or ability between men and women, Mill says, are learned, not innate, differences.

Most recent research has verified Mill's belief that girls are, at least to begin with, as scholastically able as boys. In fact, before fifth or sixth grade girls "seem to be slightly ahead of boys" in speaking, counting, learning to read, and after the years of prepuberty girls are still somewhat more verbally fluent than boys. While "highly specified tests" have begun to chart "consistent sex differences," especially with regard to "cognitive abilities," Alice Rossi summarized in 1964, "what is known is that the key to the difference between boys and girls lies in the kind and degree of *independence training* the child receives in childhood."[6] (Italics ours.) In the last few years, research on the relationship between sex hormones and behavior patterns has again attempted to produce evidence for innate sex differences. The work, largely done with primates, concerns the "association" between "aggressiveness"—conceived as a typically masculine form of behavior—and the male hormone. Whether biochemical differences may be said to "determine" behavior or to provide what Eleanor Maccoby calls "rough boundaries for the shaping of individual personalities through learning" remains doubtful.[7] A thoroughgoing skeptic, psychologist Naomi Weisstein contends that "the only thing this argument [about hormonal differences] tells us is that there are differences in the physiological state. The problem is whether these differences are at all relevant to behavior."[8] Stanley Shachter and others have created experiments which demonstrate that social conditions in the immediate environment of subjects controlled their behavior regardless of hormonal injections. Hence, Eleanor Maccoby cautions, "It is important to be clear that biochemical factors of this kind cannot determine exactly what characteristics a human being will develop."

Despite several decades of experimental failure to verify assumptions about the innate nature of woman,[9] despite the cautions of informed scientists and social scientists, the biological mythmakers continue to pursue woman. The recent tack is subtler than the old. There are disclaimers about "proof." The word "intelligence" rarely appears, or women are declared "intelligent." It's not a matter of brain at all, or of inferiority as such, but rather of necessary, "legitimate," even delightful "difference" *(vive la difference!)*. Such differences, however disguised, continue to hearken back to the limiting associations of the words "female" or "feminine" with biblical and Freudian mythology. As the myth comes down to us today, it is more determinedly than ever before connected to woman's traditional role as wife and mother. For it holds not that woman is incapable of mental activity; rather, that she is happier, more "natural" when she is fulfilling her biological destiny.

Erik Erikson's approach to sex differences is apparently clinical. "Over a span of two years," he writes in a now famous article published in 1964,[10] "I saw 150 boys and 150 girls three times and presented them, one at a time, with the task of constructing a 'scene' with toys on a table." Though he did not begin the research with sex differences in mind, but rather with an interest in "spatial behavior," he discovered that "girls and boys used space differently": "the girls emphasized inner and the boys outer space." Erikson uses the following words to describe typical female scenes: "interior," "simple," "static," "enclosure," "low walls," "peaceful"; for male, "exterior," "elaborate," "moving," "high towers," "downfall," "ruins," "accidents." Finally, he concludes:

It may come as a surprise to some, and seem a matter of course to others, that here sexual differences in the organization of a play space seem to parallel the morphology of genital differentiation itself: in the male, an *external* organ, *erectible* and *intrusive* in character, serving the channelization of *mobile* sperm cells; *internal* organs in the female, with vestibular *access,* leading to *statically expectant* ova.

Why do the scenes so vividly described as social settings inevitably remind Erikson of genitalia? Erikson is an honest man: before he began to describe his experiments of the early 1950's to an audience in 1963, he described himself as "the kind of clinical worker in whose mind a few observations linger for a long time." "Such observations," he elaborated, "are marked by a combination of being surprised by the unexpected and yet somehow *confirmed by something long awaited*" (italics added). Erikson had not been convinced by Freudian accounts of "penis envy." He had not found it "reasonable" to assume that girls "would so exclusively focus on what is *not* there." But what if there were some other way of reading and hence believing in anatomical destiny? Hence the experience of recognition that Erikson so honestly reports. He found new equivalents for the mythic models: inner and outer space, new metaphors for passive and active, christened elaborately as "the experience of the groundplan of the human body." And who can argue with experience?

In fact, the arguments challenging Erikson's interpretations are perfectly obvious. Since he observed children, some of whom "went about the task with the somewhat contemptuous attitude of one doing something which was not exactly worth the effort of a young person already in his teens," is it not more reasonable to assume that they were recording a dozen years of social conditioning? They were asked to "imagine that the table was a moving picture studio; the toys, actors and props; and they themselves, moving picture directors." Their job was to arrange an "exciting" scene and tell the plot. It is hardly surprising that their spatial arrangements reflected sexual stereotyping to be found also not only in the children's literature they had read (which we will report on later in the chapter), but in films as well! We would interpret Erikson's pictures of "male" and "female" space sociologically. "Inner space" records the social condition that confines woman to Adam's house. Girls build little rooms in which they can feel comfortable. Boys think in terms of and occupy "outer space": thus, they become explorers, scientists, builders, leaders. Women tend the fire and dream. As Erikson concludes his essay, he brings us back to Eve, and the belief in woman's "natural dispositions," especially her "procreative task."

THE WORK OF WOMEN

The belief in woman's natural destiny as homemaker and mother controls her social experience even in 1970. Social and economic institutions—marriage and the family, a consumer economy, and a tight job market—have codified those beliefs. They function to preserve a family structure and a male-centered society that oppresses women. Simply to complain, therefore, about the system's "inequities" or to assume in the usual American way that more education will "end discrimination" is naïve; or, to imagine that through some series of small adjustments the system of male supremacy might be made more just is to miss the point. For institutional arrangements suit dominant social needs, or they would not persist.

Women play one support role as the essential "shock absorbers" (other sociologists have called them soft "cushions") for a hardening, tense male-centered society, providing comfort for the warrior home from his fields. They are also an expendable source of cheap, available labor. During World War II, women filled many jobs formerly occupied by men, most of which they willingly relinquished to them at the end of the war. But the point had been made: women could work as riveters or taxi drivers or even executives; and at least in wartime, they could raise children and enjoy useful work-lives. It was, therefore, most extraordinary to find, less than twenty years later, as Alice Rossi reported, that "for the first time in the history of any known society, motherhood has become a full-time occupation for adult women."[11] In 1963, Mrs. Rossi named as culprits responsible for the dependency of middle-class women "the experts"—Benjamin Spock among others—to whom mothers "turned for guidance" in child care. Most of these had asserted the need for mothers to stay home with their babies. But a review of fifteen years of research produced no evidence that mothers who work thereby harm their children. Mrs. Rossi found the results "hardly surprising," since she maintained that "the crucial question is not whether the mother is employed . . . [but] the quality of care given to the children." Mothers themselves may be loving or neglectful, overprotective or alert to a child's need for independence. Pointing to the dependency of middle-class children, their concomitant difficulties as adolescents in establishing separate identities, as well as to the increase in mental illness among the young, Mrs. Rossi concluded that full-time motherhood had hardly shown itself a successful mode of child rearing. She also dramatized the particular effect of full-time motherhood on women:

> Psychiatric counselors of college students frequently have as their chief task that of helping their young patients to free themselves from the entangling web of dependence upon their parents, primarily their mothers, and encouraging them to form stable independent lives of their own. In other words, if the patient is eighteen years old the analyst tries to help her free herself from her mother, but if the next patient is twenty-five years old with young children at home, the analyst tells her the children would suffer emotional damage if she left them on a regular basis to hold down a job. [Pp. 113–14.]

The contradictory advice encapsulates woman's socialization in the United States, since she is taught her position so thoroughly that she becomes its chief purveyor to her offspring. "Freeing" herself from her mother ironically does not prevent her from fostering dependency in her children. In fact, forcing full-time motherhood on her insists upon a pattern wasteful of her energies and one possibly destructive to her children as well.[12] Why, then, perpetuate the institution if it operates for no one's ultimate benefit?

The demands of a consumer economy provide one obvious answer. We need only note the rapid growth of a massive promotion and magazine industry designed to sell the consuming housewife in an economy geared to waste, excrescence, and obsolescence. Betty Friedan reports the conversation of a man who runs a "motivational-research operation":

> In a free enterprise economy . . . we have to develop the need for new products. And to do that we have to liberate women to desire these new products. We help them rediscover that

home-making is more creative than to compete with men. This can be manipulated. We sell them what they ought to want, speed up the unconscious, move it along.[13]

The language is reminiscent of the Selective Service channeling memorandum, which describes the "indirect" American manipulation of young men into college or particular industries essential to the "national interest." The young woman, maneuvered into the kitchen, "serves" society by buying its goods. Indeed, she is the vital human link in the chain of production and consumption that powers the U.S. economy.

Interestingly, however, though she has the enormous power of spending (we have seen estimates up to 75 percent of the consumer dollar), the role of spender-consumer does not seem to alter her view of herself as "only" a housewife. Apparently, to stay at home is to be passive and dependent; to be, in other words, inferior. A recent analysis by Margaret Benston connects the economic function of housework and its debased value.[14] The work of women "constitutes a huge amount of socially necessary production," Miss Benston maintains, among other reasons because many men could not function in their work without the resources and comfort at least of a wife. Yet "in a society based on commodity production [housework] is not usually considered even as 'real work' since it is outside of trade and the marketplace." The assignment of such work to women consigns them to inferiority: "In a society in which money determines value, women are a group who work outside the money economy. Their work is not worth money, it is therefore valueless, is therefore not even real work." If women do "valueless work," it is no wonder that they feel valueless. Even domestics hired as labor by bachelors and by professional women receive wages, however inadequate. But not women who work in their own homes: they are unpaid labor, requiring no preparation and taken utterly for granted. As the analysis helps us understand the masculine aversion to housework, it also illuminates the concomitant social need to convince women of their duty, even their desire, to serve in the kitchen. Crassly put: if someone has to do the chores, why not someone "willing"? Indeed, how else? If you cannot afford to pay them, nor wish to use force, what is there but to tempt and to persuade?

Keeping women in the household has other important economic virtues: the economy simply could not absorb into the labor force any significant number of the 34,000,000 women over sixteen who did not work in 1966.[15] The household is thus not only a prime consumer of goods, but a major absorber of surplus womanpower. Furthermore, because many women do sense housework as "valueless"—and not just because they do not get paid—they are easily exploited when they go out to work for money: any salary is better than none; and any form of production that distinguishes them from the cooking, cleaning, shopping round of those who are "only housewives" is gratifying. No wonder, then, that when President John Kennedy alluded to the need for increasing opportunities for women he called for them to be "used as effectively as they can be to provide a better life for our people—in addition to meeting their primary responsibility, which is in the home."[16] Using women "effectively"—as consumer, unpaid worker, reserve labor force—indeed depends upon maintaining the home as their "primary responsibility."

Given the demands of this "primary responsibility," it is not surprising to find that most working women take part-time, not full-time jobs. In 1966, only 40 percent of women workers had full-time jobs for the whole year (as contrasted with 70 percent of male workers); the rest worked part-time or only a small portion of the year. One means for reducing labor costs is to cut a full-time job into several part-time ones, paying only minimum wages without many fringe benefits. Part-time workers can be expected not to organize for annual raises in salary, much less for promotion or additional responsibility. And what is more, an employer of married women can feel that he is doing something for the cause of bored womanhood. If he makes additional profit on their part-time labor, he is only, as President Kennedy said, using women "effectively."[17]

By contrast, most professions have refused to consider the part-time employment of women, perhaps as a means of excluding them precisely where their work might be competitive with men's. Law is one of these professions, Caroline Bird notes,[18] and we would add university teaching at any but the most menial levels. Thus, the part-time arrangement, reasonable if the major family responsibility is to continue as a woman's, operates effectively at her expense, never for her benefit. The woman interested in a few dollars more of purchasing power or a few hours' relief from boredom can find them in part-time work, in a store or a plant. But the woman who wants to pursue a career with some continuity while fulfilling obligations that the institution of marriage places upon her cannot.

In fact a woman's work years are inevitably split: most women do no work outside the home at all during the years that they are bearing and rearing children, even though they may have worked for several years before and after marriage. In the past decade, about a hundred adjunct institutions and programs have been established to encourage the woman over thirty-five to reeducate herself for careers or professions. More recently still have come proposals that women regularly slice their educational and professional development in two: dividing their college years from their graduate-school years with child bearing and rearing; coming to their profession at thirty-five or forty, say, rather than at twenty-five, as most men do. Interestingly, many women accept the idea quickly and rather thoughtlessly, though, as Caroline Bird notes, the idea "puts rather heavy demands on the imagination and talent of college girls . . . to plan what they are going to do when they have reared children whose fathers they have not yet met." Nor, of course, can anyone predict the future of particular careers a decade or two hence (p. 131). More skeptical still, Alice Rossi argues on the basis of studies of prime years of creativity that asking women to confine their twenties and early thirties to housework and child rearing deprives them of significant creative years, thus making it more certain that they will become at best career women of a special, lower caste—fifteen years behind their male colleagues or those females who chose not to marry at all. We dwell on this seemingly minor detail since it is evident to us that in the years to come institutional chicanery of the sort we have not yet seen or thought of will be possible and probable—anything rather than to alter the basic confinement of women to the home.

But what of the woman, married or not, who out of choice or economic necessity seeks full-time employment in a free U.S. market? What are her chances for a job she wants at a salary equal to a man's and with some opportunities for promotion? There are at least two versions of the current job situation for women. First, the view of those who say, "You've come a long way, baby," the optimists who cheer as each job category—from garage attendant to engineer to bank president—achieves the distinction of its token woman and its article on the woman's page of *The New York Times*. These optimists also express satisfaction with the brilliant and energetic individuals who have (at what cost nobody knows) managed to combine distinguished professional careers and family lives—these ladies also grace such pages.

While individual heroines may begin to make history, statistics about the masses of women workers are largely ignored. Nearly half of all women are in the work force—two of five workers: most are married, and 38 percent have children under eighteen. In 1966, half the women who worked full time earned less than $4,000; the parallel statistic for men was $7,000.[19] Similar discrepancies obtain across the salary scale: toward the bottom, the 2,000,000 women working in sales in 1960 earned an average of $2,389; the 3,000,000 sales-men earned $5,842 on average. At the other end, male managers, officials, and proprietors averaged $7,421; women, less than half: $3,514.[20] Caroline Bird reports that if one includes "all the rich widows and the five former wives of Jean Paul Getty," the proportion of women who have incomes of more than $10,000 a year is still only 5 percent (pp. 82–83); only one percent of women take down *salaries* of $10,000 or more, one-twentieth of the proportion for males. Most employed women are at the bottom of both salary scales and job classifications. With it all, their rate of unemployment is higher than men's: in 1968, 4.8 percent as opposed to 2.9 percent, figures that probably conceal the large number of women who, in the Labor Department's view, have given up and dropped out of the work force and are thus not counted.[21]

The differential between men's and women's salaries is greater than it appears, since most employers fail to provide pension or retirement plans for women, even when they do provide them for men. To add insult to injury, in thirty-seven states, a woman fired for pregnancy is ineligible for unemployment insurance. As Caroline Bird puts it, the "sex map of the world" increases the "cleavage" between first-class workers "who have rights to their jobs and the benefits that go with them" and second-class workers—mostly "docile wives and mothers," black and white women who "outnumber men in restaurants, hotels, stores, and many other fields where the work is not steady."[22]

At the bottom are black women, caught in the double jaws of race and sex. As Marlene Dixon has written recently:

Black women constitute the largest minority in the U.S., and they are the most disadvantaged group in the labor force. . . . In 1900, 41 per cent of black women were employed, as compared to 17 per cent for white women. In 1963, the proportion of black women employed was still a fourth greater than that of whites. In 1960, 44 per cent of black married women with children under six were in the labor force, in contrast to 29 per cent for white women.

Black women hold proportionately more menial jobs than white women. Whereas nearly 60 percent of white women employed in 1966 held white-collar jobs, 26 percent of black women held such positions. On the other hand, whereas 5 percent of white women could be classified as domestics, 25 percent of black women fit that category. It is not surprising, therefore, that though proportionately more black women than white are sole supporters of their families, their annual earnings fall significantly below those of white women.[23]

Nor are women with educational qualifications treated any differently from other women. In 1966, for example, the U.S. government employed 650,000 women, mostly at lower grades: women constituted only 1.5 percent of those earning federal salaries of $20,000 or more (Bird, p. 82). In 1968, approximately one-fifth of working women who had completed four years of college were employed in nonprofessional jobs as salesgirls, clerks, and household workers.[24] As a professional, a woman is usually the last to be hired, despite the fact that she may be both overqualified and underpaid. For example, the university's record as an employer of women is particularly dismal: 22 percent of the faculties of four-year institutions are women (a figure not very different from 1900, when the statistic was 19.7 percent), and these women are chiefly to be found in nonelite institutions, undergraduate departments, and in nontenured or lower-ranking positions.[25]

And, tokens notwithstanding, things have been getting worse. While more women are going to college, the proportion of women choosing *any* career or profession at all has been declining. In the 1940's women earned an average of 15 percent of all doctorates; in the 1950's, 10 percent; in the 1960's, 11 percent. Even the proportion of women who are high-school teachers has declined from 68 percent in the 1920's to 46 percent in 1966. Figures for other professions are more appalling still: in 1960, 0.9 percent of employed engineers (*down* from 1.2 percent in 1950); 10 percent of natural scientists (down from 12 percent); 25 percent of social scientists (down from 32 percent in ten years);[26] 8 percent of all scientists; 6 percent of all physicians; 3 percent of all lawyers (Bird, p. 82). By contrast, in Finland, "women constitute 83% of the dentists, 44% of the chemists, and 23% of the surgeons. In Great Britain, 16% and in the USSR as many as 65 to 75% of the physicians are women."[27]

If one continues to ask why—why in a country where women seem so free and where many of them are indeed liberated from housework, they are not usefully, let alone gainfully, employed, one is asking how it is that women have been turned into willing slaves. Studies of college women and alumnae indicate that higher education hardly alters a woman's belief that her place is in the home and that only extraordinary women can combine marriage and a career.[28] Even for career women, moreover, the primary satisfactions are alleged to remain sexual and maternal. Women believe all that. Sociologist Shirley Angrist concludes from a recent longitudinal study of alumnae that "while marriage was an explicitly anticipated contingency, work appears to have been only vaguely prepared for."[29] But even if the lessons of college and high school were to anticipate work, they do not prepare a woman to *battle* with the work world. Either she accepts that world when she enters it, as an extension of her school world, or, if she does not enter it, she imagines, perhaps wishfully, a condition of "equality" out there where other women are brave enough to compete with men. In either case, changing the institution of marriage or the arrangements of U.S. economy seem totally utopian to her.

THE EDUCATION OF WILLING SLAVES

Before one can begin to change a condition, one must believe in the possibility of change. To prevent such belief is the purpose of the education of women, even in 1970. The methods are simple but thorough: teach girls (in the name of their "distinctive nature") that they are socially and psychologically different from boys; teach them those differences early by deflecting the natural needs, desires, and expectations that all children share; teach them, finally, that they are peculiar, ill, or even dangerous if they will not or cannot learn the chief lessons of passivity and obedience, the associated lessons of dependency and inferiority.

Because they are not stupid to begin with, young girls may ask questions. Such questions have to be answered with authority. "I remember quite clearly a day in sixth grade," Goucher College freshman Brigid Kenny writes, "when the class was discussing an article from a weekly supplementary reader. The story was about a chef, and someone in the class ventured the opinion that cooking was women's work, that a man was 'sissy' to work in the kitchen. The teacher's response surprised us all. She informed us calmly that men make the best cooks, just as they make the best dress designers, singers, and laundry workers. Yes, she said, anything a woman can do a man can do better." Sometimes the instruction has already taken place and the child reports on the lesson. "My daughter, who is eight," a friend confessed, "would not allow me to continue a story I began with 'Once upon a time there was a space-pilot named Judith,' since, she insisted, 'Space-pilots had to be boys—girls couldn't understand how to fly a space ship.'" And occasionally, a girl asks a question early and to a friendly person: Why, a six-year-old wondered, after reading the line, in *Skyscrapers,* "Architects, engineers, builders and bankers put their heads together and worked out plans," and looking at the pictures, "Why are there no ladies?" And then, noticing one, she pointed her finger at a secretary.[30]

Children learn about sex roles very early in their lives. A psychologist particularly interested in creativity, Paul Torrance maintains that "overemphasis or misplaced emphasis on sex roles . . . throughout the educational ladder makes many problems for highly creative children." The problem, put simply, is that while creativity "requires both sensitivity and independence," in our culture, these qualities are stereotyped as male or female. Thus, creative boys may "appear more effeminate" and girls "more masculine" than their peers. Studies which follow students over a number of years are finding, moreover, that children will sacrifice creativity for sex role. Torrance's own experiments indicate that girls may be more severely handicapped in this respect than boys, especially by their school experience.

Using a Product Improvement Test, Torrance asked boys and girls to make toys "more fun to play with." First-grade boys were better with fire trucks, girls with nurse's kits. Many six-year-old boys refused to try the nurse's kit, "protesting," Torrance reports, "'I'm a boy! I don't play with things like that!'" Several creative boys turned the nurse's kit into a doctor's and were then "quite free to think of improvements." By the third grade, however, "boys excelled girls even on the nurse's kit, probably because," Torrance explains, "girls have been conditioned by this time to accept toys as they are and not to manipulate or change them." A later series of experiments with third-, fourth-, and fifth-graders further verified the "inhibiting effects of sex-role conditioning":

> Girls were quite reluctant to work with these science toys and frequently protested: "I'm a girl; I'm not supposed to know anything about things like that!" Boys demonstrated and explained about twice as many ideas as girls in experiments involving these materials.

In 1959, Torrance reported his findings to parents and teachers in one school and asked for their cooperation in attempting to change the attitudes of the girls. In 1960, when he retested them, using similar science toys, the girls participated willingly, and even with apparent enjoyment, and they performed as well as the boys. But in one way, Torrance reports:

> the situation remained unchanged. The contributions of boys were more highly valued by peers [*female* as well as male] than those of girls. Apparently, the school climate has helped to make it more acceptable for girls to play around with science things, but boys' ideas about science things are still supposed to be better than those of girls.

While it is encouraging to note that a year's effort had changed *behavior* patterns significantly, it is also clear that *attitudes* of nine-, ten-, and eleven-year-olds—rooted in assumptions about girls' inferiority—are more resistant still.[31]

Most casual observers have noted that in primary school boys and girls are treated exactly alike. When we asked college students what they could remember, we had two immediate responses from girls: "I remember," the first said, "having to go to play in the doll's house corner when I really wanted to run around as the boys were doing." "I remember," the second said, "wondering on the first day of kindergarten why I had to sit still while the boys could move the chairs across the room. It looked like fun and made a lot of noise."

It is not always the content of a lesson that stamps itself on the developing child, but as we have said in Chapter 8, the "noise" of a school. For girls, the "noise" may teach them that their physical need for activity is somehow different from, less than, boys'. They may pick up cues from teachers, male or female, who expect girls to "hate" mathematics or science and to "love" reading. If girls are also taught to be "better" than boys, it is in matters that reinforce the essential pattern of passivity: they are better-behaved; they do as they are told; they learn the lesson assigned, they ask fewer searching questions; they make fewer intellectual demands. School rewards the nice girl's conformity and acquiescence.

The "noise" in inequality in elementary school becomes outright channeling in high school. No women appear in building-trades courses or in engineering, let alone auto or airplane mechanics. If girls are not college-bound, they are channeled into home economics, hair styling, or nursing. Many vocational or science-oriented schools—like Brooklyn Technical High School or Stuyvesant in New York, or Baltimore Polytechnic Institute—have been or still are restricted to boys. In the academic high school, the sex-typing is subtler: most girls will volunteer that they "can't really add well or solve complicated logical problems." And anyway, with typing and shorthand, girls can get jobs. By the time a girl gets through high school, the idea of femininity may contradict absolutely the idea of thinking, much less being a serious intellectual.

Guidance counselors advise even the brightest girls to avoid fields dominated by men. Betty Friedan reports the experience of a girl counseled not to apply "for admission anywhere in architecture, on the grounds that women are rare in that profession, and she would never get in anyhow" (p. 153). Our students who are career-minded report that their counselors, attuned to sending middle-class girls to college, did not mention such careers as law, medicine, or engineering when talking to them. A recent definitive text, *The Counselor's Role: Commentary and Readings* (1968), characterizes the state of the profession. General editor Joseph C. Bentley dedicated the volume "to the women in my life"—and five names follow. The volume contains more than fifty essays, not one of which is devoted to counseling girls or to problems related to sex differences. The index lists three references to "girls": brief allusions in three essays to the changing role of women, the fact that more women are currently working, and to the need, therefore, for counseling to change! But there is no sign of when or how.

Children's books prepare girls early for the goal of marriage, rarely for work, and never for independence. In a recent article, Sarah Spinks provides a typical example:[32]

> Primrose was playing house. Just as she finished pouring tea for her dolls she began to think. She thought and thought and she thought some more: "Whom shall I marry?"
>
> "Whomever shall I marry?"
>
> "I think I shall marry a mailman. Then I could go to everybody's house and give them their mail."
>
> "Or I might marry a policeman. I could help him take the children across the street."

Primrose thinks her way through ten more categories of employment and concludes, "But now that I think it over, maybe I'll just marry somebody I love." Love is the opiate designated to help Primrose forget to think about what she would like to do or be. With love as reinforcer, she can imagine herself helping some man in *his* work. In another children's book, Johnny says, "I think I will be a dentist when I grow up," and later, to Betsy, he offers generously, "You can be a dentist's nurse." And of course Betsy accepts gratefully, since girls are not expected to have a work identity other than as servant or helper.

A 1969 annotated catalog of children's books[33] allows us to summarize neatly the characteristics of books written "Especially for Girls" (34 titles) and "Especially for Boys" (12 titles) and "Sports: Fiction" (14 titles, also for boys). In the brief descriptions that follow each title we observe that boys "decipher and discover," "earn and train," "foil," while girls "struggle," "feel lost," "overcome difficulties," "help solve," "help out." One boy's story has "strange power," another moves "from truancy to triumph," whereas a girl "learns to face the real world" or makes a "difficult adjustment." The adjectives associated either with the boys' stories or with boys are "exciting," "lively," "hilarious," "uproarious," "action-packed." Those associated with girls (who are thrice orphans and on another occasion motherless) include, once each, "enchanting," "lovable," "meek," "homesick," "humorous," and twice or more, "lively," "sensitive," "shy," "lonely," "heart-warming" or some other variety of "warm." Though these books are listed as suitable for grades four, five, and six, the sex stereotypes are gradeless. Late or early in catalogs or on shelves, the boys of children's books are active and capable, the girls passive and in trouble.

Elementary-school readers are meant for both sexes.[34] Primers used in the first three grades offer children a view of a "typical" American family: a mother who does not work, a father who does, a brother who is always older than a sister who is always younger, a dog, and sometimes a cat. In these books, boys build or paint things; they also pull girls in wagons and push merry-go-rounds. Girls carry purses when they go shopping, they help mother cook or pretend that they are cooking, and they play with their dolls. When they are not making messes, girls are cleaning up their rooms or other people's messes. Plots in which they are involved usually depend on their inability to do something—manage a pony or roller skates. Or in another typical role, a girl named Sue admires a parachute jumper: "What a jump!" said Sue. "What a jump for a man to make!" When her brother puts on a show for the rest of the neighborhood, Sue, whose name appears as title of the chapter, is part of his admiring audience.

We have found one junior-high-school text in which girls fly planes, sail boats, solve mysteries, and rescue people. But since the book was aimed at eighth-grade readers with fifth-grade reading skills, we conclude that only nonreading girls may be interested in adventure and activity. But in ordinary junior-high texts, girls continue to appear in traditional female roles, dominated by and submitting to male characters. If a girl is very smart, she is usually plain, or at least not as popular as her beautiful dumb blonde girl friend, though it is only fair to say that in the world of texts, everyone gets a boyfriend in the end.

Social-studies texts for the youngest grades are very much like early readers, since they often use stories about families and by definition therefore focus on sex roles and work. If a child's reader can be pardoned for stereotyping because it is "only" fiction, a social-studies text has no excuse for denying reality to its readers. Yet as Jamie Kelem Frisof reports in a review of five texts,[35] sisters are still younger than brothers, brothers remain the doers, questioners, and knowers who explain things to their poor, timid sisters. Energetic boys think about "working on a train or in a broom factory" or about being President. They grow up to be doctors or factory workers or (in the five texts combined) to do some hundred different jobs (as opposed to thirty for women). "A girl's ambition," Mrs. Frisof writes, "is represented by only one statement, 'Maybe I'll design fabrics when I grow up. '" She finds but one working mother in a single story —hardly a representative view. Even when men and women are shown working at similar jobs in a single text, the woman's job is inferior: thus, waitresses work in small diners, waiters in fancy restaurants. Women are mothers, and nothing they do, not even child rearing, has either the significance or complexity of male tasks. When they are heroic, it is a rare event (in a text) and a sacrificial gesture: on one occasion, a young woman teaching in a community that is short of money agrees to work for a lower salary. On another, the three groups that can "solve" national problems are named as government (men), business (men), and volunteers (women). Women, again willing to sacrifice salary, "can see things that are wrong with society and they try to help poor people." They do not, we would add the implicit message, try to help themselves, nor do the texts even hint of problems or conflicts in their oppressively sacrificial roles, or pose questions about them.[36]

Pictures in social-studies texts are divided, as one might expect, unequally: the formula in four of the five texts discussed above was seven males to one female. In the fifth, a picture book, there were 117 pictures of males, 15 of females, and 31 of the two together. In science and mathematics texts,[37] pictures are especially important because sex-typing has so fully determined the members of those professions. Looking only at illustrations, we examined six high-school science texts published since 1966, most of them in the last two years. These included a new 740-page physics book and a biology text that is part of a new experimental series. In all of these combined, we found photographed one female lab assistant, one woman doctor, one woman scientist, and Rachel Carson.

Considering that nothing we have found in school texts teaches girls about their history as women or their potential as creative, free, socially powerful workers, it is a wonder that any of them go on to college. Given the typical college curriculum, it is more surprising still that any of them break the mold. Up until last year, a course in the history of women was offered only at Barnard College, and most college history texts ignore feminism or treat with ridicule its efforts or accomplishments. We still know of only one course in the psychology of sex and one in the sociology of sex. Most psychology courses teach Freudian doctrine uncritically, and most sociology courses do the same for marriage and the family. Though 60 percent of all B.A.'s in sociology were women in 1968, we know only a few sociologists who include in the traditional course on "social inequalities" a unit on sex.

But worst of all are English courses, through which almost every student passes. Unlike history or political-science texts, where women are simply absent, women fill stories, novels, poems, and plays, even if they are omitted as authors. Though literature may be read as a record of women's oppression and (more rarely) awakening, and though blacks have set a useful precedent here, we know of few courses on literature by or about women, even at women's colleges, even though more women than men major in English. Writing courses offer a different set of problems to the college women who are provided with male models and taught nothing about their oppressive conditioning as women. It should surprise no one, then, if they write badly or without freedom, confidence, and independence. Those are qualities necessary to writers but trained out of women. Our experience suggests that freshmen women enter college already convinced that women are, in general, poorer writers than men. They consistently query (or change), for example, any course that offers them a selection of books by women. How, then, can they think of themselves as potentially able writers? The best a woman can be is second-rate. Black students brought up on white literature experience similar problems, and one of the concomitants of their revolution (as well as of others in the past) has been black literature. In some small measure women have begun to write about their revolution, though their literature thus far is still largely didactic rather than imaginative, and though it is chiefly available only through the underground press. Certainly, it has made no impact on freshman composition texts. This year, for example, several of the most prestigious publishing houses have issued competing anthologies aiming to capture youth's interest in the contemporary or the "radical." We have examined eight of these, most of which offer a generous sampling of black writers or public figures—Baldwin, King, Cleaver, Carmichael, and so on. Most of the texts use such subheadings as identity, new life styles, equality, the revolt of youth. None of the headings and none of the essays touch on women—with one exception. A text called *Representative Men: Culture Heroes of Our Time* uniquely includes two women as "representative in the present age": "The Actress: Elizabeth Taylor" and "The Existential Heroine: Jacqueline Onassis."

Perhaps we can return through these women—obviously suitable heroines for college *men* or textbook editors and publishers—to where we began. By the time women reach college, the family of their third-grade reader has been absorbed into their patterns of assumption and belief. The education of women teaches them, as we have said, a particular version of their natural distinctiveness from men: deprived of energy and power, they remain bodies waiting for fulfillment from husbands and then babies. They are sleeping beauties, useless without men to stir them into motion and sexuality.

In a single image, the fairy tale catches woman's history and her alleged sexual dependency. The work of Masters and Johnson on human sexuality has been known at least by the experts for more than ten years. It has been available popularly through the writing of Ruth and Edward Brecher at least since 1966. But only in the past year, and only in the underground literature of the women's liberation movement, have we found "the myth of the vaginal orgasm" (the notion that women are dependent on the phallus for full or mature sexuality) beginning to loosen its hold on women's minds.[38] The popular press, ready enough to exploit female sexuality, has ignored the explosion of this particularly invidious myth. Why should *Glamour* (August, 1969), for example, publish a Freudian essay called "The American Girl's Search for Sexual Identity" that continues to promote her dependency:

> But the classical Freudian analysis is practically immutable, based on the biological fact that the female has no penis and that little girls repeatedly react to this discovery with intense fear. This anatomical difference is hardly one to be affected by cultural change. . . . Another displacement [for the absent penis] fixes on the intellect, especially in very gifted girls. They develop their minds to an extraordinary degree in an attempt to masculinize the intelligence as a substitute for the penis, then become very anxious and competitive at the slightest intellectual attack.

What is the future of girls who are constantly in danger—if they are tomboyish, if they are intelligent, if they are competitive? More space is spent on (terrifying) pathology than prescription, but the message is clear: "there is no escape from womanhood but real womanhood." "To help her accept and respect her sex," another passage prescribes, "one of the most valuable things a father can do is to give his daughter a doll when she is about five. . . ."

WOMEN "IN SERVICE"

As we have conceived it in this book, service is a humane and voluntary response to needs of people outside one's class and kind. Beyond that definition, in the 1960's, service has come also to be connected with movements for social and political change. Ideally, those who "serve" are eventually to be replaced by those they are serving; the relationship between those in service and those being served is dynamic, even potentially revolutionary. In contrast, the slave's service is static, hierarchical, changeless. The slave, willing or otherwise, perverts the ideal by serving not voluntarily, but in fear or ignorance.

A slave's concept of service is so deeply ingrained in women's understanding of themselves and their roles that it operates effectively to portray any deviation, however enlightened, as "selfishness." We think, for example, of our own attitudes toward those young women who, after 1965, separated themselves from such organizations as SDS and SNCC or from the adult peace movement to begin women's liberation groups. We thought then that their activities were diversionary, divisive, "selfish." We argued that the priorities of peace and civil rights took precedence over the rights of women. Some of us were not well enough educated then to know that we were repeating history. More than a hundred years earlier, women had also been asked to put their minds and bodies at the service of the abolitionist movement (which some of them had, in fact, helped begin), to serve the blacks first, then themselves. What happened was, for a time, lost even to history: women did not gain the right to vote when blacks did (theoretically) at the end of the

Civil War. They had to battle once again, and for more than another fifty years. And there we were in 1966 saying the same thing to different women: wait until we've won rights for blacks and have ended the Vietnam war. Don't be selfish. Women really aren't suffering as blacks and Vietnamese are. Don't be selfish.

Years of teaching women persuade us that the phenomenon is characteristic, that women have an idea of service built into their models of reality. Recently, for example, freshmen at Goucher were discussing a novel by Kate Chopin. In *The Awakening*,[39] a married woman with three children leaves them and her husband to devote herself for several months to thinking about herself and to painting. She had done nothing like this before in all of her twenty-nine years. The students liked Edna, sympathized with her problems, even empathized to some extent. But one of them admitted "in all honesty" (and the rest agreed) that Edna's "selfishness" made her feel very uncomfortable: after all, it wasn't right for Edna to spend full time on herself—she should have divided herself, if she felt that she couldn't spend all of her time with her family.

We emphasize the idea of discomfort: college women, who were beginning four years that might seem to resemble self-indulgence, who spend hours on hair and clothes and cosmetics, and who may seem totally self-absorbed, felt discomfort at the view of a fictional heroine's devotion to self and denial of service to her husband and children. Perhaps that discomfort allowed them to view Edna's suicide at the end of the novel without indignation but with a profound sense of resignation. As one student said somewhat cheerfully, "It's the only way to happiness for her." If you reject husband and children, you have no reason to live. Service or death—these are a woman's options, at least for "happiness." This view fits them supremely for a life of self-abnegation and dedication—when they are saintly. More typically, the denial or dilution of self produces parasites dependent on others for vicarious pleasures or in need of other satisfactions—the devious control or the manipulation of husbands and children. The idea that all women *ought* to serve husbands and children is as rational a notion as that all men *ought* to be ministers. And yet it is impossible for most women to recognize the absurdity of their condition, so deeply are they taught to believe in its inevitability.

A woman's idea of "servitude," moreover, has little if anything to do with the idea of work. In another undergraduate discussion, this one two years ago, a student tried to make a point about the complexities of motivation. She had come to Goucher, she said, only because her parents had wanted her to go to college, and this was as good a place as any. For nearly a whole term she had been wondering what she was doing here, but now she understood what her purpose might be, not only here but for the rest of her life. The class hung on her words, but she grew suddenly shy of naming her discovery. Finally she said, "Enjoyment. I think that I am here to enjoy not myself but life—and also later on, after I get out of college." Joan was immediately chastised for "selfishness": "The purpose of life," another student said, "is to help other people." Most of the twenty students sitting in the circle proceeded to take sides; a few tried to reconcile the two positions: "helping other people" might itself be "enjoyable." "If you enjoyed tutoring in Baltimore slums," one girl retorted, "then you weren't doing your job properly." In more than an hour, no one mentioned earning money or having a vocation; no one talked about the fulfillment of her identity in terms of satisfying and useful work. Most of them thought that "service" or "helping people" should be performed for its own sake, because that was morally correct, not as an enjoyable act an individual might wish to do, nor for any other reason. This is the woman-slave mentality that Mill was describing a hundred years ago.

David Riesman reports similar concepts among Radcliffe College students discussing "ideal" careers for women:

> One girl going into medicine said that her ideal would be a marriage to a physician serving in Africa who needed her to help take care of his medical clinic; they could serve together, both of them needed, and each needing the other. . . . The group of girls seemed to agree that this would be idyllic: the situation of danger and service, not competitive as between the two spouses nor between them as a couple and the surrounding community. Here the wife could extend herself to the fullest without raising problems for her identification as a women or as a professionally useful individual. The uniqueness of the marriage and of the couple's mission could substitute for the marginal surrender of uniqueness of the hypothetical wife.[40]

The girl's ideal pictures a man in "service" to a special community, the wife in service *to him* ("who needed her to help take care of *his* medical clinic") and *through him* to the community. The portrait is apt, precisely suited to a culture bound to hierarchy nowhere more rigidly than in relations between the sexes. Men serve society or the state; women *serve* men. Most women believe that the hierarchy is correct; if they have some questions about it, or doubt their capacity to subordinate themselves completely enough, they must, as the Radcliffe student did, work out some means of easing the relationship, perhaps through disguise. A form of make-believe, for example, labels the wife's "surrender of uniqueness" a "marginal" matter; even so compromised, however, the imagined relationship needs an exotic African environment.

For a few, like Kate Chopin's heroine Edna, however, self-deception and compromise won't do. While consciousness, it may be said with some truth, killed Edna, these days it transforms the young into new feminists who march on an underground paper and produce an issue of *Rat* that spares no "hero" from damnation, not even Uncle Dave (Dellinger). When Norman Mailer took members of the Conspiracy Eight to lunch in a Chicago male club, dim lighting concealed, at a nearby table, Judge Julius Hoffman. *"In the dark, they are all alike":* women have begun to turn the myth around.[41] And in the end, they say, all the sexual myths must be slain, all the false gods abolished, even the language cleared of its male mystique. Why do we use "man" generically, especially when children can see it only as a word for "boy"? Why do we ask girls to "man" an office?

The discoveries possible once we have begun to demythologize the sexual universe are endless. It is no wonder that young women who have begun the process for themselves are exhilarated or angry; that even sympathetic young men are often irritated. It is, after all, unpleasant to discover that those girls you had expected to fold and staple your paper have their own paper to write, their own work to do. "Why not call some guys at Hopkins," a girl suggests cheerfully, "they may feel like helping you out."

When Edna said no, I won't do that anymore, I won't be a wife or mother, there was existentially nothing else for her to *be*. "There was no one thing in the world that she desired," Mrs. Chopin writes of her, just before the end. She is an interesting example because her rearing and the extension of her dependency into marriage do not preclude her "awakening." She is able to say no with relative ease and even with some glimpse of understanding from otherwise baffled men. But that is not the point, finally, for it is 1899 and there is nothing for Edna to *do*.

We have, elsewhere in this book, emphasized the importance of useful work. In the main, we have talked about such work as being in the service of change, revolutionary in an ultimate sense. It was revolutionary for Rosa Parks to say no, she won't go to the back of the bus, or for the draft resister to say no. In each case the refusal signaled the beginning of a new movement and new forms of work. For women, the process is not different, only more difficult. There are deeper expectations to be encountered, harsher charges of self-ishness, pettiness, envy, greed, and all the other sins of *man*kind. If we are rarely optimistic about the near future and less optimistic about the women's movement, it is only because hers is bound to be as Juliet Mitchell has named it, "the longest revolution" of them all.

Notes

[1] Sweet Pea Anderson's picture and story appeared in *The New York Times* on November 8, 1969. As far as we know, only Scandinavian Airlines has broken the sex barrier. See *The New York Times*, May 3, 1969, for an account of the employment of Miss Turi Wideroe, the daughter of "a pioneer of Norwegian aviation," "as the first woman to pilot a passenger plane for a major Western airline." The article concludes: "Miss Wideroe is not yet qualified to fly jets." See also, for the case of women pilots, "Toward Job Equality," a booklet published by the Equal Employment Opportunities Commission, Washington, D.C., 1969.

[2] We have not attempted a complete analogy. For further comparisons, see Gunnar Myrdal, *An American Dilemma,* especially the extensive appendix on women; Helen Hacker, "Women as a Minority Group," in *Social Forces,* 1951, Vol. 30; and Caroline Bird's chapter, "The Negro Parallel," in *Born Female.*

[3] *The Subjection of Women,* first published in 1869 and rarely republished since then. Mill's book was last published in this country in 1911, in an edition edited by the suffragist Carrie Chapman Catt. It is Mill's only major work unavailable in paperback today, in spite of the efforts of several people, at least for the past three years. In August 1970, the University of Chicago will bring out a new edition, edited by Alice S. Rossi.

[4] See *The New York Times,* April 13, 1969. Mrs. Chisholm is also reported saying, "Men don't like independent women." And with regard to her political battles with James Farmer, "Of course we have to help black men. But not at the expense of our own personalities as women. The black man must step forward, but that does not mean *we* have to step back. Where have we ever been? For the last 15 years, black men have held political office, not women."

[5] *The Psychology of Woman—A Psychoanalytical Interpretation* (New York,, 1944), pp. 224ff.

[6] In *Women and the Scientific Professions: The M.I.T. Symposium on American Women* in *Science and Engineering,* eds. Jacquelyn A. Mattfeld and Carol Q. Van Aken (Cambridge, 1965), pp. 51ff.

[7] We quote in this paragraph from a recent popular account written by Eleanor Maccoby for *Mademoiselle*'s special issue on women's liberation, February, 1970, pp. 181ff. See also her essay called "Women's Intellect," in *The Potential of Woman,* eds., Seymour M. Farber and Roger H. L. Wilson (New York, 1963).

[8] "Kinder, Kuche, Kirche as Scientific Law: Psychology Constructs the Female" has been republished many times by women's liberation groups, movement presses, and others. We use *Motive*'s special issue on the liberation of women, March/April, 1969, pp. 78ff.

[9] Convenient reviews of such material appear in Miss Weisstein's essay above and in the work of Eleanor Maccoby and Alice S. Rossi as cited in other places.

[10] "Inner and Outer Space: Reflections on Womanhood," in *Women in America,* ed., Robert Jay Lifton (Boston, 1967), pp. 1–26. The essay originally appeared in *Daedalus,* Spring, 1964. Lifton and Bruno Bettelheim, among

others, also espouse the myth of a feminine core. See, for example, Lifton's essay in the same volume and Bettelheim's contribution to the M.I.T. Symposium above.

[11] "Equality Between the Sexes: An Immodest Proposal," in *Women in America, op. cit.,* pp. 98–143.

[12] In a more recent study by Susan Orden and Norman Bradburn, called "Working Wives and Family Happiness" (*American Journal of Sociology,* January, 1969), women who worked because they wanted to enjoyed their marriages (and so did their husbands) more than those women who worked because they had to. The crucial difference, apparently, was the women's freedom to choose. So crucial a factor was free choice that the sociologists, Orden and Bradburn, see it as rescuing an otherwise failing institution.

[13] *The Feminine Mystique* (New York, 1963), pp. 217–18.

[14] "The Political Economy of Women's Liberation," in *Monthly Review,* September, 1969.

[15] By contrast, only about 8,800,000 women over sixteen did not work that year. See "Work Experience of the Population in 1966," Special Labor Force Report No. 91, U.S. Department of Labor, January, 1968. Henceforth cited as "Work Experience in 1966."

[16] Quoted by Esther Peterson in *Women in America, op. cit.,* p. 167.

[17] See "Work Experience in 1966," *op. cit.* In *Women at Work: Every Woman's Guide to Successful Employment* (New York, 1967), p. 41, Elmer Winter writes, "A full-time job away from home and a full-time job as homemaker are too much to carry unless you have superb health and executive ability or help in the home that doesn't use up all your profits from working. With this dual load, your social life probably will suffer, and possibly your health and your temper. Unless you can make practical and efficient arrangements in your home to relieve you of part of your work, unless you are so deeply involved in a career with a future that you feel you will be making a mistake to give it up even for a few years, unless your husband is in favor of your dividing yourself and your energies, then my advice to your is: Stop. Think. Is a full-time job necessary right now? Might not some other time pattern be better for you and those close to you? . . . Part-time work is in the air. It is regarded by the experts as the coming solution of the shortage of skilled labor." Mr. Winter also writes, in a chapter called "Let's Get Acquainted," that he is one of the founders of Manpower, a part-time employment agency that has grown, in the years since 1948, into 484 offices in the United States and abroad.

[18] *Born Female,* first published in 1968. We use the paperback printed in New York, 1969 (p. 130) and cite pages henceforth within.

[19] See "Toward Job Equality for Women," *op cit.*

[20] From tables prepared by Marlene Dixon in "Why Women's Liberation," *Ramparts,* December, 1969, pp. 57ff. Miss Dixon's sources are U.S. Department of Commerce, Bureau of the Census: "Current Population Reports," 1960, No. 37, and U.S. Department of Labor, Bureau of Labor Statistics. We are grateful to Miss Dixon for the additional material on black women quoted in the text.

[21] See "Toward Job Equality for Women," *op. cit.*

[22] Pp. 66–67. Women's salaries are kept low also by sex-typing particular jobs in harmony with woman's mythic "nature." Thus, more than 90 percent of all nurses, baby-sitters, domestics, hotel maids, dressmakers, milliners, and

dietitians are women; more than 90 percent of receptionists and other institutionalized hostesses; more than 80 percent of persons employed to wait on tables; more than 75 percent of cashiers; not to mention the secretaries, typists, clerks (Bird, pp. 70–71). By contrast, in 1966, 1,165,000 men were engineers or technical workers, compared with 11,000 women; 6,392,000 men managers, officials, and proprietors, 1,305,000 women. Statistics from Carolyn Bird, *op. cit.*, and "Work Experience in 1966," *op. cit.*

23 "Work Experience in 1966," *op. cit.*

24 For women with five or more years of college, the similar statistic is 8 percent. See Paula Stern, "When's It Going to Be Ladies' Day?" in *The New Republic,* July 5, 1969, pp. 14ff.

25 See Jessie Bernard's *Academic Women,* 1964. For more recent accounts, see Alice S. Rossi, "Status of Women in Graduate Sociology Departments: 1968–69," in *The American Sociologist,* February, 1970; and essays by J. Collins and members of the Columbia Women's Liberation Committee in *The Radical Teacher,* eds. Florence Howe and Paul Lauter, #2, and a pamphlet called "Free Women," available through the New University Conference, 622 West Diversey Parkway, Chicago, Illinois 60614.

26 *Science,* Vol. 145 (September 25, 1964), p. 1389.

27 Kate Hevner Mueller, "Education: the Realistic Approach," in Seymour M. Farber and Roger H. L. Wilson, eds., *The Challenge to Women* (New York, 1966), p. 116.

28 See Alice S. Rossi, Report of Conference on the Undergraduate Education of Women, July, 1969, at Cedar Crest College, Allentown, Pennsylvania. And earlier studies, particularly of Vassar women (*The American College,* ed., Nevitt Sanford, 1962).

29 "The Study of Sex Roles," *Journal of Social Issues,* Vol. XXV, No. 1 (January, 1969), pp. 215–32.

30 Leah Heyn, "Children's Books," *Women: A Journal of Liberation,* Fall, 1969, pp. 22ff.

31 *Guiding Creative Talent* (New Jersey, 1962), pp. 111ff.

32 "Sugar 'n Spice," in *This Magazine Is About Schools,* Summer, 1969.

33 Distributed at the 1969 Convention, National Council of Teachers of English and used widely in school systems to promote the purchase of paperbacks (with federal funds).

34 The following discussion of textbooks, with an exception noted below, is based on an examination of texts in use in the Baltimore City Public Schools. We are grateful to Mr. L. Earl Wellemeyer, supervisor of English, and others who made these texts available to us. We hope it will be understood that our discussion is in no way to be considered judgmental with regard to Baltimore. We are certain that an examination of texts in other cities would reveal similar or identical texts in use. We are convinced that there are no "other" texts to be had. The textbook industry, barely beginning to respond to the black revolution, has not yet heard of women. The only exception we found was a 1968 first-grade social-studies text that was "multiethnic" and that asked the question: "What jobs do mothers do away from home?" The answers they offer: teach, work as receptionists or as telephone operators.

35 "Textbooks and Channeling," in *Woman: A Journal of Liberation,* Fall, 1969, pp. 26ff.

[36] We have surveyed more advanced social-studies texts only enough to know that one has to search for pictures or stories about women in them, and that one is rewarded decreasingly as one goes through the grades. Occasionally women appear in pictures (spinning, sewing the first flag) or as token heroines in collections of historical biographies of heroes (Clara Barton, Louisa May Alcott, Harriet Tubman, Susan B. Anthony).

[37] Beyond typical pictorial stereotyping, one finds the same process in arithmetic questions. When boys' names are used, the problems have to do with sports; when girls', it is a matter of cooking or buying something. The conditioning is sometimes somewhat more subtle, as in the following series of problems from a third-grade text:

> Tom *earned* $3.03 last week. If he buys this rocket, about how much money will he have left?
> Alice *would like to have* a silk dress. The silk she wants costs 98¢ a yard. She needs three yards. About how much would the silk for her dress cost?
> Bobby *is making* a chest. He spent 37¢ for hinges and 59¢ for a lock. He spent   ?   in all. [Italics added.]

We are grateful to Goucher freshman Barbara Polikoff for this ingeniously discovered example.

[38] The myth is, of course, Freud's—that true or mature sexuality depends for women on a vaginal orgasm achieved only in coitus with a man and for the most part passively. Clitoral orgasm was labeled variously as immature or inadequate, thus condemning the masturbation, homosexuality, and active heterosexuality of women all at once as well as frightening those who said they could not achieve vaginal orgasm. The research of Masters and Johnson conclusively debunked the hierarchical Freudian theory that would keep the mature woman passively dependent on man for her sexuality. "There is neither a purely clitoral orgasm nor a purely vaginal orgasm," the Brechers write. "There is only one kind of orgasm from the physiological point of view —a sexual orgasm." See *An Analysis of Human Sexual Response,* Signet paperback, 1966.

[39] An American novel of 1899, *The Awakening* was republished in paperback in 1964.

[40] "Two Generations," in *Women in America, op. cit.,* pp. 92–93.

[41] See "Goodbye to All That" by Robin Morgan in *Rat,* February 6, 1970, pp. 6ff.

11

National Service

The United States remains saddled with human problems. These need hardly be enumerated: poor housing, hunger, pollution, overcrowding of hospitals, understaffing of social services, unemployment, demoralization. At the same time, this country is blessed—as July 4 rhetoric has it—with riches: fertile land, natural resources, enormous productive facilities, and above all, active, forward-looking young people. There is very compelling logic, therefore, in devoting some of these resources to fulfilling the human needs of people in the United States and elsewhere. Proposals for national service, whatever else they contain, start from this premise: we must use the energy, initiative, and spirit of youth to deal with the problems of the poor and downtrodden. The idea is undeniably attractive. Its reasonableness diminishes when one observes that it is probably less justifiable under our Constitution, and less practical given our economy, to nationalize the labor of youth than it would be to nationalize the mines and factories of the steel industry for the same ends. Older people, whose lives and labor are not threatened with conscription, like to call the former "national service"; their name for the latter is "socialism."

To be sure, sundry other benefits are attributed to national service by its promoters, both for the society generally and for youth in particular. Margaret Mead, one of the strongest proponents of national service, has suggested that it would help do away with juve-

nile delinquents by the "reeducation and rehabilitation" of such individuals and by deploying them into specialties that presumably
fulfilled their desires. National service would also lower the number
of school dropouts, proponents argue, by offering incentives to potential draftees interested in particular programs of "service." If the
program included women, it would help eliminate the problem of
early marriages as well as discrimination against women in employment.[1] As if these were not sufficient benefits, national service has
also been presented as a means for eliminating unemployment
problems among the young, abating pollution and achieving road-
side beautification, humanizing professionals by exposing them in
youth to the real needs of their potential clients, relocating young
people who might not otherwise wish to move from farm to city,
providing "an exact inventory of human assets and liabilities and
. . . [creating] machinery to sharpen the assets and thereby reduce
the stockpile of liabilities," and, *mirabile dictu,* alleviating the "fear
of 'long, hot summers' which yearly plagues the urban centers of
the nation" by providing opportunities "for all citizens to become
involved in and to contribute to the well-being of the national and
international communities." And—how could one forget the universities—national service would also "encourage badly needed
curricular reform in undergraduate institutions. . . ."[2]

Such claims must provoke skepticism. So does the summary of
one panel, on "Preparation for Service," at a 1967 national service
conference:

> Some people would enter primarily so they could serve;
> others would enter so they could learn. Some would seek an
> assignment closely related to their career goals; others would
> welcome an opportunity to investigate new job areas. Some
> would value the diversity of social contacts open to them; others
> would be indifferent to such opportunities. Some would welcome
> the challenge of vigorous physical demands; others would pre-
> fer intellectual challenges. Some would want to be members of
> a structured, highly disciplined unit; others would choose to
> serve on their own. [*National Service,* p. 464.]

In short, national service—like other social panaceas from commu-
nitarian living to universal schooling, and from the single tax to puritan abstinence—must be all things to all men. But it is not. The exaggerated claims of its promoters mask what a program of universal

conscription could really accomplish. But perhaps more to the point, such hopeful claims obscure the dangers of such a program, though at the same time their stridency suggests something of the decay of the liberal social ideology from which national-service programs, with all their optimistic rhetoric, spring.

How would national service work?[3] At age sixteen, perhaps a year or two earlier, all young Americans—boys and girls—would register with local national-service boards. Soon thereafter, they would be subjected to a series of physical and mental tests to pinpoint "defects," and they would be directed—or perhaps assigned—to programs designed to remedy such defects. In high school, they might be able to specialize in certain courses to prepare them for special national-service assignments. Upon graduation from high school (or, for dropouts, at age eighteen), young people would be sent to National Service Training Centers, probably at some distance from their homes, to begin their two-year stints. Most promoters of national service picture training camps as woodsy. Young people would have the chance to build their bodies over obstacle courses, in the forests, and on lakes; and they would exchange experiences with their fellows from all places and all backgrounds in the United States. Meanwhile, they would be given a series of tests to match their abilities and the needs of various agencies approved by a central National Service Board for use of servitors. And they would be assigned to classes on the spirit of service, the dangers of sex and pot, and, presumably, appropriate loyalty to the society. The atmosphere of camps would vary from the depersonalized rigors of boot camp to the intensively scruntinized groupy experience of the Peace Corps. At some point, after lectures and films about the various forms of service available, the young men and women would be given the chance to submit their first, second, and third choices. The military would get first pick, and if there were insufficient volunteers, they would dip into those who hadn't chosen military service. Computers would shuffle choices, placements, talents, needs—and then one tense day, assignments would be posted on camp bulletin boards, and the servitors would prepare themselves to move on to the cities and towns where they will work.

For those going to the Army, the routine would change little from what it is now—basic and special training, then combat or support assignment. The others, many of them assigned to new cities, might be given a choice between finding separate living quarters or putting up in special quarters run by National Service. They would then report to the agency to which they had been assigned—a hospital, the Red Cross, the welfare department, a school program for troubled children. And their work, for the next twenty-one months or so, would follow the pattern established by conscientious objectors under the present draft law in their civilian alternative service. That is, they would be junior staff members in the agency; they would undergo some job training, its amount or quality depending on the agency and on the servitors' talents; they would be subject to monthly reviews by their superiors, and they would be continued in their jobs or returned to camp for reassignment depending on overall performance.

Of course, what would actually happen, especially in large cities where hundreds and perhaps thousands of young people would be assigned, is seldom envisaged by promoters of national service. Would individuals be free evenings and weekends—and free for what? It is hard to imagine young people simply carrying out their jobs as hospital orderlies, teaching aides, welfare drivers, or even as police cadets, as they began to rub hard against the social injustices whose symptoms most of these programs are designed simply to alleviate. Like VISTA volunteers, who are comparatively few and far between and recruited for shorter terms, some would, we expect, begin to try to organize for change, both in the agencies to which they are assigned and in the cities and towns around them. National-service promoters don't talk about how much scope young people might have to work for social change: Could they organize welfare recipients to demand a guaranteed income? Could they help unionize Charleston, South Carolina, hospital workers, or lead protests against insufficient medical care for the poor? Could they help the Black Panthers in breakfast programs or in liberation schools when they found how destructive the usual public-school programs were for ghetto kids? Could they do any of this while working in a government program, on a federal subsistence salary? Would they be returned to camps if they worked actively for social change? Or would other mechanisms for control be instituted—the threat of being sent into the military or organizing servitors into disciplined squads, or separating out "agitators"? From one point of view, a national-service program might well stir up more intense agitation among young people—even if they were subject to strong controls, even if they were taken before the supposedly liberating experience of college—to work for social change. But that is not, it ought to be clear, the intention of those promoting national service. Indeed, there are many reasons to believe that national service would be organized precisely to limit or prevent a social rebellion of the young.

The more serious proponents of national service see it performing on a somewhat larger scale what VISTA, the Peace Corps, and some voluntary programs do. For the young servitor, providing an extended, nonacademic educational experience; for the society, providing semiskilled and generally enthusiastic manpower to do jobs for which either manpower is unavailable or the cost is high.

Former Labor Secretary W. Willard Wirtz listed the domestic priorities for national-service efforts in this order: state and local government internships; medical and health services; welfare services; educational programs; conservation and beautification programs; urban renewal programs.[4] The order of priorities is significant, as is the omission of community organizing, one of the fundamental ingredients of social change. With the possible exception of Secretary Wirtz's first item, the programs he names would benefit from an infusion of manpower, not to speak of money. But one cannot avoid certain questions of motive. If such services are so important that we must draft our youth for them, why, one wonders, have we not already met those social needs? Why do health and conservation and education still need so many practitioners if, in fact, they are national priorities? One might query further: Why, if such services are so important to American society, should they be put into the hands of millions of semiskilled generalists who will be around hardly long enough to learn the basic problems? One cannot help but speculate about whether the real energy behind national-service proposals comes not from a commitment to supply social services like those the Secretary enumerates, but from a desire to structure and direct the lives of young people; whether national service, presented under the rationale of providing "solutions" to every horror in America, is not an elaboration of all the institutions for controlling youth we have examined in the last few chapters; whether, in short, national service is not compulsory schooling and the draft writ large?

Certainly its advocates stress its virtues for education and training. They talk, for example, of the practical education young people, especially from America's middle class, can get working in the ghettos and reservations, in Mississippi, Appalachia, and Harlem. Of course, no ideology for national service need be erected to support that idea. Indeed, it is one of the main contentions of this book that such education has brought young people to rebellion against the American institutions they have confronted. And it is precisely such "practical education" that has made students judge as sterile and irrelevant their university courses. Obviously, therefore, we grant the value of education through service—that is, provided that one understands service more broadly than bringing soup to old ladies or driving patients to therapy, provided that one understands the idea of service for change. On the other hand, considering that the rebellion of young people today is rooted precisely in the experience of service *for change*—from the Peace Corps to SDS's JOIN project, from Mississippi to McCarthy—it is hard to imagine a government mounting programs which, by their own nature, produce challenges to that government and to the social structure which supports it. Such questions were raised about the poverty program and its notion of control by the poor. The recent emasculation of the war on poverty, with the return of control over most programs to local political machines, lends credence to such doubts.

National-service advocates emphasize two other educational possibilities: cross-cultural experience, as it is called, and remediation of the disabilities of those from "deprived" backgrounds. The first, a euphemism for "seeing how the other half lives," might be envisioned in terms of where national servitors do their jobs. But, interestingly, most promoters of the program describe it as taking place in training centers:

> National Service Placement Centers can be expected to fulfill the important role of enlarging a young man's environment and social experience by exposing him to, at least for a limited period of time, young men of diverse economic, racial, and educational backgrounds. This experience must not be lost under any circumstances; it will probably prove to be the most important aspect of the entire nonmilitary service program. [*National Service*, p. 443; cf. p. 472.]

On reflection, it is clear that such training centers alone can be truly "cross-cultural," since the jobs conceived by national-service advocates are, with the possible exception of beautification projects, mostly designed to relieve the lot of the poor—which would provide little "cross-cultural experience" for young people from the ghettos. No doubt it would be a work of supreme imagination to conceive jobs in Scarsdale sufficiently urgent to justify drafting all young Americans. Moreover, as Michael Katz has pointed out, the same idea of "cross-cultural experience," the same desire for "attaining greater social harmony" and integration, was proposed to rationalize universal education in the nineteenth century. It did not work in the schools, unfortunately—for working-class children mostly didn't attend—and there is little in that precedent to suggest that a device like national service would be any more successful in producing the social integration that American society as a whole has failed to achieve.[5]

Senator Jacob K. Javits of New York, one of many liberals who has spoken in favor of national service, proposed another educational objective, which is especially pertinent now that those taken into military service are selected by lot:

> In fairness to those who are included in the lottery, and in an effort to help the rejectees, I believe that we should require these rejects to accept rehabilitative medical treatment, or to enter remedial education and training courses as the case may be. Upon successful completion of such a course, or upon completion of medical treatment, they should be deemed fit for military service and their names should be placed in the lottery along with those who needed no rehabilitation. . . . It is simply an extension of the compulsory education concept to those whom the system had bypassed. It would be a step in the direction of compulsory education to a certain level of achievement—that set by the Armed Forces Qualification Test—rather than to the arbitrary biological age of 16. [*National Service*, p. 509.]

In this way, as another writer put it, "the program could provide remedial education toward social integration and adjustment for disadvantaged youths" (*National Service*, p. 470). As we have indicated elsewhere, this concept of remediation, directed by white and middle-class reformers to change the behavior, attitudes, and values of working-class, poor, and often black people, has proved a source of strife in public education, has been in practice a failure, and has increasingly fallen from favor even among professional educators.

The fundamental failure of the remedial strategy is what might be called "cultural chauvinism." That is, measuring by the standards of his own race and class, the cultural chauvinist can judge the "disadvantaged" person only as defective or dumb. The chauvinist's view of differences leads him to compel allegedly "defective" youth to shape up to a set of uniform standards devised not in terms of his own individual or group needs, but in other terms altogether. Thus, those wishing to use national service as a device for remedial education assert that all young people must be measured by, to use Senator Javits' suggestion, the minimal standards that would make them useful to the armed forces: the willingness to follow orders unquestioningly; the willingness to kill a whole population if need be. And if they do not measure up, presumably they would be put into "rehabilitation camps" until they do.

Any lingering doubt that the standards being proposed are only the essentials of health and literacy is dispersed by the language of the proposals: "Education toward social integration and adjustment," and to "fit into military service." Taken seriously, these words mean that young people would have to emerge from "rehabilitation" washed of bellicose attitudes toward American society, adjusted to their racial, social, and economic positions, and willing to take up tasks set by the "national interest." In this view the disadvantaged have "fallen off the track," and the process of "rehabilitation" would serve to make them useful to the Army or to industry. Thus, clothed in the liberal rhetoric of helping the poor is a fundamental social conservatism, concerned primarily to maintain its own privilege and power while removing the symptoms—"maladjustment," "alienation," "delinquency"—of class and racial conflict.

Nor is this paternalistic and conservative ideology of national service directed only to the "disadvantaged." Secretary Wirtz is again revealing: "The basic 'demand' is the need of the approximately two million young Americans for the opportunity to do something because it is worthwhile and for some reason other than financial remuneration." His figures are far too small; over 3,500,000 young people turn eighteen every year now; by 1976 the figure will be 4,250,000. What is thus proposed is that a government bureaucracy of unimaginable size be constructed in order to provide "worthwhile" opportunities for all these otherwise presumably toilless masses.

As if young people were skulking about in the corners of American society. There is an arrogance about the idea peculiarly character-istic of bureaucrats—regardless of nation. It is expressed most elo-quently in the words of one national-service panelist: "All in all, the great slush of this country doesn't move until the government says move" (*National Service,* p. 160). The statement is objectively un-true, for all movements to better the lot of people—abolitionism, women's suffrage, trade unionism, civil rights, socialism—have arisen from the "great slush," with little help from, and often in defiance of, government. Federal legislation and action have generally been forced by public agitation. The voice which speaks such fictions should be familiar to us from the Channeling Memorandum or from the PA systems in our schools: it is the voice of Big Brother, who knows what is best for people, and whose only understanding of a problem is how to accomplish what he has decided is necessary.

Like Selective Service and the schools, too, national service as conceived by its promoters would establish an ever-increasing, rigid, and self-justifying bureaucracy to carry out its programs. In these respects the most damaging criticisms of national service have been made by Roland M. Bixler, president of J-B-T Instruments, Inc., and a member of the board of directors of the National Association of Manufacturers; and by Eli Ginzberg, Hepburn Professor of Econom-ics at Columbia University, chairman of the National Manpower Ad-visory Committee, and during World War II Pentagon adviser to Gen-eral Somervell on manpower and personnel (*National Service,* pp. 29–41, 50–60). Bixler, aside from criticizing national service as a "moral concept . . . inconsistent within a society that seeks to pro-mote freedom and initiative," points out that estimates of its cost—some two billion dollars for the third year of operation—are far too low considering the spiraling price of other federal agencies. Both he and Ginzberg point to the supervisory problems inherent in any large organization, but especially crucial in one dealing with young people. "A Plan for National Service," prepared by the National Service Secretariat (a highly appropriate name), suggests that "Over a period of time, a dialogue should be developed between National Service Boards, clerical assistants, and registrants concerning the most appropriate way in which the registrant could fulfill his service obli-gation."[6] In other words, the present intolerable and irresponsible way in which draft-board clerks "advise" registrants, often inaccurately, about the few options available under Selective Service, would be extended to cover at least three times as many registrants having to be channeled into an enormous variety of jobs. Ginzberg comments, from his "background in the Pentagon, [that] it is naïve to think, as many apparently do, that it is easy to deal with large numbers of people and to work out balances between their aptitudes, their locations, the times they become available, and the jobs that need doing. The balance between jobs and people represents the most complex kind of challenge even to a military organization" (p. 55). He points out that during his Pentagon service, those in charge discovered that "although Congress had allowed us 7,700,000 soldiers, we actually had 8,300,000 on board at that time. I submit that if a centralized military organization can make a mistake of 600,000 in controlling its personnel, I would not like to have a large number of volunteer organizations in the middle of this most critical of all our human resources" (p. 60). Actually, such mass errors were the very least for which the Army was notorious during World War II; far more widespread was the simple, arbitrary misuse and waste of talent—and it is strange that most national-service promoters, who lived through that era, conveniently forget the legion of true stories of men trained in Chinese sent to fire mortars in Italy.

There are other problems of size. Effective use of short-term labor (whether voluntary or not) requires meaningful and sensitive supervision, if the new people are not to end just doing what everyone else wants to avoid. The same can be said of training: somewhere between 10% and 25% of military personnel and resources are devoted just to that;[7] the corps of supervisors and trainers, of administrators and other bureaucrats, needed for a national-service program would thus rival, if it did not surpass, the swollen bureaucracies of the Pentagon and the public-education establishment. The Selective Service System and the schools lack precisely those qualities demanded by any national-service program—flexibility, responsiveness to individual distinction and initiative, openness to change, awareness of class and racial differences.

The point here is not simply that young people in the United States are increasingly hostile to bureaucracy. It is rather that people all over the world have come in recent years to find in bureaucracy and organizational size, and their concomitants—irrationally rational rules, procedures, IBM cards and paperwork—fundamental enemies of humane ideals, of spontaneity, of the irregular processes of living, learning, and growth. In the United States the thrust of the left has shifted from working for central, federal planning to a demand for "decentralization" of schools, urban development, resource planning. Increasingly, people have been willing to risk the old problems of local chauvinism, corruption, not to speak of inefficiency, to rid themselves of Big Brother's arrogance. Similarly, in Cuba, most nationally imposed production goals have been replaced by goals established within factory units by workers. This tendency toward localism and control of decisions by the people whose lives are immediately affected by them may or may not make economic and social sense in an increasingly crowded and heated world. But there is no question that among young Americans the idea has growing strength that is reflected in youth's institutions, from insistently independent local SDS chapters to proliferating communes, and from the slogan "let the people decide" to the demand for community control of schools and police. National service, which purports to be an effort to enlist the enthusiasm and motion of young people, thus reveals itself as blind to their real enthusiasms and their real movement. Does the contradiction arise from adult ignorance, from the desire of adults to impose their own, long-held ideas on the next generation, or as part of the struggle between the order of bureaucrats and the anarchism of youth?

A suspicion that the fundamental social purposes and underlying ideology of national service are masked can be confirmed by a close look at the debate among its advocates about voluntarism or compulsion. In the first place, as voluntarist Leon Bramson points out, there are distinct social limits to the idea of voluntarism. "The concept of service, taken by itself," he writes, "has appeal only for a small part of the population: those lineal descendants of the bearers of the service ethic whose self-definition is posed in terms of work and stewardship" (*National Service*, p. 130). To phrase it differently, working-class youth, on the whole, find the ideals of service silly, and it is not therefore surprising that the Peace Corps and VISTA have recruited very few volunteers out of their ranks. A voluntary system would be useful, therefore, only if one wished to attract chiefly middle-class youth, those now directed to liberal-arts colleges. Bramson's own proposals—an expanded job corps, for example—only underscore the practical limits of voluntarism. Its practice would place severe limitations on the coveted goal of "cross-cultural experience," not to mention its dislocation altogether of plans for remediation of the "disadvantaged."

A voluntary program would be vulnerable to the same charges of privilege as the Peace Corps, especially with regard to its use as a politically acceptable alternative to the draft. It would become a special haven for those trained for or attuned to the idea of service, thus continuing to force the burden of military service onto blacks and working-class youth. It has even been argued by an opponent of national service that the idea of voluntarism would operate to enforce rigid class patterns much as schools and universities do. If some young people from working-class backgrounds or some blacks or Chicanos were recruited, a voluntary system would, Michael Katz suggests, separate them from others: "If the best use of each recruit's talents is to be made and a degree of voluntarism in choice of service is to be preserved, then social difference, as reflected in educational attainment and vocational aspiration, will result in quite as much social separation as the 'tracking' system in public schools" (*National Service,* p. 177). Moreover, professional administrators and social workers are justifiably suspicious of voluntarism's efficacy:

> We have had a lot of experience with voluntarism. It doesn't work, really. It's very nice for the middle-class and upper-society level. But their affluence doesn't make them effective because the hospital operates 24 hours a day, 7 days a week. . . .[8]

The charge that no voluntary program can guarantee manpower from year to year, that no voluntary program can permit long-range planning at the operational level of a particular hospital or legal-aid center, is difficult to meet.

And yet it is not easy for proponents of national service to support compulsion directly, primarily because it violates both the letter of the American Constitution and the spirit of individual freedom that has informed the social and political life of the country.[9] The Marshall Commission report, reviewing the possibility of proposing national service as an alternative to the draft, concluded that "there are difficult questions of public policy—and a lack of constitutional basis— involved in compulsory national service." Businessman Roland Bixler was more direct: "As a moral concept it is inconsistent within a society that seeks to promote freedom and initiative" (*National Service*, p. 4l).

Because the constitutional and social arguments against compulsion are powerful, and because their schemes are not at all "voluntary," the proponents of national service have tended to blur those distinctions, even to use the words "voluntary" and "compulsory" as though they were identical. A summary of a workshop on the question describes Margaret Mead's attempt to dissolve the two categories:

> She pointed to three levels of service: that rooted in the private initiative of the individual and given freely as an act of love, that given not lovingly but dutifully in recognition of one's social responsibility, and that required of all citizens and given grudgingly. In terms of national service, the question becomes whether it should take the form of spontaneous contributions from individuals, a citizenship responsibility voluntarily accepted by the majority, or a citizenship duty indiscriminately imposed on all. [*National Service,* pp. 503–04.]

It is clear, from other accounts, that the voluntary acceptance "by the majority" of national service would *ipso facto* inflict such service on all, since those who did not choose responsibly to participate would be subject to the draft. In "A Plan for National Service," Donald Eberly makes this clearer still:

> So long as the will to serve was manifested by the volunteer, he would remain as a national service volunteer. Servicemen not accepted by a particular agency could return to Placement Centers for further guidance and reassignment. A person would thus not be dismissed solely through inability to perform a task but could be dismissed for misbehavior or unwillingness to perform a reasonable task. The latter might occur if a person entered nonmilitary service solely to avoid military duty. This evasion mentality could be deterred by placing at the top of the military draft pool a young man not satisfactorily completing nonmilitary service. [10]

An individual who did not, first, volunteer and, second, maintain the correct attitudes, the appropriate "will," would be subject, as in schools, to "guidance" and retracking. An individual still recalcitrant would be denied deferment and taken by the military. The individual who might reject service for a society he finds deplorable, or because he wishes to exercise the supposedly treasured American prerogatives to write, roam, turn on, or fall out—such an individual would have no legitimacy whatever in this system, though it be known as "voluntary." Voluntarism, of course, is not a matter of deciding which bunk in a jail you "choose" to occupy, but whether or not you will enter the jail at all. National-service schemes invariably deny voluntarism and thus move a step beyond General Hershey's "indirect" channeling into a totalitarian program that would control the lives of all young people.

A favorite disguise for proponents of compulsion is to propose such programs as "opportunities." Thus, a representative from *Sports International* is reported as speaking "of the urgent need to bring young people into the mainstream of life by giving them 'on a compulsory basis the opportunity to "serve"'" (*National Service,* p. 453). Glaring paradoxes emerge: "service," whose historical meaning, in contrast to "servitude," has always implied "freely given" or "voluntary," undergoes a sporty change; "compulsion" emerges as "opportunity," "demand" as "voluntarism," "slavery" as "freedom." We are in 1984. It is only in such a world that one can understand Margaret Mead's response at another conference to the question whether young people in a universal service program wouldn't be compelled into service: no, she answered, it "would be voluntary, but they would have to serve."

The world of 1984 is also the setting for the argument that if we can compel young people to attend school up to age sixteen and to serve in the military, why not institute a program that combines extended education and military or equivalent service? But the constitutional authority even for a peacetime draft has recently been brought into question; and compulsory schooling, imposed by states and not the federal government, rests at least in theory on the role of the state in fulfilling individual needs rather than in supplying cheap manpower for emptying bedpans or cleaning up the roadsides. Yet there is a certain reasonableness in the analogy between national service and compulsory education and the draft. The very arguments against national service, some of which have been summarized above, are also applicable to conscription and public education; and the oppressive character of the draft and the schools, documented in other chapters, would characterize also an endlessly larger, more bureaucratized, totalitarian operation like national service. What vistas for the small-minded and powerful, the draft-board clerks and assistant principals: the many thousands to counsel, channel, and coerce; the righteousness of *national* service; and even rehabilitation centers for the slacker or the disruptive student. Brave new world!

Debates about voluntarism or compulsion tend to dress a totalitarian program in the rhetoric of social justice. Such debates also obscure other important issues, ones provoked by the idea that national service would solve crucial social problems—apart from the problem of what to do with the young. Why, for example, propose nationalizing the labor of youth as a means of dealing with poverty and pollution, rather than nationalizing the productive capacity of the steel industry? Why not propose the hiring of career personnel in serious programs to combat racism or miseducation rather than use young people in patchwork fashion and at token salaries? Are there reasons and issues unmentioned in national-service proposals that have little to do with either solving problems of poverty or extending the education of the young?

A number of interesting answers to such questions are indirectly suggested by John and Margaret Rowntree in a pamphlet called "The Political Economy of Youth."[11] The Rowntrees point out that one problem for advanced capitalist countries like the United States is the absorption of economic surplus, and especially surplus manpower, created by the very dynamism of the economy. The problem of surplus manpower is particularly acute, as we have already had occasion to discuss, among young people, whose unemployment rates are as much as three times higher than those of their elders. The Rowntrees show that two industries peculiarly suited to absorb the surplus manpower of youth are education and defense. These are, in fact, the two largest growth industries in the American economy, especially with respect to employment. One table makes this startlingly clear (Rowntree, p. 11).

Utilization of 1950–1965 increase in laboring population,
18–64 years old

	Millions	
Increase in School Enrollment	3.68	25%
Increase in Armed Forces	.96	6%
Total increase in students and military	4.64	31%
Increase in Defense Employment (civilian)	2.25	15%
Increase in Education Employment	3.19	21%
Total increase in Defense and Education	5.44	36%
Increase in Private Employment and Government Employment not directly related to Defense or Education (including unemployment)	4.92	33%
Total increase in laboring population	15.00	100%

The Rowntrees comment: "Public and private employment not direct-ly related to defense or education created only one-third of the total new employment created during the 15-year period ending in 1965. This is less than the new employment absorbed by the civilian de-fense and education employment (36% of the total increase) and only slightly greater than that created by increased school enrollment and military enlistment (31% of the total increase)" (Rowntree, p. 12). Another way to grasp the magnitude of the growth of the defense and education industries is to realize that if in 1965 the proportion of the population in school or the military were reduced to the 1950 level, 8.7 million young people would be added to the ranks of the unem-ployed. That would increase "the 1965 unemployment figures 3.5 *times,* even if the teachers and officers were kept at their posts" (Rowntree, p. 12).

More and more students spend more and more time in school. In 1966–67 the cost of educating them absorbed about $49 billion, or 6½% of the Gross National Product. In addition, because students do not get paid, they forgo the earnings they might have made in the market. In short, in money terms, education absorbs about 10% of potential GNP. Similarly, men in the military make, on the average, some $1,916 less than those in civilian employment ($4,773 per year, compared with $6,689), and their relative position has declined be-

tween 1955 and 1965. Draftees and enlisted men forgo the higher
civilian earnings they might have added to GNP. It is hardly necessary to point out, beyond that, how military operations, even without
Vietnam, expend enormous sums in ways that—to say the least of
them—do not produce additional wealth.

Besides these economic factors, the education and defense
industries serve American capitalism in other respects, since it has
come to depend more and more upon the production and utilization
of knowledge—technology, intelligence, systems design—for growth
and profit. The economy, therefore, demands from the education industry a supply of trained and socialized knowledge-producers. The
military's role in maintaining American interests around the world
does not require further elaboration here. The Rowntrees conclude
that the education and defense industries have grown so enormously
in the last twenty years in response to fundamental needs of the
American economic system.

Seen in the context of the national economy, the reasons for
nationalizing the service of young people rather than the productivity of the steel industry become clearer. Adoption of national service would support the creaky mechanisms of the draft and compulsory schooling, increasingly under attack, as well as formalize and
strengthen the channeling mechanisms by an elaborate extension
of tracked training. It would increase centralized control over that
training, thus carrying a step further the process by which government through support of the school systems has increasingly taken
responsibility for the costs of training industry's manpower. Most
important, national service would also absorb even more surplus
manpower than education and the military do now, since *every*
young person, including women (rather than the less than half of the
men who serve in the military), would be kept off the labor market
for two "service" years. Finally, since many young people would be
channeled into unproductive service jobs (just as many students today are trained for unproductive bureaucratic jobs), a "service"
industry could join education and defense as another principal
area for growth and absorption of manpower. To put it in its simplest
terms, nationalization of steel (or any other basic industry) to achieve
the desirable social purposes of ending poverty, decay, and pollution
would be a first step to ending capitalism. Whereas nationalizing the
time and labor of youth would solve several immediate problems of

maintaining private enterprise. In short, if one were committed to the preservation of capitalism at the expense of imposing totalitarian controls over youth and of erecting another giant federal bureaucracy, national service would seem attractive.

It is not surprising, therefore, that many liberals in both national parties, the heirs of the New Deal, should be among those supporting national service. Although Franklin Roosevelt was attacked by the right for instituting "socialist" policies in the United States, it is clear enough today that the basic strategy of the New Deal was not to socialize the means of production and distribution under a central government, but rather to use federal power to preserve the institutions of private profit, relieving pressure for change through welfare legislation. Pursued by every administration since the thirties, Republican or Democrat, that strategy—corporate liberalism—has succeeded in increasing the federal government's role in the economy, especially in the training and control of manpower. National service is one more step along this road, not toward socialism at all, but toward national socialism, a rather different breed of cat. For it was national socialism, at least as conceived by Mussolini, which placed the central government in the role of regulating labor while maintaining private profit. If the picture of National Service Training Camps, of "rehabilitation centers," of squads and corps and uniforms, conjured up by many promoters of national service, recalls Hitler Youth, it is thus not entirely happenstance.

National service may thus be seen as a potentially useful tool for those wishing to solve certain problems of the corporate economy. Liberal educators and others have also been attracted to the idea as a means of social control, especially of youth. It is to this use of national service that we would devote the last section of this chapter, particularly because it exemplifies the approach of those in power to the young and to the problems of U.S. society. As we have illustrated, promoters of national service slip effortlessly from the idealism of a voluntary program to the totalitarianism of a compulsory system. That movement, we suggest, also characterizes the recent development of corporate liberal ideology, especially during the last ten years. For those to whom compulsion and force seem increasingly reasonable solutions to social problems, national service will naturally appear a convenient means of enforcing their assumptions, or at least their power. And while the talk about national service is, at least so far, mainly talk,[12] the language may augur an increasingly repressive future, especially if, as we expect, tensions and conflict heighten between young and old.

Corporate liberalism has been committed since the New Deal to broad public education as a primary tool for ending poverty and, in the meantime, to welfare as a means of relieving its symptoms; to the gradual elimination of racism through ending public discrimination and enforcing the right to vote; to a foreign policy constructed around anti-Communist military alliances; and to a system of two-party government in which decisions are made by the jostling of established but "pluralistic" interests. Liberalism has moved to upgrade education by infusing federally collected funds, initiating a variety of federal programs, and encouraging the acceptance of national norms. It has established laws to eliminate discrimination in public accommodations and to ensure the rights of black voters in the South. It has placed American soldiers on the soil of at least thirty-two countries around the world, most notably in Vietnam, to enforce what used to be called "mutual security." And yet, liberalism finds the very recipients of its beneficence most in rebellion against it. Schools and colleges are at the boiling point; blacks are determined on welfare rights and black power, if not on revolution; insurgencies exist in precisely those countries where American military aid has been a prop to governmental "stability." Even critics from within liberalism's own ranks account American education a "failure"; the welfare system a "disaster"; discover a rise in racism, a nation increasingly separate and unequal; and view foreign policy, as exemplified by Vietnam, a useless drain on American lives and treasure.

Liberalism and all its achievements have been attacked as never before in the last forty years, and there are few successes to bolster its case. Yet the response to incipient and actual rebellions among the custodians of liberal institutions and ideology has been to blunder straight ahead. For there is built into liberalism, as into any ruling ideology, an explanation of failure that exculpates the powerful. Barbara Bailey Kessel recently portrayed the "logic" of that explanation:

A "liberal" American values justice, equal opportunity, and freedom, and he also believes that these social qualities are built into the structure of things so that if all men act rationally, with good will, and with energetic concern, the result will be liberty and justice for all. Since we have obviously not arrived at this result, the fault must be in the irrationality, bad faith, and apathy of you and me. An educator in the liberal tradition starts from this premise to work on the irrationality and misanthropy of Man—embodied concretely in his unregenerate students. He does this by pointing to the "self-evident truths" of his subject matter, be it English, history, art, or biology. These truths appear to him as objective, ethically neutral, and given. His articulation of them to a younger generation seems to be pure public service. Any alternatives, such as teaching dialects in place of Standard English or Cuban poetry under Contemporary Literature, appears to him highly partisan and political, while his own acquiescence to a tradition appears to be an act of reason.[13]

The liberal men and women Mrs. Kessel describes do not challenge an institution's assumptions: their job is to improve its functions, its technology, or its manpower. Thus proponents of national service have been quick to insist that its "work will parallel the work and even be conducted under the auspices of existing institutions" (*National Service,* p. 366; cf. p. 356). Presumably such a disclaimer is in part a response to the fears of welfare agencies, hospitals, and schools that national service might be seen as promoting new forms of institutional power, rather than helping to entrench old ones:

In the last decade we have made impressive progress in setting up a whole range of new social welfare systems. Pressed by the problems of urban concentrations, minority protests, poverty and educational shortcomings, the growth in our aged population, and a number of other challenges, we have developed a variety of services to promote income, health, and personal well-being. Just who is going to play out this concert of welfare and social security we have not really determined, and this may be a tragic omission. The prospect may be regimentation in some areas and disturbing shortages in others.[14]

The self-congratulatory tone and the rosy perspective assume that the "range of new social welfare systems" will continue as national policy: the only problem is training the necessary manpower. If only men, as Mrs. Kessel writes, were less irrational.

Since man is "irrational," however, liberalism needs means—

perhaps carrots—to move him along; and when carrots don't work, there are sticks. "Channeling," for example, holds the carrot of deferment, college education, good job, against the stick of induction, Vietnam, death. As the institutions and ideology of liberalism have broken down, as their viability has been challenged, those dependent on them for power and position have increasingly resorted to the stick, to more violent attempts to impose the old solutions. Indeed, the history of the United States in the past decade records the substitution of the gun and MACE for the fireside chat and Camelot. Or perhaps the revelation of the sound of the police whistle beneath the cultured accents. That is the story of half a million American troops in Vietnam, of more rules and more National Guardsmen on campus, of more and more heavily armed police in the ghettos and even in the schools, and of the ideas behind national service.

Back in the spring of 1967, shortly after he testified before the Marshall Commission in favor of national service, Secretary of Labor W. Willard Wirtz asserted that men who did not qualify for military service should be taken "by the scruff of the neck" and forced to be "rehabilitated," whether they wished it or not. The Secretary's approach is typical. If the educational system has failed to instill in the young a sense of "service" or an understanding of the real world, then tack onto that educational system two years of forced "opportunity" for young people, in which another educational establishment can have a shot at "straightening them out." If America has failed to achieve a society integrated by class and race to the point where militant blacks espouse separatism, then impose on young people gathered into camps a "cross-cultural experience." And if they are so foolish or ungrateful as to resist what you know is good for them, why, take them "by the scruff of the neck." Thus at a time when old solutions and old institutions are themselves being called into question, national service provides a method for pushing them even more forcibly down people's gullets.

The cleverest advocates of national service have, of course, presented it as a carrot for inducing young people to swallow the system. The National Commission on the Causes and Prevention of Violence, for example, has proposed a five-billion-dollar program to put one million young volunteers to work in public-service jobs. In a November, 1969, report entitled "Challenging Our Youth," the Commission presented its version of voluntary national service as an explicit alternative to "attacks aimed at the destruction of useful institutions." Seeing that "one key to much of the violence in our society lies with the young," the Violence Commission proposed giving youth "meaningful opportunities" to reform society; these "meaningful opportunities" included jobs—approved by federal authorities—as teaching assistants and tutors, hospital orderlies, law-enforcement auxiliaries, and unspecified opportunities in neighborhood-service centers. The commission thought, in a fashion characteristic of national-service promoters, that its plan would "contribute to reduction of the large backlog of unmet social needs" and "signify to the young that our nation is committed to the achievement of social justice." But it leaves to the imagination how making work at subsistence pay for young people as assistants in oppressive schools, orderlies in inadequate hospitals, and auxiliary cops would persuade them that a commitment to "social justice" exists. Perhaps that is why it threw into its report the added incentive of an eighteen-year-old vote, which, it thought, would provide young people "with a direct, constructive and democratic channel [of all words] for making their views felt and for giving them a responsible stake in the future of the nation."

Again, Leon Bramson of Swarthmore College proposes that national service "could provide new sources of integration in the society. I see it not merely as serving the system but as serving the needs of the system by serving the individual" (*National Service*, p. 163). In a paper called "The Social Impact of Voluntary National Service," Bramson develops a set of fairly elementary programs, based upon the principle of what he calls "complementarity of needs," designed to intergrate "relatively deprived groups" like blacks, Puerto Ricans, and women into the society. These include a modified Job Corps language tutorials, and child-care centers in which young women accumulate credits for work to be used for their own future child care. These programs are unexceptional and modest enough: indeed, it is hard to see how they can bear the weight of social amelioration that Bramson and others lay on them. At the same time, however, they do reveal the fundamental assumptions of even the most idealistic and modest of national service's proponents. For Bramson suggests a series of devices by which some of those most alienated from American society might be bought off, and at the trifling cost of day-care credits, might be induced to work for U.S. society as it exists rather than for its change. The problem is not so much Bramson's cooptative tactic, for many would share with him the liberal's analysis that American society needs improvement, not basic reconstruction. The problem is one to be anticipated: What if young people do not, in fact, share Bramson's analysis that the old solutions must more cleverly, more enthusiastically, be pursued? What if they have learned already that the social problems themselves resist the old solutions being forced on them? Welfare mothers don't, after all, want "welfare" as it exists. What recourse would Bramson have, finally, but coercion? When a large number of young people— those queried and discussed in *Fortune's* issue on youth, for example —do no share with those who rule (or with their elders) a particular analysis of the present, a vision of the future, or a picture of the disposition of their own lives or the society's resources, then a set of programs based on the assumption of political consensus can be little more than a diversion at best; at worst, a fraud and an imposition.

In U.S. society, the thrust of the old liberalism is centrifugal, toward order, organization, centralization, productivity, toward molding individuals through the schools or the military to fit the determined needs of society. But the thrust of increasing numbers of young people is centripetal, toward self-determination, decentralization, spontaneity, toward using the resources of society to improve the quality of all human life. Were these differences not so profound, there would be little need for the integrating techniques proposed by Bramson, let alone for the compulsory mechanisms devised by most other promoters of national service. But so long as the differences exist and grow, no system of universal service can be expected to function outside a context of totalitarian control, since assumptions about the nature and purposes of service are not shared.

Moreover, as the nation's liberal leadership has attempted to reassert the viability of its solutions by the use, increasingly, of force, its very authority has come under question. Writing about Berkeley's "Battle of People's Park," Sheldon Wolin and John Schaar suggest that "University authorities, administrators and faculty alike, have lost the respect of very many of the students. When authority leaves, power enters—first in the form of more and tougher rules, then as sheer physical force, and finally as violence, which is force unrestrained by any thought of healing and saving, force whose aim is to cleanse by devastation."[15] Thus the aims and procedures of liberal university administrators become indistinguishable from those of the political right, from Governor Reagan to the Alameda County sheriff—a phenomenon familiar to those who observed the Kennedy-Johnson position on Vietnam melt indistinguishably into the Goldwater position, and flow on the same polluted course into the Nixon policy. In short, the very processes by which the liberal establishment has attempted to reestablish its authority increasingly have undermined its legitimacy, especially among young people. Those who heckled Mr. Humphrey through much of the 1968 campaign were questioning its assumptions and authority to begin with.

In this tableau of war in Vietnam, pitched battles in the streets of Chicago and Berkeley, massive confrontations at Columbia and Harvard, the notion of national service may seem remote, a spectral horse already too much beaten. Why the expense of space and passion? Because one can see in proposals for national service so much that is at fault with other institutions, like the schools and the draft; and in the dynamic that creates plans for compulsory universal service, the same momentum that has led to the cycle of undermined legitimacy, violent assertion of power and control, and further attack, in which we find ourselves. But perhaps most significantly, national service remains a thoroughly debased manipulation of youthful idealism. We began by talking about the apparently compelling logic in devoting the resources of youth to the solution of national problems; and we have tried to suggest how, in a variety of ways, the notion has about the same cruel and destructive rationality as modern war. But there is another kind of logic to be built from the idealistic desire of millions of young people to serve, not society or the state or other abstractions, but people. It is precisely this impulse which national service betrays into the hands of the bureaucrats, the secretariats, and the masters of war, who wish only to use and control the young.

Notes

[1] "National Service as a Solution to a Variety of National Problems," in Sol Tax, ed., *The Draft: A Handbook of Facts and Alternatives* (Chicago: University of Chicago Press, 1967), pp. 104–08. Hereafter referred to as Tax.

[2] Donald J. Eberly, ed., *National Service—A Report of a Conference* (New York: Russell Sage Foundation, 1968), pp. 250, 210, 52, 48, 163, 118. Hereafter this volume is referred to as *National Service*.

[3] The composite picture that follows combines elements from a number of proposals presented in Tax, *National Service*, and elsewhere.

[4] Testimony before the National Advisory Commission on Selective Service, Burke Marshall, chairman, October 6, 1966.

[5] "National Service as Popular Education," *National Service*, pp. 180–89.

[6] From "A Plan for National Service," prepared by the National Service Secretariat, November, 1966, and reproduced in *National Service*, pp. 532–33.

[7] See Walter Oi, "The Costs and Implications of an All-Volunteer Force," Tax, p. 238, and Ralph J. Cordiner, Report of the Defense Advisory Committee on Professional and Technical Compensation, "A Modern Concept of Compensation for Personnel of the Uniformed Services," March, 1967, quoted in Bruce K. Chapman, "Politics and Conscription: A Proposal to Replace the Draft," Tax, p. 214.

[8] Comment by Angelo P. Angelides, director of Medical Education, Lankenau Hospital, Philadelphia, *National Service*, p. 71.

[9] See, for example, Robert Bird, "The Case for Voluntary Service," *National Service*, pp. 485–502. Bird quotes paper #51 of *The Federalist* and comments, "A compulsory national service violates this tradition of checking one government department by another. It is contemplated that vast powers over individual lives be granted to one authority, and it is hard to see how any effective check can be built into the system. Grafted on to the present draft law, a single agency of government would review every citizen in the nation and make decisions about his future that might affect him for the remainder of his life. Appeal of the decision, if present practices continue, would be only to the same agency. Where in this system are the checks and balances by which citizens can defend themselves against a government hungry for power?" (p. 492). Bird goes on to illustrate the arbitrariness of Selective Service decisions regarding conscientious objectors and alternative service. He comments, "None of these examples is one of threatened loss of life or liberty on the grand scale that one thinks of in our nation's history. . . . In their very ordinariness these examples illustrate vividly the loss of life, liberty, and pursuit of happiness that a compulsory national service contemplates and that the nation's founders struggled to prevent" (p. 494). He also cites the report of the National Advisory Commission on Selective Service, which concluded that "there are difficult questions of public policy—and a lack of constitutional basis—involved in compulsory national service. . . ."

[10] "A Plan for National Service," *National Service*, p. 535. The version presented in *National Service* differs somewhat from the original language reproduced here.

[11] Published by the Radical Education Project, Box 561-A, Detroit, Michigan 48232. The article first appeared in *Our Generation,* VI (1968), Nos. 1 and 2. John Rowntree is an economist at York University and Margaret Rowntree a political scientist at the University of Toronto.

[12] President Nixon's Youth Advisory Council on Selective Service has considered proposals to establish "national volunteer work services as an alternative to the draft" (*The New York Times,* June 30, 1969). A *Seventeen* magazine survey (July, 1969) suggested that their readers "strongly believe females as well as males should give at least one year to non-military national needs." Of course, such surveys seldom ask whether or not the individuals being surveyed are themselves prepared to be conscripted for such programs, or to serve voluntarily. In California a group begun by national-service advocates that called itself the Involvement Corps has placed volunteers into a variety of projects in the San Francisco area as a pilot project. Money for their efforts is provided by, among others, private foundations, a few businessmen, and women recruited from "encounter groups."

[13] "Free, Classless and Urbane?" in *The Radical Teacher,* eds. Florence Howe and Paul Lauter, December 30, 1969, p. 8.

[14] Felix J. Rimberg and Dennis J. Clark, "Careerists in Human Services: Formula for Change," *National Service,* p. 341. The writers are co-directors of the Human Services Manpower Project at the "Center for Community Studies" of Temple University.

[15] *The New York Review of Books,* XII (June 19, 1969), p. 30.

12

From Service to Solidarity

"All right! So what are you going to do when you grow up?" The angry parental question aimed at an already quite grown nineteen-year-old is at once barbed and irrelevant. The barb lies behind the assumption that at nineteen young Americans are still necessarily more like children than adults. The question implies a sharp discontinuity between what the nineteen-year-old is doing now and what he may be doing in half a dozen years; or between him and those who were nineteen in 1964. In fact, because the movement coheres less around generations than around values, young people cannot be said to graduate out of it at all. Instead, they may carry their concerns about the war and imperialism, for example, from school or the campus to new forms of work and into counterinstitutions. The rapid growth of the New University Conference, for example, an organization primarily of radical faculty members and graduate students, suggests that the concerns and strategies of the student movement have been spreading upward in age. We devote most of this chapter to the work of activists now in their late twenties. In part we are responding to adults skeptical of continuity; in part, to nineteen-year-olds interested in service for change and in its dual commitments to social reconstruction and immediately meaningful work.

We do not wish to imply that it is easy for young people to find meaningful work *and* earn money and raise a family. Nor do we wish to give the impression that transforming the patterns of service for change formed in the civil-rights movement into "professions" or vocations has been a smooth and simple process. There has been a great deal of thrashing about—retreats to isolated farms, "radicals-in-the-professions" conferences, and some dropouts as well. There has also been much that we won't describe—the work, for example, of former student activists now faculty members in schools and colleges; or fresh energies generated by ecology teach-ins and Chicago's Citizens Respond Against Pollution (CRAP) organized for legal and direct action against industrial polluters. Instead, we will first describe several counterinstitutions, and in later sections of this chapter focus on the useful functions and limitations of "advocacy" among social workers, teachers, lawyers, and health workers.

Many counterinstitutions have developed in response to needs within the movement—for information, political training, legal care—and new ones will continue to appear as such needs broaden—schools, underground papers, community-controlled health centers, research organizations, groups of radical professionals, and the like.[1] These are shaped by values we discussed in Chapter 1: that is, they function in the service of institutional change at the same time that they provide meaning for those who work in them. Most also emphasize communality of work, the dedication of one's skills to collective rather than career goals.

"Vocations for Social Change," for example, began in the head of an early movement activist, George Brosi. His early experiences in CORE, in antipoverty work with SDS and in Appalachia, and in traveling for the American Friends Service Committee and for the Council of the Southern Mountains persuaded him of the need for an agency that might encourage and direct young Americans committed to service into full-time, long-term work for social change. With five friends, he established in 1968 an office in Hayward, California, and began to issue the *Vocations for Social Change Newsletter.*

The *VSC Newsletter* and the office (now in Canyon, California) constitute a movement employment exchange. The *Newsletter* lists jobs which try to answer the question, "How can people earn a living in America . . . and ensure that their social impact is going to effect basic humanistic change in our social, political and economic institutions?" Many of the jobs that we have discussed in earlier portions of this book are described as available in particular locations: organizing in communities or with antiwar groups, draft counseling, serving in coffeehouses around military bases. Newer varieties of work described later in this chapter are also listed: office and field jobs for the National Welfare Rights Organization or the United Farm Workers Organizing Committee; jobs for lawyers or for teachers in free schools; for nurses and doctors in community-controlled clinics or traveling health teams; as well as for apprentice printers in underground papers. Besides openings in ongoing organizations, the *Newsletter* carries proposals for new institutions—chiefly intentional communities and cooperatives, though occasionally such proposals as "A Mixed Media Experiment" to create television tapes developing new life styles. In attempts to be useful to readers who have jobs, the *Newsletter* also prints suggestions about how to survive on subsistence "salaries" ($25–80/week): eat "garbage," heat with wood, gather "miner's lettuce." "Monthly Report" also describes the ongoing experience of VSC's communal style of life as a model for others to examine and perhaps adopt.

The counterinstitution that perhaps most fully meets the current "service and political needs" of the movement is the network of underground newspapers which extends into every corner of the United States, and even overseas where groups of Americans collect. There are now more than 100 regular underground newspapers, perhaps another 150 on college campuses, at least 500 in high schools and junior high schools, and some 60 on or around military bases.[2] These are connected primarily by the Liberation News Service, whose biweekly packets bring to the remotest of its 400 subscribers a radical perspective on national and international events as well as political commentary, cartoons, and graphics of great skill. The underground media obviously shape as well as serve the counterculture by supplying information, ideas, and perspective not available through established channels. High-school students read about high-school rebellions elsewhere—and also about rebellion in Angola; freeway opponents in many cities learn about protests against New York City subway-fare increases or attacks on the Three Sisters Bridge site in Washington, D.C.; readers of the *Great Speckled Bird* in Atlanta find out what they cannot in the Atlanta *Constitution* about the harassment of *The Seed* in Chicago, about a wildcat strike in Flint, or about Cuba's "Isle of Youth." At the same time, the underground papers—together with underground filmmakers and, of course, folk and rock music—express the alternative culture and the concerns of their million and a half readers: repression by authorities and how to avoid it; the draft, the law, bad trips; folk and rock music and underground films; organic gardening and the price of grass; antiwar and other social-protest activities; reports of local communes, and especially from "frontiers" like New Mexico, Vermont, the Venceremos Brigade in Cuba cutting sugarcane; interviews with Peter Fonda, Joan Baez, Jerry Rubin, or other heroes. Their concept of journalism, substituting frank involvement for the supposed values of detached professionalism, embodies movement values, Jeff Shero, former editor of *Rat* in New York, put it this way:

> My experiment in journalism also represents the idea of participatory journalism; I have writers who write from within themselves, about their involvement. Participation and advocacy in journalism doesn't mean dishonesty; it implies writing from a set of common values held by the paper and the movement.[3]

Because of their visibility, the underground papers often serve as youth's community center, dispensing information, messages, advice, providing a means to make money by hawking copies, offering opportunities to work and learn as reporters, editors, and printers, as well as a place that kids from in town or out can find. Precisely because they serve such substantive purposes, the papers have become foci for repression by local powers, typically on the grounds of obscenity, corrupting minors, and even sedition. That is perhaps a measure of their success.

While the underground press and Vocations for Social Change are visible examples of counterinstitutions that offer young people a place to work and live in their new styles, other modes are also possible. In the four sections that follow, we will examine first social work and law, two professions traditionally attractive to those concerned with social problems. Then we will turn to free schools, probably involving the energies of more young Americans than any other counterinstitution except the media; and finally, to the health professions, the most active new area in which young people are working for change.

THE DILEMMA OF SOCIAL WORK

The spring, 1969, meeting of the National Conference on Social Welfare was repeatedly disrupted by members of the National Welfare Rights Organization (NWRO), who (in the words of George Wiley, executive director of the NWRO) charged that social workers "serve the system and not the poor." The welfare recipients were joined by members of the Social Welfare Workers Movement, a small new radical organization of welfare workers, who actually opened the convention doors for the mothers. NWRO mothers and the radical welfare workers did manage to take along a few of the conference members in a march on Sears, Roebuck to demand credit for welfare recipients, and they did elicit a promise that the conference would raise funds for NWRO. But reactions of many conference participants to the disruptions were, to say the least of it, hostile. "Blah, blah, blabber, blabber," an elderly social worker shouted as Wiley demanded that the conference put up $35,000 to help NWRO organize the poor. "Blackmail, blackmail," others called. Wiley responded, "You're hostile, angry. Get it out. This is why poor people are here!" And a welfare mother from North Carolina shouted, "You've been taking from us all these years."[4]

In *Democracy and Social Ethics* (1902), Jane Addams warned that those working to dispense charity could too easily find themselves engaged in imposing alien values:

The charity visitor, let us assume, is a young college woman, well-bred and open-minded; when she visits the family assigned to her, she is often embarrassed to find herself obliged to lay all the stress of her teaching and advice upon the industrial virtues, and to treat the members of the family almost exclusively as factors in the industrial system. She insists that they must work and be self-supporting, that the most dangerous of all situations is idleness, that seeking one's own pleasure, while ignoring claims and responsibilities, is the most ignoble of actions. The members of her assigned family may have other charms and virtues—they may possibly be kind and considerate of each other, generous to their friends, but it is her business to stick to the industrial side. As she daily holds up these standards, it often occurs to the mind of the sensitive visitor, whose conscience has been made tender by much talk of brotherhood and equality, that she has no right to say these things; that her untrained hands are no more fitted to cope with actual conditions than those of her broken-down family.[5]

The language may have changed, but the dilemma of the social worker has remained much the same. Committed to the amelioration of suffering, she finds herself rather an instrument by which dominant social classes attempt to fix their cultural values on the poor. Or worse, she finds herself part of an increasingly elaborate machine designed as much to control the poor as to relieve them. Such conflicts of class, culture, and expectation are by no means abstractions to the caseworker fresh from NYU or the VISTA volunteer from Appleton College.

Work in urban welfare departments was for a long time one of the relatively few means by which young people could express impulses toward service. Requirements for employment as a caseworker were not high; a B.A. generally sufficed. Permanent commitment wasn't necessary, and the tiny salaries didn't encourage stability of staff. Thus there were always openings, and during the 1950's and early 1960's many young people, aside from those who saw social work as a career, put in time tramping from landlord to office to client.

They discovered in practice what had long been an open secret among social-work bureaucrats: that the Aid to Dependent Children program (ADC), which took up the bulk of the caseworker's time, was more a cause of misery than a relief. In the first place, the demeaning "man-in-the-house" rule usually meant that only mothers and children without husbands or boyfriends around could qualify. As a result, many men left their families, who might receive more welfare money than the men could make in wages—if they were even lucky enough to get jobs. Second, recipients were actively discouraged from finding work because two-thirds of any monthly earnings over thirty dollars was deductible from welfare benefits. If you made "too much," pittance though it was, your welfare would go down. Moreover, there are sharp differentials in benefits, mainly between the South and the North—$9.50 a month for each person in Mississippi to $65.45 a month in Massachusetts. Southerners had come to use these differentials to drive blacks north, thus exacerbating racial and financial problems in the big cities. In short, as Mr. Nixon said in his message on welfare (August 8, 1969), "It breaks up homes. It often penalizes work. It robs recipients of dignity. And it grows."

Such a system also turned the caseworker into a spy. She had to discover if there was a man around, if anyone was earning "too much," if applicants satisfied residence requirements, if a claim for supplementary benefits—like beds—was "legitimate." The primary question imposed on her by the system, her superiors, and increasingly nervous politicians was not "what is needed?" but rather "do they fit the rules?" Her own proper upbringing told her that rules aren't bad in themselves: "These may not be very good, but they're all we have and it could always be worse." And she was told, if her load of fast visits and slow paperwork ever gave her time to inquire, "Of course the system isn't entirely adequate, but what agency ever gets all the money it needs?"

Under these circumstances, some young people sought alternatives outside the system, where, freed from conflicting ties to the welfare bureaucracy, they might become advocates for the poor. From the outside, they might also organize to attack that system. During 1964 and 1965 Students for a Democratic Society began to establish Economic Research and Action Projects (ERAP) in Cleveland, Chicago, Boston, Newark, and other cities. In Chicago, for example, the project was called JOIN (Jobs or Income Now). A group of college students moved into "Uptown" to organize white Appalachians—young street guys, day laborers, and especially welfare mothers. They canvassed the neighborhood, asking about people's problems, inviting them to their storefront office and to meetings, explaining their commitment to help people oppose gouging landlords and to obtain their welfare and unemployment rights. In Boston, a copy of the Welfare Department's manual was pilfered, and simplified guides to procedures and benefits were prepared and distributed. In various cities, organizers worked with welfare mothers on applications for benefits, accompanied them as advocates when they met with caseworkers, helped arrange for groups to confront local welfare offices, and participated in demonstrations for rule changes or new benefits.

ERAP projects were transitional. For a time, they absorbed temporary volunteers, as in Mississippi Summer, though a core of organizers remained attached to projects, in some cases for two or three years. Yet even they were, on the whole, "in service" to people of another class: life on ADC was simply not their life, and people in the neighborhood continued—after long acquaintance, mutual support, and even joint arrest—to refer to them as the "students." When the "students" moved on to other work, at least in part because they were no longer needed, local people replaced them, in various new organizations. In Chicago's Uptown, for example, white street guys formed the Young Patriots, partly in imitation of the Black Panthers, partly because of their prior experiences in and around JOIN. The early SDS projects had emphasized the primacy of local needs and local priorities, and they had generated a certain unity between the "students" and the people with whom they worked, a sense of human and personal relationships peculiar to small projects. Local welfare mothers' organizations continued in the same spirit of autonomy, sometimes with sporadic aid from former ERAP organizers still in the neighborhood. But it gradually became clear that local autonomy might in some degree have to be sacrificed for the impact of a national organization.

In 1966 a general strategy for attacking the welfare system as a whole was articulated by Richard A. Cloward and Frances Fox Pivan of the Columbia University School of Social Work.[6] And a national group, the National Welfare Rights Organization (NWRO), developed to implement a coordinated attack, soon drew off much of the energy of local groups. The first part of the Cloward-Pivan strategy aimed to convert people who thought of welfare as a fortunate handout to believe in it as a right guaranteed by society. Despite the language of the Declaration of Independence, there is nothing God-given about people's "rights"; rather, societies decide, in response to political pressures, what these are to be. In the nineteenth century, for example, working men who gathered together were considered a conspiracy; today, they are a union with a legally established "right" to bargain collectively. Welfare strategists pressed the idea that all members of a society, and especially a society as affluent as America's, had rights to food, clothing, shelter; and that the society as a whole had not an option to provide charity, but an obligation to fulfill those rights.

Cloward and Pivan were aware, moreover, both of the inadequacies of welfare payments and of the mounting financial burden to states and cities of the system. They proposed, therefore, that by demanding all of their rights, all the payments and supplemental benefits to which law entitled them (but which the welfare bureaucracy carefully hid from them), recipients might break down the present system (by spiraling its costs) and thus force its replacement by a guaranteed annual income. A guaranteed annual income would not only be more adequate financially, they hoped, but it also would end demeaning welfare investigations, the "man-in-the-house" rule, and much of the rest of the bureaucratic horror. They also thought that a guaranteed income would break, once and for all—as Robert Theobold, one of its main proponents, put it—the link between work and income, increasingly absurd in a wealthy, advanced technological society. The National Welfare Rights Organization and associated organizations therefore pressed for higher benefits for more people, adopting militant tactics often focused on local welfare offices. In the short run they expected the tactics to bring recipients more benefits; in the long run they hoped to force a new approach to meeting the needs of the poor.

Like ERAP before it, NWRO has recruited many young people to work on this strategy. During the summer of 1969, for example, the national organization recruited students who wanted "to learn better where poor people are at and help them get to where they have a right to be." Volunteers and subsistence workers were assigned to local groups or NWRO offices to perform, under the supervision of NWRO staff, all the service tasks with which ERAP people had been familiar: canvassing, helping write applications, organizing demonstrations. Some of these students worried, in their turn, that NWRO left too little room for local autonomy and local growth, was too concerned with bread-and-butter issues, with attacking the welfare bureaucracy itself, to the exclusion of larger political concerns like the structure of American economic institutions. They questioned, for example, whether a guaranteed annual income might not turn into another way of buying off, instead of satisfying, the poor. But like a generation of students before them, they were learning about the realities of poverty and the tactics of struggle.

The growing welfare rights movement has not only recruited many new students into political work, but it has begun to generate new attitudes and actions among professionals in social-welfare agencies. In October, 1968, thirty-four social workers and social-work students were arrested after sitting on the sidewalk in front of New York's Social Services Department to protest a new system of "simplified" welfare payments. The new system, Richard Cloward had said, might provide $90–100 million in benefits, but the old system would have provided $200 million. In September, welfare recipients had disrupted many of New York's thirty-eight welfare centers to protest such a massive cutback. But the October demonstration, led by the group called Social Work Action for Welfare, was probably therefore unique in the history of professional social workers.[7] To be sure, ERAP welfare organizers had often been arrested with the mothers. But for young professionals working in the system, the demonstration arrest represented a serious effort to break out of the traditional dilemma.

Such efforts are salutary and may, indeed, provide a way out of that dilemma. For while President Nixon has proposed desirable departures from the worst features of welfare, his system, seriously inadequate,[8] would still confront the social worker with the old question: How can you serve the poor and the system? Perhaps groups like the Social Work Action for Welfare and the Social Welfare Workers Movement will provide answers for young people determined to serve the poor even if they must organize against the system that employs them.

LAW—THE LIMITS OF ADVOCACY

We tend to equate the professions, as if they were roughly the same sorts of beasts. It is true, of course, that they all involve specialized knowledge, mystification that exaggerates the importance of such knowledge, and ambiguous professional-client relationships. But their differences are at least as significant. As a "commodity," health care is rather like food. People must have a sufficiency, differing with size and age and metabolism, for survival. Legal care is more like a gun—a gun in someone else's hands. In theory, the law is meant to protect individuals from antisocial behavior, and, in part, of course, it does that. But the definitions of antisocial behavior are by no means chiseled in marble; quite the contrary, they are on the whole determined by those who have power in a particular society. For that reason, to take one instance, the legal concept "all property is theft" has not gained wide acceptance in the United States.

Lawyers wishing to carry their commitments to social change into their professional work face particularly grievous difficulties. In the first place, access to legal help has always been unequal; like most other people, lawyers have served power. The initial problem, then, has been how to place talents at the service of those who could not generally afford them; and how to train those talents. But even then, the best-intentioned lawyers had to meet the fact that particular laws are generally written to the advantage of those with wealth and influence. Individual "rights" or the civil rights of groups of disadvantaged people do not simply exist; they have to be *won,* often against power and property entrenched behind established laws. We easily forget that organizing workers or breaking the color bar were once *illegal.* The lawyer who will be advocate for the poor and the dispossessed must thus create new law not only in courtrooms, but perhaps by joining political struggles in public forums, or even in the streets. Such creative advocacy has required new ways of organizing legal resources into counterinstitutions. More difficult still is the question of whether the law itself, as an institution, is not structurally an expression of preservative rather than popular interests within the society, and hence ultimately resistant to strategists trying to use law to accomplish basic change.

As late as 1964, a law student entering Harvard was being told by Dean Erwin Griswold that "The law firm is the backbone of the legal profession," and the vast majority of law-school graduates joined Wall Street firms or their local equivalents. But even then, some of the largest of firms were beginning to provide younger staff with time for socially relevant, nonprofit work. During Mississippi Summer, for example, prestigious law firms in Philadelphia, New York, and Washington financed their staff members who wished to work for a week or two with the Lawyers Constitutional Defense Committee. And law students themselves organized the Law Students Civil Rights Research Council for research and action: they clerked for the few southern attorneys (mainly black) willing to handle civil-rights cases and provided legal research and emergency service to community organizations elsewhere.

In the last few years, law students interested in contending with social problems, instead of, as one law professor put it, "just helping some corporation cut down on its income taxes," have affected the profession. Many former activists, particularly blacks and now women, are coming to law schools intending to put their skills at the service of dispossessed people. A *New York Times* survey, head-lined "New Lawyers Bypass Wall Street,"[9] reported that at Harvard none of the thirty-nine *Law Review* editors of 1969 seemed likely to enter private practice, and that overall the proportion of graduates going into private firms had fallen from 65 percent in 1950 to 44 per-cent in 1968. Similar figures could be cited for other law schools. The schools themselves have added courses both to sensitize stu-dents to social problems and better to prepare them to represent a different set of clients. Such courses deal, among other things, with "Race, Racism, and American Law," "Law for the Poor in an Affluent Society," and "Consumer Protection," as well as with urban problems, drugs, even rent strikes. Law students are also being given more practical experience while in school. A group at the University of Maryland, for example, have worked as interns in the Baltimore state attorney's office helping prosecutors prepare briefs, accom-panying police in patrol cars, and visiting the morgue. A project in Los Angeles funded by the National Institute for Mental Health pairs law students with young people from Watts. The law students' job is to inform their ghetto friends about their legal rights as they go about visiting courts and hangouts or perhaps following police cars on their rounds. In turn, young black people inform law students about life in the ghetto.

Within the profession, both private firms and the government have helped institutionalize efforts to provide equal access to the law for poor people. Firms continue, as they did during Mississippi Summer, to offer company time to staff for public service, mostly with disadvantaged clients. Neighborhood legal services, funded through the Office of Economic Opportunity (OEO), have spread more widely than in thirty years. There are some eighteen hundred OEO lawyers located in eight hundred local offices in forty-nine states, and, to increase their national effectiveness, they have re-cently banded together into the Poverty Lawyers for Effective Advo-cacy.

But part-time volunteer work out of Wall Street offices and the case-by-case representation of poor people done by most neighbor-hood service attorneys have proved frustrating to young activist law-yers. Such measures do not redress the imbalance of legal resources in favor of the well-to-do and corporations. "Case-by-case legal aid," the chairman of the Poverty Lawyers group has said, "is only a band-aid." Nor, of course, can laws that operate to the disadvantage of most poor and working people, not to speak of consumers or political activists, be challenged simply by defending individual client after individual client. "'Where do you go if you want to represent consumers against Con Edison?'" asked Robert Hornick, a twenty-five-year-old student from Pittsburgh.[10] Though several legal collectives, like the Law Office in Chicago, have been organized specifically to provide defense for movement activists, what group or firm has the personnel or can afford to provide individual defense for the hundreds of black people arrested during urban rebellions or the young people during uprisings like those at San Francisco State or Chicago? Partly to answer such questions, partly to resolve the frustrations of neighborhood legal aid and criminal defense, lawyers have begun to create or renew a series of counterinstitutions designed for full-time service to people rather than to corporate power.

These counterinstitutions have had a double task: to design offensive strategies that might focus on new legal "rights" and to devise both organizational forms and legal-political means for establishing them. There were a number of precedents upon which to draw, notably the NAACP's Legal Defense and Education Fund, Inc., the American Civil Liberties Union, and the Emergency Civil Liberties Committee, founded in earlier periods of social conflict to extend constitutional guarantees to blacks or other persecuted minorities or to defend such people from repressive governmental attack. All three have usefully combined a lay constituency, a mixed lay and professional board, and a talented legal staff that understood the value both of court action and publicity.

Areas recently included in the efforts of legal counterinstitutions are welfare and more recently patients' rights, the draft and military law, and the representation of poor people before federal agencies. After the political task of persuading legislators, judges, and ordinary people that the word "right" might be linked with "welfare" had been begun, for example, affirmative actions could be brought into court. By bypassing dozens of individual cases in favor of a direct attack, on behalf of all people "similarly situated," against a rule or practice itself, the strategy of "the affirmative action" provides one fundamental approach to using law for social change. Without such strategy, an individual client might be brought to court on criminal charges for violating the "man-in-the-house" rule; or, if she had been deprived of payments on that basis, she might have to go to court to recover her position on the welfare roles. In either case, a neighborhood aid lawyer would be tied up in the details of a single case. The "affirmative action" brought to declare the "man-in-the-house" rule unconstitutional cuts through endless separate instances.

Draft law presented a different sort of problem. In 1965 there were not more than a few dozen attorneys in the United States (most of them related to the Central Committee for Conscientious Objectors) familiar with Selective Service regulations and precedents, and most of these would defend only an occasional conscientious objector. The law seemed to prohibit most court tests of draft boards' administrative decisions, on the one hand, and on the other, the social climate stigmatized those willing to help "draft dodgers." When we tried in 1965–66 to organize a panel of Chicago lawyers to deal with draft cases, we found little enthusiasm and less commitment of time. The first problem, therefore, was to create the political will among lawyers themselves to take up draft work, and thus a lawyer's organization with political principles was needed. The National Lawyers Guild, a politically left equivalent of the American Bar Association, has for many years carried on legal programs related to its political objectives. In 1967–68, with Kenneth Cloke as its executive secretary, the Guild urged lawyers and law students to relate to the antiwar movement, especially by attending to the growing number of draft-refusal cases. At about the same time, the Civil Liberties Legal Defense Fund, Inc., was organized to raise funds for the legal defense of draft resisters, and in Washington, a group of young lawyers organized a nonprofit fund to publish a *Selective Service Law Reporter.* In the course of the next two years, these groups and older civil-liberties organizations assembled a number of local panels of lawyers willing to take on draft cases, often in the role of public defender. The initial need for legal resources was, of course, created by resisters. Once lawyers had been activated, organizations followed to supply them with needed resources. In turn, the American Civil Liberties Union took an active role in test cases—the results of which have changed the legal standing of draft registrants more in two years than in the previous twenty. Now that draft law is a legitimate legal area, however, private attorneys are demanding retainers of up to $500 to handle draft cases—and that's only to help a registrant establish his file with his local board, let alone to litigate a case. Ironically, now a poor draft registrant is doubly disadvantaged, unable either to raise that kind of money or to command the time of Selective Service law specialists who concentrate on important test cases.

Among the institutions that have been formed by young lawyers to further legal-political advocacy for poor people and consumers are the Citizens' Advocate Center and the Center for the Study of Responsive Law, both in Washington, D.C. The former, a "public-interest law firm," grew out of the work of Jean Camper Cahn and Edgar S. Cahn to institutionalize and facilitate the process of representing poor people before grant-making agencies like the Office of Economic Opportunity; Housing and Urban Development; Health, Education and Welfare; and so on. The Center for the Study of Responsive Law was organized by Ralph Nader and his associates to facilitate research on federal regulatory agencies. Both organizations aim ultimately to ensure fair representation before federal agencies for ordinary people, and especially for poor people; to provide information about such agencies; where necessary, to investigate and reveal deficiencies in their work; and, through pressure or court action, to make them more responsive to those they are supposed to help. Nancy and John Esposito describe the concerns of both organizations in the following terms:

> Legal services as a concept is only part of an answer; that helps people at a local level. But so many of the larger problems . . . the policy problems are developed right here in Washington, especially administrative discretion. And businesses can affect that administrative discretion because they've got Covington and Burling sitting there watching everything for them. But poor people, despite the fact that they might have a great legal services program at home, have no way of affecting policy here in Washington. And that's what both of these firms are about.
>
> Consider the food stamp program; think about it as a subsidy. Then think about the subsidy to the aircraft industry. Now you know when the aircraft industry is going to get a subsidy that from minute one they're going to be sitting in the appropriate offices and negotiating the terms of that subsidy. But when poor people are subsidized, there's no one sitting in other offices negotiating the terms of a food stamp program. You have to wait for Rev. Abernathy to come along.

Nancy Esposito came to the Citizens' Advocate Center out of graduate school, where she had found study of American intellectual history sterile. She worked first as a volunteer for Ralph Nader, with whom her husband was associated, made a number of field trips to Indian reservations, and soon began to lobby on their behalf before such agencies as the Public Health Service. Research in preparation for some Nader testimony, before the House Indian Education Subcommittee brought her into contact with Edgar Cahn, who was preparing a devastating report on the treatment of Indians as the first official project for a newly formed Citizens' Advocate Center. The idea for a Citizens' Advocate Center had come not only from the work of Edgar Cahn on Indian affairs, but from Jean Camper Cahn's on the legal problems of the Child Development Group of Mississippi (CDGM). In October, 1966, Sargent Shriver's Poverty Program office had announced that it would not fund CDGM again despite its two-year history of successfully running a Head Start program, largely in rural Mississippi and almost wholly for poor, black children. As special counsel to CDGM, Jean Camper Cahn had to establish first that the organization had "rights" before a federal granting agency (the OEO) and, second, that those rights were being violated. She had, that is, to lay a legal groundwork not only for a possibly successful suit in the courts, but as a sufficient political instrument for forcing OEO to change its mind. Out of this case in particular Jean Cahn and her husband developed the basis for extending democratic process and the rule of law into areas in which administrative procedure had previously reigned supreme. In a 1968 article in the *Harvard Law Review*, "The New Sovereign Immunity,"[11] the Cahns proposed founding the Citizens' Advocate Center.

The Center for the Study of Responsive Law has not yet, as its name implies, taken on a direct advocacy role. Its four lawyers and one political scientist have concentrated on answering questions about the means by which citizens can gain access to regulatory agencies like the Department of Agriculture or the Federal Trade Commission. Staff member John Esposito supervised a group of "Nader's Raiders" in their study, for example, of the differences in treatment received by two batches of letters on air pollution. Those written by ordinary citizens to "Clean Air, Washington, D.C.," the address widely advertised on radio, received essentially uninformative form-letter responses. Whereas letters forwarded from constituents by their congressmen got detailed and sympathetic responses with useful information. On the basis of such understanding of how agencies work, the center can then supply information—in the form, for example, of a "Citizen's Access Handbook"—so that local people can themselves learn to use the agencies to solve their problems or, at least, learn to bring such problems directly before the agencies. The center's staff has so far hesitated to extend its functions from investigation and making proposals to direct advocacy for clients. Washington-based lawyers, they argue, may very well not be familiar with the concrete problems produced among local people by decisions of such agencies. Moreover, to step between citizens and the agency would put the center into a very elitist role, perhaps determining *for* people their objectives rather than helping them to achieve goals on which they have decided.

The Espositos are quite clear on the reformist nature of their work. Coming from working-class backgrounds in New York, they did not enter into the essentially middle-class movement of the mid-sixties, and they retain the sense that the system can be affected. "Our feeling," they said, "is that before you discard the system entirely, try it out. It's really never been tried out. All the guns have been on the other side. . . ." But, they acknowledge, "It might not work. We may all have to be on the streets in four years or five years."

Some lawyers are, of course, effectively there. Or at any rate, some have begun to regard law as an instrument of politics rather than a means only for protecting political activists. Many lawyers who experienced Mississippi or northern Florida courtrooms understood this distinction: they knew that within the court they had little chance of winning a case—that might occur on appeal, and laying the grounds for appeal was not an extraordinarily complicated matter. But they might use the court as a political instrument if, for example, they cross-examined a racist policeman very carefully about his views or challenged—"for the sake of appeal"—racist practices within the courtroom or racist remarks by the judge.[12] Such tactics helped confirm the movement's propaganda about racist institutions, as well as to provide pleasure and encouragement for activists and local people in the courtroom. To be sure, a lawyer thus engaged in turning the court into a political forum walked a narrow line. Civil-rights lawyers in the South, as Ken Cloke has pointed out, "were all but outside the reach of customary court privilege, and were all but members of the damned themselves. . . ." If they became too obvious, they were faced with contempt or, since many came from out of the state, with exclusion from the court. But if they did not press the political issues and try to break through the desires of prosecutors and judges to restrict discussion to narrow points of evidence—"were you present at such and such a place" not "why were you there"—they might lend credibility to the procedural farce used by many local courtrooms to uphold segregation.

That dilemma has more and more sharply confronted movement lawyers all over the country in recent times. On the one hand, they have been warned by judges, as in the New York case of the Panther 21, that they are "officers of the court" and thus responsible for the behavior of their clients. On the other, lawyers have been faced with the reality that their clients will not "behave," not if they are determined to challenge the law as one more instrument of privilege and control. The courtroom becomes for them, therefore, at best a forum within which to continue the purposes of those political "crimes" with which they are charged, at worst a charade designed to give pretexts for confining them. All the previous skills of lawyers—using "the law to confound the law . . . creating new remedies, stalling for time," laying the ground for appeal, creating new rights (Cloke, pp. 31–32)—become inadequate. He and his clients are faced with what amounts to the choice of his joining them in the docket or establishing a contradictory tension between his legal case and their political objectives.

Some political defendants, like the "Milwaukee 14" in their draft-file destruction case, have therefore chosen to defend themselves. For, as Francine Gray has suggested:

> Defense counsels provide an emotional buffer zone between the accused and the system. An increasing number of State and Federal jurists are turning against the war. The absence of counsel confronts them directly with their own personal allegiances and can lead to greater leniency.[13]

In that particular instance self-defense also helped lead to a decision by one of the prosecutors to give up his state post and take up full-time civil-rights law. But the trial of the Chicago "Conspiracy Eight" has had quite different results. It was not so much a matter there of going into the streets, as it was of the streets having come into the courtroom: for the government and the defendants replayed the objectives of the clashes before the Conrad Hilton in August, 1968, by different means in the court. Writing after the case, one of the jurors correctly perceived the outcome:

> I had the feeling sometimes that Kunstler was a man who had to become what he was defending in order to defend it. And maybe in this case it destroyed him. But I can not criticize him for that. He believed in what he did there.[14]

And thus, if the contempt sentences are upheld, Mr. Kunstler will join his "clients" in jail as he joined their political efforts in the courtroom. William Kunstler is not, of course, a young lawyer; indeed, he was one of the attorneys primarily responsible for working out the strategy of affirmative, offensive action in the civil-rights struggle. His dilemma in the Chicago case suggests, therefore, how much sharper the challenge will be for younger activists moving, to use Ken Cloke's distinction, from being "attorneys for the partisan" to being "partisan attorneys."

NEW SCHOOLS

The 1964 Mississippi freedom schools and the first free universities were among the earliest counterinstitutions developed by the youth movement. Given that fact, the domination of institutional education over the lives of young people, and the widespread sense that public education was a spreading disaster, a variety of new forms for organizing teachers and schools has come into being in the past few years. In the first place, increasing numbers of young people have chosen to teach as a form of service, in "difficult" schools, generally in the ghetto. Where once new teachers shunned assignment to inner-city schools, some eighty MAT candidates at the Harvard Graduate School of Education in 1968 wanted such assignments instead of the usual half-dozen. Similarly, while the increase in the number of young, male teachers in New York City's public schools can initially be accounted for by a desire to avoid the draft, the rate at which they have remained at such jobs suggests at least the growth of a commitment beyond draft dodging.

Groups of young teachers, defining their needs primarily in terms of a relevant new curriculum, have organized themselves essentially to produce such materials—on the role of the common man in American history, on the Vietnam war, on new literature for classroom use, and, of course, on black and Chicano culture and history.[15] Other groups have focused on the failings of traditional teacher-education programs. Even the new Master of Arts in Teaching schemes, they charge, have not prepared them to cope with inner-city classrooms, let alone with school or community politics. The Teachers, Inc., represents one attempt to establish alternative teacher-education institutions responsive primarily to the needs of teachers themselves rather than to educational bureaucracies.[16] A few teachers' groups have also tried to organize along political lines, to support efforts at achieving community control of schools in New York, for example. The Teachers' Freedom Party in New York constituted, in effect, a radical caucus within the United Federation of Teachers. But their success has been negligible, in part, we suspect, because it has been hard for many young teachers committed to fundamental change to believe that educational bureaucracies—either those of the union or of the school system—can be reformed.

Indeed, for many young people concerned with education, attempts to alter the entrenched school systems is rather like resurrecting dinosaurs. Some have taken teaching jobs only because they present opportunities to help students organize, especially in white, working-class areas. But many have turned away from the public system altogether to establish small, independent schools, in "free" and experimental forms. They have existed, or do exist, up and down the West Coast, in Ann Arbor, Boston, and New York, as well as in Canada, among other places. An initial conference of free schools on the West Coast was held early in 1969, and a *New Schools Newsletter* is now circulating nationally. A Harvard Graduate School of Education research group on the status of independent schools reported that although many private Catholic and other parochial schools have been closing down, the total number of independents has remained roughly stable because so many small, new free schools have been founded.

Joel Denker is one of the young founders of such a free school, and his story is in many respects typical. At Yale, where he majored in history, he initially became involved in 1962 with programs of the

Northern Student Movement: wearing black armbands to show support of James Meredith's entrance to the University of Mississippi, tutoring black kids in New Haven's schools, participating in a small seminar on racism and the problems of the ghetto. During the summer of 1964 he coordinated a freedom school in St. Augustine, Florida, as part of the Southern Christian Leadership Conference's efforts to integrate facilities in that city. When his young black students participated in demonstrations after freedom school, Joel had his first taste of rural southern violence at the old St. Augustine slave market. Though he judged the summer program only mildly successful, the experience made Yale's campus life seem more sterile and disconnected. With a small group of undergraduates, Joel therefore chose to live off campus in New Haven's black Hill district and to begin an ERAP-style organizing project. He returned to St. Augustine in the summer of 1965 and then moved on to a school for black African political refugees in Dar es Salaam. The sum of his experiences—of attempting to make connections between teaching and freedom—convinced him that he needed more training, and so he returned to the United States and enrolled in the Antioch-Putney Master of Arts in Teaching program as an intern.

Antioch-Putney, which is loosely affiliated with Antioch College, had recently begun to prepare teachers for urban assignments by establishing centers in Washington and Philadelphia where interns were to teach, supposedly half-time, study, and involve themselves in ghetto communities. Joel was assigned, much against his preference, to an almost all-white high school in plush, suburban Montgomery County, Maryland. It was a very difficult teaching assignment for him. In the first place, the students were either compulsive about "covering the material," achieving good grades, and getting into good colleges, or they were totally turned off by school, hostile to the institution and to anyone connected with it. Sometimes they were both. Joel himself was torn by two conflicting desires. On the one hand, he wanted to share what he knew, especially about American history, the connections between abolitionism, for example, and the civil-rights movement today. The standard curiculum gave him little opportunity for that, in any case.

On the other hand, he had been reading John Holt, A. S. Neill, and Carl Rogers, among others. What Rogers had written in *On Becoming a Person* struck Joel as true:

I have come to feel that the only learning which significantly influences behavior is self-discovered, self-appropriated learning. . . . When I try to teach, as I do sometimes, I am appalled by the results, which seem a little more than inconsequential, because sometimes the teaching appears to succeed. When this happens I find that the results are damaging. It seems to cause the individual to distrust his own experience, and to stifle significant learning. Hence I have come to feel that the outcomes of teaching are either unimportant or harmful.

Joel tried therefore not only to move away from the syllabus, but from the teacher-centered, authoritarian classroom. He asked his students to determine what would go on in class, to decide on important matters for discussions. Joel was silent, and the results were generally chaotic. Some students felt he was tricking them or trifling with them; others that he was cheating them. Occasionally discussions were vital and exhilarating, but usually classes were traumatic experiences for Joel and the students, exercises in tense silences or shrieking arguments. Only one thing seemed clear: if students were seldom capable of handling freedom in class creatively, that incapacity had been trained into them *by* school. It was a result neither of native stupidity nor ignorance, especially since they could be quite different outside of school. And if a teacher could not create vital learning situations steadily, that also might not signal incompetence, but rather the nature and conditions of school itself. In short, Joel theorized that the roots of his and his students' problems lay in the character of the institution, and further, that given public high schools, it was more useful to create a new institution than reform the old.

We will not describe the months of discussion with other teaching interns, older teachers, students and their parents that preceded the free school's first leaflets and its eventual establishment late in August when five "teachers" and seven "students" (who had persuaded their parents to let them enroll) moved into a house in an integrated, middle-class neighborhood in Washington. The school, one of its leaflets said, was to be a kind of "learning center" at which a group of teachers would live and to which students would come according to their interests and desires. A variety of studies might be arranged within the educational philosophy established:

The school will break down the arbitrary distinctions between teachers and students. We will all be students, we will
all be teachers. The learning process should be one in which we
share our knowledge and experience. Education goes beyond
the classroom and involves the whole person. All necessary
policy would be voted on and students and teachers would be involved in the decision-making process.[17]

Translating these ideals into practice was no easy task, for many
educational dilemmas followed the teachers and students from Mont-
gomery-Blair High School to their Mount Pleasant commune. The six
staff members and twenty-five full-time and ten part-time students
participated in courses—dance, art, drawing, nonverbal communication, Spanish, French, creative writing, Utopianism—that met with
differing regularity and with curricula that grew, when they did grow,
from the developing interests of participants. The teachers found,
sometimes disappointingly, that students did not often share their
interests. A "free school" did not any more than a public school
guarantee that teachers would know what mattered to students,
though students could in this case more easily express their interests
or boredom by choosing whether or not to attend. To be sure, "these
core courses," as Joel wrote in an article, were "intended to complement rather than serve as substitutes for the direct involvement
that is central to the school." The main purpose, he continued, was

to explode the classroom, to create the feeling that learning
is more than a formal academic exercise, that to be worth anything it must be organically related to the person's most immediate needs and concerns. Students have done a variety of things
this year: Several of the kids are working in apprenticeships
with local artists—a metal sculptor and welder and a potter, for
example. A trip to Baltimore to attend the trial of the Catonsville
Nine got us involved in a demonstration protesting the mockery
of justice in federal court and in picketing the courthouse. We
went to the City Council to hear a friend protest against their
avoidance of the police issue and heard the city fathers spend
40 minutes discussing the question of civilian escorts for funeral
processions. . . .

But such a reunification of learning and life, however appropriate and
desirable, raised a new set of possibilities and problems. If life *is*

learning, and learning life, the students argued, why have a "school"? Wasn't that itself an artificial barrier, and weren't the teachers in effect hung up on "having a school"? A couple of the more adventuresome students decided in the first year that they did not have to be *in* school to be students, and so they took off, wandering and working while remaining "enrolled." Their enrollment supplied them with the credentials necessary to get past police, truant officers, the draft, and employment certificates; more important, they remained members of a supportive community to which they might return for encouragement, comfort, reflection, and discussion.

It was not life on the road, but the experience of communal living that, for most of the students and teachers, brought life and learning together. Joel wrote:

> for myself, the ideal is to become a co-learner, a co-participant in the learning process. The intimate relationships we have with each other in the community help to make this possible. For many of us the living situation—the communal living—and the learning experience cannot be separated.

After a year and a half, it is certainly true that many of the students in the Washington school are confirmed communards. More confirmed, our observation suggests, than some of the teachers. Day-to-day life with forty intense fourteen- and fifteen-year-olds offers little relaxation and less privacy. Teachers who never left the "job" for the ease of "home," found that in close quarters, differences in life style (as between postponers and compulsives) become exaggerated and intense, finally destructive of community. Though by its second winter the Washington school had budded into four communes, some of the original staff, for reasons of health and survival, found it necessary to live with only one or two others.

There are other difficulties beyond the transparent problems of adjustment many family-raised Americans have to communal life styles. The emphasis on communality focuses the primary effects of the school on those, as it were, passing through it. The school becomes "a place where people are developing to build new kinds of institutions in other places." That clearly requires of teachers and students the unlearning of many of the patterns of response drilled in by years of private living and public schooling, learning to live and to study responsively to other human beings.[18] A number of free schools have therefore emphasized as part of their curriculum the internal processes of learning, inside and outside a "classroom." As in some "free universities," an emphasis on process, group dynamics, and sensitivity training may degenerate into elaborately self-involved, "touchy-feely" sessions. People may emerge from such encounters warmly loving each other, but they may also be no more capable than before of dealing with a world neither warm nor sensitive. An observer at the 1969 Summerhill Conference in the Santa Cruz mountains suggested that "Many of the people there seemed more into creating shelters against reality than in encouraging their kids to experience the world outside the cloister."[19] They may also forget that their ability to enjoy the sharing of such experiences is rooted in their privilege as middle-class Americans. When the educational reform movement began in the mid-sixties, the needs for examining the dynamics of classrooms and the processes of learning absorbed much of the movement's energy, understandably, in view of the impersonal nature of multiversities and of large urban classrooms. But within the last year or two people have become once again concerned more directly with analysis and the content of curriculum. Thus at meetings of teachers and students trying to discover new directions for their education, the sharpest debates, as we write, are between those emphasizing process, in the classroom, in communal living, and in the meetings themselves, and those emphasizing analysis.

Within the Washington school, the conflict about curriculum has come slowly to the center of tensions among the staff and students. Steve Baehrman, one of the original teachers, said early in the first year that the school can't be an island: "There are realities outside the building we have to deal with. What we're doing is part of a common struggle with what others are doing. If not, the people here will leave without bearings." Steve was saying that the school should be more directly involved in efforts to change the society pressing in upon it. But the Washington school has not had great success in this respect. Like most free schools, its members were interested in demonstrating that education without the usual compulsion of tests, grades, attendance, curriculum, and the rest of the system's paraphernalia could offer students a legal alternative to the system. When the Washington school moved into a middle-class but not especially well-to-do suburb, some of the staff expected that they and students might focus on the same problems as all the residents: high food prices and poor public services; pressure from real-estate developers to assemble land parcels for high-rise apartments and shopping centers that would destroy the woody character of the neighborhood, raise taxes and land costs, and drive people out of their homes; the ever-encroaching freeways. If the school was to survive in such a neighborhood, it must usefully work out solutions to such problems, perhaps by experimenting with food cooperatives or studying zoning and realty laws. These concerns were, however, more central to some of the staff members than to the younger students, who were much more involved in discovering themselves and each other and in communal life itself. The idea of becoming a true "community school" has not consequently come to fruition, and Joel, wearied by these frustrations and by increasing tensions over differences in life style, decided to leave, at least temporarily.

We chose to describe one free school's early life because its problems are characteristic of many schools we observed or read about. From the outside, their programs often seem more fun and games than school. In fact, however, open classrooms and flexible educational programs demand enormous resources of imagination, patience, and determination. That's one of their problems—they require a degree of staff commitment which may not be balanced by results,[20] at least not immediately observable ones. Who knows what students ever learn, or when, or whether a school is "good" for them? The worst one can say about "free" schools is that, on the whole, they do not have the capacity to harm students that public school systems do. Indeed, as long as there are public schools, there will fortunately be insurgent schools.

PEOPLE'S HEALTH

One of the horror stories of Mississippi Summer concerned a northern minister from Iowa, in Mississippi for a week, who accompanied a student volunteer to the office of a physician in Madden. In the waiting room the doctor first berated the clergyman for his civil-rights activities, then pushed him into the punches of a group of assailants who had entered the room from behind. Both men were severely beaten for five minutes or more and later arrested for disturbing the peace. The doctor claimed they had used profanity; he also refused to treat their injuries.

To be sure, medical practice in America has not been so transparently brutal. But the stories are legion of patients, usually poor, refused admission to private hospitals because they could not afford to pay or because their cases were not of sufficient interest to teachers or researchers. Or of such patients who, when they finally reach one of the few public hospitals which must accept all comers—in Chicago, for example, Cook County Hospital is the only such institution—must wait for hours, even in emergencies, to receive cursory and impersonal service from a doctor they will never see again. Or about service so fragmented that an infant girl treated forty-four times at a New York municipal hospital during the first nine months of her life *never* saw the same doctor twice; or of an elderly man given tests costing $4,000 that showed he had a heart condition, who was then discharged and sent home to climb five flights to his apartment. Or of the dean of Columbia University's famed College of Physicians and Surgeons rushing off to treat Portuguese dictator Salazar for a severe stroke when most Harlem stroke victims are considered scientifically too uninteresting for admission to the college's Presbyterian Hospital.[21]

The fiscal brutality of medicine in America is more familiar to all of us. In the last decade, living costs have risen about 20 percent. During the same period, hospital costs have leaped 120 percent and medical costs 45 percent. Only about 8 percent of Americans have anything like comprehensive medical insurance coverage; and even those with the partial Blue Cross/Blue Shield plans have been facing rate rises in the last year of from 30 to 85 percent, and cutbacks in services covered. When the Medicaid plan began in 1966 it was touted as a giant step toward comprehensive health care for all Americans. Two years later its costs were found to be double the estimates, and it was sharply cut, until today it amounts to little more than a welfare supplement. Did it improve the lot of the poor, the "medically indigent" (those not on welfare but who cannot afford health care), let alone the rest of us? In New York City, its results can be seen from the following table:

	Before Medicaid (1966)	After Medicaid (1969)
Eligibility for free care *(upper income for a family of 4)*	about $5,200, was to be raised to $5,700 in 1966	$5,000
Charge for a clinic visit *(municipal hospitals)*	0	$2–16
Charge for a day in a hospital *(doctors's fees are extra for private hospitals)*	about $50	about $100
City tax money for municipal hospitals	$192 million (72% of the total city hospital budget)	$206 million (50% of the total city hospital budget)
City tax money for private providers	$60 million	$120 million

Eligibility limits were, at least for a time, held down, but costs to patients and taxpayers, even the poorest, soared. Municipal hospitals, which treat most poor people, were even more fund-starved than ever. Services which had been free were now provided on a fee basis—and fewer people utilized them. Those who benefited most were private hospitals—and the doctors![22] The White House Report on Health Care Needs (July 10, 1969) pointed out that "Physicians' fees, which were increasing at a rate of about 3 percent a year up to 1965, have since the introduction of Medicare and Medicaid been rising at 6 percent a year." A *New York Times* survey reported that some doctors charge up to *four* times normal fees for Medicaid patients.[23] The administrative actions taken by Health, Education and Welfare Secretary Robert H. Finch suggest where the primary responsibilities for this incredible medical inflation lie: these included eliminating allowances to hospitals and nursing homes for "unidentified costs," "limiting payment to individual practitioners under Medicaid," more tightly reviewing hospital care and doctors' bills, reviewing "drug utilization, drug pricing, drug efficacy

and safety," proposing legislation to "bar from participation practitioners who have consistently abused the program," and to shift
emphasis from general hospital construction, most of it private, to
"the development of facilities for preventive care, outpatient care,
and to the modernization of inner-city hospitals."

Few people would complain if this escalation of health costs
brought decent care to Americans. But as Milton Levenson, former
director of the office of public information of New York City's Health
Services Administration, has pointed out:

> only 25 percent of the population receives the kind of care that
> is now possible and which is rated top quality. Perhaps half the
> population gets the kind of care that can be damned with faint
> praise as "not bad." The remaining 50,000,000 people might
> just as well have no care, considering what they receive.[24]

The infant-mortality rate in the United States, for all its industrial
wealth and medical know-how, has risen in the last decade from
fourth to fourteenth (thirty-seventh among persons in the bottom
third of income) in the world and its longevity rate for men is seventeenth. And, of course, blacks suffer disease rates higher in almost all
categories than whites. In short, most people in the United States are
probably like us with respect to medical care: we see doctors less
frequently than we should or perhaps did in the past, and then only
when we are already ill; one serious illness or even minor surgery
puts us in debt for months, even with insurance, and a major medical
catastrophe can mean permanent indebtedness; and even finding
physicians willing to treat new patients is a problem.

These realities about health care in America were brought
sharply to the awareness of the doctors and medical students who
spent a week or more in Mississippi (or elsewhere in the South) during the summer of 1964. They also recognized how largely irrelevant
their education and, for the most part, their practice was to the life
of poor people. They were highly trained in biomedical sciences and
often attracted to the intellectual challenges of research or "frontier
surgery," but they knew little of the needs of the poor nor of their
experiences as patients. They worked mostly to cure illness, but
hardly at all to cure its social causes. Lucrative practices held out

easy rationalizations about suburban doctor "shortages." In Mississippi, moreover, they had had to practice a kind of battlefield and underground medicine. They had to patch up casualties and to find ways of evading threatened malpractice suits and arrest for treating people from the black community. The experience established for some medical people indissoluble connections between politics and health care, but most were slower to learn that lesson. In the beginning, the Medical Committee for Human Rights (MCHR) and Student Health Organizations (SHO) set as early goals changing the quality of medical care, especially that provided for poor people, and the character of their own education and work as professionals. Only later did they see that to accomplish their goals they would not only need to establish alternative health-care institutions, but to challenge directly the guild structure and profit motive of their tight, hierarchical profession. And it is only within the past year or so that demands for structural change have brought students and mainly young practitioners into open conflict not only with the conservative American Medical Association but with supposedly liberal medical-school empire builders.

The beginnings of the student health movement were, however, quite modest.[25] During the 1964–65 school year, students at a number of medical centers organized lecture series, featuring people like Michael Harrington, and printed magazines to inform themselves about social realities in America and to exchange ideas about more socially relevant medical curricula. In the summer of 1965 students joined with the Medical Committee for Human Rights in a Mississippi project, and a group, mostly nurses, worked with migrants in California's San Joaquin valley. The success of these projects and the growth of student health groups led to the initial "Assembly" of the Student Health Organizations at the University of Chicago during the fall of that year, and to an expanded summer program for 1966. A grant from the Office of Economic Opportunity provided fellowships for some ninety medical, dental, nursing, and social-work students in northern ghetto projects. At that time, leaders of the Student Health Projects were interested chiefly in educating other student-participants. By giving them direct experience with people used to fragmented, inconvenient, and humiliating health care, the student, as one account has put it, was "pressed to begin defining his identity as a member of the health professions," and thus he "began a process of self-discovery and redirection of professional commitment."[26] To be sure, the projects also aimed to improve community health services, but the main effects were on the students themselves.

The 1967 summer projects brought students much more directly into health politics. In San Francisco and the Bronx they focused their efforts on patients' rights, preparing a *Health Rights Handbook,* and trying to overcome fragmented clinic care.[27] In Chicago, where students were assigned to community organization, their efforts—in a campaign against lead poisoning widespread among ghetto children—brought them more immediately against one of the city machine's ward leaders, who preferred a street-sweeping program, and into lobbying with the Chicago Board of Health (successfully) for the publication of a brochure on lead poisoning.

From the point of view of health professionals, these summer projects were quite successful. Introducing students to the problems of poor people; initiating some changes in hospital procedures; giving medicine an image of "caring"—these aspects were soon taken up by the Student American Medical Association, and thereafter received sustained support from leaders of the medical establishment, including Dr. Roger Egeberg, President Nixon's new Assistant Secretary for Health and Scientific Affairs. Indeed, the principles on which the summer projects were organized have been extended. Dr. Egeberg has proposed, for example, that some physicians, chosen by lot from among those drafted each year, might serve for one year in city slums or Indian reservations (which is roughly what doctors serving in the Public Health Service now do). And there are now an increasing number of sustained service projects, like PACE, Inc., in eastern Kentucky, and the Migrant Nurse project, which works with Chicano migrant laborers in Texas and elsewhere in the Southwest.

But for many health students, such projects fail to respond to questions raised by 150 black high-school-age "interns" in the Chicago project. Many of the interns had gained experience in ghetto medicine by participating in earlier stages of the anti-lead-poisoning campaign. They were suspicious of summer visitations from students on fellowships, whose attitudes were those of temporary do-gooders, incapable of hearing their ghetto patients. Ghetto medicine has been bad medicine, some of the students might have learned from the interns, in some measure *because* of the approach embodied in such projects. Health problems are not to be dealt with by means of doctors who spend three years' residency at a municipal hospital or a year's alternative to the Army in the ghetto and then leave for suburban or private hospital practice or for administrative positions. Projects, moreover, seldom begin to prod at the underlying causes of ill health. Medical practice among poor people remains rather like bailing the ocean: social conditions create far more disease than one can begin to treat. Yet even the *New England Journal of Medicine*, a magazine generally sympathetic to the student health movement, editorialized that "to the extent that SHO deviates from medical education, practice and service, its benefits to the creation and distribution of health knowledge will suffer."[28]

Many students whose project experiences brought them to understand the need to "deviate from medical education, practice and service" have been drawn into the Medical Committee for Human Rights (MCHR) and into efforts at community-worker control of health facilities. MCHR was politically motivated from its origins as the health arm of the Mississippi movement. Since 1964 one of its members' main tasks has been to respond to movement medical needs. They have established draft-physical clinics to help men—recently ghetto and southern rural blacks—obtain 4-F classifications. During demonstrations at San Francisco State, Columbia, Harvard, and elsewhere they have been beaten even while treating wounded students and faculty. More recently, they have helped the Black Panther party to set up health clinics, and have run educational forums to explain the Panthers' program and provide support for them. Thus MCHR may be viewed as a small but serious political alternative to the ponderous AMA.

Another form of political activity among health professionals has developed on a national scale. Dr. Howard Levy, who went to jail rather than train Green Berets to use medicine for counterinsurgency, thereby suggested political roles for health professionals different from those long established by the self-interest of the American Medical Association. In 1968, some 400 health students formed the Medical Resistance Union, pledging to refuse service in the war and organizing support in medical schools. In the summer of 1969, various insurgent medical groups, including MCHR, SHO, Health-PAC, and others, demonstrated at the American Medical Association's House of Delegates meeting in New York. They disrupted the opening patriotic exercises, claimed the microphone on one occasion, and picketed with signs reading "Health Not Wealth," "Free Health," and "AMA Needs a Heart Transplant."[29]

Perhaps the most important development in health-related work, however, is the spread of a movement for worker-community control of health facilities. This has taken two forms: agitation and action for control of existing health facilities; and the establishment of community-controlled "People's Clinics." In 1968 a group of nonprofessionals, most of them black, took over the facilities of Topeka State Hospital in Kansas, and ran the programs for twelve hours, until they were arrested. They wished to demonstrate that nonprofessionals could do most, if not all, of the work of professionals paid four times and more their salaries. And they wished to establish the principle that workers had the right to participate in decisions about the character and organization of mental health care. In a similar effort, workers at the Lincoln Hospital Mental Health Service, in the South Bronx, ousted the clinic's professional staff in the spring of 1969 and ran the service for two weeks before they, too, were arrested. The Lincoln Hospital dispute involved people from the community and clinic workers, Puerto Ricans and blacks, in occasionally uneasy alliance, against the white hierarchy of the hospital. Thus their demand was more broadly for "worker-community control" of the facility. The situation at Lincoln Hospital remains unresolved, but the principles involved are clear enough. People from the community want service that is adequate, not fragmented, and oriented to care for the full range of a ghetto patient's problems and not merely to alleviate the grossest symptoms and encourage him to adjust. They are seeking the power to determine the facility's allocation of funds— into drug-abuse clinics or research, for example—and to choose leadership responsive to their community's customs and attitudes. The workers add to those demands their own for a breakthrough in the tight hierarchy of the medical profession, which forever seals off nonprofessionals from professional responsibilities, power, and salary. In both the Topeka and Lincoln Hospital struggles, workers and people from the community have received the strong support of young hospital residents and interns, as well as that of organizations like the Medical Committee for Human Rights.

Efforts to develop locally based and community-controlled clinics have been developing in all parts of the country. They already exist in the San Joaquin Valley of California and in New York, and they are being organized in Palo Alto, Baltimore, and Portland, among other places.[30] Indeed, the Black Panther party has made establishing People's Clinics one major part of their program. On New York's Lower East Side, the Northeast Neighborhoods Association (NENA), under a grant from the Public Health Service, recently opened a community health center that stresses a team approach to continuity in medical care: adults will see the same internist and children the same pediatrician each time they visit the clinic. Specialty clinics are being eliminated, and patients will be referred to specialists by the clinic team. Such efforts will provide models for the establishment of similar counterinstitutions in other communities, for the community control of health care and for an integrated, interdisciplinary approach to patients. But like all models, their impact on established institutions—the AMA, the huge private hospital and medical-school complexes—remains small or at best uncertain. Such clinics are deflected somewhat from organizing around health issues in order to survive: they must spend energy raising money, locating staff, fighting Blue Cross for payments or federal and state bureaucracies for grants, even keeping police and building inspectors from closing them down. Like the organizers of free schools and others engaged in service for change, organizers of community clinics must learn to alter the disadvantageous political terms on which they are forced to operate. In the future, therefore, health clinics may become centers for organizing against such underlying causes of poor health as housing and malnutrition, as well as more directly on political issues.

The Health Policy Advisory Center, or Health-PAC, is not an organization of health professionals, nor does it provide health care. Yet in New York City it has had a hand in many of the developments we have been describing. A Health-PAC staff member has served as medical adviser to the Northeast Neighborhoods Association, another in a support role for the Lincoln Hospital community. The demonstrations against AMA were organized from its office, as were more recent actions against Blue Cross/Blue Shield rate increases. It might be described as a "Movement Center" for activity directed toward change in health care.

Health-PAC's staff includes two M.D.'s, a Ph.D. in microbiology, a city planner, an intinerant journalist and antipoverty worker, and

Dr. Howard Levy, now out of jail. Their roles in Health-PAC are almost as varied as their backgrounds, though they all share the work of propaganda, research, and teaching. These include issuing a monthly *Bulletin* and occasional single-issue-oriented Health-Raps; running, with a few other health organizations, a Health Free University, a series of open lectures and discussion on issues like "Medical Professionalism; Medical and Paramedical Education as the Perfect Tracking System"; conducting a set of specialized workshops in areas like environmental health, medical "empires," and women in the health professions. They also direct demonstrations, organize a variety of health workers, and attempt to set similar organizations going in other cities. Especially in New York, Health-PAC also stores health information, much of which has been fed to them, sometimes anonymously, by friends in hospitals, city and state agencies, and industry.

The organization began two years ago as a kind of radical resource for concerned professionals. Robb Burlage, an early SDS member and a fellow at the Institute for Policy Studies in Washington, had prepared a thick, muckraking study of New York City's hospitals. To disseminate aspects of the study, he and Maxine Kenny opened an office and began issuing the *Bulletin,* functioning as an information center, and serving in various advisory capacities, and they began to build a communications network among New York health professionals. It rapidly became clear that a two-person office could not hope to follow up on the ideas and contacts being generated. They were faced with the need to expand or die. Support of a friendly foundation was obtained, and the organization rapidly tripled its staff and began to function as the counterinstitution we have described.

Health-PAC's function, translating research into public action, runs counter to traditional ideas of appropriate professional behavior. Indeed, people in Health-PAC have pretty well had to rid themselves of professional aspirations and values, and to reject normal "career trajectories." Barbara Ehrenreich, for example, had been a professional cell biologist at the Rockefeller University. Involved in the antiwar movement, she had attempted to combine radical activity with full-time research. When she began to receive many requests for a paper she had written from Edgewood Arsenal, the government's germ-warfare center, she began to question the value of her biological work, and finally abandoned it, since its results were being used in ways she could not control and would disapprove. Like an increasing number of young people, she felt it necessary to work for change first in the political conditions that determined how her professional skills might be used.

Trained as a city planner, Ruth Glick finds the framework of health issues especially pertinent to environmental problems. She has been concentrating on health problems of automobile workers who breathe paint fumes and of subway workers and vehicle tunnel guards whose rate of heart attacks has evidently increased from the polluted air they are forced to breathe. Obviously, such health problems can be translated into broader issues of clean air and a decent environment for all. Her problem involves organizing support, not only for abused workers but for more fundamental changes in decision-making power over the environment and the public's health.

During 1969, one major interest of Health-PAC was in exposing "medical empires," the systems of "affiliation" by which major medical centers control health care in whole areas of the city. A workshop to study the problem was set up, and two detailed issues of the *Bulletin* devoted to the Columbia-Presbyterian and the Einstein-Montefiore "empires" were issued. Muckraking was part of the job: exposing, for example, Columbia-Presbyterian's use of Harlem Hospital as a dumping ground for patients too poor or too uninteresting for research or teaching; or the exclusion of black physicians from decision-making; or conflicts of interest in those with strong private hospital ties who also serve as municipal administrators. But those in the workshop also wished to establish analytical models that might explain how such "service" institutions as hospitals function, how and where they get funds, how their power controls people. Such analyses are important, because health care and education absorb increasing portions of national income, and because a simple profit motive, still suitable for most corporations, does not fully explain the economics or structure of services.

Questions of control and power are not intellectual abstractions. Who controls health services—that is, who makes decisions about whether to emphasize primary care and preventive medicine or advanced research and "frontier" surgery—is literally a matter of life and death. More precisely, a matter of who lives and who dies. Even more than most services, medicine has been wrapped in professional mystification, but decisions of this sort are not, as Robb Burlage has pointed out, "technical or scientific at all, but political, or even moral. This is so because, like every other resource, medical resources are limited."[31] The question then becomes: To whose benefit shall such limited resources be devoted? That question cannot be answered until one finds out for whom they are now used, how those decisions are made, and how to change them. Analyses by Health-PAC staff members helped reveal, for example, how much Medicaid *cost* low-income familes, and how much of New York City's health budget is channeled into private hospitals and clinics, many of which are not open to the bulk of the city's people and none of which are seriously accountable to the public for their use of money.

The next step, clearly, is how, or whether, such analyses of planning, power, and control can be translated into public issues and significant actions. That will test the fundamental assumption of Health-PAC: that masses of people can be set in motion over questions of health care.

SOLIDARITY AND WORK

Toward the end of *Man's Fate,* his novel about the Chinese revolution, André Malraux talks of the inner character of revolutionary change. "A civilization becomes transformed," he has one of his characters write in a letter,

> when its most oppressed element—the humiliation of the slave, the work of the modern worker—suddenly becomes a *value,* when the oppressed ceases to attempt to escape this humiliation, and seeks his salvation in it, when the worker ceases to attempt to escape this work, and seeks in it his reason for being.

Two processes come together here. One can give them technical names, but these may obscure how live the concepts are for us. One spring of change is the discovery of value in what one inescapably is: by black people, for example, that their color is not a badge of shame, but a source of beauty and vigor, not a misfortune shared, but the basis of unity and thereby power. Or by women, that they are not defective males, but separate, distinct, and equal; and that coming together on the basis of their oppressed lives as women is, likewise, the root of their strength. This is one crucial part of what Raymond Williams calls "solidarity."[32]

Malraux's second point concerns what may be called the "alienation of labor." Elsewhere in *Man's Fate* he explains the meaning of that phrase by citing the workers of the Hankow arsenal, who are manufacturing the very weapons which will be used to suppress them. Few of us in the United States are so dramatically "alienated" from the fruits of our labor. But for most of us, a job remains primarily a way of making money so that we can do elsewhere what we enjoy or find really important. We put in our time, or make it pass as best we can, passive or hostile to the meaningless demands put upon us from "on high," indifferent whether the car we put together chokes our air, or the bus we drive arrives on time, or the course we teach touches our students' lives. Or we attack a job as an object which, through frenzied effort, can be converted into wealth; it hardly matters what the object is—making girdles, oleomargarine, napalm, toasters. The exchange value, not the product, matters. Many of our students, and certainly their parents, find it almost impossible still to think of work which is *itself* fulfilling, in whose results they have a stake.

They might think of the "paraprofessionals" who do the hard and dirty work in mental-health clinics, and who have led the struggle for worker-community control of such facilities. One discovers in talking with some of them that they do not aspire to become professionals. They have appropriated much of the professional's technique—can do most of his job, they say simply, if given the opportunity. Yet they remain part of the black or brown community from which most of them come, enjoy that solidarity, and define their work in that context. Some see ahead a time in which black and brown poor people will need the skills of health workers, not just a few charitable "movement doctors." These workers' skills will then be their peoples'. A few, to be sure, may be offered an alternative, characteristic of middle-class society: climb the "new careers" ladder into near-professionalism. But in fact that ladder is lowered to few; and even those who choose to mount have learned an insistent message from their brothers and sisters these recent years: "Don't desert; we move, but we move together."

Does that sound optimistic? No doubt it is, and yet we find here the ground of confidence. Back in the first chapter, we quoted a passage from the *Vocations for Social Change Newsletter:*

> Vocations for Social Change is based on two great hopes. We feel that there is a great need for institutional change in this country so that ordinary citizens can have greater control over the forces that limit their lives. We believe that it is possible for far-reaching change to occur in this country if enough human energy is devoted to the task. At the same time, we are greatly concerned about the quality of our lives and the lives of our fellow citizens. We want our work to produce change in the society and we also want it to provide meaning for us. Similarly we hope that others can work towards and achieve this kind of confluence.
>
> This means that we view a job as a focus for individual involvement, not as a way to earn some money to do things with.

What we have tried to suggest in this chapter is that the two "great hopes" of Vocations for Social Change depend upon the two great perceptions outlined by Malraux. First, that the basis of institutional change as they describe it is not this or that federal program or foundation plan. It is, rather, an emerging solidarity, a solidarity organized around the "humiliation" of the oppressed. And second, that society is already being transformed when men and women create jobs that are extensions of their hopes and ideals, or when many of us as workers begin to see in our work our "reason for being."

To create counterinstitutions which embody such work is, in effect, to establish "liberated zones" within the old society. They are more permanent than the still symbolic Berkeley People's Park, the Young Lords' possession of churches in Chicago and New York, or the Indian encampment on Alcatraz. But like these temporary institutions, they are bases from which to move out on what Daniel Cohn-Bendit called "the long march through the institutions of society." These two perceptions, then, of solidarity and work, and one other from Malraux—"our people will never forget that they suffer because of other men, and not because of their previous lives"—generate the revolutionary optimism we find in *Man's Fate.* And, we think, among many young people in America today.

There has been established in the past decade a kind of tradition for books which, like this one, lay out certain social problems in America. They are expected to end with a more or less elaborate set of proposals, usually calling upon the federal government to adopt some new legislation, for the "private sector" to follow federal leads, and for the rest of us to support the latest attempt at social engineering. So deep-rooted and pervasive is this expectation that even an early advertisement for this book said that we would "offer proposals for bringing youth back into the national mainstream"—although we had been very clear, we thought, that we neither intended such proposals nor wished to bring youth "back" to anything, certainly not to the mainstream of war, racism, male and class privilege that has characterized United States society. If anything, we would wish to disabuse our readers of the notion that a set of federally organized programs will "solve" the "youth problem." Indeed, we would argue that even to pose the situation as a problem of *youth* to be dealt with through mechanisms designed by adults is to misconceive the situation. Significant federal initiatives are, we think, rather limited; it may be that the directions in which young people are themselves moving will prove more significant. And in the second place, the problem is not, as we proposed in Chapter 1, that of a "generation gap," but is rooted, rather, in the values of American society itself.

The limitations of federal action can be observed in the dilemmas of the present administration with respect to marijuana, the draft, schooling. Some social commentators have suggested that no better way of pacifying youth could be found than by legalizing pot. Life could than be, for those who wanted it that way, a continuing Woodstock Festival, unhindered by any Blue Meanies. Pot busts, which have been a source of increasing friction between authority and youth, would be eliminated. One can easily imagine an even more profitable industry developing around the production and packaging of joints than exists already for psychedelic supplies and music; as a matter of fact, the names of popular strains of marijuana, like Acapulco Gold, have already been copyrighted! In this way, permissiveness could be turned to profit and to social control, the issue of political repression of drug users would be taken away from the Yippies, and the likelihood of young people fighting to maintain the drug culture diminished. One might call it the "Brave New World" solution.

In fact, however, an alternative approach to young people—call it the "1984" solution—is at least as likely to prevail. While marijuana convictions have, in some places, been reduced from felonies to misdemeanors, there appears to be no diminution of governmental efforts to seal off supplies of grass or to prosecute users as well as sellers. The Puritan virtues of sobriety, industry, and piety may initially have been generated by the need in an economy of scarcity for a dependable and diligent work force. But it is clear that Puritan imperatives prevail in much of the United States today, even if they have outlived their economic roots, even if they become a basis for strife rather than restraint. One can as little imagine Mr. Nixon legalizing pot, given his political constituency, as his smoking it. Legalization might mean less trouble from some young people, but it would surely mean more from the majority of those who vote for President.

Similar dilemmas exist with respect to the draft and the war. Any form of selective service has built-in inequities; the only way finally to eliminate the discrimination implicit in student deferments, for example, is to eliminate the draft itself. But the Vietnam war, the escalating conflict in Laos, the revolutionary threats in Latin America and in Greece, all demand a level of American manpower that has been difficult to supply without the draft. To be sure, Vietnamization and other means of substituting Asian mercenaries for American boys attempt to overcome this dilemma. But each account of Vietnamization by independent reporters or by researchers for the Senate Foreign Relations Committee suggests the unlikeliness that such a strategy will work or that hundreds of thousands of American troops will not be necessary to maintain the war into the foreseeable future. Thus draft reform comes up against the limits imposed by the manpower demands of American imperial strategy, and by the ideological anticommunism and the economic needs which undergird it. Eliminating student deferments may placate some who feel their children discriminated against, but it will also antagonize many middle-class families so long as the war or similar adventures threaten their children's lives. Thus, while the Nixon administration, fulfilling its campaign promise, has proposed the creation of an all-volunteer Army, it remains to be seen whether the idea will be pushed through a skeptical Congress. Or whether it depends upon raising unemployment rates, especially among young people, more especially among blacks, to ensure in an even more cynical—"indirect"—fashion a sufficiency of channeled manpower.

Similarly, with respect to education. Government at all levels is verbally committed to equalization of educational opportunity. That is coming to mean, because of the phenomenon of "upgrading," providing some education beyond high school for all students wishing to have it. But how to meet the costs of such a program? Private colleges are short of funds: predictions of their financial demise appear in educational trade magazines. And even state-supported schools have suffered severe cutbacks, in part stemming from war-related reductions of federal grants, in part from the rigors of state finances. Mr. Nixon's veto of the congressional appropriation for health, education, and welfare early in 1970 suggests that the federal government cannot now be expected to foot the bill; indeed, some administration spokesmen have suggested that we should try to reverse the trend toward more higher education for more people, substituting instead "meaningful" vocational and on-the-job training programs. That signals not only to the education lobby but to poor and working people an injunction to keep their places and not aspire.

One plan for financing universal higher education, suggested by James Tobin and Leonard Ross in a 1969 *New Republic* article, called "Paying for the Costs of Higher Education: A National Youth Endowment," helps focus the dilemmas of federal power. Tobin and Ross propose establishing a National Youth Endowment as a public corporation. Every young person would be entitled to an endowment credit of, say, $5,000 to finance his education past high school. After he reaches age twenty-eight, he would begin to repay the "credit" through a surtax on his federal income tax. "The terms of this repayment," Tobin and Ross explain (for example, one percent of income per $3,000 borrowed), "would be set so that the average individual would over his lifetime repay the fund in full, plus interest at the government's borrowing rate." A well-to-do borrower would pay more. Thus the Endowment would ultimately become self-financing. The Tobin and Ross proposal seems to be a reasonable method for meeting the 132-percent increase in the costs of higher education which the Carnegie Corporation's Commission on Higher Education has predicted for the next nine years. It seems to provide a means whereby post-high-school technical and vocational education, which have received little solid financing, can be aided. And it appears to give the children of the poor a leg up the education ladder.

But the economic realities of the program, at least as these seem to be assessed in the present mood of the country, deny its promise. Every year, three and a half million people turn eighteen; they would have drawing rights on the Endowment of $17.5 *billion.* Money would have to come either from Congress or from bonds sold to private lenders. Either would, no doubt, be regarded as seriously inflationary, as Tobin and Ross acknowledge. They argue that:

> The inflationary impact of these initial cash deficits would have to be neutralized somehow. This could be done by taxation. But since the Endowment is a social investment project it would be entirely appropriate to borrow the funds from private lenders. The monetary authorities would have to let the Endowment's drafts on the capital market tighten credit and raise interest rates to other borrowers, temporarily displacing other investments of lower social priority.

But that is the nub of the political problem: United States society has been, to say the least of it, reluctant to elevate social investment over military or private spending. It seems even less inclined to do so in 1970 than it did in 1965; one can conceive billion-dollar programs to build supersonic transports or nuclear missiles, but not to send already troublesome students off to college. Acknowledging such realities, Tobin and Ross suggest a "more modest pilot project," limiting loans to "vocational or professional school students" or, less desirably, applying a means test. But all such limiting devices risk alienation of one or another large segment of American society: middle-class families with incomes of better than $10,000 might, for example, be excluded; but financing a college education is by no means an easy task for them, especially if they are paying through taxes for educating others' children, and one could quickly expect political repercussions from them.

The experience of Medicaid suggests, moreover, that as money for services becomes available to poor people, the cost of such services spirals upward. If Medicaid doctors and hospitals fed so heartily at the public trough, why not colleges and professors—who have been more starved than physicians. If students were put in a position to pay the full costs of their education, it is hard to believe that those costs would not rapidly increase. In the end, probably the poor would be worse off relatively—and perhaps absolutely—than before. It is hard, therefore, to see how such a program could be instituted without broad federal control over costs, and such controls would inevitably extend to eligible institutions. Tobin and Ross cite the experience of the Veterans' Administration in accrediting institutions under the GI Bill to suggest that controls offer no major difficulties. But to the usual problems of accreditation, the 1960's development of a counterculture would be adding insurgent institutions. Experience with the poverty program suggests that federal funds will not be allowed to go for long to organizations—whether they're called schools, apprentice programs, or intentional communities—which will look suspicious if not dangerous to their established neighbors. Could Malcolm X Liberation University be accredited, teaching black nationhood?

Similar objections of cost, inflation, and resistance of hardest-hit taxpayers have been brought against proposals like providing a guaranteed annual income not only to poor Americans but to all young people for a period of four years. Young people could use such income for school, for self-learning, or even to buy paints and canvas. Like the Tobin-Ross proposal, this one has a number of merits, even or perhaps especially from the point of view of those wishing to cool off or even buy off youth rebellion. There is nothing like receiving money, even if it is not finally very much money, to tame angry impulses. But the costs of such programs would demand the most thoroughgoing reconstruction of American priorities. A look at recent history tells us that even the liberal Kennedy and Johnson administrations did nothing like that; indeed, military spending and private profit grew enormously under them.

Our point here, however, is not to argue the merits of the Tobin-Ross proposal or of a guaranteed youth income; nor is it to counterpoise liberal and radical ideas about the possibility of altering United States social and economic priorities. What we want to point out is that the government's freedom to establish programs for coping with social problems is more apparent than real. It is seriously constrained by the conflicting demands, the "contradictions," of our society. Legalizing pot might cool youthful heads, but it would heat up many of their elders. Ending the draft would be a large step toward eliminating domestic unrest among youth, but it would finally seem to require a serious withdrawal from imperial expansion, or a major increase in unemployment to provide a sufficiently motivated pool of volunteers. Offering all young people some education beyond high school would buy off many demands for equalization of opportunity—and produce a better socialized work force—but it would require an unimaginable reorganization of social priorities. As a matter of fact, as we look at the scene, the "Brave New World" solution—Soma, the feelies, and tranquillity—seems still available, but increasingly unlikely. The "1984" solution of increased repression, continued war, and government-insured profit seems the more likely to be pursued.

The federal government's role in all this is, needless to say, a powerful one. But though the government can strongly influence the forms, for instance, in which conflicts are played out, it does not control social forces. Nor can it wipe away those conflicts, or even definitively set the terms for them. The depth and persistence of Vietnamese resistance to American and French attempts to impose imperialist governments on them was, so far as one can tell, quite unexpected to U.S. policymakers. Had that resistance been quickly overcome, as it was, for example, in Guatemala or in the Dominican Republic after U.S. intervention, this country would be far different from what it is now—or is likely to be. It has been, after all, the Vietnamese resistance that has produced such enormous discord in the U.S. over the war, given heart to the antiwar movement, and helped also to stimulate movements for national liberation elsewhere in the world. These, in turn, place further constraints on American policymakers.

Similarly, the progressive demands of black people in the United States for integration, for Freedom Now, for black power, and for liberation have been the major stimulants to efforts to end racism and to federal policies designed to eliminate discrimination and poverty. There is no question in our minds that the black movement, as fragmented as it has often been, is more responsible for having shaped and changed the character of American society today than federal administrations, for all their apparent authority.

The anger that the blacks, women, and the young feel is rooted in their experience of local institutions—their schools, their draft boards, their local police. While they may continue to be drawn by national leaders and national rhetoric—as they were once drawn by the call to "ask what you can do for your country"—national *programs* will have to be translated into real changes that affect people's lives in significant and visible ways. National "commitments" to end slums and change schools help to *generate* rebellion when they do not effect significant local change; and, on the whole, they have not done so. Indeed, it remains to be seen what federal administration can change the administration of justice or the organization of schools in the city of Chicago, to take just one prominent example.

With all their power of repression, we would maintain, no federal administration can chart the future. No administration can control the social and political force of the insurgent counterculture. Time, history, and even numbers tell us that the future is on the side of the Vietnamese, the blacks, women, and the young.

Notes

[1] For a useful distinction between parallel institutions, like free universities, and counterinstitutions, like those named, see Marge Piercy and Bob Gottlieb, "Movement for a Democratic Society," in *Radicals in the Professions Newsletter,* I (March, 1968), p. 20. This chapter describes a number of these counterinstitutions, but there are many which we do not have the space to describe in detail. It is worth noting, however, the proliferation of research groups within the past year: joining the three-year-old North American Committee on Latin America have been the Africa Research Group, the Pacific Studies Center, NARMIC (National Action/Research on the Military-Industrial Complex), and even, at Carleton College, a Radical Research Center. These groups and others suggest that movement organizations are developing deep and permanent roots of information and analysis.

[2] Estimates from Liberation News Service, GI Press Service, College Press Service, and Seth S. King, "Defiant Students Keep the Underground Presses Rolling," in *The New York Times,* May 19, 1969.

[3] Martin Abramson, "Rat's Radical Editor Majored in Protesting," in Baltimore *Evening Sun,* September 9, 1969.

[4] See *The New York Times,* May 26–28, 1969.

[5] *Democracy and Social Ethics* (New York: The Macmillan Company, 1907), pp. 17–18.

[6] "A Strategy to End Poverty," in *The Nation,* 202 (1966), pp. 508–11.

[7] See *The New York Times,* October 10, 1968.

[8] The amounts to be provided, especially for city dwellers, neither meet minimum income standards nor relieve the fiscal burden of cities. The repeated assertions that recipients must work reinforce erroneous assumptions held by many angry at the rise in welfare costs that most do not, and very likely will have the effect of forcing the mainly black people now on ADC into low-paying jobs. Thus the new system can develop a new set of coercions to replace the old—meanwhile injecting more cheap labor into a market already difficult for blacks and many other working people. It has been argued, moreover, that even the objective of the Cloward-Pivan strategy, a guaranteed annual income, may turn out to be a step backward. Transformed into a negative income tax and set at inadequate levels, it could provide both a carrot and a stick to buy off and to coerce poor people from challenging the basic causes of economic exploitation in the United States.

[9] Robert Reinhold, in *The New York Times,* November 19, 1969.

[10] *The New York Times,* November 19, 1969.

[11] Edgar S. and Jean Camper Cahn, "The New Sovereign Immunity," in *Harvard Law Review,* 81 (March, 1968), pp. 929–91.

[12] See Ken Cloke, "Law and the Radical Lawyer," in *Radicals in the Professions—Selected Papers* (Ann Arbor: Radical Education Project, 1967), p. 33.

[13] "The Ultra-Resistance," in *The New York Review of Books,* XIII (September 25, 1969), p. 17.

[14] Kay S. Richards, "Chicago 7 Juror's Inside Story," in Philadelphia *Inquirer*, February 26, 1970.

[15] In Boston, a group of young teachers worked up detailed curriculum materials called *Teaching About Vietnam*. Their four mimeographed volumes were circulated among teachers not only in the Boston area but in other cities. Finally, *The New York Review of Books* printed the Vietnam curriculum, and the Boston group launched a second project, an integrated social-studies and English curriculum on the social identity of kids in school.

[16] The Teachers, Inc., a cooperative corporation, trains young recruits in summer work-study programs that emphasize, besides curriculum development and classroom management, involvement in ongoing community action. The corporation then arranges for group placement in schools or systems open to innovation, and carries on curriculum workshops and consultations on classroom teaching during the year.

[17] Very similar schools have been described by other movement activists: Helen Garvey, associate national secretary of SDS in one of its earlier years, wrote of the Shire School in San Francisco:

> There is almost no formal structure. We don't divide up the kids by grades or any other way [though the 75 students range in age from 4 to 14]. There is no fixed schedule of classes and activities and no compulsory attendance. That doesn't mean there is absolutely no structure—but that it is informal. The basic structure is defined by teachers and activities that are available each day. Everyone begins in the same building [when the school had a building] and there are things to do and adults to help. Kids gravitate to activities, certain parts of the building that they like, certain teachers, or other kids. That determines what they will do. And when they get tired of one thing, they are free to leave and try something else. The kids know who the teachers are and what they do. When they see Nan, they know there will be something happening in the field of biology. And Nan may make an announcement about exactly what she will do that day. Bob teaches math and the kids know they just have to ask and he'll work with them—at their own level and their speed. Karen often works with clay and the kids know what days she comes. [*Radicals in the Professions Newsletter*, I (December, 1967), #2, p. 3.]

Bill Ayres and Terry Robbins, presently among the leadership of the SDS Weatherman faction, have written similarly about their Ann Arbor Children's Community in "Turn Toward Children."

[18] "The main problem for us," says Mickey Freedman, a teacher at Encounter House, a free school in New York, "is we've been buried by the debris of our own education. We don't know how to react in the classroom. It takes such an enormous effort to have teachers and students react to each other as people and decide for themselves how they want to proceed." *The New York Times*, December 1, 1968.

[19] *New Schools Newsletter*, Issue #21, October 9, 1969.

[20] In 1967–68 the Shire School not only had no building, but it paid its staff of eight full-time and about twenty-five part-time teachers no salaries. In order not to exclude the children of poor families, it charged no tuition. Some of the teachers maintained other part-time jobs, some lived on savings from a year at a "straight" job or were supported by others, some scrounged from supermarket garbage cans in order to be able to teach.

[21] See Martin Tolchin, "The Changing City: A Medical Challenge," in *The New York Times*, June 2, 1969, and *Health-PAC Bulletin*, #6 (November–December, 1968).

[22] Barbara Ehrenreich, "New York City Medicaid—Five Steps Backward, One Forward," *Health-PAC Bulletin*, June, 1969, p. 3.

[23] *The New York Times*, February 9, 1970.

[24] "The Health Industry—An Ailing Giant," in Chicago *Sun-Times Viewpoint*, November 2, 1969.

[25] Many details of this account are drawn from Drs. Michael R. McGarvey, Fitzhugh Mullan, and Steven S. Sharfstein, "A Study in Medical Action—The Student Health Organizations," in *New England Journal of Medicine*, 279 (July 11, 1968), pp. 74–79; and from interviews with participants in SHO, Medical Committee for Human Rights, and other health organizations.

[26] McGarvey, *et al.*, p. 76.

[27] Students .in New York acted as "patient advocates": they met with patients in the admitting room, worked with them to cut through bureaucratic forms and shuttling from office to office, and generally to focus the usually fragmented clinic care on the patient's particular needs.

[28] "Activists in Medical School," 279 (July 11, 1968), p. 102.

[29] Nothing could so well dramatize the gulf between the medical establishment and the young health movement than the contrast between such signs and an AMA official's account of the demonstrations. "At the opening session of our House of Delegates this summer, we had a score of distinguished guests from foreign countries and presidents of allied organizations on stage. We knew the young people had something in mind. . . . They didn't stand for the National Anthem or when the flag passed by. They hissed introductions of the Minister of Health from [South] Vietnam and the President of the South African Medical Society. What really infuriated our people, though, was the fact that the Marine Corps flag pageantry had been so inspirational, and right on its heels came their demonstration. . . . We had a man raving that the association was 'illegitimate.' He called it the 'American Murder Association.' We can't have people like that repelling our audience. If they have nothing constructive to say, I think they should be restricted." Quoted in Charles Louis Schafer, "What to Do About Convention Protesters?" *Association Management* (October, 1969), pp. 35–36.

[30] In 1967, for example, the San Joaquin Valley of California had one half-time doctor for some 10,000 people. A young medical resident, who was donating evening time to the grape strikers in Delano, and a woman who had been working for the poverty program setting up clinics felt the need for a new, community-oriented medical clinic in the valley. Joined by a public-health nurse, they went back to their regular jobs for three months in order to raise enough money to get such a clinic started. They found an empty building in Woodville that had, in the past, been a gambling hall, a restaurant, a barber shop; John Steinbeck had know it as the Alhambra; old-timers remembered a romantic past. The three set about clearing title. And while they waited, they went about organizing community support: "Many helped with the remodeling necessary to convert it to something resembling a medical office. Women made examining gowns and drapes, brought used furniture. Teenagers helped with construction and other heavy work. Minimal medical equipment was bought, all second hand." Leona Judson, "Salud Medical

Clinic," *Vocations for Social Change,* #7 (December, 1968), pp. 25–26. Salud opened in October, 1967, and by the following October was serving more than 1,700 families, including some 8,000 people.

All of this is traditionally service-oriented, but Salud has also tried to break nonmedical ground. Decisions about the clinic are in the hands of a community board, and people from the community are trained and employed in the clinic at a ratio of two community people to each outside professional; of the sixteen staff members in early 1969, eleven were from the Valley.

[31] "Staying Alive in New York," in New York *Advocate* (December, 1968).

[32] *Culture and Society* (New York, 1969), pp. 328ff.

About the Authors

Paul Lauter and Florence Howe have grown with and taught the young people of the late fifties and the sixties. Their dedication to both educational and social change and liberation took them to Mississippi and the freedom schools, Upward Bound and other private and federal experiments in education, to draft resistance and SDS, and more recently, to Resist and the New University Conference.

Florence Howe attended Hunter College (A.B. 1950), Smith College (A.M. 1951), and the University of Wisconsin (A.B.D. 1954). Paul Lauter attended New York University (A.B. 1953), Indiana University (A.M. 1955), and Yale University (Ph.D. 1958). Both teach at colleges in Maryland and are frequent contributors to *The New York Review of Books, Harvard Educational Review, The Nation,* and *Saturday Review.* Together they have edited two issues of *The Radical Teacher* for the New University Conference. Mr. Lauter's last book was *Theories of Comedy.* Miss Howe is working on a study of Virginia Woolf.